Fool's Gold?:

The Bruce Schuler Murder

By

Graeme Crowley

Copyright 2025 Graeme Crowley layout and design
Copyright 2025 Graeme Crowley cover and art
First Published 2025

This book is a work of non-fiction. All rights reserved. No part of this book may be reproduced or transmitted in any form or by any means, electronic or mechanical, including photocopying, recording, or by information storage and retrieval system, without the author's permission.

Once again, I dedicate this work to my wife Susan for inspiration, support and steadfastly standing by me all these years.

I also thank my friends Max Barrington, Kelli Condon and Greg Cary for all your unconditional help and support with this project.

Table of Contents

Foreword *16*
Preface *17*
Cast of Characters *19*
Background to a Murder *21*
Crime Scene Location *24*
Where is Bruce Schuler Podcast *25*
Our mate is missing *33*
FNQ *52*
Bruce Schuler *56*
Fiona and Lisa *59*
Tsunami *65*
Palmerville Station *67*
Dianne Wilson – Struber *70*
Stephen Struber *73*
George Wilson *86*
The Prospectors *93*
Struberville *100*
Sovereign Citizens *106*

12

The Vehicles *110*

The Weapons *113*

Confrontation at the Croc Hole *116*

Sunday 8 July 2012 .... *120*

Boots on the Ground *122*

Monday 9 July 2012 .... *128*

The Phone Calls *140*

Tuesday 10 July 2012 .... *144*

Wednesday 11 July 2012 .... *149*

The Neighbour *152*

Thursday 12 July 2012 .... *158*

Friday 13 July 2012 .... *163*

Saturday 14 July 2012 .... *166*

Lost and Found *169*

Sunday 15 July 2012 .... *173*

Thursday 19 July 2012 .... *174*

Monday 8 October 2012 .... *175*

CCC Hearing *177*

Arrested! Again *179*

Committed for Trial *181*

The Murder Trial *183*

The Media *206*

Ezard's Concerns *212*

Court of Appeal 2016 .... *217*

No Body No Parole *224*

The Coroner's Court 2018...*226*

Something to Boast About..*228*

Bob Haydon *231*

The Evidence *239*

A Scientific Principle Challenged *243*

The only thing I regret Sarge *247*

Knocking on Heaven's Door..*257*

Bruce Phone Home *262*

Kevin and Tremain meet up *264*

Shots Fired *267*

Was Dan Bidner even there?...*278*

Stephen and Dianne were there! *282*

A Hat for every occasion *285*

Struck by a Bull..*290*

Dead or Alive?..*294*

Video does not lie *296*

The Reader *303*

Ghost Evidence..*308*

Teleporting..*330*

Trees, Pats and Tracks..*339*

Crime Scene Staging...*346*

Window Dressing...*357*

A Very Stressful Situation, or was it?..................................*358*

RoboCop *368*

Back to Court 2025 .... *379*

MOJ *384*

Appendix A *391*

Appendix B *401*

Appendix C *407*

Appendix D *439*

Appendix E *445*

Appendix F *465*

Foreword

I was both honoured and surprised when asked to write the foreword for Graeme Crowley's book, *Fool's Gold?*

Honoured, because I have long admired Graeme's work, particularly his compelling podcast, *Where is Bruce Schuler?* which he so expertly researched, scripted and presented.

Surprised, because, as a writer of fiction, I am accustomed to crafting stories from imagination. Yet, when I consider the true story that Graeme unfolds in *Fool's Gold?* I realise that no work of fiction I could conceive would ever match the sheer intrigue, complexity, and unsettling reality of this case.

As the old saying goes, *you just can't make this stuff up.*

How tragic it is that a man, Bruce Schuler, could simply vanish without a trace, and how much more tragic still that the pursuit of justice in his case has been so deeply flawed. We live in 2025, and yet the handling of this case by the Queensland legal system defies belief. The failures, the missteps, and the unanswered questions are nothing short of astonishing.

Graeme Crowley's *Fool's Gold?* is more than just a book, it is an unflinching examination of justice denied, an investigation that demands attention, and a story that will leave you questioning everything you thought you knew about how the system is supposed to work.

Max Barrington.

Preface

Only once in a lifetime would a case like the disappearance of Bruce Schuler cross your desk. A 'straightforward' murder, (if such a beast ever existed) and this murder was anything but straightforward. Isolation and lawlessness reign supreme on a cattle property the size of Hong Kong, in Australia's vast, still untamed, arid north. Claims of gold fever, drug cultivation, murder and trespass have coexisted for decades on one of Australia's biggest and most famous goldfields.

It was a murder by two 'bushies' who seemingly descended into madness, but who managed to leave no evidence, at all, behind. No eyewitnesses, no physical evidence, no forensic evidence, no body. They made no admissions and continue to deny any involvement in his disappearance to this day. No motive was offered. It was a solid circumstantial case.

Or was it something completely different?

It is not known what happened on Palmerville Station that Monday 9 July 2012, but it is known the story told by the prospectors was embraced with gusto and adopted as fact by police and prosecutors alike, despite the known and acknowledged discrepancies within the evidence. The story that played out in the Cairns Supreme Court murder trial in July 2015 was very unlikely to be the same story that occurred on Palmerville Station that fateful Monday three years earlier.

Is it possible experienced detectives were seemingly blindsided by gold prospectors with limited education but unlimited cunning, with a hidden agenda telling a story nothing short of incredulous?

Husband and wife leaseholders who describe themselves as kidnapped. Convicted of murder and sentenced to life in prison with no chance of parole for a crime they vehemently claim they did not commit; their claims strongly supported by the now uncovered (but previously ghost) evidence. The bizarre story continues to this day.

This is a work of non-fiction. But what if the entire story, as told to the jury, was fabricated, from start to finish?

Fool's Gold? has it all.

This is the definitive account of what became known as The Bruce Schuler Murder.

Cast of Characters

The main characters in this tragedy are:

Bruce Schuler	Victim, body has never been found
Fiona Splitt	Bruce Schuler's partner of 28 years
Lisa Schuler	Their daughter
Stephen Struber	Palmerville Station Lease Holder
Dianne Wilson-Struber	Palmerville Station Lease Holder
George Wilson	Palmerville Station resident
Bertie Callaghan	Next door neighbour
Daniel Bidner	Prospector and witness
Jo Bidner	Dan Bidner's wife
Tremain Anderson	Prospector and witness
Kevin 'Rusty' Groth	Prospector and witness
Detective Sergeant Brad McLeish	Police Investigator
Acting Detective Sergeant Nicholas O'Brien	Police Investigator
Detective Sergeant Graham Camp	Police Investigator
Detective Senior Constable Alina Bell	Police Investigator
Senior Constable Scott Ezard	Forensic Investigator
Nigel Rees	Crown Prosecutor

Peter Feeney				Barrister for Stephen Struber

Joshua Trevino				Barrister for Dianne Wilson

I refer to Dianne Wilson-Struber as Dianne Wilson.

Background to a Murder

Set on Palmerville Station on remote Cape York, Queensland in July 2012. Station Lease Holders Stephen Struber and Dianne Wilson claimed they were going about their business, unaware of the disappearance of Bruce Schuler on their property, until their arrest. Both lease holders were ultimately convicted of his murder and sentenced to life imprisonment and destined to die in prison due to no body no parole legislation.

Four prospectors were trespassing and gold detecting on Palmerville Station when the lease holders, Stephen Struber and Dianne Wilson came across them. Prospectors Daniel Bidner and his mate of more than twenty years Tremain Anderson, Bruce Schuler and Bruce's long time mate Kevin Groth. Groth had only met Bidner and Anderson for the first time, the previous day. The three prospectors told police they heard gunfire and now Bruce was missing.

The three prospectors never saw anyone fire a weapon. Never saw Bruce Schuler shot or killed. Never saw the offenders removing the body. They heard two shots, very little else. Police arrived the next day and spoke with the lease holders who denied any knowledge of the matter and claimed they had spent the day on another party of their holdings. The police arrested and charged the Strubers with Bruce Schuler's murder there and then.

The subsequent trial was circumstantial: no body, no cause of death, no admissions, no actual witnesses, blood stains on leaves and rocks identified as Schuler's and a small amount of other forensic evidence. The Crown claimed the Strubers murdered Bruce Schuler using a .22 calibre rifle and a .357 magnum revolver. Both weapons are suspiciously now missing.

I became involved as a true crime podcaster in 2023, to tell the story of the murder. Hoping to perhaps, find some evidence that may lead to the whereabouts of Bruce Schuler's remains. Not just a one episode per murder type podcast, but as many episodes as it took to cover the case. Almost immediately, there was difficulty scripting the story as the prospectors' versions of events consistently changed and did not align. Initially confusing, it turned to concern and dismay as more discrepancies in their evidence were identified.

The police investigators were obviously aware of the discrepancies as it was difficult to ignore them. The prosecutor was aware of *some* discrepancies[1], as h acknowledged at trial.

The murder of Bruce Schuler and the conviction of the Strubers is a story that needs to be told. The problems with the evidence in this case casts serious doubt on the credibility and honesty of the three main witnesses and by default, on the guilt of the convicted murderers.

As the result of a legislation change in Queensland from these very convictions, the Strubers have been handed a death sentence. They will die in prison unless they reveal the whereabouts of Bruce Schuler's body. A claim they continue to hold to this day that they do not know the whereabouts of his remains.

If they did not murder Bruce Schuler, who did?

On the following page you will find a photograph of the crime scene to help you orientate yourself. I have simplified it as much as possible. As you will learn, there were no nearby street names to help you understand the location. I have kept with the basics where possible, including where Schuler was supposedly last seen and where he allegedly ran towards and where the Struber vehicle allegedly came from and travelled to. I have purposefully left out any reference to where the witnesses were when they first allegedly saw the Struber vehicle, where they said they ran to when they heard the shots etc. You will read the witnesses say where they went. It is not really relevant. What is important is what they said they saw and heard. Or, mostly

---

[1] Crown Prosecutor summing up at trial

what they did not see or hear. I have marked an X where the vehicle turned around based on the versions Bidner and Anderson told police over several interviews. It could have been twenty metres either way, but unlikely to have been any more. You can make up your own mind as to whether it was fair and reasonable to tell the jury they could infer the Struber vehicle went to the second crime scene[2] referred to as the Burnt Patches in the photograph.

There are four main points of reference in this case. It is that simple:

1. The '**X**' where the Struber vehicle allegedly first stopped, located near the old mining plant, where a shot was fired (First Crime Scene). NO evidence of any kind recovered here[3].
2. The '**u-turn**' 'where the alleged vehicle, according to the three witnesses, turned around after firing two shots[4].
3. The '**Ear Lobe**' where the vehicle had to travel to reach the Burnt Patches.
4. The '**Burnt Patches**' (Second Crime Scene) located at the bottom of a steep ravine from the Ear Lobe. Bruce Schuler's blood and DNA were located there[5]. The vehicle had to drive down and up that ravine to murder Bruce Schuler and remove his body[6].

---

[2] Crown Prosecutor summing up at trial
[3] Evidence of Bidner and Anderson
[4] Evidence of Bidner, Anderson and Groth
[5] Police evidence.
[6] Inferred by the prosecutor

Crime Scene Location

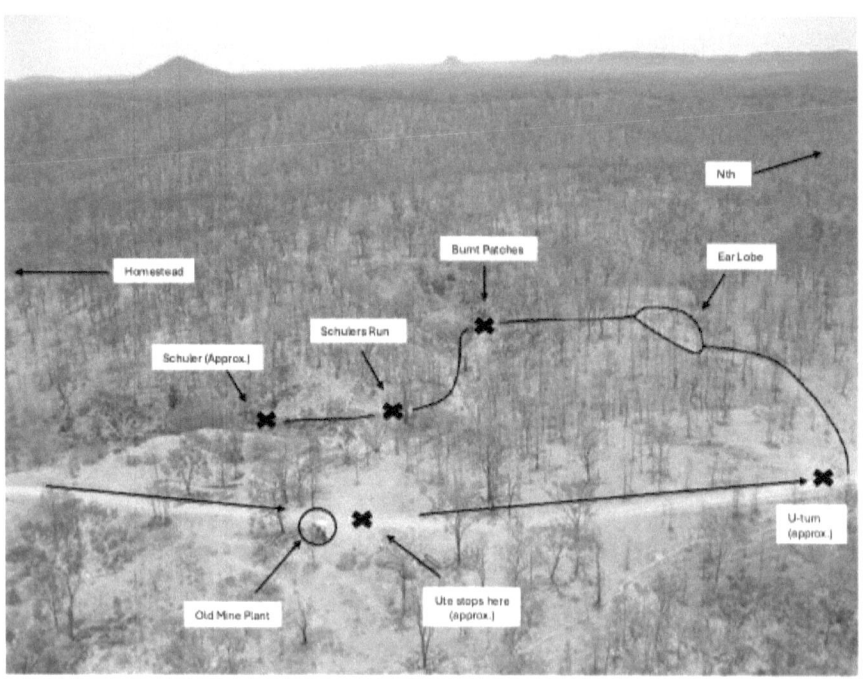

Where is Bruce Schuler Podcast

My name is Graeme Crowley. I investigate true crime through my podcasts. I have over forty years' experience as a police investigator, private investigator for criminal and civil cases and other associated fields. I enjoy analysing the evidence in cold cases, particularly violent crime, and determining *'if the system got it right.'* As of 2025, I have researched, scripted and recorded seven true crime podcasts covering almost 100 episodes from missing persons to murder. It is my fervent hope that my work will lead to police forces improving their procedures, not just in Queensland. My feedback is police do not like true crime podcasts, so I feel I am doing something right.

I do believe in the justice system, even with its many faults. I may be described as a Justice tragic – '*Do the crime, do the time*.' But equally, if you didn't do the crime, you shouldn't do the time. My passion is wrongful convictions – Miscarriages of Justice. As I said, I am a justice tragic. If there is one thing I have learned, the justice system does not always get it right. We live in the 21st Century and in some ways, it irks me that the legal system can and does rely, at times, on legal decisions from the 18th, 19th and 20th Centuries for precedence. I believe the Justice System can do better and needs to modernise. I do not profess to know the answers, but I do like asking the questions.

If there is one thing, I have learned over the years it is '*there are always problems with circumstantial cases*.' That does not mean the offender is innocent in every circumstantial case. Not by any stretch. That is well proven. What it does mean is if there are going to be questions about the evidence, it will usually be in a circumstantial case. By its very name you know there may be problems with the evidence. By coincidence perhaps, an anagram for '*circumstantial evidence'* is '*can ruin a selected victim.'* But remember the motto. *Do the crime, do the time*. I have no interest in giving killers oxygen, to give them a platform to spread their claims of '*I didn't do it.*' As more than one person has quipped '*Everyone in prison claims to be innocent.*'

By 2022, I had podcasted two brutal murders in detail with over fifty podcast episodes between them. One, '*Who Killed Leanne Holland*' I had investigated for over twenty years. The conviction of Graham Stafford was ultimately quashed for the murder of Leanne Holland in 2009. I spent two years researching the 2003 brutal triple murder in Brisbane of the Singh children, covered in "*Loose Ends: the Singh Family Tragedy*', a crime that garnered significant media attention. The new evidence surrounding the conviction of Massimo Sica for the Singh murders is very concerning and disturbing. You will be hearing more about that case as an Appeal to the Court of Appeal against his conviction has been lodged in 2025.

The trial and conviction of Graham Stafford for the murder of Leanne Holland was, according to the trial Judge and the Court of Appeal, a '*strong circumstantial and forensic case,*' until it wasn't. The trial and conviction of Massimo Sica was a strong circumstantial case. I believe it too will eventually reach the status of '*until it wasn't.*'

In 2021 I became aware of the Bruce Schuler case. It was suggested to me that it would be suitable for a podcast. It sounded interesting but I was also occupied with other podcasts. I did not have the opportunity to focus on this until 2023 and when I did, my initial research suggested it was a '*slam dunk*'. The police had got their man; or man and woman in this case. The case against Stephen Struber and Dianne Wilson was circumstantial but compelling. I read everything I could on the subject. Books, newspaper articles, television and YouTube stories. I then read the trial transcript and Appeal documents. My wife did the same and agreed with me, the police got it right. This made me even more curious about the suggestion made to me that there had been a wrongful conviction.

The Bruce Schuler murder was a classic case to review. It is very hard to cross check the evidence of a solo witness to a crime. But when you have *three* witnesses to a crime, it opens pandora's box. No two witnesses are ever going to be able to give accounts that are consistent in every aspect, and you would not want them to be. That is human nature. I would be concerned if that were the case. You would expect some divergence in the finer details, but for the big-ticket items, the significant events, where they were all present at the same time, you'd want there to be some level of consistency between their accounts. There are any number of commonalities where you should see consistency. I was excited to get into the nitty-gritty.

As a podcaster, another reason this case fascinated me was the position the killers have sustained. They refuse (or are unable) to disclose the whereabouts of the body. I was certain they understood the ramifications of this. It was over six years since the 'no body, no parole' legislation had been passed, led by these very convictions. There's been a lot of water under the bridge since that time. I wondered if, by speaking with their family members they may be persuaded to give up the body. As far as I was able to determine, the last time anyone asked them face to face to disclose the whereabouts of Bruce Schuler was 2019[7]. Plenty of time to reconsider their fate.

I wanted to find out whether anyone – relatives or friends had recently spoken to them to see if they had reconsidered their position. If they had not spoken to them, whether they would be willing to speak to them now, and ask them, to find out where Bruce Schuler's remains lay.

By 2023, it had been over eleven years since Bruce's disappearance and more than eight years since Struber and Wilson were convicted of his murder. Plenty of time to consider their bleak future. Plenty of time to decide whether they wished to die in prison or perhaps see the outside world sometime before they die.

Stephen Struber has apparently always refused to talk. Dianne Wilson maintains her innocence and that of her husband. A wife's loyalty perhaps? I have since ascertained that this was the first incorrect rumour. Stephen Struber does talk, just, not to everyone.

---

[7] Journalist Robert Reid and retired policeman Robert Haydon

I was able to speak with relatives of both prisoners, and they agreed to talk to Stephen and Dianne on my behalf. They have weekly contact with them, I was told. Prison regulations prohibit me from interviewing incarcerated criminals. The families were more than willing to assist. Everyone I have spoken to were grateful that someone was taking an interest in the case. The common theme was that they just want the truth to be heard. Families of both convicted persons believe a grave injustice has been done. Not one of their families believe they are guilty. The families do speak with both prisoners by telephone at least weekly. They also visit in-person when they can. I asked them a simple question to pass on to both Dianne and Stephen:

'*Do you still maintain your innocence and claim not to know the whereabouts of Bruce Schuler's body?*'

The answer was a resounding **YES** from both Dianne and Stephen. That answered that question. Both parties were aware of the '*No body no parole*' legislation and understood the implications. They could not disclose the whereabouts of Bruce Schuler's body because they did not kill him, and they do not know where it lay, they said.

Then there was the suggestion of a wrongful conviction. Some people believe the Strubers did not commit the murder. If they didn't commit the murder, then who did? I wanted to explore those claims and see whether there was any truth to them or whether it was just rumour and gossip. As I began researching the case, I became amazed at the incredible amount of rumour, gossip and innuendo swirling around this case and around Palmerville Station, as well.

Wrongful convictions fascinate me for a variety of reasons. What causes them? How to identify them? How to prevent them? How to make the system better? More than anything, I hate the thought that someone has committed a brutal murder and is roaming around free, whilst someone else is paying the penalty.

In case you are wondering, what can cause a wrongful conviction, it varies from case to case. I believe however, it is never just one factor: it is always several issues that align, like the planets. From my experience and research, common factors include (but are not limited to):

- Tunnel vision by investigators.
- Witness misidentification.
- Witnesses lying under oath.
- Poor Police procedures or investigations.
- Misconduct by police or prosecutors.
- Poor legal representation of the defendants.

I still had the ever-growing list of questions regarding the evidence given by the prospectors to deal with, as well as the suggestion that the Strubers were wrongfully convicted.

At the time of publication, twenty-three episodes of the podcast have aired. If you are interested in listening to the podcast, you will find it wherever you find your podcasts, and it is called *'Where is Bruce Schuler?'* Whilst researching this case, I was stunned at the anger, the resentment and the bitterness in the communities in Far North Queensland over this case. The communities are divided over the Schuler case. Some people I spoke with believed the leaseholders were responsible for the murder, whilst others believed the prospectors were implicated in the disappearance of Bruce Schuler. There was no other variance proffered. Everyone had an opinion on the case. As I dug deeper, I was surprised at the number of people, residents, many of them prospectors themselves, who had taken it upon themselves to investigate the case. Some knew the Strubers, some didn't. They didn't believe the evidence. Some were making inquiries because they knew the Palmerville area. They knew the location where the murder allegedly happened. They had doubts. Others were making inquiries because they knew at least two of the prospector witnesses and they didn't believe their claims.

Not that everyone knew all the details of the murder. Most people, (even Bruce Schuler's family knew only the barest of details). The media had been very selective in their reporting, as you will read, and I believe that was the reason the rumour and gossip festered and thrived. To be fair though, the media can only report what they are told.

The other thing that really surprised me was the position that the Cairns based media adopted. They did not have a nice word to say about the Strubers. In fact, they did not have any word at all to say about the suspects. I could not find any balanced reporting on the case. The police case was the only story going. That led to gossip, rumour and questions.

People had heard rumours that there were problems with the case, with the evidence, but there was nothing to support those rumours. The defendants were on bail for almost three years, but it did not appear any reporters had researched the case, spoken with the defendants or their family to find out why they would be in this situation. Bizarre!

Perhaps it was their isolation. Perhaps it was difficult to write a story around '*we weren't there.*' I believe that claim would have opened up a whole world of questions. My experience has been that journalists would usually sniff around a story such as this and background the defendants. That did not appear to have happened here.

As the podcast progressed, the discrepancies mounted. The police and prosecution did not seem concerned about them. I struggled with the idea that you could have three witnesses whose story lines were so divergent. I research true crime cases and record podcasts covering them. I tell the story as reported by the people involved. When the stories do not align, I cannot just make the story up. I go looking for the truth. That is what my listeners want to hear. Simple. I was fascinated by the police position of '*nothing to see here.*' There were two books written on the case based on the *trial evidence*. My podcast was the first to tell both sides of the story and to question the Crown version of events. How dare I!

I was immediately swamped with feedback from listeners with their own concerns about the evidence. I was not the only one suspicious of the evidence I found. I produced ten episodes of the podcast and although I had covered all the apparent evidence, I had a feeling of unease about the case.

In December 2023, I spoke to one of the arresting officers, Detective Sergeant McLeish and interviewed him for the podcast. In earlier correspondence with him, he reiterated the Crown position – '*I strongly disagree with you (*sic*) assertion that there are numerous inconsistencies in the evidence of the boys. They were put under enormous pressure by us during the investigation and were forced to given (*sic*) numerous versions/statements. Of course there are inconsistencies because they are human beings not robots. I would challenge you to find a witness in any court case where there are NOT inconsistencies when the witness has given multiple accounts/statements and then gives evidence in. court.*'

I agree there would be inconsistencies. There should be inconsistencies. I expected that. But so many? For such significant events? Of the almost 150 inconsistencies I identified in the witnesses' evidence, the police could see nothing amiss. I could see everything wrong with them.

In March 2024, I wrote to Sergeant McLeish and Crown Prosecutor Nigel Rees and invited them to participate in an interview for the podcast. I forwarded to both a list of twenty-one matters of concern I had identified with the evidence from the prospectors. As at the time of publication, I have not received a response from either person. You can find the full email with the list of matters in Appendix D.

I also forwarded emails to Defence Barristers P Feeney and now Cairns District Court Judge J Trevino with a list of eight matters concerning their former clients at trial and requested an interview for the podcast. I did not receive a reply from either barrister. You can find the full email with the list of matters in Appendix D.

I moved on to my next podcast but retained this unsettling feeling about the Schuler matter. That was March 2024. Five months later, the unease had not left me. I was back to researching the Schuler case. That led to a further thirteen episodes of the podcast being produced. By then, I had looked under every rock and in every crevice but was still not happy with the evidence of the prospectors. In fact, my suspicions had only increased.

To my mind, all three prospectors had zero credibility as witnesses. It seemed to me that either the Strubers had murdered Bruce Schuler and for some bizarre reason, at least two of the prospectors were lying about their evidence; or the Strubers were not involved in the murder, and it had been completely fabricated by the prospectors, a position which was bordering on the absurd.

How to deal with the 142 discrepancies with their evidence, some minor, some very significant. I did not view it as my role to decide what was a minor or major discrepancy. My role was to present them, '*warts and all.*' The full list of discrepancies identified in the evidence in this case can be found as Appendix A.

When I was researching the 1991 Leanne Holland case and co-wrote the non-fiction book '*Who Killed Leanne Holland*' in the year 2000, I understood the impact the public exposure had on the case. It suddenly propelled the story into people's consciousness. The media started taking an interest in the case. That was eight years after the murder and conviction of Graham Stafford. It would be a further nine years before his conviction was overturned. The case is still ongoing today. If you are interested in reading about that case, I wrote an updated version of the book in 2024 under the title '*The Leanne Holland Murder.*' You will find it on Amazon as an E book or soft cover printed version.

The Bruce Schuler podcast has had amazing interest and feedback. There would now be scant community members of Far North Queensland who would not be familiar with the controversial nature of this case, as these details were not published by local media. But it is still just basically an on-demand radio show, which attracts only a small percentage of the population. As a fascinating story and potentially a huge miscarriage of justice, I wanted to reach a larger portion of the population.

And here we are. You will read of matters that were not raised at trial. This is the '*warts and all*' story of the disappearance and murder of Bruce Schuler.

Our mate is missing

The phone call that started it all. The precursor for a drama that is still unfolding today, some thirteen years later. A sad and initially plausible story made potentially implausible with the ever-changing story line by the witnesses, initially on a daily basis. The contents of the conversation contained in this phone call become significant and referenced in many later chapters. This conversation occurred, for the main part, only twelve hours after the main events. Why does it change so often? I also refer to the conversation when I explore stressful situations and whether Dan Bidner was exhibiting any signs of stress or trauma.

The time was 7.12 p.m. The date was Monday 9 July 2012. The place was Maytown, Far North Queensland. The three prospectors gave varying accounts of who they called to report Bruce missing.

They said they rang all the police stations in the district. Cooktown Police Station, 250 kilometres away did not answer. Chillagoe Police Station, 400 kilometres away, also did not answer. They said they rang the national emergency number, 000. Eventually, Tremain Anderson called Laura Police Station, also the nearest police at eighty kilometres distance. Officer Tome spoke with both Tremain Anderson and Daniel Bidner and wrote contemporaneous and comprehensive notes of both conversations. I have reduced them to bullet form for ease of reference and I have not reproduced all notes. These are the officers own words.

Officer Tome first spoke with Tremain Anderson:

- Anderson stated at approx. 10.30 a.m. he & 3 mates were prospecting on the Palmer River approx. 1.5 klm from homestead.
- Anderson observed a light fawn coloured Toyota utility with no side boards travel nearby and Anderson identified this vehicle as belonging to Stephen Struber.

- Utility has pulled up near to where Schuler was prospecting.
- Anderson has sat down to avoid being seen.
- After approx. 5 minutes a shot was heard.
- After approx. 10 minutes the vehicle has moved a short distance before stopping and another shot was heard.
- After approx. half an hour the vehicle departed.
- A search of the area was conducted by Anderson however no trace of the MP or his property was located.

Officer Tome then spoke with Daniel Bidner:
- Bidner stated he had a better view than Anderson.
- He was 50 metres from MP when he saw vehicle pull up.
- He saw Schuler & his dog hiding in a gully.
- When the vehicle stopped the dog started barking.
- Bidner saw Wilson & Struber exit the vehicle, Wilson was carrying a rifle. Wilson & Struber have walked over to the gully.
- Bidner has squatted down and could no longer see.
- Bidner heard at least one shot.
- After approx. 10 minutes vehicle started & drove a short distance before stopping.
- Another gunshot heard.
- Vehicle then started after approx. half an hour and drove off.

Officer Tome informed the witnesses that someone would be in touch. When I research a case, I like to set out the story line in a chronological order, where possible. I find that the best way to cover it. I was not to know it at the time, but the versions given by both witnesses to Officer Tome were to change repeatedly, and almost immediately.

At 9.10 p.m. that same night, Acting Detective Sergeant Nick O'Brien from Cooktown police called Daniel Bidner, who was at his home in Maytown. Although the call lasted twenty-five minutes, the detective recorded call ending at 9.26 p.m.[8]

---

[8] Police Diary of A/Det Sgt O'Brien

The following is a transcript of part of that conversation, audio recorded by O'Brien:

'Today's date is the 9th day of July 2012; the time is now 10 minutes past 9 p.m. in the evening. For the record, my name is Acting Detective Sergeant Nick O'Brien of the Cooktown CIB. About to contact the informants in relation to this matter, in relation to the missing person and disappearance of Bruce Schuler, believed to be 48 years of age, was in the company of a Daniel Bidner, a Kevin Groth and a Tremain Anderson at the vicinity of Maytown and possibly at the Maytown Crossing.

Attempting to contact the informants now who are believed to be at the Butcher Creek Mining Camp, a phone number has been provided of 4060-2---.'

'**Hello?**'

'Hello, it's Detective Acting Sergeant Nick O'Brien from the Cooktown CIB. How are you?'

'**Nick O'Brien, how are you going?**'

(**Author note** - Was this a social call or a 000 Emergency call?)

'Good, Daniel, is it?'

'*Yes.*'

'Daniel, mate, I'm the Acting Detective Sergeant of the Cooktown CIB.'

'*Yep.*'

'I've just been advised by the Laura Police in relation to what's occurred today.'

'*Yep.*'

'Mate, I'm just ringing to touch base with you. I know you've obviously spoken to Ben Tome, the officer there.'

'*Yes.*'

'Mate, I'm the detective, so what I want to do, if I can just have a quick chat to you. I know you've probably spoken to him already, but if we can go back to the start and if you can let me know what's happened.'

'Yep.'

'OK, can you tell me what's happened today, mate?'

'Um, what happened was we were out detecting.'

'Yep.'

'Down on the main crossing of the, where the main Palmerville road crosses Palmerville, crosses the Palmer.'

'Yep, that's that main that's quite big, isn't it?'

'Yes.'

'OK, yep.'

'And all the tourists, as we went through, there was tourists behind us and in front of us, you know, a couple of four-wheel drives with caravans and, or the camper vans, you know.'

'Yep.'

'Or, what do you call, camper trailers.'

'OK, yep.'

'And we went through and said, oh, I said to the boys, look, let's not hide out here, you know?'

'Yep.'

'Let's just camp right here on the river where the river's not part of his land, you know?'

'OK.'

'Let's just camp here and that way, if he comes along, we'll just chat to him, you know?'

'And who's that, mate? Obviously, you've got concerns of someone for the land. Who is that?'

'The person we're worried about?'

'Yeah.'

'Yeah, Struber.'

'Struber. Do you know his first name, mate?'

'Stephen.'

'Yep. OK. OK, yeah, go on.'

'And we got down into the crossing. We said, right, let's just camp here. So we set up camp last night. A couple of us walked upstream. And two of us walked downstream. There's four of us all up.'

'OK, yep.'

'Two walked upstream, two walked downstream. We got back to camp. I got back a little bit early. I got back about five. I collected a little bit of firewood for the fire that night.'

'OK, yep.'

'And I'm talking we're within 100 metres of the crossing.'

'OK, yep. Right there at the tourist crossing. OK.'

'And then I got a bit of firewood together, and it would have been about 5.30, the other boys walked in.'

'OK, yep.'

'Yeah, and none of us had gold. One of the lads found a couple of pieces.'

'Yep, righto.'

'We're like, oh, yeah, well, where'd you get that, bud? Tomorrow morning, hey, we'll hit that, you know.'

'Yep.'

'But he said, yeah, he just found it down the river here, which is a little bit closer to Palmerville, which would have been another 200 metres downstream.'

'OK.'

'And so next morning, we had no trouble that night. We slept through till 5.30 in the morning.'

'OK.'

'Had a fire going. We weren't hiding or anything, you know.'

'Righto, yep.'

'And then next morning, we got up 5.30. We would have hung around camp, I reckon, till about 6.30, quarter to seven. All right, off we went, and because we had to cross the creek, we took our boots off. We hadn't put our boots on yet. We put our boots on when we crossed the creek.'

'OK, yep.'

(**Author note** – O'Brien and Bidner were talking to each other on the very same day this murder occurred, that very morning, yet Daniel Bidner was speaking as if it happened on another day. That is regularly referenced by language experts as a fabrication.)

'Because we had to walk through the water a little bit. And off we went, and we would have only been out probably an hour, if that.'

'Yep.'

'If that. Probably more like three-quarters of an hour.'

'OK, yep.'

'And the other bloke said, oh, this is where I got that gold here, you know.'

'OK.'

'So, and, you know, those metal detector machines, they can't operate together.'

'Oh, OK.'

'Because they're noisy with each other.'

'Righto.'

'So one bloke said, oh, well, he'd never found a piece of gold. So we said, oh, you have a look here, matey, aye.'

'Righto.'

'And we'll go and just walk down the creek and have a look around, you know.'

'Yep.'

'So we're just walking down the creek, looking around. I'd only just not, I'd probably half an hour left there.'

'Righto.'

'And then I thought, oh, bugger this, they should be finished by now. I'm going to go back to where the gold was found, you know.'

'OK, yep.'

'So I started walking back to where the gold was found.'

'Yep.'

'And I looked down, I came up on a high spur.'

'Yep.'

'Looked down into the ravine and saw me mate down there, metal detector, which is the bloke that's missing.'

'Yep.'

'And I said, oh, yeah, bloody Bruce is down there, yeah, oh, yeah. I'll just sit here and see if he, you know, because I'm waiting for him to piss off so I can go and have a little look there, you know.'

'Yep, yep.'

'And just while I sat, I just sat down on me bum.'

'Yep.'

'And I heard a car coming. So I went, oh, shit, here comes the bloody, probably that station owner, you know.'

'Yep.'

'Stephen Struber. So I squatted down and yep, fair enough, up the little spur comes Struber with his missus. And at the very same moment I heard Bruce's dog bark.'

'OK, yep.'

'And at the same time Bruce said quiet, you know, like telling his dog to be quiet.'

'Yep.'

'And that was what made Struber stop. He heard the dog.'

'OK, yep.'

'And I couldn't see Stephen but I saw his wife's arm out the window, like the two of them in the car.'

'Yep.'

'I could see him but as they came up I lost vision because she was on the passenger side.'

'Yep.'

'So she was my most vision.'

'Yep.'

'I reckon I was probably 150 metres from them.'

(This distance changes regularly as the days pass.)

'OK.'

'Sitting in the bush and, you know, I'm still, I'm thinking, oh, they won't see me, I'm dead still and I'm dressed in camo gear.'

'Yep.'

'And not camo but just khaki, you know.'

'Yep, yep.'

'Normal bloody khaki gear. Anyway, and then I saw her bring the gun out of the car and I went, oh, shit. So I sort of, I got up and I thought I'll take the risk here of moving, you know what I mean?'

'OK, yep.'

'I thought they might see movement, you know.'

'Yep.'

'So I thought, nah, I seen that gun, I went, I know I'm going to make a move here. So I walked probably 50 metres away.'

(The distance he moves also changes regularly.)

'OK.'

'And squatted down at that point. I lost vision.'

'OK.'

'Right. Because I'd walked 50 metres away.'

'OK.'

'It cost me vision. But at one point my last vision was him and her getting out of the car, her with the gun.'

'What sort of gun did she have, mate?'

'Oh, look, I'm not sure, bro.

'OK.'

'Long rifle, it was a rifle.'

'OK, yep, that's fine, yep.'

'All I know, a long gun.'

'Yep.'

'I thought it was a shottie (shotgun) myself, but the boys said, nah, Dan, that was a high-powered rifle. And I said, oh, I really thought it was a 12-gauge or something, you know.'

(The type of weapon Bidner claims he saw and heard also changes often.)

'OK, yep.'

'But we dispute that between ourselves.'

'That's fine, that's fine.'

'And then, like I said, I squatted down there at the 50, after moving 50 metres, I stayed still.'

'Yep.'

'And that's when I heard the first gunshot. And I went, oh, shit, they're letting guns off. I thought they might have seen me as I moved.'

(As you will read, he told Officer Tome that he heard at least one shot.)

'Yep.'

'And they were shooting a gun to let me know that they know I'm in there, you know what I mean?'

'OK, yep.'

'But now I doubt that because nobody come looking for us. He never came looking for us or anything.'

'Yep.'

'And then within probably another 20 minutes, I moved another, after that second, the first shot. I moved another 50 metres away. And then I crouched in a gully. And I stayed there probably at least 20 minutes. And then probably would only have been 15, 20 minutes, I heard the second gunshot.'

'Yep.'

'And I heard voices. I know that.'

'Yeah, what sort of voices, mate? Were they male, female?'

'To be honest, bro, they didn't sound raised to me but it was definitely voices.'

'OK.'

'Three people talked, like, a couple of voices, you know?'

'Yep.'

'Can't be sure on the three, but I definitely heard a couple of voices.'

'OK.'

'And as I'm trying to listen, all I can hear is my heart beating, you know what I mean?'

'Yep.'

'So I'm in a bit of a scare.'

'Yeah, that's understandable.'

'Yep. And as I'm trying to listen, I'm thinking, it's pretty quiet out there except for a few birds, you know?'

'Yep.'

'And so, I just crouched down and then, like I said, the second gunshot went off.'

'OK.'

'So, I just stayed where I was and stayed there. And then I heard the car started, moved a little bit, and then it stopped again. And I heard a clang on the back of the ute, like someone dropping a crowbar or some bit of steel on the back of a black bed tray. And then they moved *off. And then I heard the car, would have been like 20 minutes, again, half hour before that car moved the second time.'*

'OK.'

'And when it started up to move the second time, it turned around and drove back down the spur, along the river, back towards the homestead. The only thing I regret, Sarge, is I didn't lift my head up to, because I was scared, you know, worried.'

'But that's understandable.'

'I didn't lift my head high to visually get a visual. I lifted my head a little bit, but I didn't stand up. And I just saw, like, the top bars of the car, you know, like the roof and the top bars.'

'Yep.'

(I devote an upcoming chapter to *'The only thing I regret, Sarge.'*)

'And I went, oh, yeah, there they go. Hopefully thinking, oh, well, Bruce will be there. I'll go back and see him, you know?'

'Yep.'

'So, I waited about five minutes. I got up and started walking back towards where I last saw him.'

'OK.'

'And he was gone. And we haven't seen him since.'

Detective O'Brien had been taking notes as well as recording the conversation. These are part of those notes he read back to Bidner:

'And you heard a car coming.'

'Yep.

'And you believe that car to possibly be Stephen's car?'

'I don't believe. I saw it, and I know that it is his car.'

(This becomes relevant – no doubt, no confusion. No memory fog.)

'OK, yep.'

'I witnessed them in visual. I had not long seen them a couple of weeks beforehand.'

'Now, just make sure I've got this right. You hear the second gunshot, the car starts up and it moves, but it only goes a short distance?'

'*Exactly.*'

'At this point in time, you can't see the vehicle?'

'*No.*'

'OK, so you can't say whether it was 100, 200, 300 metres?'

'*No, it sounded like 100 metres.*'

'OK, all right. It sounded like.'

'*Yep. It moved about 100 metres.*'

(That too becomes very significant and is covered in the chapter 'Ghost Evidence.')

'Then the car stops for a period of time?'

'*Yep, and I heard like a clang, like someone dropping a crowbar or a bit of steel or something on the back of a tray. It's got a tray on the back of it with no side gates on it. They don't have side gates on the Ute.*'

'No side gates.'

'*And then off it went back towards Palmerville Station.*'

'Did it do a u-turn or just go straight ahead?'

'*A full u-turn.*'

(This becomes very relevant).

'Yep, OK, righto then.'

'*And I even went and tracked that u-turn. Like, after they left, I went right. I'll go and see what they said to Bruce, you know what I mean?*'

(Bidner at trial vigorously denies this happening and retracts his own evidence.)

'Yep.'

'*So, I gave it another 10 minutes after the car left me.*'

'Yep.'

'And I got up out of my position.'

'Yep.'

'And I walked back to exactly which, as you know, as I've just said, I was only 100 metres from.'

'Yep.'

'So, I walked back to that position, looked down, I couldn't see Bruce. And I went, oh, maybe he's walked back to the car.'

'Yep.'

'So, I crossed through the exact spot that I last saw Bruce.'

'OK.'

'Because we'd found gold there.'

'Yep.'

'And I was tempted to even metal detect. And I thought, no, I won't because I want to see Bruce first, you know?'

'Yep.'

'So, and he had a dog with him and the dog wasn't around. So, I kept walking and probably, it's probably only another 300 metres back to the car.'

'Yep.'

'And I kept going. I was up on a high spur looking, our car was in the centre of the river.'

'Yep.'

'I looked down in the river and I saw nothing. And I went, oh, no one's at the car at the moment. So, I probably walked around for another five minutes and I looked down at the car and I saw the dog there.'

'OK, yep.'

'And I went, oh, Bruce must be back at the car.'

'OK, yep.'

'*So, I crossed the creek, as I said, wading to take my boots off again.*'
'*Yep.*'

'*You get across the creek because it's all water. So, I waded across, you know, you get wet up to your crotch.*'
'*Yep.*'

'*Got across, put my bloody, hung my boots up, walked up to the car. There's a dog there and no Bruce to be seen.*'
'*OK.*'

'*Never saw or heard Struber again after that.*'

'*OK. And I've obviously been told, but just for my own records, you're in the company of two other blokes?*'

'**Three other blokes, yep.**'

'*Yep. So, you're with Bruce?*'

'**I was with Bruce, my mate Tremain, and the other bloke, which is Rusty, nickname is.**'

'*Yep, what's Rusty's full name, mate?*'

'**Rusty, what's your name again? Kevin Groth, G-R-O-T-H.**'

'*OK. All right. Mate, I know this is a little bit difficult. I just want to take you back to you walked up to...*'

'**I'm happy to answer anything.**'

'*OK, you said that you walked back to where you last saw Bruce?*'

'**Yep.**'

'*Did you see any signs or anything? Did you...*'

'**No, I didn't really think to look much then, you know what I mean?**'
'*OK, yep.*'

'**But I didn't see any sign.**'
'*Yep.*'

'**But after I went back to the car and waited for a while...**'
'*Yep.*'

'Me and Tremain went... Oh, Tremain went back first. I also went back.'

'Yep.'

'And looking for blood, you know, we thought, oh, maybe he shot him, you know?'

'Yep.'

'So, we went back to the site separately.'

(Another statement Bidner strenuously denies having said, at trial).

'OK, yep.'

'And looked. Tremain kept going towards the homestead.'

'Yep.'

'And thinking that maybe down that way a bit.'

'Yep.'

'We couldn't find any sign of blood or anything. But that's what I said to you. We did track where the car turned around. We went, yeah. I said, yeah, that's right, bro. I saw it. I didn't see it turn around, but I heard it turn around.'

'OK, yep. And was Bruce still in possession of the prospecting utensil or...?'

'When I last witnessed him, yes.'

'And you didn't find that?'

'No.'

'So that's missing as well?'

'OK'

'Bro, we're worried, eh?

'I can understand that. How long have you known Bruce for?'

'Probably the last six months. He's sort of bought a lease up the road here, just been getting his plant going, and we've sort of had a few discussions about what he's doing and that, you know, mining and that.'

'Yep. OK. And, yeah, you're staying at this place, obviously, tonight?'

'Yeah, bro, we live here, yep.'

'OK, you live there?'

'Yep.'

'All right. Now, tomorrow, myself and some other officers are going to be out there. We'll come take up with you.'

'Yep.'

'So, mate, if I can get you to stay at that property...'

'Yep.'

'OK, now, Daniel, to the best of your recollection, now, Tremain and Rusty, they were over in the creek, is that right, from where you were when you heard the first gunshot?'

'Well, I wasn't sure where they were until after I'd seen them, you know, but they were within 100 metres, yes.'

'OK, all right.'

'They were within 100 metres. After the first gunshot, we all sort of bolted, you know.'

'Understandable, understandable. All right, Daniel, thank you very...'

'And then we waited, bro, like eight hours. This happened at 10 o'clock this morning. At least. We argue about whether it was 9.30 or 10.'

'OK.'

'But it was between 9.30 and 10.30. I don't even think it was 10.30, more like 9.30, 10.'

'OK, yeah.'

'And then we sat at the car till 1 o'clock and I left, because Bruce had the keys to his car, see?'

'Yeah.'

'So we had no access to his vehicle, which had all that stuff in it.'

'OK, yeah.'

'So then I jumped on, Tremain had a little motorbike here, a little 125.'

'Yeah.'

'I jumped on that and rode back to Maytown, which is about, back to my place, which is about an hour.'

'OK, yeah.'

'Exactly an hour's ride.'

'Righto.'

'And I jumped in my car, and I waited here till 3 o'clock for Tremain's got a satphone...'

'Yeah.'

'...to ring me and say whether he'd turned up or not, you know.'

'OK.'

'And when he said, no, bro, no-one's turned up, I said, right, I'll be there to pick you up.'

'Righto.'

'So, then we left Bruce's car there with a foolscap note under the front wiper blade...'

'Yeah...'

'saying looking forward to you contacting us, ring us on your satphone, we've got your dog and we've got a bit of our gear.'

'Yeah.'

'Because he's got a ute, so some of our gear was in the back that wasn't locked, you know what I mean?'

'All right. All right. Mate, to your knowledge, is there been any tension directly between Bruce and Stephen? Obviously, I'm picking up that Stephen doesn't like people on his...'

'**Bruce has never met him.**'

'Bruce has never met him, OK.'

'But with the new road going through, sarge, they have had, you know Struber's probably had his fair share of people coming down that way, you know what I mean?'

'OK, yep.'

'Because the road's been opened up and there's tourists camping everywhere.'

' Yep.'

'Even around Maytown, I noticed this year, there's Winnebago's, there's all sorts of stuff, you know?'

'OK. All right, um, Dan, um, mate, we'll leave it at that tonight.'

'Now, listen, Sarge, one thing I didn't give Ben at Laura was his wife's phone number. He asked me for it.'

'Yep.'

'She's in Cooktown. She runs a video shop in Cooktown.'

'In Cooktown?'

'Yes.'

'And is Bruce from Cooktown as well?'

'Yes.'

'OK. What's her first name there, Dan?'

'Fiona. Fiona. And we haven't... Look, bro, we've told her that we can't find him.'

'Yep.'

'We didn't mention the gunshots.'

'OK, all right.'

'I just... Because we're hoping he'll turn up, you know? And he's also got a satphone in his car and all that.'

'Yep.'

'So, if he got back there now and he got to that note, then he would ring us, Sarge, you know?'

'Yep, yep.'

'So, I don't know, mate.'

'OK. All right, Dan, I'll leave it at that tonight. We'll see you early in the morning. So, um, we've got your number. We'll have satt phones, so we'll also be in touch with you.'

'Yep.'

'But we'll come take up with you in the morning, OK?'

'Righto, see you. All right.'

'If you hear anything, just leave a message at the Laura Police Station. See you, mate. The time is now 9.26 p.m. Just finished speaking to Dan Bidner.'

If evidence was a commodity such as gold, and so appropriate given the setting of this mystery, then a large amount of gold was on display and offered freely. A double murder arrest will always look good on your CV when the opportunity for a promotion comes around. By sleight of hand, was the glittering, sparkling commodity presented so abundantly just iron pyrite. Fool's Gold?

FNQ

This geographical corridor is known to many, from local residents to those who call Australia home, as FNQ. Far North Queensland. Spanning nearly 280,000 square kilometres, FNQ is larger than New Zealand which is only slightly smaller at 270,000 square kilometres. FNQ stretches from Cape York in the north, to Cardwell in the south, which lies roughly halfway between Cairns and Townsville. The region is home to some of Australia's most remarkable natural wonders, including the Great Barrier Reef and the Wet Tropics of Queensland world heritage site.

The main city is Cairns, with a population close to 200,000. About eighty kilometres to the west of Cairns, is the Atherton Tablelands, with Mareeba and Atherton the largest towns. To the west and north of the Atherton Tablelands is where the true remoteness of FNQ becomes apparent.

For many Australians, Cape York is a bucket list destination, a journey that demands careful planning to ensure a safe return. After all, it is 1000 kilometres from Cairns to the northernmost point of Australia by road. The roads are rough, mostly dirt with many creek crossings, and impassable in the wet season which lasts from around November to April each year. Those who fail to prepare for such a journey properly often don't make it without encountering breakdowns, injuries or misfortune.

People come to FNQ for many reasons: tourism, cattle farming, gold detecting, mining, fishing and the pure remoteness of the area. Unless you have an interest in mining, or gold, or live in the Cook Shire, you may be unaware of the history of the area as you pass through.

Cook Shire, where this murder occurred, covers the area around Cooktown and goes all the way to the northern tip of Australia but does not include the Torres Strait Islands. It was named after James Cook who chartered this unforgiving coastline. The shire has an estimated population of 4700 people, of which around half live in Cooktown, with the rest scattered across small, remote settlements, including Palmerville Station.

The geographical expanse of Palmerville is staggering.

Cooktown is about 200 kilometres to the northeast, by road. Mareeba is approximately 200 kilometres to the southeast, again by road. A further 100 kilometres past Mareeba is Cairns. Cairns is situated around 1700 kilometres north of the state capital of Brisbane. In the 2016 census, Palmerville recorded a zero population. By then, the only two occupants were in prison.

Palmerville cattle station was, in 2012, around 1360 square kilometres in area (or roughly the same size as Hong Kong), with a rich history of gold. At the time of the murder, there were about 5000 head of cattle on Palmerville Station. The property was run by husband-and-wife team Stephen Struber and Dianne Wilson, with some help. It must have been an enormous workload for all concerned. To gain an idea of the size of Palmerville Station, there are around seventy cattle properties of 50000 hectares or less in the Cook shire[9]. By comparison, Palmerville Station has 135000 hectares. Immense, wild country in an isolated and at times, lawless part of Australia.

Adding to the isolation, is an extreme climate. This whole area boasts an unforgiving tropical climate. Hot, monsoonal summers followed by warm, dry winters. The entire area becomes impassable by road from November to April. The daytime temperature, in winter, is usually around 30 deg C.

Many prospectors and tourists do visit the area, but Palmerville Station is a very remote part of FNQ. The area is a mecca for grey nomads,

---

[9] Cook Shire

gold miners with legitimate leases, prospectors with a valid permit and trespassers looking to strike it rich.

The Palmer River and the surrounding area was the site of a gold rush starting in 1873. The area became known as The Palmer River Goldfields. Over 35000 Chinese and European prospectors rushed to the area, hoping to find another Klondike. Although the fever pitch died down by the 1920's, the allure rush has never really left. It was claimed that Cooktown had 94 hotels during the gold rush era. In 2025, there are two hotels. Maytown was the main township on the Palmer River Goldfields between 1874 to the 1920's. It was located on the northern side of the Palmer River near the junction with Butcher's Creek. The closure of the post office in 1945 sounded the death knell for the town. Maytown was added to the Queensland Heritage Register in 2004.

It was never established how much gold was found on the Palmer River Goldfields, but estimates have been given at around one million ounces. In today's price that would be more than $3 Billion dollars. An extraordinary amount of money in anyone's language. A big incentive to put up with the deprivations and the risks of mining in Australia's far north in the late 1800s.

Some believe there are still big gold deposits to be discovered around the Palmer River Goldfields. Judging by the number of prospectors who flock to the area every season, they may be correct. By comments I receive from listeners to the podcast, there is a lot of gold still to be found in the region.

The Palmer River Roadhouse is located on the main, and only road to Cape York and rests on the banks of the Palmer River. Anyone who has been to the Cape would have passed by the Palmer River Roadhouse, but not necessarily Palmerville. To reach there, you must first travel to Maytown, around seventy kilometres to the west of the roadhouse, over a rough dirt road. Palmerville lies another forty kilometres west of where Maytown stood.

Palmerville Station falls within the Laura Police Division, Queensland's only one-man police station. Or it was at the time of this murder. Imagine an area the size of Hong Kong with one police officer patrolling. It is an eighty-kilometre drive from Laura Police Station to Palmerville Station. A drive that would normally take perhaps forty-five minutes. In this area over rough, dirt roads and tracks, allow around two hours – three hours to cover the eighty-kilometre distance. Welcome to Palmerville Station.

To say that Palmerville is isolated is an understatement. Despite the huge area and the isolation, there is barely a resident of FNQ who is not aware of the Bruce Schuler murder.

It was a story that tore through Palmerville and Far North Queensland like a class five cyclone that this part of Australia is notorious for, devastating multiple families along the way. A story that has left the local communities across FNQ bitterly divided, squarely into two camps – the 'leaseholders' camp and the 'prospectors' camp. There appears to be no one 'sitting on the fence'.

And everyone was happy to talk to me, to share their thoughts and knowledge of the case. Well, almost everyone, apart from the actual prospectors involved.

Bruce Schuler

Bruce Gavin Schuler was born on 29 December 1963 at Wondai in Queensland's Burnett region and he grew up on Queensland's Sunshine Coast. He met his partner, Fiona Splitt, in Tennant Creek, Northern Territory. At the time of his disappearance, they had been together twenty-seven years, and had two children, a daughter Lisa and son Bruce jnr. At the time of his disappearance and presumed murder, Bruce was 48 years of age[10].

Bruce and Fiona owned a residential property outside Mareeba. Fiona's parents also lived on the property, in a separate house. Bruce and Fiona owned a rental video store in Cooktown that required Fiona to travel there three days per week. She was planning on moving to Cooktown to live full time to run the video shop, as the manager had resigned. Bruce and Fiona also owned a commercial property in Cooktown, which was leased out.

Bruce was a builder by occupation, but retired early. He was an avid gold prospector and had been prospecting for around fifteen years[11].

In 2011, Bruce paid $50000 for a mining lease known as Rosie's Gully in the Palmer River Gold Reserve and spent a further $70000 on equipment and improvements. Bruce had poured a concrete slab and built a 10-metre x 10-metre shed on the property[12]. He had moved a substantial amount of equipment to the site in preparation for serious mining operations including a 4x4 truck, a bobcat, an excavator, and a 4-wheel motorbike.

---

[10] Interview with Fiona Splitt
[11] Statement by Kevin Groth
[12] Fiona Splitt records

Like everywhere in this area, Rosie's Gully was remote, accessible only via a rough dirt road, and difficult to get to. The travel time from the Palmer River Roadhouse to Rosie's Gully was around 2.5 hours, although it was only about ninety kilometres distance. Mobile or cell phone communications were non-existent. There was a landline connected to the shed, but the main means of contact was by satellite phone. Bruce and Fiona each carried a satellite phone.

Bruce was spending up to one month at a time at Rosie's Gully during the dry season. Fiona told investigators that she would speak to Bruce daily, and she had visited Rosie's Gully twice before Bruce disappeared[13].

About six months prior to purchasing the lease, Bruce had approached his friend, Bruce Parker. Schuler was aware Parker knew Stephen Struber, as he had carted cattle for him in the past. Bruce Schuler wanted to go detecting on Palmerville Station. He wanted Bruce Parker to ask Stephen Struber for permission to go onto the property for prospecting. Parker did contact Stephen Struber, who granted them permission, but with stipulations. These included that Parker was responsible for all those who went onto the property, that Struber wanted to be informed what they found, and he wanted to initially go with them so Struber could show them the areas where they were and were not to prospect[14]. As it happened, nothing ever came of it. At the time of this incident, Bruce Schuler was under no illusion of the requirements to go prospecting on Palmerville Station.

A Mining Registrar told police that none of the prospectors had permission or authority to fossick with metal detectors in the location where Bruce Schuler's vehicle was found. The only place they could lawfully use metal detectors was on mining leases within the Palmer Resources Reserve, where Schuler and Bidner held mining leases, or, on other mining leases within the Palmerville Station with the lease holders consent.[15]

---

[13] Statement by Fiona Splitt
[14] Statement by Bruce Parker
[15] Statement by Peter Wilson

This is a link to the Australian Missing Persons Register containing details of Bruce Schuler's disappearance, including photographs and newspaper articles:

https://australianmissingpersonsregister.com/ampr/Schuler.htm

Fiona and Lisa

As part of my research, I spoke with members of Bruce Schuler's family. I had a few conversations with daughter Lisa and numerous conversations with Bruce's widow, Fiona Splitt. Many of those phone calls and Zoom meetings occurred October through December 2023. None of Bruce's other family members ever contacted me or commented on the podcast that I am aware of.

We had open and frank conversations. We discussed Palmerville Station's sale and the implications. We discussed the suggestion of pressuring the government to offer a reward for information. We discussed the steps the family have taken to find Bruce and could take to find Bruce. I shared with them some of the goals I had for the podcast. Through these discussions, I was able to glean a lot of helpful information for the podcast.

Fiona firmly believed the Strubers murdered Bruce. She believed the Strubers had mistaken Bruce for Dan Bidner or Tremain Anderson. *'He was in the wrong place at the wrong time,'* was said often by Fiona. The reason the Strubers were refusing to disclose the location of Bruce Schuler's body, she said, was because where his body was located, other bodies would be found. This was not the first time they had killed, she claimed (another common rumour to which I found no basis.) Even Detective Sergeant McLeish stoked that fire as you will read. The media referred to the Strubers as serial killers.

Fiona told me she was surprised when she first heard Bruce had gone gold prospecting onto Palmerville Station, as they were both aware of Strubers reputation for evicting trespassers. He had been specifically told of the requirements to go detecting there in the recent past.

Fiona stayed in regular contact with Kevin Groth, Bruce Schuler's long-time friend and one of the three prospectors present the day Bruce disappeared. Their regular contact has recently dropped off. She never spoke with Dan Bidner. Tremain Anderson would not even look her in the eye. She did not know why but asked '*guilt maybe?*'. Which of course could mean many things including he was implicated in Bruce's murder or perhaps he was suffering survivor guilt.

Bruce's daughter Lisa was more circumspect. She expressed confusion. She had questions for the prospectors which she desperately wanted answers to. She may still do and hopefully, the podcast clarified a lot of issues for her.

The following is an edited script of my first zoom meeting with Fiona Splitt and Lisa Schuler:

GC:' *I do have concerns with the evidence. No motive. This continuing declaration of innocence, despite the overwhelming evidence and the nobody, no parole legislation. I have not met either Dianne or Stephen. They seem to me like bush people with low education. Poor social skills. Her in particular. But other stuff that I struggle with, the lack of DNA, the lack of blood on or in Struber's four-wheel drive, the lack of blood on their clothes, on their bodies, in their house. How do two uneducated bush people defy the laws of science? That's one of the questions I have in the back of my mind. And that's one of the reasons, that's one of the things I want to explore. I'm not suggesting for a moment that they're innocent. They've been convicted. I'm just saying, I'm putting it out there. I have problems with the evidence. Okay.*'

FS:' *You're not alone.*'

LS:' *We've been down that road many times too. I've been in tears to Mum saying, 'do we have the right people in jail?' Are we looking in the wrong spot? What is happening? Because it just doesn't make sense. I still struggle this many years later as to what makes sense, because none of it really makes sense in my head. But yeah, I've made up quite a few stories in my own head, I suppose.*'

GC:' *So you don't have any firm idea why they killed him?*

LS:' *No, it doesn't make sense at all for me.*

FS: *Doesn't make sense to me either. We've sat Kevin down and had him in tears. Just, you know, just to say, is this, is your story true? Is everyone's story true? Are you being threatened? Are you being threatened? But nothing came of that. I think we just upset him. Yeah.'*

Lisa wanted to sit the prospectors down and ask them some difficult questions.

GC:' *Are you in contact with either of them, Lisa?'*

LS:' *No, but I've, like I said, I made up a lot of stories in my head. I would like to sit down with them one day and nut out my stories that I have in my head. It just doesn't make sense in my head. So Danny saw the car, I believe, and Tremain said that he'd saw someone get out with a gun. And then they'd heard gunshots.*

That last comment was true from what I learned from the community. Here, were members of Bruce Schuler's immediate family who were not even sure of the evidence themselves. The media coverage had been less than desirable.

LS: 'And they knew where dad was. And then they sort of fluffed around and gold detected back to camp and then called the station homestead and fluffed around a bit more. And I don't think they called the police until later that after six o'clock. And I don't know, I've never been in that situation before. But if I was somewhere with my friends, and I'd witnessed that sort of activity, knowing those people, I probably would have ran for help straight away.'

Fiona Splitt wrote a letter to Stephen Struber but this was returned unopened, from Lotus Glen Correctional Centre.

Lisa wrote a letter in 2022 to Dianne Wilson, who is an inmate at the Townsville Correctional Centre, on the ten-year anniversary of her fathers disappearance:

'Dianne, I've wondered what to say to you for nearly 10 years now and I still don't know what to say. I believe you and Stephen are up for parole soon and I don't know if it's been explained to you, but there is a new law that if you were to tell us where you left Dad's body, you would be eligible for parole.

If you don't tell us, then you have no chance of freedom at all. I need you to tell us where Dad's body is for myself and my family to lay him to rest and so we can say a proper goodbye. I want you to think about what a father is to you, your father.

Do you think he would be proud of you at this moment? Your God, the Holy Father or any other father figures you have had in your life. I want you to put yourself in my shoes. My father was my safe place.

He was my happiness and kindness in human form. Without him, I'm scared, alone, sad and in a constant state of depression. I'm tired, Dianne.

I'm tired of trying to live my life without my father. I'm tired of putting on a brave face when really I just want to hide and cry. I ask myself every day why God would allow this to happen.

Please, Dianne, please just do this for me and my family. Please tell us where my Dad's body is. If you don't know and you weren't there, just like you and Stephen said, then where is he? You must know something, anything.

Signed Lisa.'

Dianne Wilson replied to Lisa on 16 August 2022:

'Dear Lisa Schuler

Thank you for writing to me. My apologies for not answering sooner.

I would like to say I'm not the crazy person people say I am. I appreciate how confronting it must be for you to write to me. I did not shoot your father and if I did, I would have said so from the start.

There are persons out there that know what happened and as far as I know, some are still on the property. These people are not poor prospectors, miners that they innocently claim to be. These persons have been trafficking drug internationally for around this area forever, for over 35 years.

They use mining and prospecting as a cover. They would always avoid them and avoid them when they were as much as possible because we feared for our own safety. We would always avoid them.

When somebody reported them to the police, they confronted and threatened us saying they were going to sort us out because they believed it was us. The question remains unanswered as to who actually reported them and enraged them. These same individuals also began to chase tourists off our property, claiming ownership and threatening them with firearms.

As a result, as the legit owners were accused of this conduct despite having no part of it, these individuals would travel around the property in four-wheel drives, including one which closely resembles our own. Only days after the incident on the 9th of July, their vehicle was parked up on the property with a water pump in the back. I noted the only difference from ours was that it was under tires, that it had wider tires.

Another vehicle had its tyres changed right after the incident despite being an active investigation. Another point I have noted is that despite having a satellite phone with them, the individuals with your father waited nine hours before reporting anything to the police. I would think that any normal person would have called the police immediately.

Lisa, I sincerely regret that I am unable to help you find your father. You have my deepest sympathies for the loss and trauma you have experienced as a result of his disappearance. I believe we both need closure and if I ever find out anything that could provide answers needed, I will not hesitate to contact the police and yourself.

Sincerely,

Dianne Wilson-Struber.'

The original handwritten letter from Dianne Wilson will be found in Appendix F.

The fact the victim's family had concerns when I first contacted them should have been enough for a police inquiry into the case. Twelve years after the event and they still had questions. A lot of questions. Not one word from the local media about it. Hopefully, a lot of those questions were answered by the podcast, but I suspect it raised more questions than provided answers.

The first episode of the podcast '*Where is Bruce Schuler?*' was released on 29 November 2023. On 29 December 2023 I released episode 5 of the podcast '*Ghost Evidence*,' on what would have been Bruce Schuler's 60th birthday.

That episode was a turning point for me. It had taken me months to '*get my head around*' the crime scene whilst relying on GPS points and locations such as '*The One Mile*[16]' as opposed to say, the intersection of Queen Street and Edward Street in Queensland's capital of Brisbane.

Whilst researching episode 4, I watched the witness re-enactments for the first time[17]. I sat up and replayed the videos. Several times. I could not believe what I was watching! I had no recollection of this evidence coming out at trial, in such a simplified format, at least. It was very simple evidence. I had stumbled across '*the vehicle u-turn evidence*' and I started looking at the case through a different prism. I had already sketched out the scripts for episodes four, five and six. They went in the bin and I went back to scripting.

After I released episode 5, I called Fiona Splitt and told her I suspected there were serious concerns with the convictions of Struber and Wilson, as all the evidence had not aired at trial. I told her I suspected the prospectors may have been implicated in Bruce's disappearance. I suggested she listen to episode five and call me to discuss. Fiona blocked me at that point and we have not spoken to this day. She will not reply to emails. I still do not know the reason for this. It could be that police involved in the investigation told her I was wrong.

A journalist told me Fiona Splitt believed I was being paid by the Strubers, which of course was not the case as well as being nonsensical. That would not change the evidence. It occurred to me that the Schuler family had eleven years to '*hate*' the Strubers and blame them for their misfortune, and then a stranger comes along who potentially upends their beliefs. Whatever the reason, I hope the podcast (and this book) brings some closure to the Schuler family and helps answer the many questions they have. It may even help eventually bring them some justice.

---

[16] The general area where the murder allegedly occurred
[17] Police re-enactments by witnesses Bidner, Anderson and Groth

Tsunami

Tsunami is a word that, for many Australians pre–Boxing Day 2004, was relatively unknown. The Boxing Day Tsunami roared through South-East Asia and into the Australian consciousness simultaneously. Australians suddenly became aware of the potential for a tsunami to devastate entire regions, courtesy of television, news reporters and people with video cameras and mobile phones.

How does that relate to Bruce Schuler? It is very easy to think of a murder case as involving just one victim: the deceased. Any death has a ripple effect through the family involved, along with the community and ultimately touches the lives of many people. When the death is violent, it takes it to the next level. When there is no body and it was a violent death, as in this case, it becomes something of a tsunami.

Whilst Bruce will always be the true innocent victim in this mess, there are so many other innocent victims. The extended Schuler family, especially widow Fiona, daughter Lisa and son Bruce junior, have been suffering daily now for thirteen years. Bruce was one of five children. They have their own families. His father and stepmother are still alive. Bruce and Fiona had four grandchildren at the time of his disappearance. The entire extended Schuler families have all experienced the pain of Bruce's disappearance.

The same equally applies to the extended families of Stephen Struber and Dianne Wilson. Stephen Struber was one of nine children. Dianne Wilson was one of eight children. Whilst Dianne never had children, Stephen had four children from a previous marriage. He has three grandchildren and the extended Struber families have twenty-five grandchildren and thirty great grandchildren.

The extended Wilson Family have seventeen grandchildren. Those extended families live with the daily shame that comes with a family member being convicted of murder, and worse: the killers are refusing to give up the body. The Struber and Wilson families live with the ongoing search for Bruce. Most of the extended families live in small communities in Far North Queensland who must face their neighbours and friends on a daily basis.

Then, of course, the three prospectors. Some, or all, may be suffering survivor guilt. The inevitable doubts and questions: '*Maybe we shouldn't have continued prospecting after the shootings? Maybe we should have tried harder to find Bruce? Maybe we should have rung the cops at 10 a.m. instead of 7.15 p.m.*' Hindsight is always twenty-twenty, isn't it?

This disappearance, arrest and murder trial tore through the Far North Queensland communities like a tsunami.

The communities are very divided on the guilt or innocence of Stephen Struber and Dianne Wilson and will probably continue to be for many years to come. People within those communities are angry: angry that Stephen and Dianne will not give up the location of Bruce Schuler's body. Others are angry because they believe the Justice system got it very wrong. Angry because the Strubers will die in prison, and angry that the real killers are roaming around free. This division will likely take generations to heal.

Palmerville Station

Alfred (but known as George) and Doris Wilson won Palmerville Station in a ballot of unsettled, vacant agricultural land in early 1964. No buildings or improvements came with the property. The family including eight children moved to Palmerville Station in mid -1964 and set about building a house consisting of corrugated iron, bush timber, a floor made of wetted and crushed ant bed, a wood stove and kerosene refrigerator.

Initially, there was no power or running water and a few untamed cattle. The family built fences and cattle yards using crosscut saws, crow bars and shovels to dig the fence and yard posts. In 1965, friends gave the Wilsons' thirty head of short horn cattle and one bull which took a full week to drive with stock horses back to the station. In the same year, another friend gave the family 1500 pounds cash to start their business[18].

The current homestead was built in 1970, with plans in place to build a new homestead at the time of the arrest of Dianne and Stephen. Alfred Wilson passed away in 1995 aged 75 years and his wife Doris Wilson passed away in 2011 aged 82 years.

When the property was sold by the Queensland Public Trustee in 2019, there were 5000 Brahman-cross cattle on the property.

As the children of Alfred and Doris grew up, married and moved away the only children left on Palmerville Station were Dianne and George. The families always returned to the property for holidays and special family events.

Daughter Sharon recalled:

---

[18] Interviews with Wilson families

'*We would take our children back to enjoy the many things we used to do at Palmerville e.g. fishing swimming in the river creeks and dams, knee boarding and tubing behind a small boat on the big Five Mile Dam, exploring the old ruins at gold mining day at Maytown and other areas, caving in the limestone bluffs where there many aboriginal Paintings from years ago. You cannot imagine how much fun the whole family had over the years, picnics by the rivers, BBQ's with extended families grandparents showing their grandchildren how to wash gold with a gold pan and metal detector. We were so blessed with so many activities to experience and then people started travelling through Palmerville taking up gold mining leases, growing drugs, trespassing anywhere they felt like, shooting our cattle and work horses, can you imagine how having your beautiful work horses shot, 6 in total, would make you feel. This sort of thing started to happen way back in the 1970's and slowly got worse over the years. Our parents were very hospitable people with all visitors we welcomed in our home given cups of tea, coffee, home baked cakes and biscuits even for lunch and dinners at night, but people still did the wrong thing by them. Not all unexpected visitors were bad, we met and became very good friends with most of the people coming to Palmerville, it was just the minority that were very bad, every year from October on, Palmerville was deliberately burned out by people, the family would have to try to contain the fires so they would have grass to feed their stock until the wet season rains started to grow grass to feed the stock. The family would put in fire breaks in the earlier months of the year to stop the property being totally burned out, but people would go inside the fire breaks and still light it up, a no win situation for the family.*'

There would be very few rural primary producers in Australia who have not had problems with trespassers: cutting fences, stealing fuel, batteries, equipment, and killing livestock for fun or food. Prospectors were notorious for burning off the vegetation for more effective detecting. Palmerville Station suffered the same fate. Being so large, people could come and go on the property and never be seen. The Strubers were aware marihuana had been cultivated and produced on the property by others. George Wilson stated they were always concerned with being blamed if drug crops were discovered on the property. The grass that cattle and horses relied upon for fodder were always at risk of loss by bush fires that complicated management of successfully farming the land.

In 1999 this article appeared in The Age newspaper:

'The cattle queen is angry. 'I've had a gutful of the bastards' spits Doris Wilson, the 73 year old owner of the sprawling Palmerville Station on Cape York Peninsula. 'I tell you. I'm going to chuck a bomb in their car. I'm going to 'shoot the mongrels between the eyes. I don't care if I go to jail.'

Mrs Wilson is referring to amateur gold prospectors, many arriving from New South Wales and Victoria in late-model four-wheel-drives and scouring her 136,000 hectare property with metal detectors in search of riches.

Her bitter struggle with the prospectors reflects a wider conflict. Cape York has become the nation's premier four-wheel-drive destination, and visitor numbers are growing rapidly.

Landholders have had enough of illegal shooting, fishing, burning, vandalising and trespassing. Authorities are concerned about the toll on Cape York's fragile environment.

Prospectors set fire to the cape's dry woodlands so their metal detectors won't be impeded by vegetation.

Four hundred kilometres to the north, Mrs Eileen Nixon, proprietor of the 58000 square kilometre Shelburn Station is also angry. Mrs Nixon says her stock are sometimes shot for food or sport.'

During the 1980s, I was a Queensland Police Service Detective stationed in Townsville. Drug cultivation was always on our radar, and we discovered many cannabis crops in the Townsville Region. The climate in tropical Queensland was especially conducive to marihuana cultivation. But we knew the big crops were north of Cairns.

Dianne Wilson – Struber

I have been told so much about Dianne Wilson by other family members during my research, none of it negative. I found very little written material regarding Dianne apart from incorrect media reports describing her as the '*Real Life Wolf Creek killer*'.

As one of eight children, Dianne had lived her entire life on Palmerville Station. She was home schooled to the equivalent of primary school Grade Four and her education was basic. From childhood, her life was a dawn to dusk routine of farm chores and hard physical labour. Apart from any friends and strong family support, she appeared to have little social life and had a withdrawn demeanour. Her favourite television program was '*Home and Away.*'

After most of her siblings grew up and moved away, there was only Dianne and her brother George left on the station, with their parents, Alfred and Doris. Stephen Struber was her first boyfriend. They met while Stephen worked for her family. After the death of her father and with mother Dorrie aging, it fell to Dianne and George to run the business. Whilst she had no children of her own, she loved her animals.

Dianne had never travelled any further away from Palmerville than Mareeba, 200 kilometres away, in her life. It must have been with mixed emotions and probably very overwhelming for her when she was flown by Police to Brisbane to appear before the CCC Coercive hearing in October 2012. It would have been explained to her at the hearing, she had no right of refusal. Despite the hustle and bustle of Brisbane, being surrounded by police and solicitors, she continued to deny any involvement in the murder and denied any knowledge of the whereabouts of Bruce Schuler's body. She is now serving a life sentence in Townsville, a world away from her family. Whilst I am cognisant of comments such as '*she should have thought of that before* she murdered Bruce Schuler', it does add another layer of punishment to her sentence.

One of Dianne's nieces, Tanya, had this to say about her Aunty:

'I spent a lot of time at Palmerville, especially with Dianne as Sharon and Narele had left and married by the time that I was old enough to remember going to visit on holidays. I remember doing so much out there, it was hard (no electricity and having to be mindful of the water tanks running out.) But each of my siblings and cousins always enjoyed our time spent at Palmerville.

Dianne always had different animals, dogs, cats, chooks, goat, poddy calves and horses. When I visited, I loved helping Dianne do what needed to be done around the property. We would go fishing and swimming and spend time together, once I don't remember how old I was I caught a couple of black breams (more then we needed) I was excited and the thrill of successfully able to catch anything I kept trying. Dianne spoke with me and said no more you only take what you're going to use. And spoke to me about everything having the right to live, that you should not kill something just for the sake of being able to.

Over the years that's something Dianne always said everything has a right to live. As an adult and seeing some of Dianne's dogs getting older and having numerous health issues due to age I mentioned to Di that she should put them down, no she said again they're alive and still breathing they have a right to live, (she wouldn't let them suffer but never just put them down because they were old) Di has the gentlest personality she always looks at a reason why someone is acting the why they do, and gives an explanation at the way she thought they might be the way or think the way they did.

When Dianne was incarcerated my husband and I tried to keep her twenty-three dogs alive but financially couldn't and had to put them down, something that upsets my husband and I still now, as we know how much Di loved her dogs.'

There is no evidence Dianne was ever implicated in more than one murder. She is dearly loved by her extended family, who solidly stand by her and believe in her innocence. Whilst it is difficult for most of them to visit her in Townsville, (being a round trip for most of them of about 850 kilometres), she receives as many weekly phone calls as the Corrective Services system permits.

Stephen Struber

I have also read and been told much about Stephen Struber during my research. He is also loved by his extended family. They all firmly stand behind him in his claim of innocence for the murder. I found during my research that all relatives of Stephen Struber and Dianne Wilson whom I have spoken with have been very helpful. As you will learn, I have read about and spoken with people who dislike him. He was very forthright in his business dealings. He disliked tourists coming onto Palmerville Station. They left rubbish and caused environmental problems. He disliked prospectors. They lit fires to assist their detecting. They left gates open and destroyed his stock. Stephen Struber disliked miners. He believed, in most cases, they were ignoring best practice, mining outside their leases and in breach of Environmental Protection guidelines. He blamed them for polluting the river and stealing water from his dams. This reduced water availability for his cattle, with many cattle dying after becoming bogged in the mud these trespassers created. The family consistently claimed that if people approached him, he was willing to grant them access to the property, as Monte Dwyer discovered.

As a young adult, Stephen Struber was described as quietly spoken and polite. After leaving school he completed a sheet metal coppersmith apprenticeship. He was apparently a self-trained mechanic (a good one) and went on to be employed as a boilermaker. There was very little mechanically that he could not repair. His adult life was one of hard physical labour. According to family members, he regularly repaired motor vehicle and rebuilt old cars. He learnt under his father, who was very particular: a trait he instilled in his son. Long time friend, Frank Teodo, was interviewed for the podcast. He had this to say:

Graeme Crowley: *'How long have you known Stephen Struber and Dianne Wilson?'*

Frank Teodo: *'Well, Graeme, I've known Stephen for over 50 years. I knew the entire family. I knew them very well. We're all very close. We all grew up together. Dianne I've probably known for about 30 years or thereabouts. But I know Stephen really well. I know him and all his family, mother, father, everyone.'*

GC: *'Do you believe that they murdered Bruce Schuler?'*

FT: *'Graeme, I've never at any time believed that. And after listening to your podcast and all the evidence and everything like that, I'm even more convinced than ever that they are totally innocent of this crime.'*

GC: *'What made you sort of so sure, before the podcast I mean, that they weren't responsible?'*

FT: *'Well, the first thing that stuck in my mind was you've got to have a motive to want to take another person's life. And I've known Stephen all my life. They were bushies, but they lived by a code. They were good, honest people. Their mother was a good woman. Their father was a strong, honest man. He taught them to be good men, the whole family. They were all good people. And Stephen used to call down periodically. I'd hear all the stories he'd talk about. There was another thing that you didn't mention in the podcast that Stephen was always incensed when he saw litter bugs. He didn't like people camping and leaving stuff laying around. And this had gone on for a long time. And that's why the resentment built over the years. So, I don't doubt for one minute that he might have bailed up some people and been a bit forthright in telling them to clean their campsite up or pull up at the homestead in future. But he was always glad to see people because up there it's a remote area. You don't have much of a social life. So, it was always hard for me to believe what I've been reading in the papers about this bloke bailing people up. I thought, it's a load of bull. I'd known him all my life. Whenever he called in to see me, he was the same friendly, hardworking, honest, stalwart character I've always known. So, I never believed it for a minute. And to commit a crime like that, he's too smart to think he could ever get away with it. I mean, if you look at his record, I don't know that the police would be able to do all of this, of course. I don't think Stephen ever had so much as a speeding ticket. I mean, even when he was on the road, he's driving. He was always a careful man. He was never a rev head as a kid. He was never someone that would break the law. You know, their father was pretty strict with them boys. So no, I never believed it. You've got to have a motive. You don't come up and shoot somebody because they're trespassing. And as far as the motive mentioned in the podcast that they mistook Bruce Schuler for Daniel Bidner, again, that doesn't hold water. No way in the wide world. I heard about the confrontations at the Croc Hole and the fact that Stephen had walked away from that rather than have the argument escalate further. That's the bloke that I know. They were all strong men. They were all tough boys, but they'd never look for trouble. And his father used to say that. And the other thing I heard Anderson talk about how the first time he met Stephen Struber, he was thumped to the ground from behind and he thought he got hit by a scrub ball. Well, old Charlie Struber would have disowned any of his boys if they king hit anybody or seek to promote violence or anything like that. He didn't allow that nonsense. So, yeah, again, it's completely out of character. I did also, when you read the extracts from the newspaper clippings about how they said Stephen was a bully, well, ask any of the young people that he grew up with. It was the opposite. If there was some kid that was a little bit overweight or one that wasn't athletic or anything, he'd always take them under his wing and he was always extra kind to them because they weren't as athletic or as capable as the rest of us. So, again, none of it added up. It was like reading and hearing things about a completely different person. And I knew him well grown, really well. If my dear old dad was alive today, he'd tell you – he'd be over 100 years of age, dad, if he was still around – he'd tell you about the time Stephen fixed his car for nothing, how he was always doing work for pensioners and older people, always helping out. He never ripped anyone off. He'd do quality mechanical work, repairs and things, and say, you're right, mate, I won't charge you for that, or I had these parts lying around. It didn't cost me anything. Away you go. He was generous, and he wasn't a wealthy man. So, again, that speaks volumes for the character of the bloke. He* was a battler. That's the Stephen Struber I know, and if you were to come to his hometown, where he grew up here, you will find 100 people with the same sentiments as me. I saw a bloke today shopping down the IGA store, and he said, nah, no way in the wide world did Stephen Struber do that. And as for Dianne, I mean, I read that about her too in the newspapers and made her out to be some sort of a diabolical, heartless, cold person. She was nothing like that. The first time I met Dianne, I couldn't even give her a glass of water. She was very independent. She was quiet, shy. Stephen brought her here, and she didn't want to impose. She was used to being independent and out in the bush, and it took a long time before I finally, because I had to go and laugh and carry on, and eventually, once she got used to me, then she was quite articulate. She loved talking about cattle, horses, things she was familiar with. So, I found Dianne a really good woman. She loved animals. She was good with all my dogs here. She was just a good-hearted bugger. Yeah. So, yeah.

GC: Could Stephen fight?

FT: 'Stephen, well, all of them boys could take care of themselves, because old Charlie used to have, he had a shed, a mechanical workshop, and you could go down there on a Sunday afternoon and you could put the boxing gloves on. So, all the brothers used to do a bit of sparring, and we'd get other young blokes too. They might be Taekwondo fellas. They'd all come there, and you could basically have a bit of fun sparring. And old Charlie, he was like the referee and trainer at the same time. But he also liked to train people's character.

He would not tolerate, we called him Mr. Struber, but there was none of this familiarity, none of this cheekiness or anything. We all respected him. And Stephen, yeah, he never looked, of all the boys in the family, Stephen was the quiet one that would go out of his way to avoid trouble. But he did have heavy hands, and I mean, he could punch. And when I hear about these confrontations up there, after all those years, not a single punch was ever thrown. And that speaks volumes for what Stephen, yeah, he could take care of himself, don't worry about that. But he never looked for it, Graeme, never, never. Stephen and Dianne were described as wearing khaki clothes on that day.

GC: Frank. Yeah, I remember reading something about that.

FT: 'I did read that statement. Well, look, maybe I'm colourblind, Graeme, but I can remember Stephen, his favourite colour work clothes, King-Gee work clothes, it was always dark green, usually with long sleeves, because when he was welding and that, you don't get your arms burnt and everything like that. And I remember Stephen, his first wife, Janet, she used to actually make clothes. They'd buy the pattern, he'd cut the material out, and she'd make the shirts and clothes for him. So, of course, eventually they realised they weren't saving very much, you could buy them off the shelf almost for the same price. But yeah, always green. That was, I'd never been to Palmerville Station, so I got no idea what he used to wear when he was living up there and working up there. But whenever I saw him down here on the coast or when he'd come to visit, it was usually green.'

GC: 'Never saw him in khaki?'

FT: 'Not that I can remember. Like, yeah, he was always green, dark green, but not that that means anything. I mean, like I said, I've never been to Palmerville, but to me, he wore green, yeah. I tell you what, if you want character references, all I heard about when this case was coming up, though, I remember the police on the radio saying, if you had to run in with this man, come forward. I never heard anyone ask to come forward if you knew him and give another side to it, because like I said, it's that out of character for that man. He sat at my table, and if he would have committed that crime, he would have admitted to that. The Bushmen code they live by, Graeme. Old Charlie used to tell them, don't lie, don't quit, live cleanly and speak softly and fight hard and fair. That was their mantra. So, this business of, no, no way in the world, mate. Yeah. No way.'

Both Bidner and Anderson described the clothing worn by both Struber and Wilson as khaki, on several occasions. The Tuesday night when they were first arrested, they were wearing dark blue clothes. No khaki work clothes were found on Palmerville Station when it was searched by police. Were the police not concerned about that?

Stephen Struber had a fearsome reputation when it came to evicting trespassers from his property. If he came across trespassers, he ordered them off the property. Immediately. No exceptions. His reputation was known throughout the entire district. That was the most common complaint the police received. He ordered them off his property!

George Wilson told police this, in part:

'Detective Camp has asked me about any conflict Stephen has had with prospectors/trespassers. I would say more often than not prospectors upset Stephen.

With prospectors they are supposed to get a prospecting permit for an area from the mines department. This allows them to come onto the lease and prospect. It is my understanding they must first give Stephen seven days notice. My understanding is that Stephen can tell, if it's a bad time to come. A big miner is supposed to also put up a bond in case they cause damage. I don't think the small fossickers need to do this.

My understanding is that the laws say they are not allowed to interfere with the stream in a creek or gully. Prospectors do interfere with the stream though as they often build small dams to hold back water either to make it easier to prospect or to help their camp. When you speak to the mines department about this, they say that yes they know people do it but that it is hard to police. These blokes with metal detectors don't dam creeks so much. They do seem to burn the country though. They do this because it is easier to runaway metal detector across the ground without any grass in between.

So what ends up happening is that although prospectors have a right to enter they don't often tell you where they are and this causes problems. Once some prospectors turned up in the middle of a muster and spooked the cattle. This caused a massive delay.

I would say that Stephen does not get on with prospectors. I would say this is because of the reasons I mentioned above. However, any problems Stephen has with prospectors is probably made worse by the way he conducts himself. By this I mean his manner is quite intimidating and abrupt. He finds fault easily and speaks his mind rather than negotiating with people.

In fairness to Stephen, he does only expect people to comply with the letter of the law.

I have never seen Stephen or Dianne point a gun at anyone. There is always a gun in the vehicle. That is to say whichever vehicle you take out either Stephen or Dianne would make sure there is a gun in it. This is because if you come across an animal that needs to be put down you don't want to have to go back to the homestead to pick up a rifle. Also, it is handy to have a gun in case you see a pig to shoot for dog meat.

I am aware that there are a lot of stories about that Stephen has pulled guns on people. I am not saying this is not true, but I have never seen it.

I am aware of incidents with or without guns where Stephen has come across trespassers.

I know Danny BIDNER but have only met him once. He lives over on the R16. R16 is a piece of land that was taken off the Palmerville Station in 1986. It is a goldfield reserve.

*(*According to the Department of Environment and Heritage Protection that area of land now known as 'R16' was bequeathed by George Wilson, the original owner of Palmerville Station).[19]

I have never seen BIDNER on Palmerville. Dianne and Stephen told me that they saw him on the property back when I was in New Zealand in about 2005/2006.

Over the years at different times Dianne and Stephen have said that they thought BIDNER may have been on the property and that it would be nice if he asked permission.

I would say prospectors do weigh on Steves mind a bit as they do cause problems. He will see a fire and say that he thinks it's prospectors.'

Stephen Struber had a love/hate relationship with the Cook Shire Council. In 2005, the Local Government Association of Queensland

---

[19] Statement by Team Leader DEHP.

released a draft *'Guidelines for Local Government – Roads Off Alignment and Undedicated Roads.'*

The Agenda for one Cook Shire meeting in January 2005 states that *'the Guidelines will not resolve anything where there is no agreement with the landowner/lessee – which will be the case in the vast majority of cases in the Cook Shire Council.'* The Agenda went on to note:*' I propose progressing Palmerville Pastoral Holding as a test case as soon as funds become available to collect the required data.'* The Agenda concluded with a recommendation to proceed with the compulsory acquisition of such lands as are necessary to establish a legally gazetted right-of-way from the homestead of the property known as Palmerville Station to the lease boundary on Mt. Mulgrave Road[20].

The CEO of that Council, Stephen Wilton, met the Strubers in 2008 and described their relationship as polite and civil. Once the Council informed Stephen of the compulsory acquisition of land to align existing roads on Palmerville Station, the relationship became strained. Cook Shire Council resumed around 100 kilometres of Palmerville Station land to construct a road through the area. This resumption included part of the Palmerville Station airstrip, which resulted in planes being unable to land there as needed for mail and food supplies.

This was apparently a bone of contention with Stephen Struber. On Strubers side of the ledger, he did not oppose realigning the gazetted road. He believed it was in the wrong place. He wrote to Cook Shire Council stating that by resuming the required land, he would be obliged to remove and relocate horse yards, a loading ramp, saddle shed, hay shed, lick shed, fencing and a number of established mango trees. He added that it would also require the removal and relocation of Telstra and Bureau of Meteorology infrastructure[21].

Thereafter, the Cook Shire Council would find gates locked and they had to have police in attendance whilst they forced entry. Stephen Struber argued unsuccessfully that the locked gates were on his private

---

[20] Cook Shire Council Agenda/Business Papers January 2005
[21] Letter from S Struber to Cook Shire January 2005

property. There was an incident where the tyres on a Council vehicle were spiked in 2011, which was found to have been caused by Stephen Struber[22].

The CEO referenced a letter to the Queensland Commissioner of Police in 2004, detailing a claim of threats of violence by the lessee of Palmerville Station and a further letter to the Far Northern region of the Queensland Police Service in 2005, requesting confirmation that police officers would be available to accompany Council officers whilst attending Palmerville Station.[23]

The Director of Engineering for Cook Shire Council knew Stephen Struber well. He confirmed the ill feelings between him and Council were over the approximate 100 kilometres of road that the Council had compulsorily acquired from Palmerville Pastoral Holdings. He stated that all meetings with Struber were confrontational but never ended in violence.

He described them as shouting matches, with Struber 'shouting, swearing and carrying on.' He was sometimes irrational in his arguments and wouldn't heed or take advice. Often, the issue ended with Struber basically blowing his stack and storming off[24].

The Council Works Manager related an instance in 2011 where he had a friendly discussion with Stephen while they had 'smoko' and two hours later Struber was blocking the road and threatening to sue everyone, including the same Works Manager, claiming the road was not gazetted and they were all trespassing[25].

The Manager stated that Stephen Struber was so irrational and erratic, he thought Struber might be on drugs, but there was no threats of violence or weapons produced. After being challenged, he backed down and went back to his previous calm self. Quite independently and not a Council employee, another person who spoke with police

---

[22] Statement by W Hunt
[23] Statement by Stephen Wilton
[24] Statement by T Lickiss
[25] Statement S Law

commented that Stephen Struber was a bully but if confronted, backed down and behaved himself.

I was contacted by a long-term resident of Cook Shire Council. He described his own treatment over many years by the Council as 'appalling'. Eventually, he stood for and became a Councillor, to stop it.

Stephen Struber was a prodigious litigator. In 2012, there were thirty-three granted mineral exploration permits on Palmerville Station; ninety-five granted mineral production permits and twenty-three applications for mineral production permits. In the preceding three-year period, Struber had objected to almost all those applications for new leases in the Land Court.

He retained the law firm Bottoms and English to represent him. The solicitor representing him was Ann English. Struber would often complain that he knew more about the Land Court regulations than the solicitors he was paying good money to, to defend the applications. At the time of his arrest, Stephen Struber had outstanding legal fees in excess of $80000 associated with Land Court hearings on twenty-seven mining related matters.

When Stephen Struber was not in Land Court objecting to mining applications, or brawling with the Cook Shire Council, (for whom he had a particular dislike) over the disputed location of the road realignment, he was fighting with the Department of Environment and Heritage Protection (DEHP – formerly known as the EPA) or Telstra over technicians accessing Palmerville Station to service Telstra equipment. The team leader of the Mining and Heavy Industry Team within the DEHP department was on a first name basis with Stephen Struber and had been since 2002.

He had personally met Stephen on about ten occasions in that ten-year period up to 2012, because of inspections, addressing complaints relating to environmental impacts, Land Court dealings and concerns or complaints lodged by Stephen Struber. In addition, over that same period, Stephen Struber had called the Department on nearly thirty occasions in relation to his complaints. In all his dealings with Stephen

Struber, Team Leader Dean stated that there were never any threats of physical violence.

He did however, describe Struber as demeaning, verbally aggressive and made various allegations relating to incompetence. The conversations revolved around alleged trespass, loss of income, non-compliance within the EPA, contamination of drinking water, alluvial mining, impact on the river crossings and land, waterhole silting, bogged and dead stock due to sediment accumulation in mine dams, which were all causing Struber stress and hardship[26].

A Telstra Technician contractor was required to attend a tower on Palmerville Station once per year for preventative maintenance. He would often find the gate locked. As it was gazetted road and he was acting under Federal telecommunications legislation, he would use bolt cutters to gain access. He met the Strubers on the road on two occasions and the meetings were friendly. He claimed that during the 2004 meeting, Dianne was standing back near the car, about twenty metres away, resting a rifle in the gap between the car and the car door, which he found intimidating. During their discussions, he formed the opinion that Stephen Struber had a major dislike for gold prospectors. If he attended the site by helicopter, Stephen Struber would complain to CASA of a low flying helicopter.

The contractor claimed that in 2005 Telstra were forced to build a separate road from the airport to the tower at a cost of $40,000[27]. The irony of course being that if Telstra was refused entry on to Palmerville Station, it may well have been their telephone service, their only contact with the outside world, that became inoperable. I put the contractor's claims to Stephen Struber through a family member when she visited him. He claimed he always had a good working relationship with the technicians who came on to Palmerville Station, and he had no knowledge of the claims raised.

Journalist Monte Dwyer was exploring FNQ in May 2012, researching material for a story on grey nomads (people that live for extended

---

[26] Statement D Sharpe
[27] Statement S Lee

period on the road). He had heard stories of a lease holder who was terrorising prospectors and tourists in the area. He met and camped on Dan Bidner's Maytown property. Dan regaled Monte with stories about his neighbours and Palmerville Station, which Bidner had nicknamed "Struberville.'

Intrigued, Monte turned up unannounced at the homestead and interviewed Stephen Struber. He described the Strubers as polite and gracious hosts and agreed to an interview.

This was two months before Bruce Schuler's disappearance. He believed the Strubers' *'went mad from the isolation'* and Schuler's murder was the consequence of that isolation. Monte camped that night on the Palmer River, with the approval of Stephen and Dianne Struber. I interviewed Monte for the podcast. He agreed Struber was reasonable and rational during the video recorded interview he had with him.

If you watch the YouTube video of the interview, you will note Stephen Struber was wearing a long sleeve blue work shirt in that video, as he was at the time of his arrest. You have just read Frank Teodo's comments regarding their clothing. The prospectors claimed they were both wearing khaki, yet the next day they were back in blue and despite there being no khaki clothes being recovered at all from Palmerville Station, only blue and green work clothes could be found.

I have not met either Stephen Struber or Dianne Wilson. I only know what I have read about them and been told to me by family members. Stephen Struber obviously had an intense dislike for 'government' as evidenced by his history of brawling with every government agency that had anything to do with administering laws relating to Palmerville Station. He also had a dislike for prospectors, tourists and miners trespassing on the property.

To his credit, he was claiming that they were disrupting his business and not acting in an environmentally friendly manner. It was the opinion of investigating police that Strubers' conduct escalated until they graduated to murder. There were isolated instances, where Dianne Wilson was observed carrying a weapon but otherwise her behaviour would appear moderate and controlled. So did only one of the Strubers descend into criminality or insanity, or both?

Stephen Struber appeared to be perhaps eccentric, whilst Dianne Wilson may have been considered a follower. Whilst Stephen had education and learned many skills after school, they both appear to me to be hardworking bush folk with limited education and social skills.

Where did these people learn how to forensically clean a crime scene and ensure all evidence had been disposed of? Make no mistake, they definitely had those skills. They may not have heard of 'Locard's Exchange Principle' but they certainly understood the dynamics of it. More about that in the chapter '*A Scientific Principle Challenged.*'

George Wilson

George Wilson, brother to sister Dianne, was living at Cannibal Creek, an outstation of Palmerville at the time Bruce Schuler went missing. He mentioned to me on several occasions that if he had not had an alibi, he believed he would have also been charged with the murder of Bruce Schuler. After numerous conversations with George, it was noted he has incredible recall.

George was interviewed twice by police during the investigation. His statements provide an insightful window into his life and life on Palmerville Station, and his words would be difficult to replicate. These are some his words:

'I'm *a 43-year-old male, I'm currently living on Palmerville Station. I know Dianne Wilson Struber, she is my sister. I have known her all my life, I get on very well with her.*

I know Stephen Struber, he is my brother-in-law. I used to get on well with him, I don't get on with him much at all these days. My father Alfred Wilson got this Palmerville property by ballot in 1964.

I have lived at Palmerville off and on my whole life. My mother's name is Doris Wilson. Palmerville Station is a cattle station called Palmerville Holding and is 840 square kilometres by 525 square mile or roughly 136,000 hectares.

Palmerville is a pastoral holding, it is leased from the government, however these leases can be sold, that is you can sell what remains of the lease to another pastoralist at a price agreed to by both parties.

I have seven siblings. Out of the lot of us Dianne is closest to me, then probably Julie then Narele.

I don't know of any friends that Dianne has. She does get along with the neighbours.

In 1984 I was working at the Noel Adams mine about 8 miles down river from the homestead here on Palmerville. I first met Stephen Struber there as he was working there as a mechanic. In 1986 I offered Stephen some work as a mechanic on the station here at Palmerville. He would just work for hourly rate as a mechanic. In 1987 Stephen started working here full-time.

He started seeing my sister Dianne in about 1987. I believe Stephen had a missus and kids back in Malanda at the time.

Stephen worked on until about 1989 when we ran out of work for him. I think he went back to his missus for a bit and was carting Bagasse for one of the mills. Then he came back up here in around 1992 and was doing a bit of mining around here and would do a bit of work for us as well.

Dad died in 1985 at the age of 75. At that time the lease at Palmerville was transferred to my mother Doris Wilson and then she owned the lease.

In 1996 Stephen left again. He came back in 1997 and 1998 and did bits and pieces of work for us and a bit of his own work mining around here. I believe he and Dianne were on and off around this time.

In 1999 he was carting cattle for Russell POOLE. He would collect cattle from here to take to the sale yards in Mareeba. When he came to get the cattle, he would help us in the yards as well. I think he started up with Dianne again at this time.

I was on the property full-time up until the end of 2000. I had a wife back then. She is now deceased. By the end of 2000 she wanted to leave the property. She did not like the way Stephen spoke to her. This was not the only reason she left. My wife and I moved away to Dimbulah then. My wife died in 2001, June 16.

Mum continued to own the lease at Palmerville until 2001.

In 2001 the lease was transferred to Dianne and Stephen. They didn't actually purchase it but they borrowed money and paid Mum's debt and paid me some money that they felt was owed to me in wages for the work that I put into the station for free, given that I was now not able to run the property by myself as my wife would not stay.

Dianne and Stephen have had Palmerville since then. They have lived at the main homesteads here since then. They have had people working for them on and off.

Apart from that it has mostly been me.

In terms of who lives at Palmerville at the present time, I have my gear in the second room on the right. I camp in the back room on the left. Dianne is in the caravan to the left of the house. I never go inside the van. Stephen camps mostly in the van but sometimes in the house, sometimes in the shed.

I don't know why Dianne does not camp in the house. I think it is because she initially moved into the van before she was with Steve when mum and dad were still alive, and she just stayed there.

As at Monday 9 July 2012, the only people who would be available to answer the phone at Palmerville Homestead are Dianne and Stephen. There was no one else living or visiting Palmerville at the time.

About a month ago I half moved up to Cannibal Creek. This is a location within Palmerville Station about 75 kilometres away from the homestead. I basically have an agreement with Steve and Dianne to sub-lease 50 square miles around Cannibal Creek. I am in the process of starting a camp there with the idea of running my own cattle. There is an existing camp there which consists of five little two bedroom buildings. They are in a poor state of repair. There are a set of yards there.

It normally takes two and a half hours to drive from Palmerville to Cannibal Creek if you don't stop.

I helped Stephen and Dianne muster here at Palmerville on 16 and 17 June 2012. On 18 June I drove up to Cannibal Creek by road, basically moving up there to stay. I made an arrangement to speak to Dianne on the phone every afternoon at about 6 30 pm. We made that time that I would ring her, or she would ring me just to make sure I was fine, hadn't been bitten by a snake or had an accident or whatever. I have a sat phone and I would ring Di on her phone number and would speak with her up to 10 minutes each day. This was mainly just to check how I was. Dianne would talk about how the cattle were doing.

I remember speaking to Dianne on the phone on Wednesday 4 July 2012. Dianne told me that they had done a killer, that is killed a cow for meat, upriver on the property from what I could gather. She said they seen a bit of activity where motorbike and vehicle tracks had been moving around. Apart from this in the time that I had spent at Cannibal Creek, Dianne did not mention any further problems that they were having with trespassers or prospectors.

After going back to Cannibal Creek on 18 June, I stayed at the Cannibal Creek area until Wednesday 11 July 2012 and did not come home to the Palmerville homestead or anywhere up this end of the property at that time.

On Sunday afternoon 8 July 2012 my sister Sharon and her man Tony came into my camp and bought me some supplies. They stayed the night and left at about 9am Monday 9 July 2012. They were going to continue on to Lakefield to do some fishing.

On Monday 9 July 2012 Sharon and Tony left me in the morning. After this I went for a ride up to the back fence just to see what the cattle were doing. I was riding on a motorbike over there a Suzuki 200. I got back about lunchtime, had a bit of lunch and did some cleaning on the lower hut. I did that till dark and went over to the camp and knocked up a bit of food.

At about 6.30pm Monday 9 July 2012 I rang Dianne to check in as normal and told her that Sharon had got away all right.

I told her that I had a look at the cattle at my end that day and that the cattle had been getting a bit quieter. I told her it would be worth doing a muster later.

I remember Dianne told me a bit of how the station was going. I remember she mentioned having cut some mickey balls (castrated) the day before (Sunday). She hadn't mentioned it on the Sunday because Sharon had been with me and Sunday's check-in call had only been quick.

Dianne did not tell me about any problems.

I did not detect any problem in her voice.

Dianne mentioned that Stephen had been working on the loader (as in repairing it) to get it ready to do some work in the water tanks.

On Tuesday morning 10 July 2012 it was a bit drizzly, so I did not do much in the morning. At about 11 a.m. I went down to Greasy Bill Creek at the bottom of Howden Dam. Greasy Bill Creek runs into Oakey Creek which runs into Sandy Creek. I went down there and took the pan just to look for spots along the creek that might be good for prospecting. I was riding the motorbike along the creek bed and bank. It was pretty slow going. This is within the 50 square miles that I'm sub-leasing from Stephen and Dianne.

I covered about 4 or 5 miles along the creek. I did this until about 3pm in the afternoon. I went back to the camp, got some water and firewood. At about a quarter to six I saw a big helicopter heading due east. I thought this would mean trouble as this helicopter is normally only used if people are hurt or lost.

Because of this I started ringing Palmerville on the phone number. I started ringing a little bit earlier than usual at about 6.10pm. I did not get an answer. I would have rung about three times between 6.10pm and 7.30pm. Dianne watches 'Home and Away' so I did not ring between 7 and 7.30pm and tried again a little later after 7.30pm. In one of the calls, probably the second last one, I left a message on the phone and said something like 'all is okay here.' Just to let Di know I was alright. I did not call again after that.

The next morning, Wednesday 11 July 2012, I rang Palmerville at about 6.30 a.m. and a few more times until about 7am a male person answered the phone. I knew it was not Stephen Struber or Dianne. The phone dropped out a few times because I was on the sat phone. I did call again, no one answered the phone.

At about 7.30am 11 July I rang my brother-in-law Paul and asked him what was going on. He told me that Dianne and Stephen were in the watch house and could I go and look after the animals on the property. I would have gotten to Palmerville by about 3.45pm on 11 July 2012. I have been staying next door at Mick Callaghan's house since then.

I spoke to Dianne about 4 o'clock on the Wednesday afternoon. I can't recall the exact words of the conversation.

I said something like:" how are you going?'

Dianne said she was okay and asked how the dogs were pretty much straight away.

Towards the end of the conversation, I said something like' I've been up and checked everything and everything is good. The place is like a town, there's a lot of people here. This looks serious. I was talking to one of the policemen and he said if we know anything the man has a wife and children, and the kids would like to know where their dad is, and the wife would like to know where her husband is.'

Dianne said something like" I hope he's alright too.' Dianne sounded alright to me.

On Thursday Ann English rang me on Mick Callaghan's phone. I told her everything was alright. Ann got Steve on the phone on a hook up. All Steve talked about to me was the property and making sure the Police Stock Squad horses did not contaminate any of the other horses or cattle.

Stephen did not talk to me about the missing person, and I did not ask.

Detective Camp has asked me about firearms on Palmerville Station.

When I moved up to Cannibal Creek I left all the firearms (except the handgun) in the safe in the second room, on the right in the homestead at Palmerville. This is my safe. I told Dianne where the key was.

In a subsequent interview with police in October 2012 George made these comments:

'After the first time Dianne and Stephen were arrested, back in July, I took Dianne aside at home and I talked to her about this. I said" This is serious, if you know anything you've got to come forward.' She said:" We haven't done anything, we've been framed.'

I haven't spoken to Dianne about Dan BIDNER. When we talked just the other night Dianne said it was Dan BIDNER who had framed them because of a run in they had the week before at the 18 mile, some people call it the Croc Hole.

The last time I saw my lever action .22 was on the morning of the 18th of June just before I left for Cannibal Creek. At that time I put it in the gun safe in my bedroom at the homestead. I realised when I read the receipts from the police that my .22 was missing. I asked Dianne where it was, she said:" They've taken it.' I wasn't sure who she was talking about. Dianne also told me that Stephen had a gun missing, I can't really recall the words she used, she told me at the same time as she told me about my gun."

I don't know what's going to happen with the property. I'm owed money and I'm worried that I'm going to lose everything.

I am willing to speak to the police again.'

George had relatives staying overnight with him on Sunday 8 July 2012 at Cannibal Creek. Police were able to confirm that. His visitors left mid-morning on the Monday. It was at least a two-hour drive from Cannibal Creek to the homestead. George could not be in two places at once.

With George's intimate knowledge of Palmerville Station, his experience as a prospector, bushman, cattleman and with his incredible recall and his very helpful nature he became my go-to-guy for many of the questions I had. Questions about Palmerville Station's layout, the crime scene setup, and other related issues. He answered every question without hesitation or obvious avoidance. As you will read, George did get dragged into the murder investigation. Even when I asked him about his meeting with the Grey Nomad he appeared to answer honestly and openly.

The Prospectors

The prospectors were central to the prosecution case. They *were* the prosecution case! If I was being uncharitable or more pointedly, realistic, I would say two of the prospectors were *the* case whilst the third was merely window dressing.

They were an unusual mix. Dan, an avid gold prospector who hadn't worked in twenty-five years due to a back injury, which seemingly did not interfere with his fishing and gold prospecting hobbies; Tremain, a snake breeder, gold prospector and jewellery maker who did own the shirt on his back but apparently not much else; and Kevin 'Rusty' Groth, Bruce Schuler's mate of twenty years who worked full time as a lineman for a power company.

Daniel Peter Bidner was born in 1960. At the time of this incident Dan Bidner was fifty-two years old. Bidner had been on a disability pension from age twenty-six years but listed his occupation with police as a prospector. He was married and living with his wife at Butcher's Creek, Maytown. It was the only freehold property in the Palmer River Gold reserve. Bidner had two children, who were not living at home. Bidner moved out of the property and later sold it not long after the disappearance of Bruce Schuler, telling police he was frightened of Stephen Struber, after living there about six years. There were prospectors who told me they were happy to see them go. I have since been told the Bidner's did not live there fulltime but also had a property on the Atherton Tablelands.

The amount of 'police speak' in Daniel Bidner's statements and video interviews is extraordinary. I assumed he may have had some police service at some point and explored that avenue, but I found no information to support that opinion. It was only later discovered that his father was former Detective Sergeant James Bidner who was the officer in charge of the Cairns Criminal Investigation Branch at one point.

Bidner's lease was about thirty minutes' drive from Bruce Schuler's lease at Rosie's Gully, although it was only ten kilometres away. Bruce Schuler had to drive past the Bidner lease to reach his own lease. Bidner and Schuler met about one year before his disappearance, when Bidner assisted Bruce Schuler in unloading an excavator off his truck and walking it to Schuler's lease. They exchanged numbers and remained in contact.

Bidner described Tremain Anderson as 'almost family'. He stated Tremain sometimes called him uncle. They had known each other for over twenty years.

Dan Bidner met Stephen Struber and Dianne Wilson for the first time about ten days before the murder but knew of them by their reputation for evicting trespassers. As you will read, he and Tremain appeared to have intimate knowledge of the Strubers' day-to-day activities[28].

Dan Bidner's remote leasehold was raided by drug squad police in April 2012, three months before Bruce Schuler's disappearance. Police located 100 kilos of cannabis and arrested and charged Dan Bidner with cultivation of a dangerous drug. He pleaded guilty in the Cairns District Court in January 2013 and received a wholly suspended prison sentence. He blamed Stephen Struber for 'dobbing' him into police[29]. This was not his first brush with the law. He had convictions dating back to 1984.

But as with most aspects of this case, Bidner had his own version of the facts. At trial this exchange took place:

Barrister Feeney: '*Did you plead guilty to an offence of ...?*'

Bidner: '*Cultivation. Yes.*'

F: '*producing a dangerous drug?*'

---

[28] Statement by Daniel Bidner
[29] Trial Transcript

Bidner: '*Yes. But I never agreed that they - the plants were pulled out; the police never weighed it. That was an estimate on the police's behalf.*'

F: '*Seventy large plants?*'

Bidner: '*Yeah. I mean, if I could get 100 kilo out of 70 large plants, I'd be working for the CSIRO, mate.*'

In 2012 **Tremain Anderson** was 40 years old. He resided with his wife at Mutchilba, a small township about thirty-five kilometres west of Mareeba, with a population of about 600 people.

When interviewed by police, he gave his occupation as a Snake Breeder, and Gold Prospector. He made jewellery in the wet season. He confirmed he was a long-standing friend of Dan Bidner, of twenty years or more. They referred to each other as '*almost family.*' He used to stay at Bidner's camp in Maytown during the prospecting season which commenced as soon as the wet season was over and ceased when the next wet season arrived.

Tremain also had a recent conviction for cultivation of 300 kilos of cannabis. He pleaded guilty in Cairns Supreme Court in 2010 and received a wholly suspended sentence. Tremain had criminal convictions dating back to 1992. Tremain and Dan Bidner were both questioned at the 2015 murder trial and denied they were involved in the cultivation of each other's drug crop.

Anderson denied even knowing that Bidner's property was raided by police in April 2012 and Bidner arrested for cultivation of cannabis even though he was at Bidner's camp within one month of that event. Apparently, no one considered it odd that, as friends of more than twenty years and '*almost family*', he was ignorant of such a significant arrest,[30] and also ignorant of the fact Bidner was growing a crop.

Tremain had met Bruce Schuler briefly the year before; they reconnected the week before Bruce went missing when he, Dan and Bruce spent the day prospecting at Cradle Creek which is located on Palmerville Station.

---

[30] Trial evidence of Tremain Anderson

Tremain, along with two friends started a YouTube channel in 2015 called '*Gold Hounds*'. They described themselves as three friends who prospected for gold for a living. At the time of writing, this channel was still available on this link on YouTube:

@goldhoundsnuggetrecovery1630

Kevin Groth, known by all as 'Rusty,' was born and bred in Cooktown. He was 47 years old at the time his friend of more than twenty years went missing. Rusty lived in Cooktown, with his wife and children. He had worked for a local energy company for more than twenty-five years. He had visited Bruce once previously at Rosie's Gully as Bruce had apparently encouraged and mentored Rusty in gold prospecting. He and his wife sold their Cooktown property of thirty years in December 2023, and they left the only town Rusty had ever known. No one knows where they relocated to.

Rusty had been in Adelaide on holidays for a month, visiting family. He arrived back in Cooktown on Thursday 5 July 2012 and immediately contacted Bruce and arranged to visit him at Rosie's Gully the coming weekend. Rusty arrived at Rosie's Gully on Saturday 7 July and was ultimately a late addition to the pre-arranged overnight prospecting trip to Palmerville Station by Bruce, Dan and Tremain.

Dan Bidner told police that a neighbour of his had found ten ounces of gold on Palmerville Station the week before. He wanted to try his luck. He invited Tremain and Bruce[31].

I searched for, but could not determine whether this gold find was ever confirmed by police. No statements existed where a prospector confirmed he had found ten ounces of gold, or where he found it. After all, it was *the* reason the men were going on to Palmerville Station. Would not the investigators want to confirm every aspect of the circumstances leading up to the murder? Eventually, after the circumstances of the ill-fated prospecting trip were shared on the podcast, a listener refuted that story.

---

[31] Statement by Kevin Groth

The listener provided details of who made the find, where exactly the gold was found and how much gold was found. It was a very different story to the tale Dan Bidner told police. A claim that made the whole '*a neighbour found ten ounces*' story sound like an elaborate ruse. It would seem the police were, and still are, unaware of that significant fact. Gold had been found on Palmerville Station and surrounds for over 150 years. Of *course* you can find gold there!

Dan Bidner *lived* on the Palmer River Reserve. That was *why* he lived there. He was a prospector. Dan Bidner told police *this* was his first expedition on to Palmerville Station. That was shown to be a lie. He had been going there for ten years[32]. At least. He had been on Palmerville Station two times during the previous fortnight. There was much commentary from listeners about this detecting expedition. Seasoned prospectors commented that it was most unusual to travel that distance for a one-night trip. As you will learn, Bruce Schuler packed clothing for four days or more. Police never recorded how much food the prospectors took with them. As Palmerville Station was the size of Hong Kong, you would first try the exact spot the ten ounces were found, right? Not just pick a random location on Palmerville Station. Yet, the site chosen to set up base camp was nowhere near the gold discovery that allegedly inspired them to go there in the first place. Anderson and Bidner were aware of that. It is unknown whether Schuler or Groth were aware of it.

Bruce Schuler was not the first prospector invited to go to Palmerville Station, prospecting with Dan Bidner and Tremain Anderson. Two other prospectors contacted me to say they had been invited 'out of the blue', to go with Bidner but declined, being nervous of the invitation. Apparently, Dan Bidner had a reputation on the Gold Fields as someone best avoided.

Rusty allegedly first met Dan Bidner and Tremain Anderson on the morning of Sunday 8 July 2012, a mere twenty-four hours before the unlikely events unfolded on Palmerville Station. All four men were aware they would be trespassing by going onto Palmerville Station.

---

[32] Croc Hole incident

They all knew Struber's reputation for evicting trespassers, but it did not seem to faze them.

Evidence presented at trial showed that Dan Bidner and Tremain Anderson had been detecting on Palmerville Station for years[33]. Bruce Schuler had also been previously on there. Furthermore, there were claims by Anderson that he had been fired upon twice by Stephen Struber. On the evidence of Bidner, he had been involved in a confrontation with Struber only a week before. Yet, despite this, they still decided to go on to Palmerville Station and set up camp virtually in sight of the homestead. Brazen, much! They had an area the size of Hong Kong to traverse, yet they chose the alleged lion's den.

The information that Acting Detective Sergeant O'Brien received, regarding the accuracy of the witness claims, together with the knowledge that Groth had only known Bidner and Anderson for one day, would have been compelling evidence there could not have been collusion between the prospectors in retelling their version of events of Bruce Schuler's disappearance. A comforting fact for any investigator.

All three prospectors were very co-operative with the subsequent police investigation into the disappearance of Bruce Schuler. They all travelled back to the scene and met with detectives the next day, Tuesday 10 July 2012, and spent hours with them detailing their knowledge of the events of the incident. Dan Bidner went with the investigators to the gully and pointed out where and how events unfolded.

The witnesses then travelled to Mareeba Police Station that same night where they provided recorded statements. They remained in Mareeba and willingly supplied DNA samples, as well as fingerprints and consented to a forensic procedure examination (FPO). They again attended the police station as required for identification of the suspects. Police remained with Bruce Schuler's abandoned vehicle, awaiting reinforcements.

---

[33] Evidence at trial

All three prospectors returned to Palmerville Station later that same week and participated in video recorded re-enactments. The witnesses returned yet again to the crime scene on Sunday 15 July 2012 and again conducted re-enactments to enable digital mapping to be undertaken. All three witnesses returned to Palmerville Station, on 1 August 2012, to undertake yet another video recorded re-enactment of the events of Monday 9 July 2012.

In 2014, two years later, they gave evidence in the committal proceedings and of course, they all gave evidence at the Supreme Court trial held in Cairns in July 2015. *Very co-operative witnesses.* If only they could have gotten their various versions of events straight.

Struberville

There was no question Stephen Struber and the FNQ mining community were at loggerheads. The gold forums and prospecting chat rooms were abuzz with comments about Palmerville Station. Everyone knew someone, who knew someone, who had had a run in with Stephen Struber, whilst trespassing on Palmerville Station. The stories were eerily similar. The prospector had been going on to Palmerville Station for years. They would go there for three or four days, a few times during the season. They just enjoyed gold prospecting and for some, it 'topped up' their income. They never started fires. They never caused any problems, and they didn't want to go to the trouble or expense of obtaining a mining lease or a fossicking permit. They didn't see a need to advise the owners as they were only gold detecting.

They knew they were trespassing, but they were not hurting anyone. Stephen Struber evicted them. He was nasty. He wouldn't even let them stay until the next day or until when they planned to leave. On one occasion, he had a rifle slung over his shoulder, and sometimes his wife would be sitting in the car with a rifle visible. Sometimes the male would identify himself, sometimes Stephen Struber was known to the campers and sometimes they just assumed it was Stephen Struber.

On Stephen Struber's side of the ledger, he was fed up with trespassers coming onto the property unannounced, causing environmental damage, leaving their rubbish everywhere, interfering with and sometimes shooting his stock, and lighting fires to enable the detectors to work more efficiently, burning grass desperately needed for the cattle. He would tell them they should get a permit and ordered them off the property immediately. A '*Brutish Enforcer*' as the Cairns Post described him.

The entire area was well known for illegal cannabis cultivation. It was common knowledge that if prospectors or tourists strayed close to a drug crop, the growers would threaten them and force them out of the area. It was claimed that growers sometimes identified themselves as the Palmerville leaseholders when evicting them.

Was Stephen Struber obsessed with people coming onto his property? Prospectors, tourists, Cook Shire employees included. If you accept the evidence of several Shire Council employees, including a Council Surveyor, two Council Engineers, a Council Surveyor and there does not appear to be any reason why you would not accept their evidence, Stephen Struber was obsessed with people coming onto the property, particularly Cook Shire Council officers.

The Surveyor had worked for the Cook Shire Council for eleven years and knew Stephen Struber from council meetings. In 2007, he was instructed to survey Palmerville Station for compulsory land acquisition. He telephoned Stephen Struber and advised him he would need to gain access to Palmerville Station for surveying purposes. He was accompanied by a police officer from Laura Police Station. Stephen Struber met them along Whites Creek Road, and from Struber's body language ,he could tell Struber was unhappy to see Council officers or Police on his property. After discussions, he then undertook his work which occupied two full days. He said Struber was present and watched him the entire time.[34].

The Engineers described confrontations with Stephen Struber as shouting matches, but eventually, he would jump in his car and drive off. His main complaint with the Shire Council was the realignment of the road. He did not appear to be objecting to the road's construction; his argument was that it was in the wrong place. Despite the many confrontations between Struber and Council employees, there was never any violence. He was shouty, he was unreasonable, he wanted them off his property, and he regularly threatened to sue them all.

In 2007, a descendant of a person who originally found gold in the Palmer River was organising a family reunion, to include a tour of

---

[34] Statement by J VanDebBerg

Maytown. She had seen a newspaper advertisement that nobody was to go onto Palmerville Station without a permit. She called the homestead, and spoke with Stephen Struber and requested permission to go onto the property, and explained she was organising a family reunion. Her request was refused. She described Struber as very calm, but adamant in his stance of refusing permission to enter.

Police claimed some 200 people contacted them, after an appeal was made for people with information about Palmerville Station, to come forward.

Police obtained thirty-nine statements from people who alleged they had a run-in with the Strubers, over the previous two decades. The statements related to twenty-one separate instances, where Stephen Struber and Dianne Wilson confronted them on Palmerville Station.

Some of those instances involved Council employees going about their business. *All twenty-one confrontations were non-violent.* No one complained of being assaulted or threatened by Struber or Wilson. In most instances, the trespassers felt intimidated. Struber was aggressive and abusive and ordered them off his property. On one occasion Dianne Wilson was carrying a rifle. On two occasions a rifle was seen in the car, and on one of those occasions Dianne had her hand on the rifle. On another occasion Stephen Struber had a handgun in his belt with his hand on it.

On one occasion people on a mining lease heard a lot of shooting in the surrounding bush, and later Stephen Struber and (possibly his son) rolled up and told them they were shooting in the area. One person complained that an unidentified woman on horseback, with a revolver on her hip had abused them.

One man contacted police and informed them that in about 2002, he was stopped on the side of the road in Palmerville, checking his vehicle. He heard a gunshot, and dirt was kicked up about fifteen feet in front of his vehicle. He saw a vehicle driving off in the distance and he said it looked like the Strubers. He did not see who was in the vehicle or who fired the shot, just an inference.

On another occasion a man was using a dozer to build a fence on the boundary of three properties, before the wet season. One of them being Palmerville Station. Struber had telephoned him requesting he ensure the fence be built on the boundary. The man came back to Palmerville after the wet season, three or four months later, to find a .357 magnum bullet shell on the step of his dozer. He had no idea of who fired the round or left the shell there. As the statement was in the police evidence brief, the inference was it was somehow connected to Stephen Struber. Perhaps he left it there as a warning?

There was no evidence of Stephen Struber physically assaulting anyone or evidence of assault with a deadly weapon. It appeared that when someone stood up to Stephen Struber, he backed down and drove off.

Were the confrontations between Stephen Struber and Cook Shire Council, Telstra, DEHP, miners in the Land Court, prospectors, miners and visiting tourists a factor in what occurred on Monday 9 July 2012? It's possible. It would be fair to say, Stephen Struber had upset and offended a large group of people who disliked him, some intensely. Much of it by his own hand.

I have been told a few miners and prospectors downright hated him. One prospector wrote this to me, '*It seems everyone in the Maytown crew knew Struber and Wilson were innocent, I got the impression years ago and more so now, although most people are sorry for Dianne, Struber can stay where he is.*'

It sounds like FNQ's worst kept secret!

There were two notable exceptions to the apparent argumentative, but non-violent side of Struber and Wilson. One involved a local known as Coca Cola John. He used to make items out of Coca Cola cans and sell them at street markets. Whilst he could not put a date on the event, it would appear to have occurred around the year 2000, and involved George Wilson, although he said Stephen Struber and Dianne Wilson were present in the car.

He had been prospecting since 1956 but had been going to Palmerville since about 1992. He would go up there every second weekend and stay five days during the dry season. This was his main source of income apart from a disability pension.

Stephen Struber came across his camp near Dog Leg Creek. There was a big hole near a mango tree dug by prospectors, and they had been using it as a rubbish dump. Stephen Struber was angry about the rubbish, but John pointed to the rear of his utility and told him he took all his rubbish out with him. A woman, presumably Dianne, was in the passenger seat and did not get out.

After talking for a while, Stephen accepted an offer of a cup of tea. He walked back to speak with Dianne who declined, and they left. About a year later, Coca Cola John was driving into the Croc Hole (on Palmerville Station) when a vehicle passed in the opposite direction. Struber was in the passenger seat, a woman in the middle and the vehicle was driven by George Wilson. He didn't know George, but thought he looked like his mother Dorrie. The car turned around and followed him to the Croc Hole. He stated Struber stayed in the vehicle, but he could see he was holding the barrel of a rifle. George Wilson got out of the vehicle and confronted him about being on private property. George then pulled him out of the vehicle and kicked him to the ground. He said George then continued to kick him, and he crawled under his vehicle to get away. George then got back in the car, and they drove away.

I put those allegations to George Wilson. He denied ever seeing Coca Cola John at the Croc Hole or assaulting him. Everyone in the mining communities from Cairns to Cape York and beyond knew about the assault on Coca Cola John, and the incident gained folklore status. Most of the people who quoted it or had heard the tale, thought that Stephen Struber was the one who had assaulted Coca Cola John. Whatever happened, or didn't happen on that day, Coca Cola John told police he never returned to Palmerville Station after that[35].

Whilst everyone knew someone, who knew someone, who had been threatened or abused by Stephen Struber, no one had ever complained of being assaulted by him, or fired upon by him or Dianne Wilson. That

---

[35] Statement by J Tomlinson

is, until Tremain Anderson came along. Anderson told police Stephen Struber assaulted him whilst Dianne Wilson pointed a 30/30 rifle at him. Just the previous year, Stephen Struber fired a shotgun in his general direction whilst he was fishing on Palmerville Station.

Curiously, Anderson was present the day Bruce Schuler went missing. He was unlucky. Of the thousands of prospectors who go to the Gold Reserve every year, he was the only one ever assaulted by Stephen Struber, three times. You will read about Tremain's clashes with Stephen and Dianne in the chapter *'Charged by a Bull.'* Despite these repeated threats and assaults, Anderson continued to risk trespass on Palmerville Station for the elusive gold jackpot.

The majority of what is covered in this book about Stephen Struber's confrontations (with half the world) was not heard by the jury at their murder trial. That was probably just as well. They would have returned a Guilty Verdict before the trial was finished. Why have I introduced them to the story? For balance.

Those complaints did show a consistent pattern of behaviour. Struber was hot headed, he was abusive, he was at times irrational and threatening, but never violent. When confronted, he backed down. The confrontation with Dan Bidner at the Croc Hole was a classic example, as you will read shortly. After the bluff and buster, he returned to his car and left the area. Violence was not one of his trademarks. It was important to introduce all the allegations, rumour and gossip. Stephen Struber's conduct around the Palmerville Gold Reserve was legendary.

In speaking with the locals, the issue of Bruce Schuler's disappearance couldn't be raised without all the threats, arguments and confrontations beforehand. *'The Brutish Enforcer'*, as the Cairns Post referred to him.

Did Stephen Struber or Dianne Wilson 'descend into madness' as was the claim? Did the threats, intimidation, and harassment escalate to murder? That's for the evidence to prove.

Sovereign Citizens

Did initial police investigations mistake the Strubers for Sovereign Citizens?

The phrase *Sovereign Citizens* came into existence around the 1970's in America and quickly spread to the UK, Australia and other western countries. But Sovereign Citizens have been around, in one form or another since Rome was on the drawing board, and along the way that name was shortened to SovCits.

People disillusioned with governments, taxation, a grudge against councils and police, conspiracy theorists and people with their own pseudo-legal beliefs (based on misinterpretations of common law), have been doing the rounds in Australia since the first settlement. The Eureka Stockade or Eureka Rebellion of 1854 is a prime example. The miners in Ballarat, Victoria were disgruntled with the way the colonial government was administering the goldfields.

They were particularly unhappy with the exorbitant prospecting license fees. The rebellion had escalated from peaceful demonstrations and civil disobedience to fighting that resulted in twenty-seven deaths. The rebels had sworn allegiance to the Southern Cross flag. If those riots occurred today, they would likely be described as SovCits involved in a domestic terrorist event. It is noted the Southern Cross flag can still be seen flying in parts of Australia, and even featured in the 2025 Australian Federal election.

The Principality of Hutt River in Western Australia was a micronation proclaimed in 1970, when Leonard Casley declared his farm a sovereign state. The principality issued its own currency, stamps and passports which were not recognised by the Australian Government or any other nation states. The High Court of Australia and the Supreme

Court of Western Australia both rejected submissions arguing the principality was not subject to Australian laws.

The reason for the original declaration was typical of the beliefs held by SovCits. The Casley family were unhappy with what they called the draconian wheat production quotas. The Casley family and others objected to the quotas and protested. The WA Government introduced legislation to compulsorily acquire their land, and it escalated from there. In 1977, the Principality declared war on Australia, but cessation of hostilities followed several days later. After Leonard Casley's death in 2019, his son Graeme dropped the claim to sovereignty in 2020.

That has not stopped the proliferation of SovCits in Australia. In fact, if anything, it likely encouraged conspiracy theorists to continue with their anti-government agenda. They are not confined to rural or remote area. In the 1990's, I regularly conducted door knocks at Brisbane suburban addresses to find a large sign on the front gate forbidding entry and declaring the laws of the Commonwealth did not apply to the occupants or the property. With the arrival of the Internet, and particularly since Covid 19, SovCits have exploded exponentially. People with a grudge against the State or Federal government, local Councils, and police for starters, were and are fodder for SovCit recruiters.

If the Boxing Day Tsunami was a wakeup call for Australia to the power of nature, the tragic events at Wieambilla, Queensland on 12 December 2022, brought Sovereign Citizens to the Australian consciousness. That senseless act resulted in the murder of three people, two of them young Queensland police officers.

The sovereign citizens involved held strong anti-government, anti-police and anti-vaccine views and were known online conspiracy theorists. They ended up also dying in a gunfight with police.

What do Sovereign Citizens have to do with the murder of Bruce Schuler? Everything, and nothing.

I refer to an entry in the diary of Acting Detective Sergeant Nick O'Brien dated Monday 9 July 2012:

- *'Name redacted - stated he believed nominated witnesses story'.*

That diary entry was made just before Detective O'Brien placed the telephone call to witness Bidner as you read in the chapter '*Our mate is missing.*' Whomever made that comment, believed the story the witnesses were telling. Who made that comment? Obviously, Officer Tome or Detective O'Brien did not talk to the local postman, the local hotelier or a neighbouring station owner. It was likely a senior police officer at Cairns District Headquarters. Someone that Detective O'Brien trusted, and had confidence in. It was a comment that could well have influenced his decision making.

That entry never made sense to me. Why did the person believe the story? Was it based on the claims the witnesses told Officer Tome? One of the nominated witnesses had a Supreme Court criminal conviction for growing a large quantity of cannabis, and another of the witnesses was on bail for a similar offence.

I make this suggestion - was that belief not based on what the witnesses said or who they were, but on the previous conduct of residents of Palmerville Station? Stephen Struber appeared to have an irrational hatred of the Cook Shire Council in particular. Letters had been written about him to the Commissioner of Police and to the Assistant Commissioner of Police at Cairns, by the CEO of that Council.

Police had to accompany Council employees when they went to Palmerville Station. Stephen Struber and Dianne Wilson may have had a genuine gripe with the Cook Council over losing their airstrip and the resumption of 100 kilometres of their property. They blamed miners for polluting the river, and tourists for environmental damage and leaving a mess. They had a genuine gripe with prospectors trespassing on their property, destroying their stock and starting fires to assist gold detecting, but to the police and government departments were they 'nutters' and probably Sovereign Citizens? Senior police would have been aware of the many stories by prospectors of Strubers (at times) erratic behaviour. Did they perceive the shooting of Bruce Schuler as an escalation of that conduct?

That may have been a valid consideration. The evidence that came out of Bruce Schuler's murder did not support any suggestion that Stephen Struber or Dianne Wilson were Sovereign Citizens. Whilst they were certainly locked in confrontations with the Cook Council over road realignment, there may have been some legitimacy in their concerns. I am not sure the same could be argued about Telstra.

Their actions against trespassers were forthright, and at times confrontational, but there was no evidence of violence. There was no evidence they were anti-Government or anti-establishment. They were very conscious of environmental issues and perhaps obsessed with keeping Palmerville Station as it was. The world was moving on, the area was opening to tourism and development, and they were objecting. There was no evidence they were trying to create a micro nation on Palmerville Station. Right or wrong, the Strubers had reached folklore status across FNQ. Everyone knew about the leaseholders on Palmerville Station. Everyone knew to be wary about going on or across Palmerville Station land. It was the town gossip. Some of the stories about the Strubers and their conduct were accurate, many were inaccurate, which made the brazen conduct of the prospectors even more bizarre.

There was no evidence that the Strubers were communicating with other SovCits. Stephen Struber appeared to believe in Australia's legal system. I am sure not all decisions in the Land Court went in his favour, but he was happy to continue to use it for his purposes.

Whilst sovereign citizenry may have been a very valid point to consider at the time of the murder investigation, I do not believe (and have not seen) any evidence to support any suggestion that the Strubers were sovereign citizens. I would go further and say, that if the shooting of Bruce Schuler was an escalation of the Strubers resentment against 'the government', it would have played out very differently on the Tuesday night when SERT surrounded their '*stronghold.*' I expect it would have ended in a similar manner to the result at Wieambilla, with the Strubers being shot dead when they refused to surrender. If the Crown was hoping to use SovCits as a potential motive in this case, there was no evidence to support that. Whatever happened to Bruce Schuler, it had nothing to do with sovereign citizenry.

The Vehicles

The Strubers' two, four-wheel drive vehicles were to become a significant part of the Crown case. A single question about one of those 4x4 could have changed the course of this investigation, as you will learn.

Four-wheel drive vehicles dominate this story; just as they dominate all of outback Australia. The roads demand it; the weather conditions demand it; the terrain demands it. It is not unusual, just a fact of life in the bush. Typically, 4x4 'utes' or utilities are the main means of transport. They are convenient for carrying equipment as well as passengers.

Bruce Schuler drove a single cab Nissan Patrol 4x4 utility with a tray back, covered by a canopy and tarpaulin tie-down covers.

You can view photographs of both Strubers' vehicles and Bruce Schuler's vehicle in Appendix C.

Dan Bidner drove a single cab Nissan Patrol 4x4 tray back utility. Tremain Anderson drove a LandCruiser tray back 4x4 utility. He also had a small 125 cc motorcycle. Rusty Groth drove a Toyota LandCruiser 4x4 station wagon. Most police vehicles in this region were 4x4 LandCruisers.

The two 4x4 vehicles the Strubers owned were central to the Crown case against them. They were very similar Toyota LandCruiser utilities, both beige in colour. One was registered, the other an unregistered 'bush basher' for use around the property. The major (and to become significant) difference between the two utilities was the registered 4x4 had sides on the tray which formed a tub, and a crane attached behind the cabin. The unregistered bush basher had a flat metal track back with no sides.

After their arrest, investigators instructed a police mechanic to inspect both vehicles. His report was not kind to either utility[36]. Both vehicles had bull bars fitted, had poor brakes, poor suspension and poor steering. Both were in a potentially dangerous condition. The hand brake did not work on either vehicle.

The mechanic test drove both vehicles. He would only drive the 'bush basher' on level ground, as he considered it too dangerous to drive on a slope. He was unable to select first or second gear in any range, that is H2, H4 and L4, in that vehicle. All other gears operated. In layman terms, the mechanic had to start and drive the vehicle in 3rd gear, yet it was the Crown case this very vehicle drove up and down a very steep incline, as you will read.

For those with no 4x4 driving experience, the vehicle is placed in H2, high range for normal driving, say on a bitumen road. The rear wheels only are engaged in that range. For off road driving, say on a well-made dirt road, the transmission is placed in H4, where all 4 wheels are engaged. In extreme off-road conditions, the transmission is placed in L4, where all 4 wheels are engaged, but speed is sacrificed for engine torque.

Stephen Struber was awaiting arrival of parts to repair the gearbox of the 'bush basher' at the time of their arrest. Both George Wilson and Stephen Struber told the court[37]in 2015, they *could* drive the bush basher in first or second gear, but it was difficult selecting those gears. Otherwise, it was necessary to start driving in third gear.

As most people would know, that made driving extremely difficult and almost impossible if the vehicle was on any sort of an incline. The question that was not asked, by anyone, at any time, was whether the vehicle could be placed in reverse gear. The police mechanic was silent on the subject and not asked. George Wilson and Stephen Struber were not asked the question by police or at trial.

George Wilson told me that if the gearbox was placed in reverse, the gearbox became jammed, and the vehicle could not be moved out of

---

[36] Statement by M Ritchie
[37] Trial Transcript of G Wilson & S Struber

reverse. To get the vehicle out of reverse necessitated removing the top cover of the gearbox, putting a screwdriver down the inside of the gearbox, and forcing the gears out of reverse. A time consuming and tricky operation, that also becomes significant, as the ute supposedly performed a three-point turn at the bottom of a ravine, or traversed the ravine in reverse gear, at the area that became known as Crime Scene Two.

As part of the Crown case, it was alleged this bush basher ute was driven up and down a very steep ravine. If it had been determined this vehicle could not have successfully done that, where would this investigation have gone? It was later established it was not the bush basher that went up or down that ravine, but by then Struber and Wilson had been convicted, and the Court of Appeal did not consider that one aspect was sufficient to reverse the convictions.

The Weapons

It is hard to fathom why the jury were not told of the huge discrepancies in the weapons the prospectors saw and heard fired that day. This was a murder with no body and no cause of death. The Crown claimed death was caused by bullets from the missing firearms. As you will read, there was a lot of evidence about the weapons that the jury was painfully unaware of, and due to the minimal evidence presented, the jury was asked to make many inferences in this case.

It started as two of the missing weapons being central to the Crown case – a .22 bolt action rifle, and a .357 magnum revolver. But as the investigation progressed, it appeared the murder weapons may have been a .22 lever action rifle, a 12-gauge shotgun or a 30/30 rifle (*the one Dianne always carried according to Tremain Anderson*). The jury was not made aware of any of that information.

It would be rare to find a remote property anywhere in Australia without a collection of firearms. For primary producers, firearms are essential business tools, used for putting down injured or diseased stock, controlling wild animals, and general property management. Palmerville Station was no exception.

Following the Port Arthur massacre in 1996, Australia's firearm ownership laws were significantly tightened. Licensing requirements were standardised nationally, and under the new legislation, each firearm had to be identifiable, registered to a specific individual, and securely stored, typically in a gun safe when not in use.

George Wilson for instance carried a .44 magnum handgun in a holster on his hip. He explained that, when on horseback, a rifle or long arm was impractical. He may have only a split second to draw and fire on a dangerous snake, wild pig or scrub bull charging at him. Reaching for a long arm could cost precious time and injury, or worse[38].

Stephen and Dianne Struber always carried a rifle when in the vehicle. Dianne usually had it within reach between the seats, with the barrel pointing down. George Wilson confirmed any rifle in the cars was usually kept between the seats with the barrel either pointing down or up.

A Queensland Police firearms register search revealed Dianne Wilson did not hold any firearm licenses. A similar search showed that Stephen Struber was licensed to hold four weapons, whilst George Wilson was licensed to hold seven firearms.

All firearms found on Palmerville Station were seized when a search warrant was executed on Tuesday 10 July 2012.

Missing and not located was a Winchester .22 lever action rifle owned by George Wilson, and two weapons registered to Stephen Struber, a .357 handgun and an Armscor brand .22 bolt action rifle[39]. He denied ever owning or licensing an Armscor .22 rifle bearing serial number 411-2801. My inquiries in 2024 with Armscor, Nevada, USA revealed serial number 411-2801 was unknown to them and had never been manufactured by them.

Five of George Wilson's licensed weapons were found by police secured in a gun safe inside the homestead. George believed his Winchester .22 lever action rifle should have also been in the safe along with his other weapons, but he had told Dianne where he had hidden the key to the safe. Dianne later told him she had used the Winchester.

George was not happy. He was concerned he could lose his firearms license, because the rifle was not safely stored in the gun safe. Dianne could not explain what happened to his rifle. She did not know, she told him. George could not explain its disappearance and ultimately concluded it had been stolen.

---

[38] Interview with George Wilson 2023
[39] Police Firearms Register

Stephen Struber told police his .357 handgun was locked in the registered LandCruiser along with a .308 rifle. The vehicle had broken down he said, and would be found approximately one kilometre from the homestead. When police forced entry to the LandCruiser and searched it on Wednesday 11 July 2012. only the .308 rifle was found.[40] The .357 handgun was not located.

Police were then able to easily start the vehicle and drive it to the homestead. Stephen Struber and Dianne Wilson eventually made complaints both weapons had been stolen by police. Queensland Police investigated their complaints and found there was no substance to them.

Bruce Schuler, Dan Bidner, Tremain Anderson and Rusty Groth were all owners or frequent users of weapons and experienced with firearms. The various weapons the prospectors claimed they heard fired when Bruce Schuler went missing are dealt with in later chapters.[41]

---

[40] Statement by Det Sgt McLeish
[41] Trial evidence

Confrontation at the Croc Hole

The Croc Hole was located approximately fifteen kilometres to the east of the homestead, on Palmerville Station property, and was a renowned fishing spot known only to locals and tourists lucky enough to be told about it. Barramundi were plentiful in the Croc Hole, as were crocodiles. When you read about a phone call that Dianne Wilson later made to the homestead, she was referring to this place.

Around a fortnight before he went missing, Bruce Schuler went fishing at the croc hole with Dan Bidner and two friends.

On Monday 2 July, (one week before he went missing) Dan Bidner and four friends were fishing at the Croc hole when Stephen Struber and Dianne Wilson stumbled across them. This was the first time Struber and Bidner had ever met. Bidner had nicknamed Palmerville as 'Struberville,' because of the many stories he had heard about Stephen Struber. They were clearly trespassing, having failed to inform Struber of their intention to go to the Croc Hole.

Struber ordered them off the property. Immediately. The other campers started to pack up their belongings, but Bidner refused and stood his ground, and a confrontation ensued. Bidner argued they were camped on the water's edge, which was Crown land, not part of Palmerville Station, which was accurate, but incorrect. Struber pointed out they had to drive across his property to reach the fishing spot.

Struber threatened to call the police unless they left immediately. Bidner, unfazed, encouraged him to do so, stating that they planned to stay three days and would only leave if and when the police arrived. The situation became heated. What happened next depended on whose version you accept. Bidner later told police Struber and Wilson had a history of intimidating people and using firearms to threaten them.

Everyone knew about it. Tremain Anderson had been previously assaulted and shot at by them, he said. He claimed they had been doing it for years. The confrontation lasted some fifteen minutes.

Dianne Wilson was videotaping the event. She said she recorded every encounter they had with trespassers in case it was needed for court purposes, she told police. The following conversation was recorded and later recovered by police when they searched Palmerville Station:

Wilson: '*Will I get it?*'

Struber: '*Hey?*'

Wilson: '*Will I get it?*'

Struber: '*Please yourself. He is an ignorant arsehole.*'

Bidner: '*What, are you getting the gun out are ya?*'

Struber: '*He's got plenty of witnesses.*'

Eventually, Struber and Wilson returned to their vehicle and left the area. No weapon was ever produced[42]. After the Strubers drove away this conversation was allegedly recorded as the camera continued rolling:

Wilson: '*if those other cunts weren't there I'd stop and get the gun out and I'd .... (Unintelligible)...between the eyes.*'

The original audio was never made public. Dianne Wilson denied the conversation, claiming she would never say those words.[43]

Sharon, one of Dianne's sisters knew of the incident, as Dianne had called her that night. Dianne was feeling scared and anxious. Sharon recalled the conversation along these lines,

'*Sharon, we came across Bidner at the Croc Hole today. Steve told him he was trespassing, and they needed to get off his property, because they did not have his permission to be there. She said Bidner was very angry and told them flat to call the police, and that he didn't care if they were called, taunting them. Bidner said that Dianne and Stever had reported him for growing drugs to the police.*

---

[42] Trial transcript
[43] Trial transcript

He also said that police had been to his place about drugs and the police told him it was the Strubers that had reported him. Bidner then told Dianne and Steve that he was going to get them. That he (Bidner) was coming down to their homestead in the next week some time to sort them out. Dianne said if something happens to Steve and I tell the police that Bidner has threatened us. I was very concerned about Dianne and Stephen's safety and told her to call the police. She said to me that wouldn't do any good because it was our word against his, and we have called the police before about other matters, the police didn't even bother calling them back.[44]'

Some believed this was the confrontation that sent Struber or Wilson, or both, over the edge into that mental abyss where they dropped into madness. It was claimed Struber and Wilson mistook Bruce Schuler for Dan Bidner in the gully the following week.

As the Crown never put forward a motive for the murder, this seemed sort of plausible to some. Judge Henry saw it otherwise. In the absence of the jury, he made this comment to defence counsel, '*The prosecution case appears to be that the present alleged killing occurred because the deceased was trespassing*[45].'

On Wednesday 4 July 2012, only days before his disappearance, Bruce Schuler, Dan Bidner and Tremain Anderson went gold prospecting in an area known as Cradle Creek (on Palmerville Station land)[46]. The Croc Hole is part of Cradle Creek so it would appear the prospectors were not concerned about returning on to Palmerville Station just two days later and trespassing once again. '*Dan was just showing Bruce around as he had never been up to Cradle before.*[47]' No gold was found and nothing out of the ordinary occurred. There was no note of whose vehicle or vehicles they were using on 4 July. It was claimed the confrontation earlier made Dan Bidner cautious about taking his vehicle onto Palmerville Station.

---

[44] Interview with S Ferguson
[45] Trial transcript
[46] Statements D Bidner
[47] Statement by T Anderson

The Crown used this confrontation to prove to the jury the Strubers had the potential to be dangerous people. Bidner and his friends were the victims in the Croc Hole confrontation.

There is no record whether police took the Strubers' claim seriously of Bidner threatening them. Was Dan Bidner out for revenge? Were police investigating Bruce Schuler's disappearance from the wrong perspective?

Sunday 8 July 2012

The discrepancies in the prospectors' stories start.

Early Sunday morning, Rusty Groth and Bruce Schuler packed their swags and prospecting equipment in the back of Bruce Schuler's Patrol. They needed enough clothes and food supplies for two days and one night. They headed off early from Rosie's Gully on the twenty-five-minute trip to Bidner's camp[48].

Kevin Groth was the only one asked by police, and he told them they left Bidner's lease at 9 a.m.[49] '*We waited for a while as they had their breakfast.*' Jo Bidner, Dan's wife was interviewed on Saturday 14 July 2012 by police, and she stated Bruce and Kevin Groth arrived at 7.30 a.m., had a 'cuppa' and then left[50].

The first inconsistency; small but concerning.

Bidner did not want to go onto Palmerville Station in his vehicle, he said. After the fresh in his mind confrontation with Stephen Struber, he was concerned Struber would recognise his ute and there would be trouble[51]. Dan and Tremain loaded their swags, food and detecting equipment into the tray of Bruce's ute. Dan joined Bruce and Rusty in the single cabin, and Tremain rode his 125-cc motorcycle for the trip to the Palmer River crossing[52].

Although it was a ninety-minute trip to the river crossing, Bidner told police they arrived around lunchtime, however this would change as time went on. Neither Bidner nor Anderson were asked or made comment about any stops during the trip. Groth commented they

---

[48] Statement by K Groth
[49] Statement by K Groth
[50] Statement by J Bidner
[51] Statement by D Bidner
[52] Statement by T Anderson

stopped several times along the way with Tremain pointing out various landmarks, and where he had had found gold. He added that after arriving at the crossing, they prospected in a couple of locations before returning to the riverbed.

No mention was made by any of the prospectors of making a side trip to the area behind the Two-Mile gravel pit, located on Fairlight Station and about four kilometres past the river crossing. That information did not surface for over two months. It could be safely assumed the prospectors also trespassed on Fairlight Station that day.

Boots on the Ground

Discrepancies in the versions provided by the three prospectors were mounting.

The headwaters of the Palmer River rise in the Sussex Range, part of the Great Dividing Range southwest of Cooktown. The river flows west across the Cape York Peninsula towards the Gulf of Carpentaria over the 327-kilometre course.

Palmerville Homestead is situated on the southern side of the Palmer River. The station land extended north and south of the Palmer River, so it enjoyed a prestigious seventy-kilometre double river frontage. During the investigation into the disappearance of Bruce Schuler, police declared the entire Palmerville Station a crime scene. Probably the biggest crime scene in Australia's history.

It is not often that a crime scene has no nearby landmark to identify it, most commonly a street name. Most people would expect to read the incident occurred on the corner of Queen Street and Elizabeth Street. This was certainly the exception. Nearby reference points were known as 'the one mile', 'the two-mile gravel pit', 'the six mile dam', 'the big dam' and so on. The Palmerville Homestead was the nearest and most identifiable landmark, around one kilometre to the west of where the murder allegedly took place. A rough dirt track led down to the Palmer River from the homestead. As anyone with four-wheel driving experience would know, it may then be possible to negotiate a riverbed, dependent on water levels, trees, logs and other debris, as well as the depth of the sand in the bed. It was possible to drive from the homestead to the crime scene, with difficulty, and in four-wheel drive.

This remote location required police to map the entire crime scene using GPS mapping equipment and creating their own map. The general area where the crime scene was located was called The One Mile.

The prospectors set up camp on the southern side of the Palmer River (the same side as the homestead), in the riverbed, about 200 metres from the main Palmer River crossing, and about two kilometres east of the Palmerville Station Homestead. (They did not need to drive past the homestead to reach that location). It was necessary to wade across the Palmer River to access the northern bank of the river in this location.

This site was selected by Dan Bidner as it was on Crown land. He felt confident he could rebuff any demand to leave the area if they came across Stephen Struber, he told police[53]. Yet he claimed he was reluctant about taking his car there, and he was already concerned about an altercation. It was evident Stephen Struber would roll up on a camp regardless of whose car was there.

In his interview taken two days after the event, Bidner said at point 49:

'A couple of days later or maybe a week later I rang Bruce and I said,' We're heading down to Palmerville, do you want to come for a run? I said to him that we would go down there to detect it because the neighbours got 10 ounces down there and we saw the gold and we thought right let's go.'

As well as being unable to confirm the authenticity of the gold find, I was unable to confirm whether Bidner was ever asked by police the specific location of the ten-ounce gold find. After all, you would not go onto a property the size of Hong Kong based on a neighbour's claim, unless they told you where they found the gold, right?

As the prospectors set up camp in this specific location and went detecting on the northern side of the river, again in this very location, it would be reasonable to believe this was where the neighbour found the gold. It would later be learned Bidner had missed the gold location by around six kilometres and three ounces. *'We saw the gold.'* It was seven ounces, not ten. Exaggeration? A big difference in size, weight

---

[53] Statement by D Bidner

and value to an experienced prospector. The actual location of the gold find was in Fish Creek, an area about six kilometres away in a straight line from the river crossing where they parked up. Had they selected that area, it would have been a further six kilometres away from the prying eyes of the lease holders.

Why would Bidner go detecting practically under the noses of lease holders with a fearsome reputation for evicting trespassers, and around six kilometres from where the gold was found? As any number of prospectors commented, '*A long way to go for an overnight prospecting trip*'. The trip had only just begun, and the questions were starting. From the evidence, investigators did not consider or question this.

The deep gully where Bruce Schuler was last seen was generally known as the One Mile, located about one kilometre east of the homestead and on the other (northern) side of the Palmer River. The walking distance, including wading across the river, from the prospectors' camp site to the first crime scene was approximately 900 metres. Basically, that gully was located midway between the riverbed camp and the homestead, but on the opposite side of the river.

Police referred to that location as the primary crime scene and the burnt patches as a secondary scene. For ease of reference, I referred to that location as Crime Scene One, and the area where the burnt grass was eventually located as Crime Scene Two.

Approximately four kilometres (by road) to the north of the river crossing is an area known as the Two-Mile gravel pit. This area is located on neighbouring Fairlight Station. Two months later it was established the prospectors initially conducted some prospecting in this area on Sunday 8 July[54].

All three prospectors seemingly forgot to mention that not insignificant detail to investigators. During a police interview on 17 September 2012, Groth mentioned that Dan Bidner owned a video camera, and he

---

[54] Further statement by K Groth

believed Dan took some video of them setting up gear to go prospecting. '*I think he also took some video of the camp.*'

That resulted in police obtained a further statement from Dan Bidner on 1 October 2012 during which he confirmed he had taken <u>a</u> video of the camp. As it turned out, Bidner had taken two videos. The first video was in the area behind the Two-Mile gravel pit on Fairlight station, with Mt Emma in the background. His three companions can be seen sitting on the ground assembling their detecting equipment. Bruce Schuler's 4x4 can be seen in the background along with Anderson's motorcycle.

The second video was of the camp in the Palmer riverbed. Three prospectors can be briefly seen or heard in the short video. Both videos can be viewed on YouTube channel - @graemecrowley448.

The Crown submitted those two videos to the court as having been taken on Sunday 8 July 2012[55]. The first video around 9.53 a.m. and the second video around 5 p.m. That was later found to be untruthful, courtesy of the power of social media feedback, after the two videos had been posted on my group Facebook page. That significant matter is dealt with in a subsequent chapter called '*Video does not lie*'.

By the time the case went to court three years later, Bidner was stating they set up camp in the riverbed mid-afternoon, not lunchtime[56].

In the Monday night phone call to Detective O'Brien, Bidner stated '*two walked upstream, two walked downstream*' prospecting that afternoon. By the time the prospectors gave interviews twenty-four hours later, versions had changed, and a glaring discrepancy emerged.

At that time, Bidner recalled Bruce and Rusty went upriver (toward Maytown), Tremain went down river (toward Palmerville Homestead), whilst he hung around detecting close to camp. "*I'm not as fit as those boys so I don't go out as far*"[57].

---

[55] Trial transcript
[56] Trial transcript
[57] Statement D Bidner

Anderson told police Bruce and Kevin went upstream. Dan stayed near the car and 'I *went upstream towards the Strubers*'[58]. Obviously misspoken as the homestead was downstream from that location. Or perhaps they just hadn't worked the detail out by that time.

Groth told police he and Bruce went upstream and '*Danny & Tremain went downstream towards Palmerville homestead to see what they could find*[59].'

Around 5 p.m. Dan Bidner returned to camp, had a wash in the creek and collected firewood for the fire. The others returned between 5.30 p.m. and 6 p.m. with both Kevin Groth and Tremain Anderson telling police two days later they were the last one to return to camp. Dan Bidner claimed Bruce arrived first, followed by Tremain and Rusty was the last one to return to camp.

As a reader, you may ask yourself '*does it matter if the prospectors can't remember the detail? After all, they were on a prospecting trip, and it was not something they would ordinarily take note of.*'

Arriving last back in camp would stay with you. You would want to know the others were back, were safe. You would want to know if they 'struck it rich.' The prospectors were asked to provide details of their activities a little over forty-eight hours after the event. It should have been still a very fresh recollection. In the case of Dan Bidner, he was questioned just over twenty-four hours afterward.

Discrepancies are expected and normal. Lack of discrepancies where you have multiple witnesses may suggest collusion. There is a difference between small and major discrepancies, obviously. How do you value discrepancies? By analysing each statement and its value. But how do you quantify discrepancies? One, two, ten?

Ultimately there were around 140 discrepancies initially identified. Some minor. Some significant. That equates to almost fifty discrepancies per prospector, over a two-day period. Or twenty-five discrepancies per prospector, per day. Or around two per hour each

---

[58] Statement by T Anderson
[59] Statement by K Groth

during their awake time. Reasonable? Were they all high on cannabis and had no concept of what was happening around them? If you were suspicious, you may conclude the prospectors had a 'general plan' of what happened to Bruce Schuler but as investigators drilled down, the glaring differences in their stories became apparent. All discrepancies, big and small are addressed in later chapters.

Tremain Anderson had found just under one ounce of gold. Kevin Groth had not been prospecting long and had never found gold. It was decided he would get preferential treatment the following day. The prospectors sat around the fire telling stories of gold found and gold lost, and were asleep by 10 p.m.

As you read in the phone call with acting Detective Sergeant Nick O'Brien, which was recorded just twenty-four hours later, the night passed quietly. Though Tremain Anderson told police he did hear vehicles crossing the river during the night. They did not see anyone else camping near them.

Monday 9 July 2012

Bruce goes missing!

The events recorded here were as told to investigating police during the initial investigation.

Tremain Anderson was not asked and did not say what time the prospectors woke up. He did say they liked to get out early and take advantage of the cool temperatures.

Kevin Groth said they '*got up around 5.30 a.m. We headed off downstream around 7.30 a.m.*'.

Author note- would it be considered normal to loiter around camp for two hours when you are there to go gold detecting? Before the heat of the day.

Dan Bidner told police Tremain had set his alarm for 5.30 a.m. They had a pot of coffee and cold potatoes from the fire. *'We were all excited to get down there and see if we could get a piece'*. He went on to say they left camp around 6.50 a.m.

It wasn't as if they were being asked for their recollections months later, it was the next day!

They waded across the Palmer River, keeping their equipment dry over their heads, and putting on their socks and boots on the northern bank. From there, they walked along the bank, and over two or three gullies to where Tremain had found gold the previous day. Red, Bruce's dog accompanied them.

As *Kevin Groth* had never found gold, it was agreed he could detect in the area where Tremain claimed to have found the gold the previous day. As detecting machines interfere with others if too close, the prospectors separated. They agreed to meet back up in an hour or so. Groth remained there detecting. Dan went up and out of the gully.

Bruce went toward the river and Tremain went up the gully. Kevin found no gold and later walked over to Bruce, where they talked. As Bruce had a stronger detector, he decided to detect in the area the gold had been found. Kevin headed off up the ridge in the direction of Danny, and a short time later he heard a vehicle approaching.

Dan Bidner was away detecting for two hours,[60] and he told police he wanted to *'have a go'* in the area the gold had been found. He walked back along the ridge line on the other side of the deep gully, and he could see Bruce below him, detecting. He did not see Tremain or Kevin. Shortly after, he heard a vehicle approaching.

Tremain told police that after unsuccessfully searching for gold for twenty minutes, he returned to the gully[61]. He was on the ridge line on the opposite side, looking down on Bruce and they had a brief conversation. He claimed he did not see Dan or Kevin. After a short conversation, he crossed the dirt track roughly in the direction of the camp when he heard a vehicle approaching. On the evidence of both Bidner and Anderson, they should have seen each other. Bidner should have heard the exchange between Anderson and Schuler. They were less than 100 metres apart, in open country, on opposite sides of the gully Bruce was in. But they both denied it.

The elephant in the room of course was the time discrepancies. There was up to a ninety-minute gap in their stories, yet they all claimed they arrived back at the same time, which turned out to be around 9.30 a.m. They had previously said they all agreed to meet back in that area one hour later. Kevin Groth said forty-five minutes had passed. Dan Bidner said it was close to two hours before he returned. This later changed to one hour thirty minutes and then one hour. Tremain Anderson initially said he returned to the gully after twenty minutes. In later evidence this changed to forty minutes and then later to one hour, in line with Bidner's recollection. Yet, they were all within about 100 metres of each other when they heard the 4x4 and denied seeing each other.

---

[60] Statement by D Bidner
[61] Statement from T Anderson

Tremain Anderson 'climbed down into a gully just off the road'. He admitted the Strubers would have seen him, but they must not have been looking[62]. He was about 250 metres away from where Bruce Schuler was.' He identified the ute as Struber's older style fawn coloured cruiser. He glimpsed Stephen Struber driving and saw Dianne Wilson was in the passenger seat. This was important for the Crown case, as Anderson was able to identify the vehicle and both offenders.

As days passed, Bidner amended the distance he was from Schuler from 150 metres down to fifty metres. When he saw the vehicle stop, he saw the 4x4 had a steel tray with no sides. He identified Wilson as the passenger but could not see the driver. He then stated both Wilson and Struber exited the vehicle, and Wilson pulled a gun out from behind the seat. This too varied. She had the gun when she got out at one point. This too was critical for the Crown case. Two witnesses identifying both offenders and their vehicle at the scene.

As days passed, so did Bidner's recollection of whether Stephen Struber got out of the vehicle, and whether Dianne was carrying the gun or retrieved it from behind the seat. There were so many variations to those two events, I devote an entire chapter to each issue.

As you read in the Monday night phone call to Detective O'Brien in the chapter *'Our mate is missing",* Bidner believed he heard and saw a shotgun. Later this changed to a .22 rifle. By the time the case reached trial, specifically a Remington lever action rifle, that just happened to be the same as the missing rifle owned by George Wilson. A lever action rifle is reloaded by drawing the lever in a down and up motion, behind the trigger.

Anyone who has had any experience with firearms would recognise the significant difference in sound made by a shotgun, a .22 rifle, and a large calibre weapon such as a 303/30 rifle.

Kevin Groth did not specify his exact location (he was in the bush after all), but was on the ridge east of the gully when he heard a vehicle approaching. He lay down flat on the ground he told police because

---

[62] T Anderson re-enactment

'Danny and Tremain had told me that on previous occasions whilst they were fishing that they had shots fired at their fishing lines once and once in the air over his Tremain's head. Bruce had mentioned this to me before as it was common knowledge that you didn't want anyone to see where you were fossicking[63].'

He could only see the top of the vehicle as it drove past. It sounded like a Toyota diesel, but he would not be drawn on whether it was a LandCruiser, and he saw the beige coloured top of the vehicle. He could not see the occupants.

Groth then headed away from the area at a jog and a minute or two later, he heard a large calibre rifle discharge. He thought the round was fired into the air, and not into the ground. He stated it was definitely a high-powered rifle, as the shot was very clear and not muffled. It sounded like it was about 100 metres away, in the direction of the camp, and he had looked at his watch and saw it was around 9.30 a.m. As he jogged away, he heard a bang like a door shutting or something being thrown in the back of a ute. All three prospectors told police they heard a 'clang' at various times, some after the first shot as Groth just did, some after the second shot.

Dan Bidner moved to cover after seeing Dianne with a firearm. A few minutes later he heard what he believed to be a shotgun discharging. The distance he moved varied considerably, as will be discussed in a later chapter. He heard no cries for help, no screams, challenges or any other conversation. Bidner heard the clang after both shots.

Bidner claimed after the shot was fired, he ran fifty, maybe one hundred yards. But that distance varied as does the weather. He hid in a gully. After hearing a clang and muffled voices, the vehicle drove off but only went about twenty yards, and then after ten to fifteen minutes he heard a second shot.

For the uninitiated, it is suggested the prospectors were strongly hinting, but not saying, the clang sound was perhaps a metal detector or similar item being thrown onto the tray of the utility. They all heard

---

[63] Statement by K Groth

it, though the number heard changed from witness to witness and the timing also changed - after the first shot, after the second shot, after both shots.

Without rehashing everything Bidner told officer Nick O'Brien on the phone that same night, this was perhaps the most consequential part of the entire story:

'So I just stayed where I was and stayed there. And then I heard, and then the car started, moved a little bit, and then it stopped again. And I heard a clang on the back of the ute, like someone dropping a crowbar or some bit of steel on the back of a black bed tray. And then they moved off. And then I heard the car, would have been like twenty minutes, again, half hour before that car moved the second time.'

'OK.'

'And when it started up to move the second time, it turned around and drove back down the spur, along the river, back towards the homestead. The only thing I regret, Sarge, is I didn't lift my head up to, because I was scared, you know, worried.'

And the Struber vehicle doing a u-turn was introduced into the narrative on the very first contact with police and was consistently referred to - until the trial.

Tremain Anderson walked across to the next gully once the car arrived. He was still only about 200 metres away from Bruce. *'I then heard a loud gun shot. It sounded like a high powered rifle. It was probably a 30/30 which is what I have seen Dianne with in the past.'*[64] On every available opportunity, both Bidner and Anderson told the police they always saw Dianne carrying a 30/30 rifle. Around the same time as Anderson was being interviewed and making those claims about Dianne, Dan Bidner was telling police this:*' When I heard it I wasn't concerned at that time. I thought that because he's (Stephen's) done this before and he does this to everyone all the time. I was like here he goes again. It was common knowledge that he would use a gun and he*

---

[64] Statement by T Anderson

would just have a go at you, abuse you and send you on your way, send you packing.'[65]

I considered it curious that both prospectors would promote a similar story about the Strubers. A claim that was shown to be false, as you may recall Bidner had only met the Strubers for the first time, a week before.

Tremain Anderson walked further into the bush, sat down and rolled a smoke. After about fifteen minutes the vehicle drove *'a little bit further'* up the road. He then heard a second shot, and it was all quiet for about thirty minutes. The car then started up and drove back toward the homestead. By this time, it was about 10 a.m.[66].

The second crime scene was eventually located, about 200 metres away by road from where the vehicle first stopped, and the first shot was fired. Quite clearly, to this time, the prospectors were not indicating they heard the Struber vehicle travel 200 metres to the area of the second crime scene, and return. Instead, the jury would be asked to infer the Struber vehicle did travel to the second crime scene.

What the prospectors did not tell police they heard before or after the first gun shot was shouting, yelling, calling out in fear, cries of pain, arguing, pleading or challenging, nothing. The confrontation between Bruce Schuler and the prospectors played out like a scene from a western silent movie.

Kevin Groth then ran for a further five to ten minutes before he heard a second shot. He stated after the second shot, he smelt gun smoke. It was later established Groth was 300 metres from Bruce Schuler at that time. There is commentary in a later chapter about smelling gun powder over long distances.

Groth walked, lay down and walked again for over three hours and by now it was about 11a.m he said. Clearly, those times did not add up! According to him, the shooting occurred at 9.30 a.m. and therefore it should have been around 1 p.m. After that, he again wandered through

---

[65] Statement by D Bidner
[66] Statement by T Anderson

the bush, and he sat down and lay down at times. He even had a sleep. He checked his watch, and he had been there three hours. Despite the fact the time should have been 4 p.m. at least, he looked at his watch and it was 3 p.m. He saw Tremain walking near the creek, so he followed him into camp, and another *'who arrived back in camp last'* narrative was born. A narrative that was the subject of considerable confusion. I devote a chapter to it later in the book.

Despite Dan Bidner telling officer O'Brien on the phone that same night he decided against detecting back to the camp, by the following night, he changed his version of events to he *did* detect his way back to the camp.

To my mind, that was a significant discrepancy. Not only did the version of events change within twenty-four hours, but the issue also went to the very heart of the story. Bidner told O'Brien he was scared, he was hiding, he could hear his heart beating. *'He considered detecting back to camp but no, he wanted to make sure Bruce was OK.'* Then, on the next version, after not being able to find Bruce Schuler, he stands up in the open and continues gold detecting.

On the way, he met up with Tremain and they briefly discussed the situation. Even on this small aspect of events the timing changed significantly. He said they talked for two to three minutes. Anderson said they talked for a whopping thirty minutes. By trial, Bidner said they spoke for fifteen minutes. Even fifteen minutes seems like a long time to decide a course of action after a traumatic and life-changing event.

Of course, whether Bidner and Anderson walked to the location where the Struber vehicle performed u-turn before heading back to the homestead occupied much discussion, denial and dispute.

Bidner detected his way further along the ridge line until he was across the river from the camp. He could see Schuler's 4x4 across the river and no one was there. He continued detecting for ten minutes or so and when he looked again, he could see Bruce Schuler's dog at the camp.

He then made his way down to the bank, waded across the river and returned to the camp. Bidner by his calculations arrived back in camp around 10.30am. '*The incident happened about 9.30am, 10am.*' He couldn't call it for what it was. A shooting.

I went searching to see if the claim Bidner could see the 4x4 and the dog in the camp from the northern side of the river was verified. No confirmation could be found. This was a significant point. I have not been to Palmerville Station. A few prospectors who have been there made comment it may have been possible to see the vehicle through the trees, but it would be '*impossible*' to see a dog, given the vegetation.

The dog was variously described by the prospectors as being beside the vehicle or '*cowering under it*'. In Detective O'Brien's diary, Bidner walked back to the camp and found the dog there, which is a significant variation to his evidence. Which was it? Either he saw the dog across the river and *that* was why he returned to camp, or he walked back to camp and saw the dog? Investigators noted they could not see Schuler's vehicle where it was parked from the river crossing 200 metres away, yet Bidner could allegedly see a dog beside the vehicle from at least 200 metres or more, and from across the river. Regrettably, there is no evidence the police investigated that claim.

Tremain Anderson also spent about two hours detecting before he too arrived back at camp. He found two or three pieces of gold. Which was peculiar when considered. He had just heard two high powered gunshots in his immediate vicinity. He had two previous encounters with Stephen Struber where weapons were involved.

He told police after the second gunshot that he sat there for awhile
, and he thought,' *What if she's dropped Stephen off with a gun and she's driven off?'* Because that is what he used to do. He would track you to your camp*[67]*. Despite the concern that Struber may have also been hunting him Deliverance Style, Tremain Anderson stood up in full view and spent the next two hours prospecting with his detector whining loudly. Prospectors have told me external speakers on metal detectors can be heard up to one hundred metres away. I wondered if

---

[67] Anderson re-enactment

Dianne was strumming Duelling Banjos nearby at that time. That was a story the Cairns Post missed out on. Anderson then decided to head back to camp as it was *'after lunch by this time'*.

On that evidence, the time would be around 12.30 p.m. In that same Monday night phone call Bidner told O'Brien he *did* go back to where the vehicle turned around. By Tuesday night, he was claiming he did not go back to the spot on the road where the utility did the u-turn. He left that to Tremain because he was fitter than him: '*I was just sitting on the bank and wishing I had a fishing line because there was fish jumping.*[68]' By this time, I was becoming dizzy trying to keep track of the prospectors' timeline of movements.

Once again, a significant discrepancy that goes to the credibility of the witness and his state of mind. Was he distraught or concerned about a kidnapping or shooting of his mate? He was wishing he had a fishing line as the fish were jumping.

By Tuesday night, when Dan Bidner was relating to police his conversation with Tremain Anderson in camp, he said this:

106. '*I said something like,* Nah, *seen no one except you. Mate maybe he caught both of them. Maybe that's what the two shots were. He shot at both of them or was shooting above. Usually he'd shoot above you.*'

And this comment is relevant when it comes to consideration of stress and trauma. They knew Struber liked to scare prospectors, so they said. They were used to it, and they expected it, they said.

107. *Then we sat there together for probably half an hour and then Tremain said, 'Bugger this, I'm going back to look.'*

108. *Tremain's fitter than me and I said, 'Bro I'm buggered already.'*

109. *He said, 'Well, I'm going.'*

110. *I said, 'You better check for blood too bro.'*

Bidner had clearly forgotten what he said to Detective O'Brien just twenty-four hours before, or he considered it prudent to change his version of events. Is that a minor discrepancy? I do not believe it is. I

---

[68] Statement by D Bidner

consider it a significant shift in story line and the fact he obfuscated, denied and argued with the Defence barrister at trial in cross-examination, regarding what he said, indicated to me he was willing to change his evidence to suit his agenda. More importantly, why was he already distancing himself from the claim he went back to where the alleged Struber vehicle performed the u-turn. If I were being suspicious, I would consider both Bidner and Anderson saw the implication of the vehicle not heading to the second crime scene.

Whether Bidner did or didn't return to the spot the vehicle did a u-turn, was the subject of a heated and lengthy exchange with Defence Barrister Trevino during the trial. Despite Bidner's constant denials, the Crown admitted the conversation between Bidner and Detective O'Brien had occurred.[69]

When Tremain returned to camp, he told Bidner he had run all the gullies and called out but did not find Bruce. They sat down and discussed the matter for about one hour. According to Bidner it was about 12 p.m. or 12.30 p.m. when he decided he would return to Maytown on Tremain's motorcycle and bring his own ute back as they did not have keys to Bruce Schuler's car.

Yet on previous evidence the time would now be at least 1.30 p.m. or 2 p.m. On the new claim Bidner believed he arrived home around 1.30 p.m. after a one-hour motorcycle trip.

Confused by the timings given by the witnesses? So am I. The timing the witnesses gave police on that day changed constantly. So much so, I simply could not plot a timeline of events for the prospectors. If that was the only concern, I may have considered just accepting it, given the circumstances. But that was the least of the concerns with the witnesses' claims.

Arrangements were made for Dan to return to Maytown, and Tremain was to call him on his satellite phone at 3 p.m.

After Dan left, Tremain went back again to look for Bruce, looking for blood, anything. He said he went as far as opposite Palmerville

---

[69] Admission at close of Crown case

Homestead (approximately two kilometres away) and called out for Bruce and Kevin. He told police he could see trees in front of the house but not the house[70].

By 3 p.m. he was back at camp. He called Dan. He decided to do some more prospecting whilst waiting for Dan, but fifteen minutes later was returning to camp when Kevin called out to him. Kevin was near the car. The time was about 3.15 p.m., and we have Anderson's first version of Groth arriving back at camp before him[71].

At this time Tremain called a business partner, Wal Randle seeking a contact number for Stephen Struber. Randle would later tell police that Tremain had told him he heard three gun shots[72], a claim Anderson strenuously denied at trial. The Crown ultimately admitted Randle's version of events[73]. Anderson made that call within six hours of the event happening, and it is concerning he could not remember if he heard two shots or three shots.

Dan Bidner returned from Maytown around 4.30 p.m. It was never explained why he simply did not call his wife Jo and have her drive down in his vehicle to collect them. He told police they then tried to call Palmerville Homestead on Tremain's satellite phone, but it went to message bank. A message was left. They took some of their possessions out of the rear of Schuler's 4x4 and returned to Maytown. They left a note on the windscreen for Bruce. Telstra call records did not confirm Bidner's claim.

Tremain Anderson said that upon returning to Maytown, he called the Palmerville Homestead two times on his satellite phone. He left a message that if they did not hear from their mate within half an hour, they would be calling the police. He made no mention of trying to call the homestead from the riverbed camp. Nor did he make comment about walking to Palmerville Homestead and trying to contact the

---

[70] Statement by T Anderson
[71] Statement by T Anderson
[72] Statement by W Randle
[73] At close of Crown case

Strubers. Instead, he told police he went along the opposite side of the riverbank to the homestead.

Kevin Groth told police they called Palmerville Station after arriving at Maytown. He too made no mention of calling the homestead before leaving the camp. Kevin called a friend Bruce Parker, requesting he call Palmerville Station to make inquiries about Schuler.[74]

Curiously, the prospectors called any number of people but did not try calling Bruce Schuler on his satellite phone. Would that not be the first person they tried to call, and try continuously? Tremain Anderson later called police.

Whilst being interviewed, police showed Kevin Groth some maps of the area and asked him to point out the details he had just outlined of where he was, and where he went to. Groth claimed the scale of the maps was either too small or too large for him to show where he last saw Bruce, or his location when he heard the shots[75]. Seriously?

Curiously, according to his statement, he started 'going bush' before he heard the first shot. It was one or two minutes after he started walking away from the area before he heard the firearm discharge. Why did he feel the need to do that?

---

[74] Statement by B Parker
[75] Statement by K Groth

The Phone Calls

The telephones, including landlines, mobile phones and satellite phones were running hot around FNQ on Monday 9 July 2012.

It was anything but an ordinary day. But I will backtrack first to the previous day, Sunday. Stephen and Dianne were working on a dozer at the big dam, about eight kilometres to the south of the homestead. Stephen told police that. His brother Charlie Struber told police that. The telephone records confirmed that. Stephen, who could fix anything mechanical, was having trouble fixing a dozer. Charlie Struber told police he usually only heard from Stephen when he needed help with fixing something, and so it was that day. Charlie Struber also told police he and Stephen were not particularly close and usually only caught up two or three times a year. The last time he had seen him was 2011 when they bumped into each other in a shop in Cairns.

He described Stephen in these words:

'Stephen is a straight down the line kind of fella. He calls a spade a spade. He has got frustrated over the years with people coming onto his property without his permission. There is a mining town called Maytown that is near his property. I recall him getting annoyed with some of the prospectors with gold detectors who have gone onto his land without permission. Some of the prospectors light the grass causing fires to extend across his land. Stephen has also been annoyed with the local council due to road alignments and gazetted roads that were not there. I am aware that he threatened some council members because it was written up in the local rag.'

Telephone records obtained by police indicated that at 12.21 p.m. that Sunday, the Palmerville Homestead phone called Charlie Struber's mobile on four occasions, with all the calls going to message bank.

Two SMS messages were then sent to the mobile number. Four further attempts were made to call Charlie at 1.42 p.m. with the calls again going to message bank. A further SMS was sent.[76].

On Monday 9 July 2012 at 12.43 p.m., the homestead again called Charles Struber's mobile phone on four occasions with the calls going to message bank. Two SMS messages were sent. Immediately after that call, Stephen Struber called Neville Brown, a lifelong friend. Neville Brown confirmed Stephen Struber did call him and told him he was heading into Mareeba the next day, and they would catch up[77]. Immediately after that call, four further calls were placed to Charles Struber's mobile number, but they all went to message bank. A further two SMS messages were sent. At 7.38 p.m. Stephen finally spoke with his brother Charlie. Charles Struber confirmed he did speak with Stephen[78]. He explained that he was out of mobile coverage for the times Stephen was trying to call him. Stephen was asking help to fix an engine, but by the time they spoke, Stephen had worked out the problem and the engine was repaired.

At trial, Stephen Struber gave evidence that he was working on a loader at the big dam on the Sunday, eight kilometres to south of the homestead. He was briefly questioned about the phone calls to Charles Struber but there was no detail regarding the number of calls or the times the calls were made. To put all those phones calls into context, Stephen Struber claimed he was trying to reach his brother to ask his input in repairing an engine. Charles Struber confirmed they did discuss repairing an engine when they finally connected. In-between murdering Bruce Schuler, disposing of his body, thoroughly cleaning blood from their bodies, their clothing, their vehicles and anywhere else possibly contaminated by blood and DNA, Stephen Struber was either repairing an engine or going to extraordinary lengths setting up an elaborate alibi to show he was otherwise occupied at the time of Schuler's murder, including calling friend Neville. An alibi that was

---

[76] Telstra telephone records
[77] Statement by I Brown
[78] Statement by C Struber

never heard by the jury at their trial. Definite shades of Graham Stafford once again.

Whilst Graham Stafford was not murdering Leanne Holland by bashing her with a hammer around the head about ten times, or cleaning up what would have been a very bloody crime scene from which only three drops of Leanne's blood was recovered, and disposing of her body, Stafford was purchasing lunch, visiting a friend for over an hour, sighted at a shopping plaza five kilometres away, washing his car or replacing a shock absorber, all of which were independently verified by police. All between 10 a.m. and 4.15 p.m. on the same day. It was also confirmed he was wearing the same clothes at 4.15 p.m., as he was wearing at 7.30 a.m. that day.

The Strubers' telephones were not the only phones running hot on that Monday in FNQ.

You read that Tremain Anderson rang his business partner Wally Randle requesting the number for the Palmerville Homestead, so he could call Stephen Struber and demand the return of his mate Bruce. Tremain reached Wally at 3.47 p.m. on a call that lasted just two minutes. Following that call, Wally or someone using his phone, called a number registered to Dave Wright, a seafood vendor six times between 3.55 p.m. and 5.40 p.m. and sent the number an SMS. You will remember Dave, he was with Tremain when Stephen Struber allegedly fired at him at the Croc Hole in 2011.

Wally, Tremain and Dave were all shareholders of a mining company which was involved in a joint venture with a Chinese mining company undertaking prospecting and mining on Palmerville Station. Wally's number also called Dan Bidner's Maytown number at 4.27 p.m., and spoke for six minutes. Dan Bidner should have been arriving at Palmerville Station around that time to collect his prospecting friends, and not Bruce Schuler. Dave Wright's mobile called Wally back around 6 p.m. with the call lasting seven minutes. There was obviously a desperate need to discuss with Dave Wright what had happened on the Palmer that day. Once again, the jury never heard that. More curiously, apart from the stream of calls from Wally's number to Dave

Wright and Dan Bidner, Wally's mobile only called one other number for that entire twenty-four-hour period.

The telephone traffic between Tremain Anderson, Wally Randle and Dave Wright that afternoon should have deserved at least a cursory inspection in a murder investigation, but there was no indication that happened. More importantly, the telephone traffic between Stephen Struber and Charles Struber was of potential evidentiary value. The investigators should have considered perhaps Stephen Struber, and by default Dianne Wilson, had an alibi on Monday 9 July 2012. Once, again, there was no indication that happened.

Tuesday 10 July 2012

As you read of the telephone call between Nick O'Brien and Dan Bidner on the Monday night 9 July 2012, arrangements were made for police to meet the prospectors the following morning.

Eight detectives and police from Cooktown station and Cairns CIB travelled around 130 kilometres and 200 kilometres respectively, and met up with the prospectors around 10.10 a.m. at Dog Leg crossing, about sixty kilometres west of the Mulligan Highway. There was a brief discussion with the witnesses before travelling on to the Palmer River crossing. There is no record that interview was audio recorded, but some notes were made in diaries. The prospectors pointed out Bruce Schuler's Patrol, parked and locked in the sandy rived bed about 200 metres from the crossing, and not visible from the crossing.

Detective Sergeant McLeish would later say that before being instructed to attend this complaint, he had never heard of Palmerville Station nor Stephen Struber[79]. After the convictions of Stephen Struber and Dianne Wilson in 2015, the Cairns Post newspaper quoted McLeish as saying: '*I was sure from day one that they were responsible for Bruce Schuler's disappearance.*' If accurate, that is not an inspiring comment from the lead investigator, which may raise concerns of tunnel vision.

Six detectives and uniform police, together with Dan Bidner then headed off to what would become known as Crime Scene One. Bidner would only agree to accompany police if he was permitted to wear a Kevlar bullet resistant vest.[80] Groth, Anderson and two police remained at the campsite with the vehicles.

---

[79] Statement by Det Sgt B McLeish
[80] Statement by A/Det Sgt N O'Brien

After Dan Bidner pointed out where he had last seen Bruce Schuler in the gully, police conducted a foot search of the area. According to McLeish, this search focused primarily in the gully, with police walking south to the Palmer River and north for approximately 500 metres. (To remind the reader, Crime Scene Two was later located 140 metres north of Crime Scene One).

Nothing of interest was located. Specifically, no body, no abandoned personal belongings, including detecting equipment of any sort, no blood trails, drag marks, burnt grass, or other evidence of any crime. No evidence or suggestion of a panicked flight from danger. All that was pointed out to police was a hole in the ground, where it was claimed Tremain Anderson found an ounce of gold the previous day.

Bruce Schuler's vehicle was photographed insitu, and a videographer took video of the vehicle. The note left by the prospectors the previous day before heading back to Maytown was still under the windscreen wiper of the Patrol. It was photographed and seized as evidence, but did not find its way to the trial.

'Bruce. Mate ring us at base 'Maytown'. We have the dog & are waiting to hear from you! Ring on the Sat Phone. The boy's.'

By 2 p.m. the prospectors were released, and requested to travel to Mareeba Police Station to provide statements.

Following telephone consultations with superior officers, SERT (Special Emergency Response Team) was deployed to the area by helicopter from Cairns. These tactical police are engaged for any number of operations, but include where there is a high risk of offenders using firearms when resisting arrest. The helicopter initially flew around Palmerville Station, and as far as Cannibal Creek, seventy-five kilometres to the north but nothing of interest was seen. The SERT team was then deployed, and the police drove to the homestead and surrounded it.

Nick O'Brien recorded his call to the homestead:

'Attempting to call Mr. Stephen Struber or Dianne Wilson. The time is now 13 minutes past 6.'

'Hello?'

'Hello, Dianne, is it?'

'Yes, who's speaking?'

'Dianne, it's Acting Detective Sergeant Nick O'Brien from the Cooktown CIB with the police. Can you hear me?'

'It's not very good. It's a bit staticky.'

'It's a bit staticky. OK, listen very clearly. I've got something very important to say. I need yourself and your husband, Stephen, to come outside your house and walk up to the gate. The police will meet you. OK? Do you understand that?'

'Yes'.

'OK. As I said before, it's Nick O'Brien with the Cooktown CIB. I'm investigating the disappearance of a Mr. Bruce Schuler and I believe yourself or your husband may have some involvement or knowledge in relation to that matter. OK, so I need you to come outside the house and meet the police. Do you understand that?'

'Yes.'

'OK, now listen very clearly before you hang up. Can you hear me? I need you to walk out with Stephen and anybody else that's inside the house with your hands in the air and walk up to the gate and you'll be met by the police and I'll explain and I'll talk to you when you come up to the gate.

'OK.'

'You'll be met by the police. Do you understand that?'

'OK. '

'Alright, I'll see you shortly.'

Fortunately for all concerned, Stephen and Dianne Struber did exit the house with their hands in the air, and not carrying any weapons. O'Brien then arrested each for the murder of Bruce Schuler. The defendants were handcuffed and given forensic overalls to wear. The defendants were driven to Mareeba Police Station in separate vehicles for processing. Palmerville Station was declared a crime scene.

It is noted that at that time, police had no confirmation Bruce Schuler was deceased. The prospectors had not seen him shot, killed or kidnapped. Police had a crime scene but no physical evidence. No eye witnesses to date, no body, no forensic evidence, no cause of death or murder weapon and no admissions.

By the time the three prospectors had given their statements to Mareeba police that Tuesday night, discrepancies in their versions of events were beginning to appear, even though it had only been thirty-six hours since the incident, and only twenty-four hours since the phone call between Dan Bidner and Detective Nick O'Brien. Some discrepancies were minor as would be expected; some were of concern. As time went on more discrepancies became evident. As events unfolded, it was obvious police became aware of the discrepancies, but no concerns in writing were ever seen. There were some significant entries in police diaries for this day. Entries that would raise red flags when investigated.

Detective O'Brien:
- Conducted search of the gully left and right.
- Nil signs of any property.
- Nil blood.
- Nil shells.
- Nil drag marks.
- O'BRIEN/BIDNER/TOME walked right to the end, back along roadway to original place where STRUBER vehicle first observed.
- Bruce not located, nil signs of blood observed, metal detector not located.

Officer Riles who had a briefing in Mareeba:
- Anderson goes to homestead at 1630 hrs cant find anyone.
- DS McLeish took 3 x witnesses back to MP's camp. Vehicle & dog at camp - no sign of MP (missing person).

Detective McLeish diary

- 0930 - 1000 hrs first shot fired.
- Tremain to homestead **1530 hrs.**
- Struber's ute not present, yelled repeatedly.
- no one came out of house.

Wednesday 11 July 2012

Stephen Struber and Dianne Wilson arrived at Mareeba Police Station at 12.25 a.m. that morning in the back of separate police vans. Struber turned to his Land Court solicitor Ann English for advice. Solicitor English advised both Stephen and Dianne to not participate in interviews nor answer any questions. She advised them to agree to required forensic examinations. A Forensic Procedure Order (FPO) had been issued by a Magistrate for both prisoners. Their bloody clothing was seized (tests proved positive to the presence of blood which was later confirmed to be bovine blood). Swabs were obtained along with fingernail scrapings and other forensic procedures. Photographs and fingerprints were taken. Tests for GSR gunshot residue were conducted. Both persons refused to participate in formal interviews and the defendants were placed in cells at the Mareeba watch house by 3.10 a.m.

Both defendants appeared in Mareeba magistrates court that morning. Dianne was eventually released from custody at about 7 p.m. Wednesday night and Stephen was released from the watchhouse Thursday morning. As Palmerville Station was the subject of a crime scene warrant, neither defendant was allowed return there. Instead, they stayed with relatives in Mareeba.

The three prospectors had a big day Tuesday as you read, and a late night. After showing police how events unfolded on Palmerville Station, they drove to Mareeba and spent hours with police giving statements. They stayed overnight in Mareeba. Next morning, Dan Bidner replaced the four tyres on his 4x4. The police were not aware of this until 1 October 2012, when he told police he had blown a tyre and as he had mixed tread on the Patrol, they needed to be replaced.

Police later stated it was pre planned[81]. Bidner told journalist Robert Reid in a later interview he *'got busted for not roadworthy tyres'* and had to change the tyres on his car. Bravado on his part or something more sinister?

Any chance the police investigators had of eliminating Bidner's vehicle from making the tracks down the ravine at the crime scene evaporated.

Meanwhile, the investigation on Palmerville Station was ramping up. Palmerville Homestead had become the designated FCP - Forward Command Post for Operation Kilo Principle, the investigation into the disappearance of Bruce Schuler.

Ultimately, three helicopters, more than thirty police and SES volunteers, as well as stock squad officers on horseback and quad bike scoured a huge area on Palmerville Station looking for Bruce Schuler or evidence relating to his disappearance. The search lasted four days to locate a living person and a further three days for recovery of a body. Search and Rescue experience told them missing persons are almost always found within a nineteen-kilometre radius of where they were last seen.

Four crime scene warrants were executed over a period of several months. All recorded mineshafts within a nineteen-kilometre radius were searched with officers abseiling down mine shafts looking for evidence. The SES members conducted an intensive grid search of a ten square kilometre area.

At 9 a.m. that Wednesday morning, a further search of the gully where Schuler was last seen was conducted. A shoulder-to-shoulder located nothing of interest.

Searches of the homestead and outbuildings on Palmerville continued during the day. Nothing of interest was found.

Scenes of crime officers descended on the property taking photographs, testing for blood, DNA, fingerprints where necessary of the homestead, outhouses, motor vehicles and crime scenes.

---

[81] Interview with Det Sgt McLeish

The two Struber vehicles were searched and firearms found in both vehicles were seized. As you read earlier, Stephen Struber's .357 handgun was not found when the registered LandCruiser was opened and searched. Both vehicles were tested for blood with negative results. Two gouge marks were noted in the suspension of the unregistered utility and moulds were taken, as well as moulds of the tyres.

George Wilson was contacted and requested to attend the homestead, doing so at 3.45pm. After being interviewed by police, he was tasked with feeding the stock and other animals around the homestead[82].

That same afternoon, searches by SES members located some burnt patches of grass on the side of a steep ravine about 140 metres north from what was known as Crime Scene One. (This area I designated as Crime Scene Two). The burnt areas were just above the gully line, together with partially burnt matches, an empty film canister, bailing twine, blood on grass cover and drops of blood on a leaf. There were visible tyre tracks in the grass down the steep embankment to the area of the burnt grass. The area was secured for further examination in daylight hours.

Whilst there was a walking distance of 140 metres between Crime Scene One and Crime Scene Two, to drive from those scenes was quite different. The steep sides of the gully made it impossible to drive through or down to the gully in most places. From Crime Scene One (where Dianne allegedly fired the first shot), any vehicle had to travel approximately eighty metres along the dirt track on the ridge line overlooking the gully, basically in a straight line. It should be noted the track was about 100 metres away from the gully, and it was not possible to look down into the gully. The vehicle would then have to turn left and drive along a circular road known as the Ear Lobe, for approximately eighty metres, before driving down a steep incline for approximately forty metres, making a combined driving distance of some 200 metres. This was to become crucial for the case.

As daylight was fading, the search for Bruce Schuler was called off for the day. But things were looking up.

---

[82] Statement by G Wilson

The Neighbour

A potentially contentious and significant event.

Despite this being a remote, isolated cattle station the size of Hong Kong, the homestead had a close neighbour. What are the chances. Bertie Lyndon Callaghan, but known to all as 'Mick' Callaghan lived just 150 metres away from Palmerville Homestead on Fairlight Station, in a high set house. The house did not face the homestead, but there were views of the road heading toward the Palmerville homestead, and a view toward the Palmerville Station cattle yards, located past the homestead.

Mick had never married, had no children and had lived his entire life on Fairlight Station which was predominantly a cattle property approximately 400 square miles in size or 103,000 hectares and carried around 4000 head of cattle.

Mick had known Stephen Struber for around twenty years, and he had known Dianne since she was two years of age. Mick was profoundly deaf, the result of an ear infection when he was in his twenties. But there was nothing wrong with his sight nor his memory. Mick was seventy-three years of age at the time Bruce Schuler went missing, having been born in 1939.

Bert was interviewed by acting Detective Sergeant Nick O'Brien on Wednesday 11 July 2012, just two days after Bruce Schuler went missing. The statement was dated 11 July 2012, but signed 16 July 2012. It is not known if the statement was digitally recorded at his house, or prepared from notes taken by O'Brien, later typed up and Bertie signed it on the 16 July, again at Fairlight Station. No recording of Bert's statement has been located.

The following are parts of that statement:

10: '*Our properties are separated by a fence line. Even though we are neighbours I don't have much to do with the STRUBERS. I see them every now and then drive past my property on the road.*'

11:' *I haven't seen much activity over that way. I know that they were mustering a couple of weeks ago, as I could see the cattle all being moved around. I believe that only Stephen and Dianne reside at the address. On occasions I know that George WILSON comes and stays with the Strubers at the property. I know George WILSON to be the brother of Dianne WILSON-STRUBER. George is a helicopter pilot and on occasions fly's the chopper in and out of the STRUBERS property to refuel.*'

12: '*I haven't seen the helicopter in about 3 weeks or more. The helicopter never stays parked on the property for too long. It lands to only refuel before going again.*'

13: '*I know the George comes and goes from the property a little. He helps them out on the farm a lot and especially with mustering the cattle. I believe he also does a little prospecting on the property.*'

14: '*On occasions other people come and do prospecting, but I don't recall any names of the people who do that.*'

15:' *I last seen Dianne and Stephen on Tuesday the 10th July 2012. I remember seeing their vehicle coming back in on the back road and crossing the grid, just in front of their house. I only observed their vehicle and can't say that I saw Dianne and Stephen in the vehicle but it was definitely one of their vehicles. When I say it was one of their vehicle's, I mean that they have 2 x beige coloured old Toyota Land cruisers. I can't say exactly which one it was, but it definitely one of the STRUBERS vehicles driving in on their back road to the homestead.*

16: '*I can't recall seeing Stephen or Dianne on Monday the 9th of July 2012. I really don't pay too much attention, as they're my neighbours and all.*'

17: '*I don't see to much traffic coming through this way. Over the past 4-5 days I would have only see maybe 2 x cars. I remember seeing a white new car and a blue coloured car passing through. I think they may have come from the Chillagoe Road.'*

18: *'I believe that Stephen has been doing some grading work on his grader/dozer lately. Although I don't know where the grader/dozer is parked at the moment.*

19: *'I personally haven't seen Stephen do anything strange with guns.'*

20: *'I haven't spoken to Stephen over last 2 days. I haven't used my phone to make any calls over the past 2 days either.'*

Bertie Callaghan was not called to give evidence at the 2015 murder trial. He passed away in 2020 aged 81 years. One social media post stated the world lost a true gentleman with his passing.

Mick Callaghan had a good network of friends and family who would swing by and check on him when they were in the area. They included George Wilson (Dianne's sister), Jason Cardelli who was not related to him but was related to Dianne Wilson, Wayne Callaghan, a nephew of Bertie's and Wayne Joseph, a friend and no relation of any of the above.

In October 2024, after an episode of the podcast was released, I was contacted by Jason Cardelli, related to Dianne Wilson. He had this to say, in part:

I did see Bert on the …I cant remember the date or the day. But me and George went up there & we seen him. He said he told the police that Monday morning about 8.30am he seen em driving out towards the big dam which is the opposite direction to the crime scene. I cant remember the date but it was a good while after Steve & Dianne went to prison.

It was because of speaking with Jason Cardelli, I contacted George Wilson, Craig Callaghan and Wayne Joseph.

George Wilson had arrived at Palmerville Station around 3.45 p.m. that same Wednesday. As it was a crime scene, he was not permitted to stay on the property, and he stayed at Mick Callaghan's that night and for a period after.

Naturally, they discussed the situation of Stephen and Dianne's arrest. The following is a conversation I had with George Wilson in October 2024, after it became known that Mick Callaghan had told various people a different version of events to what was in his police statement. George Wilson had this to say:

'*I can tell you, Graeme, I came down on the Wednesday, then I had to go and stay with him after I'd called in and seen the police at Palmerville Homestead.*

And when I went down to Bertie, we were talking about what was going on, because he was quite, like, you know, shocked, like he said.

He didn't believe that it was happening, what was said, you know.

And he said to me then, he'd seen their movements, that was Dianne and Steve's movements, and he said on the Monday, he'd seen them go out to the south.

They went out, and obviously that's when they were to go out and work on the loader, and they went out early in the morning. And then they came back at lunch.

And he didn't know for sure if there was two, because they were over a grid, so he couldn't see, but Dianne and Steve drove pretty well away together in the vehicle.

They came back and then in the afternoon, Dianne went and got a horse, bring the mickeys up out of the square, because there was a square behind the yard.

So Dianne got down there, and then they brought up, and then they were working at the yards.

He'd seen them go up to the yards, and he'd seen even Dianne catching the horse.

And they then did the afternoon, the yard, and then they came home.

And then next morning, they went back to the yards, and they worked there the whole day until the afternoon.

And Mick's seen that as well.

Like he said, he'd seen them go up to yards in the morning, and they came back from the yards that afternoon. And that's where they were the whole time.'

And for the reader's reference, south is toward Chillagoe and the opposite direction to the Palmer River and Crime Scene One.

Wayne Joseph, also mentioned by Jason Cardelli said the following when I spoke with him:

Well, on the Monday, Bert only knew that there was somebody working over in the yards but he didn't see anything. We did have a talk about it and Craig Callaghan was there as well and he just, that's all he said, he said he knew that somebody was working over in the yards and, and it's from George and from what Dianne had said, she was working her horses over in the yards in the morning and then Stephen was working on the front end loader at the, at the new station's, you know, homestead site over at the dam, which is about another 10 minutes drive from the, the old homestead.

He believed this conversation took place about one week or so after Stephen and Dianne were convicted of the murder.

Bert was Craig Callaghan's great uncle. Craig couldn't recall being present at any conversation where Wayne was present, but he was aware the Strubers were mustering at the time and that they had cattle in the yards. Uncle Mickey had told him the Strubers were branding, and he recalled they were also dehorning. He recalled there were cattle in the yards when police turned up. At the request of police, Craig flew his helicopter around Palmerville Station looking for Bruce Schuler.

Ann English, solicitor for the Strubers emailed Queensland police on the Wednesday and Thursday confirming the Strubers were cutting and dehorning wieners on the day police arrived. She also pointed out Stock Squad horses were being held in the stock yard, and not the old horse yard. This represented a tetanus threat to all stock in the yard[83].

There was indisputable evidence Struber and Wilson were mustering, branding and dehorning during this time. On the Crown case they

---

[83] Email to COP from Ann English

stopped their mustering, went and committed a brutal murder, and then went back to branding and dehorning.

Bertie Callaghan being able to provide an alibi for the Strubers would have been an inconvenient truth for the police case. But on the Crown case, Bertie saw nothing on the Monday and little on the Tuesday. The relatives and friends of Bertie Callaghan who claimed he told them he did see the Strubers on the Monday and Tuesday did nothing with the claims. They told no one until 2024. It was not raised at trial nor appeal. That would negate any claim they were inventing an alibi.

On the evidence of four people, Bert Callaghan did witness events on the Monday and the Tuesday that were crucial to the investigation. The defendants' legal advisers accepted the claim that Callaghan did not see the Strubers on the 9th and 10th of July as you will read in a later chapter.

A truly serious concern.

Detective O'Brien's diary notes, in part, for Callaghan interview:
- they've been mustering our part for 2 weeks.
- Struber mustering up until week before last as he can see the cattle being moved & around near house.
- Departed yesterday morning went to the house returned home about 5pm.
- Observed Dianne & Stephen yesterday after about 5pm on their back yard (?) saw them at the grid saw their vehicle.
- Doesn't know if he seen Dianne or Stephen Struber on 9 July 2012 doesn't take too much notice as they're neighbours.
- Never seen Stephen do anything with guns or anything strange. (Never seen him handle a firearm).

Thursday 12 July 2012

That phone call!

With daylight, the search for Bruce Schuler commenced again on Palmerville Station. Searches were being conducted on foot, horseback and by helicopter. Nothing was found.

Straight out of left field, at around 9.30 a.m. on Thursday morning, three days after Bruce Schuler's disappearance, a phone call was received at Palmerville Station FCP. A police officer answered the phone.

'Hello?'

'Hello?'

'Hello. Is this Palmerville Station?'

'Yes, it is.'

'Is this the police?'

'Yes.'

'You're doing a search for a person?'

'Yes.'

'I have some information.'

'Okay.'

'You're looking in the wrong spot.'

'Okay. Where do you think we should be searching?'

'12 to 15 K's to the east of there.'

'Okay. Who am I speaking with?'

'I don't want to give my name.'

'Okay then. Why do you say we are looking in the wrong place?'

'I have someone that was involved.'

'Okay. If that's the case, we would like to speak to your friend to help. We might be able to sort this out. Are you there?'

The call was then disconnected.

The Croc Hole was located approximately fifteen kilometres to the east of Palmerville homestead. The same Croc Hole that had been the scene of the confrontation between Dan Bidner and Struber and Wilson less than two weeks before.

The call was traced to a public phone box in Mareeba. Investigators immediately suspected Dianne Wilson may have been the caller. Dianne Wilson had only been released from the watchhouse the previous night, and she was staying with family in Mareeba. Police approached her, but she initially denied making that call, but admitted doing so through her solicitor Ann English two hours later.

Her solicitor told police Dianne had made the call out of frustration that the police were looking at the wrong people responsible, and that the police should be looking at drug users who were mining in the area.

That phone call was to become very significant at the trial three years later. In my view, it convicted her and by default Stephen Struber.

The same day, solicitor Ann English fired off a five-page email to the Commissioner of Police. Included in that email was a belief by the Strubers that prospector Dan Bidner was trying to blame them for the disappearance of Bruce Schuler. She requested those claims be investigated.

Dianne Wilson and Stephen Struber were prevented from returning to Palmerville Station because of the crime scene declaration. Police took the opportunity to install two listening devices in the homestead, and tracking devices in the two Struber vehicles.

Meanwhile, there was an important development in the ongoing police investigation. That day, police returned to that area in the gully where the burnt patches were found late the previous afternoon.

Ultimately, evidence from a very wide area was gathered from this location which would form a significant part of the Crown case.

As noted, this area was 140 metres by foot from where it was alleged Dianne Wilson first shot Bruce Schuler. It was the Crown case Schuler, wounded, ran up the gully to this location. Struber and Wilson drove down to this location, where they shot and killed him, loaded his body onto the tray of LandCruiser, and took his body away, with all his possessions.

No evidence was discovered in the gully between scenes one and two. No physical evidence, no abandoned possessions, no blood, no DNA, no other forensic evidence.

Vehicle tracks were observed going down the steep ravine from the spur forty metres above, and going back up. One officer recorded the slope was steep and it was difficult to keep your footing[84]. Along the way there were two small saplings snapped off, and an anthill (termite mound) with a gouge mark in it. At the base of the ravine, there was no evidence the vehicle had made a three-point turn or even circled around.

At this location (Crime Scene Two), there were several very small areas of burnt grass, spread over a large area. An officer commented they could be covered by a blanket. The Crown alleged the Strubers burnt these areas to destroy Schuler's blood.

Evidence located included four partially burnt matches in one of the burnt areas, an empty film canister, black bailing twine, a drop of blood on a leaf and drops of blood on two rocks. But they were not in a tight group. The film canister was found ten metres away from one of the burnt patches. The blood on the leaf was seven metres from the canister. A small apiece of green fibre was also found.

Curiously, what was not found were footprints, drag marks, scuff marks or other marks consistent with the offenders dragging/carrying the victim's body from where he was shot, and placed on the back of the 4x4 tray. The evidence showed a vehicle had been there, but no people.

---

[84] Statement by M Vincent

One of the partially burnt matches was later found to have Bruce Schuler's DNA on it, as did the black twine; the blood drop was matched to Schuler's blood as was the blood on the rocks. Schuler had been at the crime scene. Or at the very least, his DNA and blood had visited that spot.

Late that same Thursday afternoon, Kevin Groth returned to Palmerville Station, and agreed to conduct a walk-through of the events that occurred on the Monday. The re-enactment was video and audio recorded, and was conducted by Acting Detective Sergeant O'Brien. The re-enactment was quite unremarkable and very similar to the statement he provided less than forty-eight hours earlier, as it should be. However, there was one notable differences to his statement and one significant new piece of evidence.

He described the headboard (the only part he saw), of the vehicle as a rusty dirty orangey colour (Struber vehicles were fawn). In his statement three days previously, he had described the headboard as beige. Whilst important, that claim disappeared and was never mentioned again. Groth clarified the speed of the vehicle as it moved past his position as travelling at about 10-15 kph. Once the vehicle drove past him, he stood up and headed away from the area at a jog. The first shot was two to three minutes later.

He looked at his watch when he heard the first shot and noted it was 9.30 a.m., which was important. Trying to keep track of the prospectors timings was almost impossible. The witnesses variously claimed the first shot was heard between 9.30 a.m. and 10.30 a.m.

When Kevin Groth was interviewed on the Tuesday night, Groth explained that he lay down on the ground, because he had been warned Struber was known to shoot over the heads of people he found trespassing. That may explain why he immediately ran from the area and disappeared for six hours.

Whilst doing the re-enactment he forgot that claim; he provided a different, somewhat garbled explanation of why he lay down on the ground. That explanation provided no reason why he would run away and hide for six hours. Once again, there was no evidence the police challenged him on his different versions of events.

His apparent earlier concern of being shot at by the Strubers, was replaced by a concern someone may think he was working an area where gold could be discovered:

Groth: '*Oh well um it's just a metal detecting it's a like suppose the law with them there's nobody's when they if they see you metal detecting that oh I said you must be onto something like that so you just it was a common thing knowledge to yeah get outside so nobody else know the patches you're working or you know they might think oh you might you might have got some gold so they come into your patch and like take gold.*'

Q: '*So it's a metal detecting thing? You don't want to be seen in that area?*'

Groth: '*Yeah yeah like it's just normal if like if you're up any any roads and anyone anywhere or even go um it's the thing common knowledge to just to get down don't let you know don't let be seen okay yeah people have well you know you don't want less people know where you're getting as gold as it is.*'

Groth again repeated he saw Tremain out in the open near the camp at 3 p.m. and he followed him into camp, despite Tremain claiming he found Kevin Groth in camp when he returned.

Friday 13 July 2012

Operation Kilo Principle rolled on relentlessly. Witnesses Tremain Anderson and Daniel Bidner arrived at Palmerville Station at 8.30 a.m. at request of investigators, to undertake a re-enactment of the events of Monday. The re-enactments were undertaken separately, and all were video and audio recorded. Bidner's re-enactment was conducted by Detective Sergeant Riles with assistance from Detective Sergeant O'Brien. It was Detective O'Brien who conducted the Monday night phone call with Daniel Bidner, whilst it was Detective Riles who interviewed Bidner on the Tuesday night. Surely, they must have picked up on discrepancies between what he said on the Monday and Tuesday nights, and what he was saying a few days later. However, it seems Bidner was not challenged on any issues.

Tremain Anderson's re-enactment was conducted by Detective Senior Constable Alina Bell.

The wheels had fallen off the investigation bus. Whilst detectives were diligently gathering evidence from all the witnesses, there could not have been any one nominated detective examining each statement, each re-enactment in detail, otherwise the enormous number of discrepancies would have been immediately obvious. Or perhaps the wheels had not fallen off the bus. Maybe the discrepancies were noted and not considered an issue, as claimed in later interviews.[85]

In the case of Daniel Bidner, his re-enactment was initially unremarkable. He did comment the time the four prospectors first separated as 8.30 a.m. by his watch. That was important, as Groth confirmed the shooting occurred at 9.30 a.m. Yet that was where it also became messy. You read earlier about the various lengths of time the

---

[85] By Det Sgt McLeish & former Det Sgt Furlong

prospectors were absent before returning. From two hours to twenty minutes.

On this re-enactment, Bidner was detecting for one hour. Add to that the thirty minute walk back and he still somehow managed to arrive back at the gully at 9.30 a.m.

Upon his return to the gully, he saw Schuler was standing up detecting with his headphones on, when he heard a vehicle approaching. Bidner confirmed what Schuler was wearing when he last saw him. It is important to add that when he spoke with Officer Tome on the Monday, he said he could see Schuler and his dog hiding in a gully. As just as significant was the claim that Red Dog started barking after the vehicle stopped.

'Bidner states he could see the MP & his dog hiding in a gully. When the vehicle has stopped the MP's dog started barking.'

A mere two hours later, when he spoke with O'Brien, he said the Struber vehicle stopped because the dog started barking. That was then the constant claim through to the trial, Red Dog barking was the reason the vehicle did stop.

From when the vehicle was first seen and heard was around two minutes, yet Bidner did not call out to Bruce Schuler or warn him. He told police he would have been giving away his position had he done so. Did police not wonder about that claim?

In his Tuesday interview, Bidner recognised the car as belonging to the Strubers *as he had seen it on numerous occasions, at least a dozen with Dianne in the passenger seat. I couldn't see who was driving...'*

At the re-enactment, he could '*not get a visual on the driver*' but was sure it was Stephen Struber. He was queried on that point and confirmed he could not identify the driver. He was even able to tell police the Struber ute had skinny tyres[86]. There were several other variations to his previous interactions with police that are covered in later chapters.

---

[86] Bidner re-enactment 13 July 2012

In the case of Tremain Anderson's re-enactment, there were also several discrepancies that are covered in later chapters. Of importance, he believed Bruce Schuler was wearing his wide-brimmed hat and had his headphones and prospecting pick with him. Anderson was able to positively identify Stephen Struber and the Struber utility.

And that was significant for the Crown case. Both witnesses identified the vehicle as being owned by the Strubers, and both offenders were identified as being at the scene. The Crown was well on the way to having a case against the Strubers. Never mind the ever-growing list of red flags.

Meanwhile, other police were searching outbuildings and other areas of Palmerville Station, looking for evidence to connect them to Bruce Schuler. Nothing was found.

Another shoulder-to-shoulder search was conducted. This time from the roadway to crime scene two. Evidence was found and gathered, and the briefings of all police involved continued.

Saturday 14 July 2012

Cracks in the search for Bruce Schuler appear.

By 3 p.m. that Saturday, search experts concluded there was little chance of Bruce Schuler still being alive. The search of Palmerville Station and surrounds switched from search and rescue to search and recovery (of a body) which continued for a further three days.

At 11a.m. on Saturday 14 July 2012, Senior Constable Bishop, an SAR officer working in Cairns Police Station requested satellite telephone information on Bruce Schuler's missing satellite phone. He received latitude and longitude of -16*0051S and 144.1279E as the last point on the Sunday 8th July 2012 at 9.33GMT. Reverse call data was not available.

He wrote in his statement:

'This location is consistent with the missing persons camp located near Palmerville Station, approximately 120 miles NNW of Cairns. When plotted, I determined this to be approximately 12 kilometres to the east of the missing persons LKP (last known position).

The first I became aware of the satellite phone being 'pinged', was when I read it in a 2019 report prepared by retired police officer Bob Haydon. It was never mentioned again, anywhere, other than in Officer Bishop's statement. It certainly wasn't raised at trial by either the prosecution or the defence, nor at Appeal.

09.33 GMT (Greenwich Mean Time) is 7.33 p.m. Eastern Australian Time. Bruce Schuler's satellite phone pinged at 7.33 p.m. on Sunday 8 July 2012. Officer Bishop said the GPS coordinates of where this occurred was twelve kilometres east of Schuler's last know position. That was the distance if travelled there from Palmerville Station homestead using Whites Creek Road, the main road in that area. In a straight line from where Bruce Schuler was last seen in the Palmer River bed camp, the GPS coordinates were roughly three and a half kilometres away, deep in a gully, at night, or about five kilometres by using the closest road.

The reality was that phone call at 7.33 p.m. was the last independently corroborated contact with Bruce Schuler, (or someone using his satellite phone), apart from the claims by the prospectors. According to their evidence, at 7.33 p.m. that Sunday night the prospectors were sitting around the campfire, enjoying a few beers and talking about gold found and gold lost.

There is no record that area was ever searched by police or SES after that information was received. It was searched around 2019 by friends and family of Stephen Struber and Dianne Wilson, however nothing was found.

Dan Bidner never replied to any request by me for an interview for the podcast. Of course, there was never any obligation on him or any of the other prospectors to comment on the case. He did agree to an interview with journalist Robert Reid around 2018, but Reid was not challenging him on discrepancies with his evidence. Bidner never commented on anything raised in the podcast, especially the inconsistencies in their evidence and the discrepancies in their recall of events. Except for the satellite phone ping.

In the Facebook group page '*Justice for Bruce Schuler*', run by Schuler's widow Fiona Splitt, a Facebook user with the account name '*Dman Dan*' pasted a comment from another group that said '*Our 14M vessel pinged 50k inland.*' Dman Dan commented on the '*Justice for Bruce Schuler*' Facebook page "*The answer to bruce's sat phone ping Not as accurate as they would have you believe Graham Crowley*" (sic).

Numerous listeners commented the Dman Dan Facebook page belonged to Dan Bidner. Of course, someone could have been using his page with or without his knowledge.

Handheld GPS devices need to be regularly calibrated. What Dan Bidner or whoever used his Facebook account did not understand was that it was not Bruce Schuler's satellite phone that was giving the location deep in a gully, at night, five kilometres from their camp. It was three or more satellites deep in space giving that reading. Nothing to do with Bruce's handheld GPS device.

In conversations with Daniel Wood, a cyber security specialist, he informed that an error in the location was possible, but he expected it would be in the range of 100 metres to a maximum of 1000 metres. It would definitely not be 4000 metres. Therefore, it was possible the satellite phone was in the area of the deep gully, but not necessarily in it.

But the questions linger which have never been addressed, answered or explained. What was Bruce Schuler doing four kilometres from their camp the night before he 'went missing'. Or whoever had his satellite phone. What were the other prospectors doing at that time and why did they not comment on it when they provided their statements. I contacted Kevin Groth several times, begging him to talk to me about that very issue. He never replied.

Lost and Found

This case gets weirder by the minute.

Saturday 14 July 2012 was certainly a big day in the life of Operation Kilo Principle.

Not only was there an inexplicable satellite phone ping to ponder, there was also the mysterious recovery of Bruce Schuler's satellite phone. Lost and found. How curious that they both happened on the same day, and it did not even appear to be considered a significant event.

There were any number of possessions that went missing with Bruce Schuler. His Minelab GPX 5000 metal detector weighing over three kilograms, a prospecting pick weighing one kilogram, headphones, GPS device tied onto his belt with twine, hat, a backpack containing spare detector battery and satellite phone, snacks, and frozen water bottles. Nothing has ever been recovered. Now the police have the satellite phone. Was that the reason the officer requested the satellite phone records the same day?

You will recall the note the prospectors left on the windscreen of Bruce Schuler's 4x4 the day he disappeared, Monday 9 July 2012:

Bruce. Mate, ring us at basetown Maytown. We have the dog & are waiting to hear from you. <u>Ring on sat phone</u>. The Boy's.

Fast forward to Saturday 14 July 2012.

Six detectives descended on Dan Bidner's Maytown lease by arrangement, and executed a search warrant. It is not clear if Bidner was aware police intended to execute a search warrant when arrangements were made to visit him. It is not known what was listed on the search warrant, but nothing of interest was found according to police diaries. (A recurring themes in this investigation).

Dan and his wife told police they were in the process of packing their belongings and leaving their property, out of fear of Stephen Struber.

Whilst there, police obtained a statement from Jo Bidner. You may recall she told police the previous Sunday when Bruce Schuler and Kevin Groth arrived at their property at 7.30 a.m., they had a quick 'cuppa' and left.

After leaving the Bidner property, police headed to Bruce Schuler's lease at Rosie's Gully. Along the way they came across Charlie Silver, friend and neighbour of Bruce Schuler, travelling in the opposite direction. Silver told police he had been to Schuler's lease to retrieve Bruce's .22 calibre rifle and hold it for safe keeping. The same rifle Bruce normally stored behind the driver's seat of his 4x4. Police took possession of the rifle. Police continued on to Rosie's Gully, conducted a search, took photographs, and gathered personal belongings including toothbrushes for DNA comparison purposes.

Around two hours later, Charlie Silver returned. He handed police a black carry bag containing Bruce's Iridium satellite phone, amongst other things. It transpired that after driving away from the police on the track, he went to Dan Bidner's property. There, Bidner gave him the black carry bag and satellite phone and asked him to pass them onto police. The same black bag that appeared in police photographs of the rear of Bruce Schuler's 4x4 taken in the riverbed on Tuesday 10 July, and the same black bag that was later photographed in the rear of Dan Bidner's 4x4.

Police spread out the contents of that bag at Schuler's lease at Rosie's Gully and took photographs. Apart from the clothes Schuler was wearing at the time he went missing, in the black carry bag were one pair of shorts and a short sleeve shirt; one long sleeve shirt, one pair of long trousers, three pair of underpants and three pair of socks. A lot of clothing for the one-night prospecting trip. The lost but now found Iridium satellite phone also appeared in that photograph. The same phone that pinged in the gully almost four kilometres from the prospectors' camp, on the Sunday night.

Detective Sergeant McLeish made note in his diary that Silver had handed him Bruce Schuler's satellite phone. No statement was taken from Charles Silver, and the reason for that was never specified. The investigator's role is to identify the offenders and as part of that, they must ensure the witnesses are honest and have also not forgotten any vital evidence. It would be difficult to conclude the investigators did not understand the significance of the satellite phone not having been with the missing person at the time he disappeared. It is even more difficult to understand why no statement was taken from Charles Silver.

Did this not raise a note of concern about their witnesses?

If Defence barristers had read McLeish's statement, they would have safely assumed the satellite phone was always at the camp. '*Nothing to see here,*' unless of course they had read the police diaries which obviously they hadn't.

So many unanswered questions from this one single issue. Why did Bruce Schuler leave a very valuable and expensive possession in the unlocked tray of his vehicle whilst he went prospecting? It was, and still is, a fact of life stealing is a big issue on remote, isolated gold diggings. More importantly, why didn't Schuler take his satellite phone with him? The whole purpose of have a satellite phone is to remain safe and to enable contact to be made in the event of an emergency. It would be akin to not taking his handheld GPS with him when he went detecting, and leaving it in the unsecured rear of his ute.

Why didn't Dan Bidner hand the satellite phone to police when they visited his property just two hours before? Surely, he didn't 'find' it one hour after the police left, causing him to hand it to Silver? Why not deliver it himself? Or on the previous day when he was with police? When did he realise he had Schuler's satellite phone?

He was in possession of it from Tuesday 10 July to Saturday 14 July. Why did he even remove the black bag from Schuler's ute when they left camp? If it appeared to contain just clothing why take it? If he searched it, he would have seen the satellite phone. How was Bruce Schuler going to call them if he didn't have his mobile phone with him? Is that the reason they never bothered trying to call Bruce on his satellite phone, because Bidner had it? It does not explain why investigators disguised the recovery of the satellite phone in their police brief?

It was intriguing to see how the whole saga of the satellite phone was handled at the 2015 trial. The prosecutor wanted the jury to know the prospectors left a note for their friend, but he did not want them to know they had his satellite phone. I do not believe you can tell half the story. You must tell it all or none. As I mentioned, the Defence barristers would have been none the wiser that Schuler did not even have his satellite phone, but the prosecutor was not taking any chances. The Prosecutor asked the following questions at trial:

Prosecutor: '*Did you leave any message for Bruce?*'

Bidner: '*Yes, we left a note on the windscreen.*'

P: '*And who wrote the note?*'

Bidner: '*I did.*'

P: '*Do you recall what the note said?*'

Bidner: '*I don't recall it too- word for word, but it said something to the effect of, Bruce, we've got the dog. I haven't heard from you, mate. We've headed back to main camp, to base camp, Maytown.*'

There was no mention of the satellite phone or requesting Schuler to call them. The note Bidner left and seized by police was not tendered as an exhibit. Bidner was not cross examined on the subject. Did the prospectors take Red dog? According to diary entries in at least one investigator's notebook, they left the dog tied to Bruce Schuler's 4x4. The jury being kept in the dark about the Sunday night phone call was inexcusable.

What investigations or action did the investigators undertake once they became aware of the lost and found phone? From police statements and notebooks, *nothing*.

Sunday 15 July 2012

The three prospectors returned once again to Palmerville Station, to assist with GPS mapping of the area. By now, the number of inconsistencies in their combined evidence was dwindling. Although there was still to be a significant discrepancy in where Bidner went, or didn't go, after the first gunshot, as you will read later. Those re-enactments on that day were neither video nor audio recorded. The witnesses were asked to point out where they were standing, which direction they travelled, where they saw the Struber's 4x4, which direction it travelled, and so on. Survey pegs were driven into the ground. From that, investigators were able to forensically map the area, and prepare a precise scale forensic map of the entire crime scene.

In total, seventy-eight GPS points were mapped, which covered every aspect of the movements of all involved on Monday 9 July 2012. What is not known to this day, is whether the GPS point where the alleged Struber vehicle turned around and headed back to the homestead was recorded, and whether that point was flagged and pointed out to the jury.

The police investigators seemed more focused on where the prospectors went, rather than what they saw and heard.

This forensic map would be used to show the jury where everyone was, where they went and so on. Of course, the jury also had the luxury of visiting the crime scene and seeing the lay of the land, so to speak, first hand.

Thursday 19 July 2012

The police investigation on Thursday 19 July 2012 will be remembered for all the wrong reasons. Life had moved on. There were other crimes being reported; other matters to investigate. Of course, administrative and procedural matters were ongoing in the background of Operation Kilo principle. Those matters can take month, sometimes years.

It was a small note scribbled in Detective Sergeant Riles's notebook. He was doing administrative work on Operation Kilo Principle. The background stuff:

- *S/c EZARD - tyre width - anomaly. Advise DS McLeish.*

Riles' notebook contained ninety pages of notes referencing Operation Kilo Principle. Easy to miss one entry, and anyway, what did it mean? It was never commented on again. It certainly wasn't raised at the 2015 murder trial. Nothing, anywhere. That is until the Appeal Court hearing four years later in 2016, when Senior Constable Ezard's comment from 2012 was the centre of attention.

Monday 8 October 2012

Another seemingly innocent event that likely sealed the fate of Stephen Struber and Dianne Wilson.

You may recall the problems with the transmission on the bush vehicle, the unregistered LandCruiser, not being able to engage first or second gear in any range. After the disappearance of Bruce Schuler, the parts to repair the gearbox that had been on order from before Schuler's disappearance arrived. Stephen Struber repaired the gearbox, and found the vehicle drove satisfactorily again. He also fixed the brakes and handbrake.

On 8 October 2012, Detective Sergeant Camp arrived at Palmerville Station, and took the bush basher for a drive. He drove it up and down the ravine above Crime Scene Two, along the same tracks found during the investigation. Camp wrote in his statement:

'I found I could drive the vehicle down to the bottom of the slope, turn it around and drive it back up the slope with little difficulty. This was videotaped.'

At trial, he told the court he was able to drive the vehicle in four-wheel drive, low range, first gear and did not recall any difficulty engaging gear. In relation to the speed, he travelled he replied: *'I crawled down the slope. So, you know, below five kilometres per hour.'* He confirmed the brakes were working. He drove back up the slope in four-wheel drive, low range first gear.

The videotape of Detective Camp driving up and down the ravine was played to the jury.

The Judge then went to considerable length to remind the jury of the previous evidence of George Wilson that it was difficult to engage first and second gear in that vehicle, and that according to Detective Camp, it now easily went into first and second gear[87].

The Judge said:

'That it would not be possible to drive this vehicle, that's the unregistered Landcruiser, up the slope in low-range third gear and that the vehicle would have to at least be in low-range second gear.'

It did not seem important to clarify why the police mechanic could not get the vehicle into first or second gear in any range, and here was a detective driving it normally.

And if only the question had been asked whether it was possible to drive the vehicle in reverse.

When Stephen Struber gave evidence at trial, he told the court he had repaired the gearbox in the period after Bruce Schuler went missing. The question of course would be whether the jury accepted that claim or considered Struber was lying.

The full evidence regarding whether the Struber vehicle could go up and down the ravine is covered in a later chapter. As you will read, there was legal argument in the absence of the jury that occupied twenty-three pages of transcript, regarding whether the vehicle could go up or down the ravine, and no legal argument (read zero) about whether the vehicle *did* drive up or down the ravine!

---

[87] Trial transcript day 5

CCC Hearing

The Crime and Corruption Commission (CCC) is an independent statutory body set up to combat and reduce the incidence of major crime and corruption in the public sector in Queensland. It is staffed by public servants, solicitors and police officers seconded from the Queensland Police Service. On their website www.ccc.qld.gov.au the CCC describes their reason d'etre as follows:

'*The CCC investigates major crime such as drug trafficking, fraud, money laundering, criminal paedophilia and homicide. Its role is to protect Queenslanders from major crime by using its specialist expertise and powers in cooperation with the Queensland Police Service and other law enforcement partners.*

The CCC is Queensland's anti-corruption body. We deal with corruption that affects the state's public sector, using special powers under the Crime and Corruption Act 2001 and the Police Powers and Responsibilities Act 2000.'

In a recent newspaper article by veteran journalist Des Houghton, he commented on the performance of the CCC in the financial year 2023 - 2024. Of a record number of 5139 complaints of serious and systemic corruption, there was only one person charged. His article was less than complimentary toward the CCC.

How did the CCC become involved in the disappearance of Bruce Schuler? The CCC also conducts coercive hearings as required, and usually at the request of the Queensland Police Service. Coercive hearings are not open to the media or the public, and cannot be reported upon. In other words, they are held in secret. Witnesses summonsed to a coercive hearing have no right to silence, must answer questions even if they are self-incriminatory, and cannot request the assistance of a solicitor. In the words of the CCC, they assist police with serious crime investigations *'that cannot be advanced using traditional policing powers.'* Refusal to answers questions usually results in imprisonment until the witness agrees to answer.

In the case of the disappearance of Bruce Schuler, Queensland Police had hit a wall and were unable to gather any further incriminating evidence. On 11 October 2012, almost three months to the day from when Bruce Schuler went missing, witnesses were summoned to attend a CCC hearing. As one barrister commented, *'the speed with which the investigation went to a coercive hearing was nothing short of surprising. They must have had no evidence against the Strubers.'* As is known, police had no or few witnesses apart from the prospectors, no body, no cause of death, no admissions from their main and only suspects. The listening devices planted in the homestead and tracking devices placed in their two vehicles had produced no results, and the call to the public for information had generated lots of gossip, evidence of repeated trespassing, and at times apparent over reaction by Stephen Struber, but no leads to Schuler's murder.

Stephen Struber and Dianne Wilson were required to attend the CCC hearing along with four relatives of Dianne. Lifelong friends of Stephen Struber, seventy-nine-year-old Neville Brown and his seventy-five-year-old wife were also compelled to attend. In total, nine witnesses were examined in both Cairns and Brisbane.

Obviously, the CCC hearing produced no new evidence, as no incriminating evidence was given by witnesses at the trial three years later.

Arrested! Again

On 30 October 2012, eight detectives descended on Palmerville Station, and Stephen Struber and Dianne Wilson were once again arrested for the murder of Bruce Gavin Schuler. The defendants declined to make any comment.

On this occasion, the defendants were taken separately to Cairns watchhouse where they were formally charged with the murder, and with misconduct of a corpse. DNA samples were obtained, and bail was refused. The defendants would remain in custody for some weeks, until an application for bail was successful, and they were released.

It is appropriate to compare the evidence police had when they first arrested the Strubers on 10 July 2012, compared to the evidence they had on 30 October 2012.

In the chapter *Tuesday 10 July 2012,* at the point the Strubers were arrested, I wrote in part:

It must be noted that at that time, police had no confirmation Bruce Schuler was deceased. The prospectors had not seen him shot, killed or kidnapped. Police had a crime scene but no physical evidence. No eye witnesses to date, no body, no forensic evidence, no cause of death or murder weapon and no admissions.

What was the state of play as of 30 October 2012? What further evidence did the police have against the offenders?

The police still did not have confirmation Bruce Schuler was deceased. They had no motive for the Strubers to murder Schuler. They had no body, no cause of death and no murder weapon. The defendants had made no admissions or confessions. The police still had no eyewitnesses apart from the prospectors. They still had no one who could say they saw Schuler shot, killed or kidnapped.

There was minimal DNA evidence, and there were some tyre impressions and damage to trees and an anthill consistent with, but not definitive as having been made by either the Struber's unregistered 4x4 or the registered LandCruiser. There was conclusive evidence Bruce Schuler, or at least his blood and DNA, had been at Crime Scene Two.

There was no evidence to show that Bruce Schuler had ever been at the gully – the First Crime Scene - apart from the evidence of the prospectors. There was no evidence to connect either Dianne Wilson or Stephen Struber to either crime scene. No blood, DNA, physical evidence or forensic evidence had been found, after thirty days of intensive searches, on their bodies, their clothing, in or on their vehicles, or in their homestead or outbuildings. The listening and tracking devices had not uncovered any incriminating evidence.

Apart from the damaged tress, cow pats and wheel tracks, the evidence implicating the Strubers appeared unchanged.

Defendants obtaining bail on a charge of murder is almost unprecedented, in Queensland anyway. Yet the Strubers were able to obtain bail. An application for bail is considered very closely by the Supreme Court before approving. It was Judge Henry who heard the Application for bail by the Strubers, and he presided over their trial in 2015.

He made comment during the trial, in the absence of the jury, that he recalled at the Application he said,' *one would expect, at the very least, there'd be cross-examination.*' He was referring to thorough cross-examination of the prospectors and found it extraordinary there had been no such cross-examination of all prospectors at the committal proceedings. Reading between the lines, I am suggesting Judge Henry had concerns regarding the evidence of the prospectors. I would agree.

Committed for Trial

The committal proceedings for the murder charge were held at Cairns Magistrate Court on Monday 8 December 2014. It was a hand-up brief, comprising 183 witness statements with cross examination of three witness, the prospectors. For those not familiar with the Queensland criminal judicial system, most criminal charges that go through the magistrate's court do so via a *'hand up brief.'*

It is generally acknowledged the case will be committed for trial. This is a necessary formality, in Queensland, for the charge to proceed to the District or Supreme Court. A hand-up brief saves the court a huge amount of time, and the defendant/s significant savings in legal fees. Only in rare instances are criminal charges strenuously defended at committal level, with numerous witnesses called to give evidence and examined. Usually by defendants with deep pockets.

From my experience, the cases that are strenuously defended at committal proceedings, are more likely to be found Not Guilty at trial. Or have the matter rejected by the Magistrate, and not committed for trial at all. The cases that are defended are in the minority.

The cross examination of key witnesses is not unusual or uncommon. The examination of the three prospectors went as expected, although the surliness of witness Bidner toward the Defence Barrister was obvious almost immediately. I could give examples, but I would not know where to start, there was so many. Nothing surprising came out of the cross examination.

The defendants were duly committed for trial to the Cairns Supreme Court to a date to be fixed on a charge of murdering Bruce Schuler and interfering with a dead human body.

In response to the charges Dianne Wilson entered no plea. (She was not obliged to do so). Stephen Struber entered a plea of '*Not Guilty*' to both charges. A second charge of interfering with a dead human body was later withdrawn. Bail for both defendants was continued.

The stage was set.

The Murder Trial

It is important to understand the court process. The defendants Stephen and Dianne were tried separately, but together, if that makes sense. Each defendant had their own barrister. That barrister was working for the benefit of their client, sometimes to the detriment of any co-defendants. The barrister's role is to give the best legal advice and defence to their client, regardless of any other defendants on trial. As sometimes happens, a defendant is found guilty, whilst other defendants are found not guilty. That is the Westminster system of justice.

By 2015, prosecutor Rees was ready for trial. Whilst the Crown had no motive, and no need to provide a motive, there was a claim (not heard by the jury except perhaps by innuendo) that the Strubers had mistaken Bruce Schuler for Daniel Bidner, and the shooting was revenge for the confrontation at the Croc Hole one week before.

Motive, or more to the point, the Crown not presenting a motive is a subject that has always intrigued me. I believe most people would agree that it is most unusual to have a motiveless crime, even with someone suffering a mental illness (such as listening to voices in their head). The Crown is conveniently not obliged to provide a motive, but rest assured, if they have a motive, they will promote it endlessly.

On the Crown case, the Strubers murdered Bruce Schuler for no apparent reason. By inference perhaps, the accused had been pushed to the point of madness by trespassers, as Monte Dwyer concluded. But that is a quantum leap from evicting trespassers to murdering them, and then both denying the claim for the thirteen years, to the time of publication.

The Strubers could not have known they would come across Schuler that day, at that time, in that gully. No evidence was given as to what were they doing there. As you have read, they had been mustering, branding and dehorning for the two weeks prior, in the opposite direction to this area of the property. It is well known prospectors rarely detect alone, for safety and companionship. The Strubers would have been aware of that.

Almost all the documented confrontations people claimed they had with the Strubers, the people were in company with others. In some instances, there were numerous people present. For it to have occurred in the manner described by the prospectors, it had to be an unplanned murder. Which makes the fact they were able to clean up the crime scene so meticulously even more curious, in the time frame as claimed by the prospectors. It appeared no effort was made by the killers to find Schuler's camp to dispose of his car or see if he had company. He obviously did not walk to Palmerville Station. Let me see if I have this correct. They murder Bruce, scrupulously clean up the murder scene, and dispose of all evidence, but make no effort to find his camp. When he is reported as a missing person, the fact he was camped so close to the Struber Homestead would surely cause police to focus on them.

The defendants were claiming they were not involved in the murder, and they were not there on that day. They did not know what happened to Bruce Schuler but whatever it was, it was not at their hands. As it happened, the defence position dovetailed nicely into the Crown case. The defendants had no provable alibi. Or did they, as you read in '*The Phone Calls,*' an alibi never heard by the jury.

The Crown had three witnesses that placed Stephen Struber and Dianne Wilson where Bruce Schuler was last seen. They had Dianne Wilson with a firearm, despite the confusion of the type of firearm, not that the jury was told. The witnesses heard a shot at that location, probably from the now missing .22 rifle. Whichever one that was. They had the witnesses saying they also heard a second shot. The prosecutor called this the '*killing shot*.[88]' By Struber with his now missing .357 revolver.

---

[88] Crown summing up

The prosecutor had the Struber's unregistered bush basher ute last seen heading in the direction of the burnt areas, referred to as Crime Scene Two.

But what about the claims the prospectors variously and repeatedly heard a shotgun, a large calibre rifle and a 30/30 rifle, the '*one Dianne always carries*?' The jury was extraordinarily unaware of those claims. You will read more about that in later chapters.

The Crown had tyre marks heading down the ravine to three separate areas, where bloodstains were variously found on leaves, small rocks and ground cover; the blood was confirmed to match the DNA profile of Bruce Schuler. A piece of twine and an empty film canister were found with DNA which matched Bruce Schuler's. They had two snapped saplings and an anthill with damage, *consistent* with coming from the Struber's unregistered bush basher utility[89]. (Identical according to the prosecutor).

The Crown also had tyre impressions *consistent* with having been made by the registered 4x4 (identical according to the prosecution)[90]. As well, they had the Strubers unable to independently verify their movements on that Monday. Purely circumstantial, but relatively strong.

The trial commenced on Monday 13 July 2015, in the Cairns Supreme Court. Both defendants pleaded Not Guilty to one count of murder, in front of Judge Henry.

The trial lasted eight days which was surprisingly brief for a murder trial. It is not unusual for murder trials to last one month, or longer. In this instance, day one was legal argument, the morning of day two the jury heard the evidence of two witnesses. The court was then adjourned to travel to Palmerville Station, to view the crime scene.

A logistical nightmare to transport a group of some 30 people including the Judge, three barristers, twelve jury members, the defendants and associated staff and police around 1200 kilometres. Two nights'

---

[89] Defence Admissions at Trial
[90] Claims by Prosecutor at Trial

accommodation was arranged in Cooktown. The sort of logistics for a criminal trial unprecedented in Australia.

Witnesses were heard on days four, five and six of the trial, with summing up and the verdict covering days seven and eight. A total of three-and one-half days hearing the testimony of ten witnesses, in a murder trial. Extraordinary.

The witness list had been whittled down from 183 to just ten witnesses. The case revolved around the three prospectors. They *were* the star attraction. Other witnesses included a police mechanic, George Wilson, one other relative of the defendants, the widow, two children of the victim and Detectives McLeish and Camp.

Part of the brevity of the trial may be explained by the admissions the Defence barristers made. Admissions are where the defence counsel admit facts relevant to the case. This eliminates the need for the Crown to call witnesses to prove those points of evidence. The jury can accept those claims as proven.

It is not unusual for counsel to make admissions in a case. What was unusual was the number of admissions made in this trial, and the contentious points of evidence where an admission was made.

At the end of the prosecution case, the Crown can and did also make admissions, which saved the defence the need to call witnesses to prove that point of evidence, which you will read about later.

The full list of admissions by Defence will be found as Appendix B. This is a summary of those admissions only:

Admissions by Defence:

Vehicles

All tests for blood were negative in both Struber vehicles. A 22 bolt action Norinco rifle and a Harrington & Richardson firearm in a leather case and spent cartridge cases were found in the unregistered LandCruiser. Located in the cabin of the registered LandCruiser was a bolt action firearm with scopes and unspent cartridge cases and a firearm magazine.

Clothes

All clothing seized from the Strubers tested negative for blood.

DNA testing

Swabs from an empty film canister, botanical matter, black twine, leaf, and two rocks matched the DNA profile of Bruce Schuler.

Photographs

Photographs were taken of both Struber vehicles. Tyre tracks in bushland and Palmerville Station homestead. Photographs of the location of leaf and general views of the burnt patches. Photographs were taken of anthill and scrap marks. Photographs were taken of the damaged trees, anthill and tyre tracks in grass bushland.

Map titled Palmerville River Station

The map produced by police marked with the last known position of Bruce Schuler according to Daniel Bidner. The positions marked on the map of Kevin Groth, Daniel Bidner and Tremain Anderson are positions described by themselves. Various locations were noted. Tyre tracks, broken saplings, termite mounds that had been knocked over and had gouge marks were recorded. The gouge marks are consistent with being made by a metal component on the undercarriage of the unregistered Toyota Land Cruiser owned by the accused.

An examination of the gouge marks established a positive comparison between test marks, the cast taken from the vehicle, and test marks, cast taken from termite mounds. The marks present within the termite mound was consistent with having been caused by an object such as the underneath of a vehicle or a similar type of tool capable of leaving such a mark.

Leaves with blood matching the DNA of Bruce Schuler, area of burnt grass and vegetation was noted. Located in this area were four partially burnt matchsticks. One of these matches the DNA profile match of Bruce Schuler.

Bloodstains were observed on several rocks. The bloodstains matched the DNA profile of Bruce Schuler. Blood-staining was observed in the ground cover. The ground cover in that area consisted of grass, leaves and other botanical material. The blood matched the DNA profile of Bruce Schuler. A damaged projectile was found. The projectile slug was old and had not been recently fired.

A smaller area of burnt grass, knocked down tree with gouges in the bark and grease marks on the exposed wood were noted. Knocked down tree with gouges in the bark, scratches in termite mound, gouges in the bark of two trees that were parallel to one another on either side of the tyre tracks were recorded, as were scratches on the top of the surface of a termite mound, cow pat and tyre impressions. These impressions correspond in class characteristics, tread design and wear to the tyres on the unregistered Toyota

The Land Cruiser owned by the accused and could have been made by the tyres on that vehicle or any other tyre with similar tread characteristics. There were gouges in the bark of a tree in two places, and two knocked down trees as well as damage to tree and termite mound. A piece of black twine was located. The DNA profile matches that of Bruce Schuler empty white film canister.

The admissions in relation to point 5 were interesting and relevant. The Crown was claiming the marks and gouges in the trees and ant hill were *consistent* with having been made by the Struber unregistered LandCruiser. The defence accepted those claims, and they were admitted as an admission. What about any other four-wheel drives? Particularly those that were in, on and around Palmerville Station at the time Bruce Schuler went missing? There was no evidence to suggest the police had examined the undercarriage of the Struber's registered LandCruiser. There was no evidence to suggest they examined the undercarriage of Bruce Schuler's Patrol, the many police LandCruisers that were used in the investigation. There was no reference at all to any SES vehicles present. There were tyre impressions on the Ear Lobe that were identified as having been made by one of the police vehicles. Would that not be an admission you would force the Crown to prove, if they were capable of so doing? I suspect the defendants came to regret to agreeing to those admissions.

Telephone Call:

It was accepted Dianne Wilson-Struber made the call to Palmerville Station on the 12th of July 2012 at approximately 9.27 am from a pay phone at Lawson Street, Mareeba.

Weapons

The schedule titled Seize and Missing Firearms is a list of firearms that were seized and/or are missing from Palmerville Station.

Witness

It is formally admitted that Berty Lyndon Callaghan is the neighbour of Dianne Struber - Wilson and Stephen Struber. He is profoundly deaf and did not see or hear anything on the 9th and 10th of July 2012 from his neighbour's property.

The evidence the Crown witnesses gave will be addressed in various following chapters. The witnesses covered the mechanical condition of both Struber vehicles, and its ability or otherwise to traverse the steep ravine; what the three prospectors heard and saw on the day Bruce Schuler disappeared; evidence relating to the phone call made by Dianne Wilson to Palmerville Station; evidence by three family members of the victim; and evidence by Detectives McLeish and Camp who were involved in the investigation.

Upon closing the Crown case, prosecutor Rees admitted several matters, just as the Defence had done at the commencement of the trial.

Admissions by Crown:

Daniel Bidner was interviewed by Detective Sergeant Nicholas O'Brien on the 9th of July 2012,

the interview was conducted by telephone and commenced at 9.10 pm,

Daniel Bidner has said the following:

"At the very same moment, I heard Bruce's dog bark, and at the same time, Bruce said, 'Quiet."

"I even went to track the u-turn, like, after they left. I went, 'Right, I will go and see what they said to Bruce.'

"But after I went back to the car and waiting a while, me and Tremain - oh, Tremain went back first. I also went back. So we both - we went back to see the site separately. We did track where the car turned around. We went - yeah."

Walter Randall receives a telephone call from Tremain Anderson on the afternoon of the 9th of July 2012. Tremain Anderson said to Walter Randall that he had heard two gunshots being fired and then another shot a bit later.'

Did the jury understand the implications of those admissions. Was the Crown conceding Bidner and Anderson were lying in those aspects of their evidence, or at the very least and more politely, mistaken? Particularly with point 3. Bidner repeatedly denied in evidence of going back to the u-turn point, but here was the Crown admitting that he had done just that.

Curiously, the Crown did not admit Bidner's claims about not standing up and watching the Struber vehicle drive past on its way back to the homestead. In my opinion, the evidence Bidner was lying about that part of his evidence was as strong as the u-turn evidence, but the Defence counsel did not raise object or challenge it. You will read about '*The only thing I regret Sarge*' in a later chapter.

Defendants do not have to give evidence at their trial, nor call evidence from other witnesses. They are entitled, under the Westminster system, to have the Crown prove their guilt. Nothing should be read into whether a defendant does or does not call evidence in their defence.

It is a brave defendant who gives evidence, particularly in a murder trial. I believe it is better to have the Crown prove their case, if they are capable, but it has been suggested to me that where there are two defendants, it can be a tactical advantage for the defence to have one defendant give evidence. It is all to do with being the last barrister to address the jury.

Many defence barristers jealously protect the right to be the last to address the jury, and for that reason advise their client not to enter the witness box. That way, the Crown prosecutor addresses the jury first, and the Defence counsel has the opportunity to pick the Prosecutor's jury address to pieces. In this trial, the prosecutor was wedged in the middle of the two defence barristers when it came to addressing the jury.

Dianne elected not to give evidence. I have since read she regrets that decision and wished she had given evidence. Most likely, she was relying on her barrister's advice when she made that decision. Not that I believe it would have made any difference to the outcome. Stephen Struber did give evidence. The following is part of the cross examination of Stephen Struber by the Crown prosecutor.

The first part of this exchange referred to the condition of the gearbox of the Toyota LandCruiser, the bush basher:

Prosecutor: '*And you told Mr Feeney just now that there were some difficulties with first and second gear?*'

Struber: '*That's correct.*'

You will recall a police mechanic had previously given evidence he was unable to engage the gearbox on the unregistered LandCruiser in either first or second gear, in any range.

P": '*However, on the 9th of July you could select first gear if you were careful, couldn't you?*'

Struber: '*Yes*'

P: '*And you could select second gear if you were careful?*'

Struber: '*Yes.*'

And at this point, the prosecutor questions Stephen Struber about the crime:

P: '*I want to put a number of propositions to you, and you can agree or you can disagree. Now, you know the gully we were talking about, don't you?*'

Struber: '*Yeah.*'

P: '*And to get to the gully from the homestead, you would drive over the Palmer River and go along the track along the Palmer River and then up the track, and the gully would be on your left, correct?*'

Struber: '*Yes.*'

P: '*On the 9th of July 2012, you drove up that track, didn't you?*'

Struber: '*No.*'

P: 'You drove up that track with Dianne as a passenger?'

Struber: '*No.*'

P: '*And whilst you were driving up that track, Dianne gestured down to the gully, didn't she?*'

Struber: '*No, We weren't in that area.*'

P: '*Well, I am suggesting to you, you were, and you were there about 9.30am?*'

Struber: '*Were not.*'

P: '*And I am also going to suggest to you that you stopped that ute, and Dianne got out?*'

Struber: '*we weren't in the area.*'

P: '*do you carry weapons in your ute?*'

Struber: '*Yes.*'

P: '*A .357 revolver handgun?*'

Struber: '*Yes.*'

P: '*A .22 bolt action rifle?*'

Struber: '*Yes.*'

That was despite witness Bidner given evidence he witnessed Dianne with a lever action rifle.

P: '*You had your revolver with you that day, didn't you?*'

Struber: '*No, I didn't.*'

P: '*Going back to the gully, Dianne got out of that vehicle and pulled a weapon, didn't she?*'

Struber: '*We weren't there.*'

P: '*You weren't there?*'

Struber: '*We weren't there.*'

P: '*Did Dianne shoot at Bruce Schuler?*'

Struber: '*Like I'm saying, we weren't there.*'

P: '*Did you shoot at Bruce Schuler?*'

Struber: '*I was out-both of us were out at the dam. We weren't there.*'

P: '*You then drove up the track and drove down that slope, didn't you?*'

Struber: '*We weren't there.*'

P: '*You shot Bruce Schuler didn't you?*'

Struber: '*I did not. We were out at the dame doing the work that I've already mentioned earlier.*'

P: '*So you fired the second shot at Bruce Schuler?*'

Struber: '*We weren't there.*'

P: '*Dianne's fired the second shot at Bruce Schuler?*'

Struber: '*We weren't there.*'

P: '*You drove down that slope, didn't you?*'

Struber: '*We weren't there.*'

P: "*Well, you caused the tracks that went down that slope?*

Struber: '*Couldn't have because we weren't there.*'

P: '*Are you saying to this court and to this jury?*'

Struber: '*Yes.*'

P: '*That you have never driven a vehicle down that slope?*'

Struber: '*Yes.*'

P: '*Dianne drove the vehicle down the slope?*'

Struber: '*Dianne wasn't there.*'

P: 'You disposed of Bruce Schuler's body?'

Struber: '*We weren't there.*'

P: '*You burnt the grass at that – on the bottom of that slope, didn't you?*'

Struber: '*We weren't there.*'

P: '*And you did that to dispose of evidence, didn't you?*'

Struber: '*We weren't there.*'

And later:

P: '*What did you do with that Winchester?*'

Struber: '*Never had anything to do with it.*'

P: '*What did Dianne do with that Winchester?*'

Struber: '*As far as I know, she didn't have anything to do with it either.*'

P: '*And you've got 2 weapons missing as well?*'

Struber: '*One.*'

P: '*One?*'

Struber: '*One.*'

P: '*What weapon is that?*'

Struber: '*Pistol.*'

P: '*I put to you that you disposed of both of those weapons?*'

Struber: '*I didn't.*'

P: '*I put to you that you know Dianne disposed of those weapons.*'

Struber: '*She didn't.*'

Stephen Struber's evidence left his barrister Mr Feeney with a conundrum. Where the defendant denies being the killer, the defence does not need to present an alternate proposition, but in this case, the jury would be looking for a reason why they should not believe the prospectors.

The only alternate position was the prospectors murdered Bruce. There was no other possibility, but where does that leave Kevin 'Rusty' Groth? Long time friend of Bruce. He had known Bidner and Anderson one day. Struber's barrister would be asking the jury to accept that Kevin Groth conspired with two men he had only just met, to murder his mate of twenty years. Or he was threatened by them, and he had remained mute for three years, and then did not tell the court.

It got worse. The barrister would be also asking the jury to accept Queensland Police investigators totally missed the clues, the inconsistencies, the lies, the innuendo the prospectors blindsided them, and had fabricated the entire story. Seasoned detectives missing something so obvious! A truly preposterous allegation.

That left his barrister to somehow deal with the rather dodgy hand he had been dealt. A great outcome for the Crown Prosecutor. Not so good for either Defence Counsel. If the jury was wobbly and had doubts about the Crown case before Stephen Struber gave evidence, it likely lost the wobbles after he left the witness box.

Upon the conclusion of the Defence case, and before the Crown and Defence summed up their cases to the jury, there was legal argument in the absence of the jury. It was interesting to read the arguments. The barristers were dancing around the suspicion that the prospectors were lying, but no one was willing to say *that* word.

Here are two comments that were made whilst the barristers danced, both by Judge Henry:

'in other words they've got concerns that the whole thing hasn't been the subject of generally truthful evidence than obviously that's the end of it if they think these prospectors have come up with a story and that shortcuts everything.....;'

'and I will explain to the jury why it's there but it's basically to make plain, look, if you've got a reasonable doubt, generally, about the accuracy of what these prospectors say happened,....because if they're not satisfied they've been told the truth about those matters then the case can't possibly succeed.[91]*'*

When the prosecution and defence sum up their case to the jury, they refer to parts of the evidence that supports their case. The prosecutor said this in part, to the jury:

'Now, it wouldn't have taken blind Freddy to see that my learned friend, Mr Feeney and no doubt Mr Trevino, are going to attack the credibility and reliability of Mr Anderson and Mr Bidner. I concede there were inconsistencies.'

That is both an interesting and disconcerting comment by the Prosecutor, in my view. The prosecutor was acknowledging there were

---

[91] Trial day 7-5

inconsistencies with the prospectors' evidence. Did he only just learn about the discrepancies during the trial, and possibly when his witnesses gave evidence? Had he not read the statements? Had he not watched the re-enactments?

To borrow his line, blind Freddy could see there were problems with the case. But he was not that concerned with the inconsistencies to make him pause and reflect. To reconsider his prosecution. By default, the police investigators were also aware of the inconsistencies. Nowhere did the evidence show the prosecution or the investigators attempted to clarify the discrepancies, identify how many or what they related to.

Obviously, the prosecutor did not concede the u-turn, as you will read. He did not concede that the Struber vehicle never went to Crime Scene Two. He did not concede the different weapons heard by the prospectors, as you will learn. He did not concede the '*I didn't stand up Sarge*' evidence. Would it be reasonable to conclude the prosecution was aware of all, or most, of the 142 discrepancies I identified? Yes, I believe it would be reasonable to reach that conclusion. They were all there, hiding in plain sight. I found them and I was not even involved in the investigation. Police were there, and they interviewed the witnesses. They would have heard and seen the ever-changing stories.

The jury was obviously aware of some inconsistencies in the witnesses' evidence, but if the issues were not covered during the trial, they would be unaware of the many, many other inconsistencies that emerged.

The prosecutor continued:

'*The Crown cannot say which one of these accused did the act but submit that it was one or the other and that the other was a party to that offence. The Crown say and submit that you can infer murderous intent from the second shot. You may conclude it's the kill shot.*'

'*You may have considered the following. Mr Schuler was shot in the region where he was last seen, made his way to where the burnt patches are, then there was a second shot, and as I say, ladies and gentlemen, the kill shot, you may infer. You've got the admissions, yet there was no shouting, no screaming, no trail of blood for the 150 metres from where he was last seen until those burnt patches. That's on the premise that Bruce Schuler actually remained where he was last seen.'*

The prosecutor continued:

'Remember what Daniel Bidner said to you? The vehicle came and there was a one to three-minute space in time Mr Schuler may have already been at the bottom of the slope. Mr Schuler could have been shot there. He could have laid there without making a noise, not a sound. Then the second shot, the kill shot, and this may explain the lack of scream and the lack of the blood trail. These are just possible scenarios.'

Was the prosecutor was seriously suggesting to the jury Schuler may have been shot at the first crime scene, despite there being no blood, no DNA, no yelling or screaming, no cries for help, no abandoned possessions between there and Crime Scene Two, 140 metres up the gully. As well as no spent shells, no tyre impressions or footprints connecting the Strubers or their vehicle, to that scene.

There was absolutely no evidence led that Bruce Schuler was shot or shot and killed at Crime Scene One. That scene was at the bottom of a V shaped gully, with steep sides some fifteen to twenty metres high.

Was the prosecutor seriously suggesting Struber and Wilson somehow dragged or carried Schuler's body up those steep walls without leaving blood, drag marks or other evidence on the ground or their own clothing, in the time frame available? If the murder did occur it at the first crime scene, how was Bruce's blood and DNA found at the second crime scene? A ridiculous suggestion really.

That suggestion also conflicted with the prospectors' evidence. They said the vehicle started up and drove twenty metres, followed by a second shot. So, the murder could not have occurred at Crime Scene One.

What was the purpose of suggesting that to the jury? To force them to conclude the only other option was the murder occurred 140 metres up the gully at the Burnt Patches perhaps? It may well have been. I understood counsel were supposed to stick to the facts when summing up, not speculate on what may have happened?

The prosecutor also said this:

'*Look at the admissions.*

Termite mounds that had been knocked over and had gouge marks. The gouge marks are consistent with being made by a metal component on the undercarriage of the unregistered LandCruiser. An examination of the gouge marks established a positive comparison between test marked cast taken from vehicle, test marked cast taken from the termite mound.'

The prosecutor continued:

'*Do you know what else there is? There's cowpats. Cowpats with tyre impressions that **match** the unregistered vehicle.*'

Shades of the Leanne Holland prosecution case right there. The tyre impressions did not *match* the tyres on either Struber vehicle. The tyre impressions were '*similar*'. Was the prosecutor misleading the jury?

When it came time for the defence counsel to sum up, the two barristers approached the issue from different angles.

Barrister Feeney, summing up on behalf of his client Stephen Struber was brief. About thirty minutes. He challenged that Stephen Struber was there or was identified as being there. He challenged the identifications made by Bidner and Anderson. He pointed out that Groth saw a vehicle with 'a rusty-coloured headboard,' which was not either Struber vehicle.

Frankly, Mr Feeney was doing the equivalent of rearranging deck chairs on the Titanic. Witnesses Bidner and Anderson were very strong in their identification of the vehicle, and the two defendants being at the crime scene.

Mr Feeney's address covered four pages in the transcript, and twenty-five minutes court time. Mr Trevino summing up for Dianne Wilson covered twenty-six pages and one hour twenty minutes court time.

Wedged in-between both defence counsel was prosecutor Rees, whose address was covered above.

Whilst Trevino covered all aspects of the evidence, he kept circling back to the credibility of the witnesses. It seemed the Prosecutor was not the only barrister aware of the discrepancies with the prospectors' evidence. The difference being Prosecutor Rees, whilst aware of discrepancies, was not concerned. Trevino was concerned. He thought the witnesses were lying, but he did not use *that* word.

In the first five minutes of his address, he said:

'*Can you really be satisfied that they are witnesses of truth?*'

He painted Dianne Wilson as naive and frustrated, when it came to the telephone call to the homestead. In a later chapter titled '*Something to boast About,*' further comments by Barrister Trevino and that phone call are given.

Mr Trevino then stated what you, as the reader, have no doubt already concluded:

'*It is clear that the evidence given by Daniel Bidner and Tremain Anderson is the lynchpin of the Crown case against Dianne. Indeed, without their evidence, there really is no case at all against Dianne*'.

Mr Trevino did not mention the statement by Kevin Groth that the weapon he heard fired, allegedly by Dianne Wilson, was a large calibre rifle fired into the air, not into the ground. The reason Mr Trevino never raised it was because that evidence was never heard at trial. What would the jury have made of Kevin Groth's claim, had they heard it?

When describing Groth's evidence, Trevino said: '*He saw nothing of any significance…. You might think that Groth's evidence does nothing to advance the Crown's case.*'

I commented in the podcast Kevin Groth reminded me of Sgt Schultz of Hogan's Heroes fame: '*I see nothing. I hear nothing. I know nothing.*' (You will have to imagine the German accent). During the re-enactments, Groth sounded like he wished he wasn't there. It was notable he seemed to contradict the claims by Bidner and Anderson at every opportunity. He saw a different coloured headboard on the vehicle the Strubers were driving (he never saw the occupants). He heard the high calibre round fired into the air, not into the ground. So much so that two months later when he was again interviewed, he reiterated that he believed the round was fired into the air, not into the ground. (Not that the jury ever heard that). On Groth's evidence, was there *any* case against Dianne Wilson?

Had Groth not mentioned Dan Bidner was using a video recorder that day, would that very significant evidence have ever seen the light of day? Vision that Bidner denied to police and to the court. You will read about the damning video tapes in the chapter '*Video does not lie.*

Whilst Groth's evidence did not advance the Crown case, he was very important to the Crown case. He was window dressing. He gave Bidner and Anderson desperately needed credibility. He was *their* alibi. Without him, they were just two prospectors with serious drug cultivation convictions, in an area notorious for drug cultivation and dealing, trespassing on a property when their friend mysteriously disappeared. I have often wondered what the police investigators and the jury would have made of the claims by Bidner and Anderson if Groth was not with them on that day. Snake Oil salesmen comes to mind.

Once again, Trevino circled back to the credibility of the Crown witnesses:

'*Upon analysis, upon scrutiny, significant concerns exist about both their reliability as witnesses of truth and their credibility as witnesses of truth.*' But of no concern to investigators. Trevino constantly challenged the evidence of both Bidner and Anderson in his summing up which is addressed in various chapters.

Referring to their conduct after hearing the shots and he said:

'*Bidner and Anderson, they go out prospecting for gold and for a significant period of time. That behaviour might - you might think is incongruous with their claims to have seen the defendants turn up in the gully.*' Trevino correctly queried why Anderson did not summon help immediately, as he had a satellite phone. Trevino made further comment:

'Can I deal with issues of honesty - the honesty of their evidence, their credibility as witnesses. …'

Once again Trevino focused on Bidner's ever changing story line that concerned him, but not the police nor prosecutor.

"*His evidence was littered with inconsistencies*".

Mr Trevino can find inconsistencies that cause him grave concern. I can find inconsistencies that make me very dubious of the witnesses' honesty. The prosecutor admits there were inconsistencies. But the police investigators decide there is '*nothing to see here.*' It was curious that whilst prosecutor Rees did concede there were discrepancies, he did not try to refute any of them. Where would he start?

Mr Trevino then went on to address only four inconsistencies. Perhaps there was not enough hours in the day to address them all.

The four centred around the weapon Bidner saw Dianne with, including a shotgun, a black stick, and at committal he was "*100 percent sure that it was a rifle,*' and at trial, he described the lever action loading of a rifle.

He reminded the jury of just one inconsistency with Anderson's evidence - the Randle telephone call, where he told him he heard three shots, which of course Tremain Anderson denied under oath that he said.

This comment to the jury was also telling:

'*Other matters relevant to the credibility of their accounts, which may cause you to entertain serious doubt about them, is the extent to which their accounts are inconsistent with each other and the account of Mr Groth.*'

Which of course '*blind Freddy could see*' but not the police or prosecution.

Trevino then went onto discuss the claims by both Bidner and Anderson that they were on opposite sides of the gully where Bruce Schuler was, but denied seeing each other, or hearing the conversation between Anderson and Schuler.

'*Those two accounts of the return to the gully just don't match up. They're fundamentally inconsistent. Mr Bidner would have been there to see that conversation if it occurred.*'

Other matters Mr Trevino addressed are covered in other chapters.

Trevino then visited the u-turn evidence. There is nothing to indicate the jury ever heard about the Struber vehicle doing a u-turn. There was conversation about the vehicle returning to the homestead. *You might think that this inconsistency in Mr Bidner's account is denial in respect of his earlier statement and the inconsistency all that evidence has with Mr Anderson's account is quite concerning and troubling. It certainly doesn't fit with the Crown theory about the significance of those tracks that you can see in exhibit 2.*

The problem was, as you will read in later chapters, the jury was not told the location of where this u-turn occurred. It was never introduced into evidence, courtesy of the prosecution. But of course, the defence could have and should have raised it. The jury was unaware the u-turn occurred more than 100 metres away from the top of the ravine. The Struber 4x4, on the repeated claims of the prospectors, never went to the Second Crime Scene.

Finally, he challenged the forensic evidence and finished with this fitting comment:

'*So ultimately, I suggest to you that the forensic evidence proves very little apart from, perhaps, Mr Schuler's presence in that gully.*'

It was curious that of the two barristers involved in the same trial, one was very concerned about the credibility of the witnesses, whilst the other barrister had no concerns whatsoever. Perhaps that was a tactical decision between them.

The case was dripping with irony. At no time was the allegation made that the Crown witnesses were *lying*. You read where the barristers danced around that suggestion. Their credibility was questioned. Their reliability was challenged. The inconsistencies in their evidence were pointed out. Immediately after the Defence closed their case, and in the absence of the jury, the prosecutor informed the court he wished to address the lies told by the defendants[92]:

'*And again relying on Bidner's evidence. Crown says that's a provable lie. It's a deliberate lie on her behalf.*'

Bidner was unreliable, and he was not credible. But the defendants were lying.

Before the jury was sent out to consider their verdict, the trial Judge addressed the jury on all aspects of the evidence and law they needed to consider. Judge Henry gave a comprehensive summing up to the jury, covering all facets of the trial including law and fact, unanimous decision required, and identification of the accused.

He explained the requirements where there were two accused, a circumstantial case and missing weapons. The Judge pointed out, fairly, to the jury that Dianne Wilson's phone call did not apparently have a sinister intention to it. He also summed up the missing weapons. He did address the question raised, '*Why are both so inconsistent?*" The Judge said this at one point:

'*Members of the jury, beyond those specific weaknesses in the identification evidence, there were of course broader witness reliability points raised about Bidner and Anderson in cross examination and in addresses, and of course, you may also take into account those matters and indeed any other matters you consider as bearing upon their reliability generally...*'

The Judge also commented on the issue of whether the evidence had been made up: '*The point was made, Look, none of these witnesses say they saw who fired the gun. If Bidner's making this up might he not have helped the prosecution case along a bit further and said that he'd seen it.*' He could just have easily addressed whether the prospectors were lying, when they gave evidence.

The jury returned guilty verdicts of murder against both defendants, after a surprisingly brief four hours of deliberation.

---

[92] Day 6-47 trial.

In sentencing the defendants to life imprisonment, Justice Jim Henry said: "*It has been well over a century since the turbulent, sometimes violent days of the Palmer River gold rush. But in this day and age, long removed from those frontier days, it beggars belief that station leaseholders could become so detached from standards of civilised behaviour and could've engaged in such cowardly and callous behaviour as this.*

Such explanation as seems likely for your conduct is that this probably began with one of you shooting and intending to hurt, or at best for you, scare off a prospector you perceived to be a trespasser without particular regard to the safety and welfare of that person or the consequences of your high-handed action in firing. Once it began, this conduct obviously spiralled out of control with the probably panicked but truly dreadful decision to pursue and shoot again. It was surely that callous, calculating behaviour which, in the jury's unanimous view, elevated this beyond manslaughter to a case of murder.'

In a conversation with Frank Teodo, long-time friend of more than fifty years with Stephen Struber, he had this to say about the trial:

Graeme: '*Stephen and Dianne were staying with you during the trial, weren't they?*

Frank: '*They were, morning and evening. I would see them every morning before work, half past four in the morning, we'd have breakfast together, and I'd see them in the evening when they came home, yeah.*'

G: '*And on the day of the verdict, can you just tell me what happened that day?*

Frank: '*I can. Just leading up to that, I'd ask him every afternoon, how you going there, Stephen? He said, well, I've never been to court before. He said, my bloke says something and their bloke says something. But anyway, on the morning that they were convicted, I said to him, what do you want for dinner tonight?*

And Stephen said, oh, well, hopefully it'll be over sometime after lunch, and we've been away that long, we've got that much work to do, we've got to get back on the property. And I said, look, stay one more day, you can leave first thing in the morning, we'll have a good feed, you can celebrate, whatever, and it'll be okay. And that was it. They never made it home that day.'

G: *'They must have been very confident they weren't going to be convicted.'*

Frank: *'Well, Stephen always said to me, he said, we weren't there. Just like he said in court, he said, we weren't there. And he looked me in the eye when he told me this, Graeme, and like that bloke, he did not lie. We've all got our faults, eh? But one thing I can tell you, that man was not a liar. Ask people, ask other people that have known him, they will tell you, he was not one to lie. If he would have done, just say they would have had a confrontation and the other fella fell back and hit his head accidentally, he's the sort of man that would own up to it and take responsibility for his actions.'*

Stephen Struber and Dianne Wilson had the rest of their lives in front of them to ponder. A life so different, so foreign to what they had enjoyed previously, it must have felt like they were in a horror movie.

The Media

The disappearance and murder of Bruce Schuler received extensive media coverage as would be expected. The story may not have received the full media attention it deserved, having occurred in a remote area in Far North Queensland. Once the Strubers were convicted, the media coverage became quite sensational, and at times hysterical in nature. Immediately after their conviction, the Cairns Post ran this story:

Convicted Palmerville murderers Stephen Struber and Dianne Wilson-Struber had dark past.

Cold, heartless, cruel, blank, remorseless. These are the words used to describe Palmerville murderers Stephen Struber and his wife Dianne.

One last time detectives stood outside the jail cell of Cape York graziers Stephen Struber and Dianne Wilson-Struber and asked them where Bruce Schuler's body was.

Neither made a sound as they stared stonily ahead through the bars as if they were not even there.

Minutes later they were led away, not even acknowledging each other despite likely spending the rest of their lives in separate jails.

It was the soulless end to a dark story which began long before the mysterious disappearance of Mr Schuler three years ago.

Tales of abuse, threats, weapons, booby traps and other disappearances have swirled for years.

Travellers blogs and online forums are littered with warnings about the tyrant landholders of Palmerville Station, aimed at those attempting to make the four-wheel drive trip along Palmerville Rd.

When police put out public call for anyone who had faced hostility there in the past they were inundated with complaints stretching back two decades.

In fact, it was Tremain Anderson, one of the three witnesses to Mr Schuler's murder, who described being assaulted and having a rifle pointed at him by Struber, who demanded he leave the property back round 1992.

I was sure from day one (of the case) that they were responsible for Bruce Schuler's disappearance, Detective Sergeant Sgt Brad McLeish said.

Stephen is a bully, he has a dominant personality. It's like she (Wilson-Struber) doesn't respond to anyone but him.

Detective Sergeant Alina Bell described Wilson-Struber's response when they arrived at Palmerville Station in the days after the murder to arrest them.

"The only thing she ever really cared about was the dogs, who would look after them while they were away", she said. That was the only time I ever really saw her show any emotion.

"She is just cold, she comes across as cold. I don't know that she has the ability to feel".

Some of the more confronting historic tales came from Cook Shire Council workers who had to remove illegal gates the couple had set up on Palmerville Rd to block access.

Cook Mayor Peter Scott, a friend of Mr Schuler, admitted council workers were often forced to travel under police escort for their own safety.

I was told in the past, I never saw it myself, he (Struber) has been armed and there were notices and signs displaying guns, he said.

But nobody thinks that someone would take someone's life. I guess no one really expected it and it was a big shock to the community when we heard someone had been killed.

The homestead resembles something out of the violent Gold Rush era the case has been likened to.

A small tin shack with just slits for windows and no screens, inside the floor is dirt and cement, while outside 20 dogs the couple kept as pets roamed around.

And further in the story:

The two guns police believe were used in the shooting remain missing with the only excuse Struber was able to come up with as to their absence being police had stolen them.

Until they and a body are recovered the case will never be fully closed. It is something that irks Sgt Bell.

I was happy that they found them guilty but I'm still not content they haven't found the body - that poor family, she said.

Just to front someone who has no remorse, I can't imagine it.

In July 2019, the Brisbane Courier Mail led a story with this headline:

How many other dead bodies are there? *Why did they resort to murder? Was it purely territorial? Did they have something to hide like a secret outlaw bikie drug laboratory? Or was it more macabre and did the husband-and-wife hillbillies simply like to hunt and terrorise humans? Did the deadly duo, ultimately, get caught taking a scalp in a thrill-kill?*

Convicted murderer Dianne Wilson-Struber – the now jailed outback Cape York cattle station owner found guilty of stalking, executing and disposing of the body of missing gold prospector Bruce Schuler – does not look evil.

But, by all accounts, she liked to ride shotgun, carrying a Winchester lever-action .22 rifle on her lap.

Her husband Stephen Struber, on the other hand, has the wild deranged appearance of a modern-day bearded bushranger.

Known as a brutish "enforcer", the grazier and bush mechanic wielded a fearsome reputation, driven mad and lawless by isolation and adversity, his dark eyes hard as flint in a thousand-mile stare.

He wore a .357 handgun revolver on his hip.

Later in the same article:

No body. No murder weapon. No eye witnesses. No confessions. It was a hard case to put together to convince a jury beyond all reasonable doubt. Lead investigator Detective Sergeant Brad McLeish, renowned as a straight-talking lawman, told of the circumstantial murder case.

Fellow prospectors Dan Bidner and Tremain Anderson gave evidence they saw the Strubers pull up in a farm ute. They heard two shots.

But a small burnt out patch of blood splatter, later confirmed in DNA tests to be of Schuler's blood, was the only trace to be found. 'I believe Dianne fired the first shot,' McLeish, of the Cairns CIB, said. "The second shot, the execution shot, was a different sound.

And of course that revolver is missing, and the Winchester .22 she used is missing, and they've gone missing because those bullets will be in Bruce's body.

If they fired the first shot deliberately at him, they've wounded him, they still could have walked away, but they followed up with the chase 100 metres down the creek, the execution shot, and the body disappears.

There's no doubt they put the body on the back of the ute and lit the fire to get rid of traces of blood.'

Not to be outdone, the Daily Mail ran the following story on the same day with this headline:

'***Real-life Wolf Creek killer speaks out:***

Woman who stalked and murdered outback gold prospector finally breaks her silence on crime that ended father-of-two's life.'

And this article:

'*He (Det Sgt McLeish) described Struber as an "absolute bully" with a history of domestic violence towards Wilson. Both of them "strange individuals, cold and emotionless". "Dianne is a victim of her upbringing. She kills a beast, takes it back to the house and cuts it up. That's how she's lived. She's a hard, hard woman. To look at her hands, she's got the hands of a man who has lived off the land."*

He said the body could've been dumped "five hours away, ten hours away" from the property in a cave, mineshaft or a shallow grave given the window of time the pair had to cover their tracks.

McLeish also told the journalist he could not rule out the possibility the Strubers had killed before, and where Schuler's body is, there could be more.

"They are only rumours. There's talk of a murdered backpacker up there and talk about an older body that's been there for years, but we don't have any reports of missing people in that area for decades," McLeish said.

Any sensational murder, particularly in a small community like Cairns and the Atherton Tablelands usually evokes a broad range of emotions and comment. The 'for and against' if you like. Whilst researching this case I saw no dissent, no questions regarding the evidence or convictions. The world had moved on, or the media had. The only media I had read on the case was very derogatory, and critical of the defendants.

If there was any unrest in the community, I would have expected to see something in the media. I did not become aware of any dissent or concerns with the convictions until I started speaking to residents, and after the podcast was released. The response was intriguing. I found there were a lot of concerns in the community about the convictions.

In 2024, I was contacted by a listener to a podcast episode. He lived in Cairns. He told me he was going to ring his local radio station, again, and see if he could generate some media interest in the story. I listened to the radio interview and was stunned.

The radio commentator was a long-time member of the Cairns media community. The radio station boasted they were the voice of the north. I am sure they were aware of this case, and the station probably covered it in-depth. This was the second time this caller had raised this murder with the same radio announcer. The announcer pretended not to be aware of the case. He listened to the caller, thanked him and moved on.

When I researched all the news stories on the case I saw a common theme. The journalists appeared to accept the police version of events without question. No cross checking, no looking for 'another side'. No searching for a motive, or investigating why the murder occurred. The media seemed happy with vilifying the defendants, and broadcasting sensational headlines. I could not find where any journalist investigated the case and wrote a balanced story.

Ezard's Concerns

Senior Constable Scott Ezard was a forensic crash investigator attached to Cairns District. He was instructed to investigate the vehicle tracks that were seen going down the ravine from the 'Ear Lobe' to Crime Scene Two. He measured the inner and outer tyre widths of both Struber 4x4 vehicles, as well as all vehicles that had been anywhere near Palmerville Station before, during and after the disappearance of Bruce Schuler, to identify which vehicle caused the tracks.

Except for Dan Bidner's vehicle of course, as he had swapped out his tyres the very next day at Mareeba on 11 July 2012, after giving police his statement.

At point 24 of his statement dated October 2012 Ezard concluded: *'This area was identified to lead from the top of the hill, down the side of a gully area. This track width was identified to be consistent with the track widths measured on the second Toyota LandCruiser with the tray sides and hoist crane fitted measured at the Palmer River homestead.'*

He was of course referring to the registered LandCruiser. Yet, the prospectors had consistently identified the unregistered LandCruiser as the vehicle the Strubers were driving when they murdered Bruce Schuler. It is also noteworthy, Ezard said the track widths were consistent as opposed to identical. That becomes very relevant.

You have read the admissions the Defence made at trial. Point 5 was titled '*Map titled Palmerville River Station.*'

Within that point was:

G7. *Cow pats with tyre impressions.*

Bold has been used for emphasis. The points have been numbered for ease of reference.

4. '*These **impressions correspond in class characteristics, tread design and wear** to the tyres on the unregistered Toyota.*'

5. '*Land Cruiser owned by the accused and **could have been made by the tyres on that vehicle or any other tyre** with similar tread characteristics.*'

Because they were admissions, no witnesses were called to give evidence regarding them. By default, there was no opportunity for Defence barristers to examine those witnesses on the validity and accuracy of those claims.

How confusing! On the evidence of Constable Ezard and Forensic Scientist Walker, *both* Struber vehicles had been on the track from the Ear Lobe to Crime Scene Two. The unregistered LandCruiser left impressions in cow pats, and the registered LandCruiser had left the tyre tracks in the grass. They drove both vehicles to the burnt patches!

The first obvious comment regarding those admissions was that nowhere was it said the marks or impressions were **identical,** or as you will learn, **matched** the vehicles or tyres of either LandCruiser. That is very important and relevant. If the comment was that they were identical, that would place it beyond doubt, that it was the unregistered Struber vehicle that made them. The words used were '**consistent**', '**correspond**' and '**could have.**'

The Struber vehicle may have made the marks or impressions, or as was written, '**any other tyre with similar tread characteristics**.' The underneath of Strubers 4x4 may have made the gouge or impressions or likely, and other vehicle with a similar chassis.

From that evidence, the prosecution was able to conclude the tracks down the ravine *could* have been made by Struber's *registered* utility. It was a circumstantial case after all. Where it can become useful is when those circumstantial points are added to other circumstantial points that show Struber and Wilson were responsible for the murder. That is the glaring anomaly with this case. There was no other circumstantial evidence, apart from the identification of the offenders by the prospectors, to connect the defendants to the murder.

How did Prosecutor Rees deal with this anomaly at summing up to the jury? Very easily as it transpired. He said the witnesses couldn't say which of the Struber vehicles it was. He was more definite than that:' *None of the witnesses pick out which one. They don't say whether it's the registered or the unregistered one.*' That was clearly misleading, wrong and inappropriate. The prospectors mentioned on many occasions it was the unregistered LandCruiser (by its description.)

Bidner said this in his Tuesday night interview:'

'*One of the features of it, is that has no side gates all round, it's just a flat tray*'. He repeated this in his first re-enactment on 13 July 2012. This is what Bidner had to say at his 1 August re-enactment:' *I can make out that it's a standard Toyota with a flat tray on the back.*' If you recall, the registered LandCruiser had a tub behind the cabin.

Therefore, on the evidence of Senior Constable Ezard, the unregistered vehicle did not drive down to the second crime scene. On the evidence of scientist Walker, the unregistered LandCruiser may have caused the damage to the trees and driven through the cow pats. Very clever of prosecutor Rees to muddy the water, by telling the jury it could have been either vehicle that went down the ravine.

You may recall the cryptic comment in Detective Riles's notebook on 19 July 2012 that then seemingly disappeared into the void:

- *S/c EZARD - tyre width - anomaly. Advise DS McLeish.*

What exactly did that cryptic comment mean? There is no evidence that anomaly was addressed anywhere until after the trial. After the conviction. After the Strubers' fate was sealed. It begged the question. Who ignored Ezard's concerns? The police, the prosecutor or both?

Would it be reasonable to conclude Senior Constable Ezard was so unhappy the Crown had ignored his concerns of an error he made, when calculating the tyre widths of the Struber vehicles, that he believed he needed to alert the Defence to the problem. That would seem a very reasonable conclusion to draw. It is also a very unusual position for a police officer to adopt, and a potentially detrimental one for his future police career.

To Officer Ezard's eternal credit, he approached defence solicitors after the trial, and informed them he had made an error in his original calculations. Those calculations meant the tracks down the ravine could have been made by either the registered Struber vehicle, or the unregistered Struber vehicle.

After making further calculations, he concluded the tracks in the ravine could not have been made by the unregistered Landcruiser, the bush basher. If the bush basher 4x4 did not make the tracks down the ravine and back up again, what vehicle did. As the result of that, he prepared a further statement on 30 May 2016.

The Court of Appeal made this comment regarding Ezard's new evidence:'

'After Mr Struber's conviction, Sergeant Ezard had discussions with Mr Struber's solicitor and prepared his second statement which included the following. He had made a mistake in calculating the tyre track widths. There were, in any case, a number of variables that could affect the accuracy of the measurements in his first statement, including the precision of the actions of the officer assisting him. The possible variations in the measurements "could be somewhere in the vicinity of 50mm." This meant that the tyre tracks which he originally said were consistent with the appellants' registered vehicle could have been made by either of the appellants' vehicles, or many other vehicles. If the new calculations in his second statement were precise, the tyre tracks could not have been made by the appellants' unregistered vehicle. In answer to a question from the Court, he stated that now when he provides statements about measurements of this kind he records that the measurements are approximations only and not precisely reliable.' (Overtones of the Leanne Holland case all over again!).

What does that mean for the Crown case? Other evidence aside, the Court of Appeal found the unregistered vehicle did not make the tracks from the Ear Lobe down to Crime Scene Two.

As listeners of my podcast 'Who Killed Leanne Holland?' or readers of my book '*The Leanne Holland Murder*' would know, I spent many years investigating the murder of Leanne Holland, for which Graham Stafford served life imprisonment.

Some of the strongest Crown evidence in that circumstantial case (and the most damning for the defence), were two separate and different tyre impressions found at the body disposal dump site, that matched the two different sized tyres of Stafford car. Until they didn't.

A policeman with six years' service, a science degree and no tyre experience, initially declared the two tyre impressions found at the body disposal site were *similar* to the tyres on Stafford's car, in size and tread pattern. By the time the trial came around, the two different tyre impressions were *identical* to the two different and unusual tyre sizes and tread patterns, on Graham Stafford's car.

The trial Judge was so impressed with that evidence, he referred to it seventeen times in his summing up, that the two separate tyre impressions at the scene were *identical* to the two different tyres on Stafford's car. But of course, they weren't identical, as it later came out. One impression was similar but not identical. The other impression was not even close. Stafford's conviction for murder was quashed seventeen years later.

So, forgive me if I question the '*similarity*' evidence about Strubers tyres and scrape marks on the undercarriage, without seeing strong scientific evidence to support those conclusions. Particularly in dry, arid land such as found on Palmerville Station, in mid-winter as shown in the police crime scene photographs.

Court of Appeal 2016

The appeal by Stephen Struber and Dianne Wilson to the Queensland Court of Appeal was heard on 31 May 2016, with the decision handed down on 11 November 2016.

The prosecutor made some revealing comments in his submission, by what he did not say. He did not mention the u-turn, at all, nor the Struber vehicle travelling to the Second Crime Scene (the burnt patches according to police). After the prospectors heard a second shot, the prosecutor had Bidner and Anderson returning to the camp to wait for the others.

Later, he stated that when police and SES searched the property, they found *'tyre marks matching the accused's vehicle were located coming from the direction of the top of the slope/embankment.'*

Which was factually incorrect, as you have read.

The Appeal Court Judges also made some interesting comments:'

'The jury were also entitled to reject the appellants' exculpatory account to police and Mr Struber's evidence at trial. Whilst no blood was found on the clothing seized from the appellants, or in their vehicles, Mr Struber explained in evidence that they used a tarp when killing cattle for food so as to keep the vehicle free of blood. In disposing of the deceased's body and effects, they may also have disposed of the tarp and any sullied clothing. The lack of both a body and DNA evidence implicating the appellants did not necessitate their acquittal.'

With due respect to the Justices, their area of expertise is the law. I am sure forensic scientists and scenes of crime officers would be lining up to challenge them on the comment, that using a tarp to dispose of the body may have disposed of all blood and DNA. Using a tarp to dispose of a body would not prevent the transfer of all trace evidence.

This exact same story came up in the Leanne Holland murder twenty-five years earlier, when the Crown claimed Graham Stafford bashed Leanne Holland around the head with a mallet, wrapped the victim's body in a shower curtain, and carried it down the front stairs of the house to the boot of his car, dripping a mere three drops of blood along the way.

Queensland's then chief forensic scientist gave evidence (for the defence) that he would likely be the only person who could wrap a body and prevent blood escaping. But here we have the Strubers disposing of Bruce Schuler's body using a tarpaulin, and being able to ensure no blood got on their bodies, their clothes, their boots, or on the tray of their vehicle. Has the Court of Appeal learnt nothing in twenty-five years?

And this:

'The only rational conclusion from the evidence which I have earlier summarised in some detail was that the deceased was either injured or killed in the isolated gully where the appellants and the deceased were seen on 9 July 2012, and where traces of the deceased's blood were found after two shots were heard.'

I note the Justice did not conclude the victim was shot to death.

Unfortunately, the Justice did not enlarge on this comment:

'There were some peculiar aspects to the prospectors' evidence, but none of them had guns on 9 July 2012.'

I would be interested in what the Justice was referring to as *'peculiar.'*

Dianne's appeal on the grounds she was not properly identified was unanimously refused.

You have just read the finding in relation to Constable Ezard's fresh evidence, which was one point of Stephen Struber's appeal.

If the prospectors' inability to align their evidence on the Sunday was their train wreck moment, (which progressively became worse), the

Court of Appeal application using the evidence of Stephen May was Stephen Struber's personal train wreck moment.

The evidence of Stephen David May was next level. May was a disability pensioner and grey nomad living in his motorhome. He attended Mareeba Police Station on 6 August 2015, after the trial of Stephen Struber and Dianne Wilson had concluded, and told police he had seen a body on the back of an old utility when he was on Palmerville Station on Thursday 11 July 2012, three years earlier.

He gave a five-page statement that defied belief. The body he saw on the back of the utility had only the boots showing. The rest was covered by a tarpaulin. The utility was driven by George Wilson. On the nomad's evidence, George Wilson passed him on the track whilst driving in the direction of Palmerville Station, where they stopped and had a conversation. The nomad saw the boots protruding out of the tarpaulin, which George then pulled down and covered. They both then continued on their separate journey.

The next vehicle the nomad passed was a police troop carrier. He did not flag it down as he was in *'flight mode.'* The witness kept a diary and did make general entries on and for 12 July 2012, for what he did that day, but made no reference to seeing a body. He did record it four days later on 16 July, when he *'felt safe'*. He said that he could see a *'blue tarp in back of ute, with soles of boots facing me on top.'* No further comment was made about seeing that body anywhere else in the diary.

On that evidence, George Wilson who was on his way to meet police, was carrying a dead body in the tray of his vehicle which he managed to dispose of before reaching Palmerville Station, and said body has never been discovered.

Stephen Struber was trying to throw George Wilson *under the bus*, by suggesting to the Appeal Court that it may have been George Wilson who murdered Bruce Schuler in company with Dianne Struber. The Court of Appeal seemed to seriously consider George Wilson as an alternate killer, which defies comprehension. There was no evidence to suggest George Wilson rolled up on Bruce Schuler that day. Stephen

Struber had been positively identified, in company with Dianne Wilson, by Tremain Anderson, and if Daniel Bidner had his way, positively identified by him also.

Perhaps it was Dianne Wilson's train wreck moment also.

The Court of Appeal wrote this:

'Both appellants contend that the guilty verdicts were unreasonable under s 668E(1)Criminal Code 1899 (Qld). They submit that there are many reasonable hypotheses open on the evidence consistent with their innocence. One appellant may have killed the deceased independent of the other, with the other assisting only in disposing of the body after the killing. They contend that it was impossible from the evidence to know whether either shot was directed at the deceased or actually struck him resulting in serious or fatal injury. Even if there was sufficient evidence to establish that each appellant was involved in the killing, there was insufficient evidence to infer that the killing was intentional. Either appellant may have fired the shots merely to frighten the deceased without the others knowledge or involvement. Ms Wilson-Struber may have fired the first shot as a warning, or to kill the dog, but inadvertently killed the deceased, with the second shot discharging either accidentally or after aiming and firing at the dog but missing. To conclude that one appellant knowingly aided the other in intentionally killing the deceased, in the absence of any incriminating DNA evidence, they contend, was mere speculation and conjecture.'

Were Dianne and Stephen blaming each other? Was this an admission of guilt? Gerard Baden-Clay became infamous when he changed his defence at the Court of Appeal, just the previous year, 2015. Whilst researching the Schuler, and when I first read the grounds the Strubers were using in their Appeal to the Court of Appeal, I had a moment of *'Am I giving killers a platform to spread their lies of innocence.'* That is definitely not in my playbook.

The prospectors' eyewitness testimony made it a compelling case the Strubers murdered Bruce Schuler, the circumstantial evidence that went with it, not so much. But for the disturbing and contradictory evidence of all three prospectors, I would have walked away from the case at that point.

For those not familiar with the Baden-Clay case, his 43-year-old wife Alison, mother of two children, went missing whilst out on a morning walk on 20 April 2012, three months before the murder of Bruce Schuler. Gerard Baden-Clay was a successful real estate agent; the family lived in the upmarket Brookfield area in Brisbane's western suburbs. He had political connections.

Alison was successful in her own right in her employment at Flight Centre. Her body was found ten days later in a creek, thirteen kilometres away from their home. Baden-Clay denied any knowledge or involvement in her death. The disappearance received massive media coverage, both in Southeast Queensland and nationally, notably due to Gerard's arrogance and attempts to control the narrative, and his long-standing affair with an employee made for salacious headlines.

Gerard Baden-Clay strenuously denied the allegations, but was found guilty of murder at trial. In the Court of Appeal, his legal team argued her death may have been the result of an altercation between husband and wife, where he did not mean to cause serious harm. The conviction was reduced to manslaughter.

As the result of a huge groundswell of public backlash, the DPP appealed the case to the High Court of Australia, and the murder conviction was reinstated. Baden-Clay is serving a life sentence. It did not help his cause that he dumped her body in a creek.

There are two notable take-aways from that case. Gerard Baden-Clay talked himself into a murder conviction. He denied any involvement in her death and then changed that to *'well, maybe I accidentally killed her.'* Australia has an appalling record when it comes to the death of women in intimate violence cases.

As of 2025, a woman is killed by an intimate partner on average about every four days. A male is killed by an intimate partner around every ninety days. The daily papers across Australia are full of DV cases where the female, usually, is killed. The male admits he killed her, but claims he did not mean to cause serious harm. A conviction for manslaughter follows in many, many instances. Had Gerard Baden-Clay put his hand up and said just that, he would likely have been given a seven-year prison sentence.

And compare that case to that of Sandrine Jourdan. Less than three months after Alison Baden-Clay went missing, Sandrine Jourdan, a 38-year-old mother of three children went missing whilst standing at the front gate of a friend's house in Caboolture, Queensland. She has never been found.

The first media article appeared about two weeks later, followed by sporadic articles thereafter. The difference I believe can be partly attributed to their social standing. Sandrine was a single mother living in a lower socio-economic area. The Baden-Clays were a successful couple in an upper middle-class area. Queensland Police ruled Sandrine's disappearance a suicide, even without a body and once again the Queensland Coroner agreed[93]. Sandrine's disappearance is covered in my podcast *'Bring Home Sandrine.'* Sandrine's disappearance is now back before the coroner.

In the Strubers case, it made no sense. If Stephen was willing to *point the finger* at Dianne and George for the murder during the appeal, the obvious next step would be for one of them to give up the whereabouts of Bruce Schuler's body to gain parole, and let the other die in prison, yet that has not happened.

Fiona Splitt believes Stephen Struber still has a hold over Dianne Wilson, and she is under his influence[94]. I reject that. They have lived separate lives for ten years, in separate prisons, five hundred kilometres apart. Whenever she has been asked about the murder, she states she *and* Stephen are innocent. That is a quantum leap from claiming innocence and *'you will need to ask Stephen his position.'*

Stephen's appeal to the Court of Appeal was refused by a two to one majority[95]. The dissenting Judge recommended acquittal and retrial.

---

[93] Bring Home Sandrine podcast
[94] Interview with Fiona Splitt November 2023
[95] Qld Court of Appeal

Stephen Struber later sought leave to appeal to the High Court of Australia, however, his application was rejected.

That was the end of the legal road for Stephen Struber and Dianne Wilson. They had exhausted their legal options. They have to serve out their punishment of life in prison. Stephen is incarcerated at Lotus Glen Correctional Centre on the Atherton Tablelands, whilst Dianne Wilson is destined to serve her life sentence at Townsville Correctional Centre at Stuart, outside Townsville.

Since releasing the podcast, I have been messaged by prison officers from both prisons to say they believed both persons to be innocent. One Stuart Creek prison guard wrote '*you could let Dianne Wilson out the gate at 8 a.m. and tell her to come back at 5 p.m. and I guarantee she would be there*[96].'

---

[96] Where is Bruce Schuler podcast

No Body No Parole

By October 2015, more than three years after Bruce disappeared and three months after Stephen Struber and Dianne Wilson had been convicted of his murder, Fiona Splitt had had enough. Struber and Wilson were refusing to disclose the whereabouts of her partner's body.

'We don't know where he is. We were not involved', they both said whenever asked by police, media or family.

Fiona started a Queensland Parliamentary petition. She eventually obtained 8775 signatures demanding a change to the state's laws. The petition was lodged in Queensland's Parliament as the Corrective Services Amendment Bill 2017. It passed through Parliament on 8 August 2017 and became known as *'the no body, no parole'* legislation.

Under the legislation the parole board must refuse to grant an application for parole where the offender is serving imprisonment for a 'homicide offence' and the body or remains of the victim have not been located. The legislation has not been without its problems. There was a case where the killer disposed of the body; he told police where to find the remains but only around 90% of the remains were recovered. Under the legislation, parole had to be refused because of the wording of the Act. I believe the Act was amended or that case was was overturned on Appeal.

What it meant for Stephen Struber and Dianne Wilson was simple. They would never obtain parole from prison until they provided the location of Bruce Schuler's body. A big incentive to talk both Dianne Wilson and Stephen Struber refuse to accept.

As of 2025, both Stephen Struber and Dianne Wilson maintain their innocence. They maintain they were not involved in the disappearance of Bruce Schuler and do not know where his body is.

They are destined to die in prison.

As of 2025 they have now each served ten years of their life sentence. They could be eligible for parole in the next five to ten years but with this legislation in place that will not occur unless they provide whereabouts of Schuler's remains.

Stephen Struber is currently 68 years of age whilst Dianne Wilson is 62 years of age. They potentially could have another fifteen to twenty years in prison before their deaths. Both prisoners had exhausted their legal redress. Ordinarily, the two murderers would be eligible for parole around the year 2030 or perhaps even before that.

In 2019, journalist Robert Reid interviewed Dianne Wilson in Townsville Correction Centre. She denied being involved in the murder and denied knowing the whereabouts of Bruce Schuler's body. Robert Reid concluded she was telling the truth, but he later decided she had been telling herself for so long that she was not involved in the murder, that she had started believing it herself.[97]

There was also allegedly a claim that Stephen Struber may have disposed of the body himself, and Dianne have no knowledge of the disposal site. I do not accept that claim, based on the evidence.

---

[97] Interview with Robert Reid 2023

The Coroner's Court 2018

In August 2018, Coroner Nerida Wilson held a Non-Inquest investigation into the disappearance of Bruce Gavin Schuler.

She found he *likely* died on 9 July 2012, *likely* at Palmerville Station, Palmerville in the State of Queensland and his *likely* cause of death was from fatal shotgun wounds inflicted by Stephen Struber and/or Dianne Wilson. After reading the Coroner's eight-page report, I am no closer to establishing why she concluded Bruce Schuler died from wounds inflicted by a shotgun. She had commented about the missing firearms, none of which was a shotgun. That decision did not clarify anything.

What happened to the claims Dianne shot him with a .22 rifle and Stephen Struber finished him off with a .357 handgun?

As officer McLeish was quoted by a journalist as saying:

'And of course that revolver is missing, and the Winchester .22 she used is missing, and they've gone missing because those bullets will be in Bruce's body.'

And Kevin Groth was very specific. Insistent. He heard a high-powered rifle, whilst Dan Bidner claimed he heard a shotgun. Tremain Anderson believed he heard a .30/30 rifle which would be consistent with a high-powered rifle.

What was the view of that coronial non-Inquest finding by the Queensland Police Service and Director of Public Prosecutions?

In March 2025, Sharon Wilson, sister to Dianne lodged a Queensland Parliamentary petition to hold an inquest into the death of Bruce Schuler. The closing date for signatures is 28 July 2025. In future updates of this book, I will post the outcome of that petition.

Unfortunately, Fiona Splitt opposed the Parliamentary Petition. She spoke publicly saying '*Not a murder mystery. Push for inquest hurtful and futile says widow.*[98]'

---

[98] Cairns Post 28 April 2025

Something to Boast About

In 2022 whilst researching this case, I came across the details of that telephone call Dianne Wilson made to Palmerville Station on the 14th of July 2012:

'*I have someone that was involved.*'

Dianne's solicitor did not seem fazed by the contents of the call. It was made Admission number 6 at trial in 2015. I felt this was an unusual comment. I considered a more likely wording would be:

'*I know someone that was involved.*'

To use '*have*' implied ownership. (Such as …I have a family member that was involved')

The wording of the phone call was very precise and was consistent with the officer having recorded the phone call. A search for the audio was fruitless.

The jury was also troubled by this comment. They sent a note to the Judge querying whether there had been a mistake, or a typo in the wording of that call. They queried whether the call had been recorded. The answer came back, 'no', the phone call was not recorded which was even more perplexing. The trial Judge was equally surprised. He said this at trial:

'*I mean, I understand, gentlemen, it must've been a tape recorded phone call for the transcript to be so precise.*'

The prosecutor replied: '*It was not recorded.*'

Defence Barrister Trevino raised the subject in his summing up to the jury:

'*There was a query from the jury about the statement:*

"*I have someone that was involved.*"

It is a peculiar thing to say. Its ambiguous. Its loosely expressed. Its ambiguous in the sense of what the word "have" could possibly mean in the context of that sentence, and whether it means "I know someone that is involved" or "have information about someone who was involved".

It's an ambiguous statement. But one way in which it is not ambiguous, one interpretation that those words cannot sustain is that she, herself, was involved. She's certainly not speaking about her own involvement in that conversation with Det Sgt Groen.

She is clearly speaking about someone else. The inference that could be more easily drawn, having regard to the circumstances that you know of, might be that's she's referring to Daniel Bidner.'

I considered that comment convicted Dianne Wilson in the eyes of the jury. I believed Dianne Wilson had probably made the call out of frustration. Although I have never met her, I did not believe she had the cunning or know how to try and mislead the police. I could not see how she was misleading them by making that call.

What benefit could she possibly gain by sending the searchers out to the Croc Hole? It seemed illogical. As of that Thursday, three days after Bruce Schuler went missing, Dianne would not have been aware of the claims by the prospectors and the One Mile location of the crime (unless of course she was involved).

As her solicitor suggested in her email to the Commissioner of Police, the Strubers suspected Daniel Bidner was behind the disappearance of Bruce Schuler.

Contained in the police file was a presentation held at James Cook University (JCU) Campus in Cairns in 2018. It was organised by a community policing support group and was titled '*Behind the Crime: The Gold Prospector who vanished*'. It was advertised publicly and around 500 people attended. This sort of presentation is quite unique and not something the Queensland Police Service is known to usually engage in.

The presenters were (by then) Detective Sergeant Alina Bell, Sergeant Lesley Walker and Principal Crown Prosecutor Nigel Rees. The power point presentation consisted of twenty-nine slides and was a detailed insight into the murder and investigation of Bruce Schuler. A Cairns resident who attended the presentation commented that he thought the police were somehow trying to justify the conviction. Perhaps there was community unrest that had been ignored by the media.

The transcript of the phone call that Dianne Wilson made to Palmerville Station was read out as part of that presentation:

'I **know** someone that was involved.'

Between the 2015 trial and the 2018 JCU presentation the evidence had morphed from '*I have some involv*ed' to '*I know someone involved.*' How did that happen! There is obviously a huge difference of meaning between "*I have someone that was involved*' to '*I know someone that was involved'*. Would the defence have so readily agreed to that evidence being admitted into trial had they been aware of that difference?

That phone call was answered by Detective Senior Sergeant Goan. It was not recorded. He must have made notes (in his notebook) and prepared a statement based on those notes. Goan's notebook was not in discovery so we will never know whether he wrote '*have*' or '*know*'. But it does raise the question. Whoever wrote the script for the JCU presentation obtained the phone call information from somewhere. What and where did they obtain it, and more importantly, why the variation with what was heard at trial.

That JCU presentation can be found as Appendix C, and it also contains photographs referencing the case.

Bob Haydon

Bob Haydon was a police officer for thirty-six years, with both the Northern Territory Police Force and Queensland Police Service. He served at Laura Police Station from 1991 until his retirement in 2002. Eleven years. I have never met Bob Haydon or spoken with him, but I wished I had. He would have some amazing stories of his police career, particularly in FNQ. Bob also had a mining lease, Jessop Creek, in the Palmer River Gold Fields from 2000 to 2007.

As a working police officer, and as one of the 'locals' on the Palmer River Gold Fields, Bob Haydon had a good knowledge of the area and a good rapport with the community. Bob Haydon had seen, lived and worked the Gold Fields from both sides of the fence. Bob knew Stephen Struber and Dianne Wilson. He knew Dianne's parents when they owned the property, as he had stayed overnight on Palmerville Station, whilst patrolling his division.

In 2019, Bob Haydon read a book on the murder of Bruce Schuler. In his words he wrote in his subsequent report:

'*After reading the book and from my local knowledge of the Palmer River Gold Fields and its inhabitants, I became acutely aware of numerous discrepancies in the prosecution evidence and the defence of the Strubers, and I believe a blatant miscarriage of justice has occurred.*'

Someone else who became aware of the discrepancies! He was suspicious of the claims made by the prospectors, and critical of the police investigation that resulted. He set about conducting his own investigations into the case. He was seventy-six years of age at the time. His subsequent report covered almost fifty pages. He handed his findings to Dianne Wilson's family, and those notes are now in the possession of the defence team.

Haydon re-enacted the alleged drive made by and from the homestead, to the One Mile as claimed made by the prospectors, using an identical Toyota LandCruiser, and was assisted by Dianne's brother George Wilson. He had access to the police measurements of the crime scenes.

Several matters stood out from his investigations. Haydon described the track across and along the Palmer River as rough and stony, and through very deep loose sand that was difficult to negotiate. The LandCruiser needed to be in four-wheel drive, low range, second gear with the engine revving between 1500 and 2000 revolutions to drive through the conditions. He added that at times, the vehicle became bogged, which required the vehicle reversing and crossing the soft sand at a higher speed. The deep sand started about one kilometre from the turn off to the road, to the alleged murder site and continued all the way to the turnoff. He described the vehicle as very noisy, and he had no doubt the prospectors would have heard the vehicle approaching, from a long way off. He concluded that there was a high probability Bruce Schuler would have heard some noise from the approaching vehicle, even if both headphones were in place.

And if you recall, George Wilson claimed if the unregistered LandCruiser was placed in reverse gear, it would need the top of the gearbox to be removed, to get the vehicle out of reverse. How could the Strubers have even made it to where they were alleged to have first stopped, on that evidence?

Haydon believed Dan Bidner would have heard the vehicle approaching for a kilometre, and that he would have seen the vehicle for 300 metres, as it crossed the creek and climbed up the steep hill to where the group were detecting. Yet Bidner claimed he did not alert Schuler to the impending danger because the Strubers would have seen him. It would have taken at least two minutes for the Struber vehicle to reach that destination, from the bed of the Palmer River.

Haydon was in the passenger seat. He had to grip the handle above the door because the track was that rough. He did not have time to look out the window but was more concerned with bracing himself for the next bump. He could only catch a glimpse of the gully and after calculations he believed Dianne had about four metres and one second, to see Bruce

Schuler in the gully, and only if Schuler was standing to his full erect height. On Daniel Bidner's evidence, it was the dog bark that alerted Dianne. A claim that changed from his first contact with police. Haydon did not believe anyone in the cabin would have heard a dog bark.

In relation to the distance between Crime Scene One and Crime Scene Two, Haydon commented there was excellent cover to hide from anyone shooting from up on the spur. He questioned that Schuler would leave this cover and concealment, and run up a forty-five-degree incline onto an open ridge, in full view of anyone on the road where the Strubers had allegedly parked their vehicle. (And I note Haydon did not suggest the Struber vehicle drove down and up the ridge line. Did he also not understand the evidence regarding the vehicle turn around point?).

In his words, the three prospectors ran away from the shooter, yet Bruce Schuler ran toward the shooter. Had Schuler run downstream, the Strubers would have had to turn the vehicle around to pursue him.

Haydon obviously did not have a high opinion of prospectors Bidner and Anderson. It would appear he knew them. He said this in relation to these witnesses:

14. '*Danny Bidner and Tremain Anderson are people who live their lives in country where you cannot move without a four-wheel drive vehicle. Their knowledge of those vehicles and the identification of them would have been acute. But they neither mention nor were they questioned about an 'orangey headboard rail' on the Toyota tray back LandCruiser that they allegedly saw and identified as the Strubers' work ute.*

14(a) Danny Bidner and Tremain Anderson's evidence was so changeable, unreliable and inconsistent with the established facts that it should have been rigorously destroyed in cross examination.

14(b) They are either expert blatant liars or they were so convinced that the vehicle they saw was the Struber's work ute, and the occupants of the vehicle were Steve and Dianne Struber that their imagination and perhaps fear overcame and distorted their powers of observation.'

Haydon repeated a story he had heard several times from various members of the Wilson family. It was in 2009 or 2010 when Dorrie Wilson (Dianne's mother) was still alive.

At that time, only Stephen and Dianne were living on Palmerville Station. Dorrie had been living there but was in Mareeba Hospital where she had been hospitalised for shingles and other associated medical conditions.

Eventually, Dorrie returned home from hospital. The next day Stephen and Dianne left the homestead about six a.m. to go to work, which was their usual routine and practise. They left Dorrie at the homestead asleep in her bedroom. Dorrie related the story to Dianne and Stephen when they returned to the homestead. She also told George Wilson and other family members before she died in 2011.

At about 8 a.m., Dorrie heard a noise and got out of bed to investigate. She saw a man sitting at the table on the back verandah, drinking coffee from one of her kitchen mugs. Dorrie walked up to the man, and he said to her in a surprised and shocked manner, '*What are you doing here?*'

Dorrie replied:' *More to the point. What the fuck are you doing here. I live here.*'

The man did not say another word, but just got up and put down the mug of coffee, and left the house by the back gate and walked north towards the Palmer River. Dorrie later recognised the man as Tremain Anderson when she saw him in a YouTube video.

In September 2019, Bob Haydon drove to Townsville Correctional Centre at Stuart, outside Townsville and spoke with Dianne Wilson for over five hours, spread over three visits. He was unable to take notes or record the conversation due to prison regulations. Dianne was very willing to speak with him and according to Bob, wanted the '*truth to be known.*' She denied she and Stephen were involved in the murder of Bruce Schuler.

She gave Bob a detailed breakdown of their movements on the Monday and the Tuesday, which included working on a loader at the big dam, and working horses in the paddock. She told Bob that after George

Wilson purchased a helicopter in 2009, the threats and intimidation by trespassers and prospectors increased. George could quickly fly over the property and see where everyone was and what they were doing. In 2011 or 2012, someone tried to set fire to the helicopter.

In their final meeting, Dianne said to Bob, *'Please tell Bruce Schuler's widow that I pray for her every night, and I pray she will find her husband. But Steve and I didn't do it.'* Bob wrote that during all their conversations, Dianne appeared to be very honest and straight forward with her answers. She did not hesitate or attempt to sidestep any question, and she answered with conviction and apparent honesty.

Sold!

In 2012, Stephen Struber and Dianne Wilson both signed an Enduring Power of Attorney (EPA), giving George Wilson and Kathleen Struber control of their financial affairs if needed. The next business day after their murder convictions, officers from the Queensland Public Trustees Office (QPT) visited Dianne in the Cairns Watchhouse and informed her the EPA was not valid for anyone sentenced to more than three years imprisonment, and they persuaded her to have the Queensland Public Trustee manage her financial affairs.

Stephen Struber was just a few cells away but for some reason they did not approach him. I have been informed it didn't matter, as he would not have signed anything anyway. He believed if he signed a consent form, that was an acknowledgement of his guilt for the murder, which he denied.

As time passed, the QPT wrote to Stephen and Dianne and indicated they wanted to sell the property to settle Stephen and Dianne's debts. Both parties signed a letter addressed to the QPT, informing them they did not want to sell Palmerville Station; they were innocent of the crime, and believed their innocence would be proven. They would then be able to return to their home. The QPT replied, advising them they would be selling the property.

George Wilson wanted to buy Palmerville Station, and Stephen and Dianne were willing to sell it to him. He arranged $4 million finance and made a written offer. Stephen and Dianne accepted the offer, and they wrote to the QPT informing them of the contract. The QPT refused to sell the property to George Wilson, claiming the sale had to go to auction. Eventually, the QPT took the matter to the Supreme Court and obtained a Court Order to sell.

When Palmerville Station was advertised for sale in 2019, the real estate agents advertised it this way:

'Palmerville Station is a lower peninsula grazing property located within the established beef cattle breeding area of North Queensland, located just 70 kilometres southwest of Laura.

Offering a total land area of 134,000 Hectares of predominately a mix of undulating ridge country comprising rough broken ranges associated with the Great Dividing Range through the northern section intersected by several creeks and gullies extending to the south across eroded plains with the main feature being the 70 kilometres double frontage to the Palmer River.

Palmerville Station is known as one of Queensland's largest alluvial gold deposits and hosts 30+ mining leases.'

The property sold the same year for $4.07 million, just $70000 more than George Wilson would have paid, and it would have remained in the family. The new owners, Diversified Agriculture Pty Ltd continued to maintain the property as a pastoral lease. However, they also opened the property to gold prospecting.

I had a wide-ranging interview with a senior member of the management team of Palmerville Station. They have several goals. They intend to maintain the property as a cattle station. They wanted to make the property family friendly and family safe. They were aware of a small group of gold prospectors, miners, drug dealers and criminals causing havoc on Palmerville Station, and the place resembled the Wild West. These people were trespassing, growing drugs, terrorising prospectors, and lighting fires to better detect gold.

In 2023 fires burnt out sixty percent of the property, and the owners were forced to close the Station to prospecting, for safety reasons. Through concerted efforts that figure reduced to four percent in 2024.

The owners introduced CCTV throughout the property, and they also have Aboriginal rangers stationed permanently on the property patrolling in helicopters. Any drug crops found are burnt, and there were many. The number of drug crops have decreased significantly since Rangers have been patrolling the property.

The rangers monitor traffic and who is coming and going on the property. They also have a Savannah burning project where they burn twenty per cent of the property each year. That way, no one needs to torch the vegetation to go prospecting.

The current owners run 5000 head of cattle. Through a legal test case all the miners with a lease on Palmerville Station are now required to abide by the Farm Holders Biosecurity Program and the miners are also required to have their own Biosecurity Program in place. An initiative started by Stephen Struber when he took a miner to the Land Court.

The company is working with the Mines Department to ensure those miners who hold a lease do not have criminal convictions. The manager quoted an example where two convicted drug growers held mining leases, but they have now been forced out.

The website www.palmerville.com.au was registered and has a lot of information regarding Palmerville Station.

The webpage www.diversifiedagriculture.com.au also has some stunning photographs of Palmerville Station.

The Evidence

What you have read to this point represents the history of the Bruce Schuler case up to and including 2019. We have seen the history of Palmerville Station and at times, the erratic behaviour of Stephen Struber. We have seen their efforts to force miners, prospectors and tourists to abide by the law, and Stephen Struber's never-ending battles with the Cook Shire Council.

We saw Bruce Schuler's disappearance, the police investigation, the arrest and prosecution of Stephen Struber and Dianne Wilson for murder, their convictions by a jury which were upheld on appeal by the Queensland Court of Appeal. The legislation changes known as '*no body no parole*' had been implemented, Palmerville Station had been sold, and Bob Haydon had conducted investigations and had concerns. Stephen Struber and Dianne Wilson were still refusing to provide the whereabouts of Bruce Schuler's remains, claiming they were not involved in his disappearance. With each passing year, the likelihood of Bruce Schuler having been murdered, increases exponentially.

The world moved on. It would be accurate to say the case went cold from that time on, but efforts were being made in the background to have a further Court Appeal by the defendants. However, the world had not moved on for the Schuler families, the Struber families and the Wilson families who are all in a living nightmare.

The next event in this story was 2022, when I began researching the case. I wanted to know why the offenders continued to maintain their claim from day one that they were not involved in the murder and did not know where Bruce Schuler's remains lay.

To my surprise, I found a circumstantial case with no body, no cause of death, no admissions by the convicted persons, either before during or after, very little forensic evidence, no physical evidence, a lot of speculation, a lot of unsupported inferences, and many discrepancies in the evidence of the three main Crown witnesses, which left their credibility in tatters.

I was curious to know the reason why the Strubers were arrested on day one, released on day three and then rearrested months later. Obtaining bail on a murder charge is virtually unheard of, yet the Strubers managed to obtain it. I was disturbed to note the jury were not told compelling evidence including the type of weapons heard fired, and the fact the witnesses repeatedly told police the Struber vehicle did a u-turn on the track, a long way away from crime scene two. I was curious about the disturbing number of discrepancies in the evidence of the prospectors. If they were witnesses to the crime, why were they seemingly lying about it?

I was concerned by the evidence that was not found during the comprehensive search by more than thirty Police and SES, including footprints, boot prints, broken twigs and branches, drag marks, blood trails, and lack of spent ammunition. I was disturbed there had been no evidence of yelling, screaming, arguing or cries for help by the victim.

I was perplexed by the complete lack of abandoned personal belongings during a flight of fear. Surely, Bruce Schuler would have dropped something during his run along the gully, as he was weighed down with many individual belongings. I was also concerned when I found it was around fifteen minutes between the first and second shot, and Bruce Schuler had only managed to run 140 metres. I wondered how the Strubers knew which way he ran, and where to find him. From their position on the spur, they had no vision into the gully. It was a perfect hiding spot for Bruce Schuler.

Instead of maintaining cover, he allegedly left the gully and ran toward the shooters whilst his companions ran away for the shooters. He did not have a weapon, or a military background and training to do just that. He then dropped a single, solitary small film cannister and a few small pieces of twine, whilst the Struber 4x4 was crawling down the ravine at about five kph, yet he seemingly stood there awaiting his fate. So many questions. Later, I was concerned by the tyre tracks on the spur that did not appear until at least the Tuesday, if not the Wednesday, after his disappearance.

I felt the first and second crime scenes were never satisfactorily explained. There was no evidence to connect the Strubers to either scene, yet Bruce Schuler's blood and DNA were at scene two. How did his DNA get there? You would seriously not gold detect and burn vegetation whilst being hunted by a shooter. The police investigators told me they believed the Strubers had just disposed of his body and had his DNA on their hands, when they lit the matches to burn his blood. That would mean they shed *his* DNA but not their own. That explanation would be better suited in a work of fiction. From the very wide area containing the burnt vegetation, the only non-sensical conclusion is, Bruce Schuler staggered around whilst bleeding, without letting out a shout or cry for help, without leaving footprints, boot prints, drag marks or blood. But he still managed to hold on to all his equipment.

I was disturbed by the matter-of-fact attitude of the witnesses, after allegedly enduring a very traumatic event, then continued their gold detecting, not bothering to ring anyone, particularly Bruce, for around nine hours. I read an Aboriginal Police Tracker spent three days on the ground and found nothing to support the murder having occurred there. '*I could not find any signs to follow. We were looking for boot prints, bits of clothing, his pick, shovel or metal detector, stuff like that.*[99]' I was curious how the Crown case morphed to include the missing weapons, when there was no evidence to show Bruce Schuler was shot to death.

I read the trial evidence and saw the witnesses, particularly Bidner, obfuscate, dissemble, evade and be outright deceitful in his answers. Tremain Anderson did also, but to a lesser degree. That did not inspire confidence in their credibility. But every time I considered the possibility this story had been fabricated, I would circle back to Kevin Groth. He knew his prospecting companions for one day. Why would a twenty-year friend of the victim conspire with two persons he had

---

[99] Newspaper article 2012

only just met to commit murder? A question I cannot answer to this day.

And how best to present the evidence unearthed during my research? You have already heard a significant amount including the neighbour Bertie Callaghan, the lost and then found satellite phone, Constable Ezard's tyre evidence, together with the Court of Appeal decision and Dianne's phone call to the homestead.

I considered the easiest way to present the findings, was to treat each discrepancy separately, and lay them out in no particular order, though I have left the strongest and most compelling evidence until last.

You, the reader can formulate your own decision as to whether the discrepancies are minor, and of no consequence, which is the position of police investigators, past and present. Or perhaps you may reach the conclusion those discrepancies cast real doubt on the credibility and integrity, of the three main Crown witnesses. Or perhaps somewhere in-between.

I will start with a Scientific Principle. A backbone of forensic science.

A Scientific Principle Challenged

Dr Edmond Locard (1877 - 1966) was a pioneer of forensic science. He formulated the basic principle of forensic science as *"Every contact leaves a trace'*.

The principle holds that the perpetrator of a crime will bring something into a crime scene and leave with something from it, and that both can be used as forensic evidence. The principle can also hold true for victims of crime. They too will take something into a crime scene and will take something away.

Examples would include leaving a fingerprint at a crime scene whilst leaving the scene with blood on their clothing or bodies. This principle has been a driving force behind modern forensic techniques; however, it should be noted that it is not absolute. A trace is not left in every instance. Factors such as environmental conditions, the type of materials involved, and the passage of time can affect whether a trace is left or detected. With the introduction of television shows such as CSI, offenders are developing *'forensic awareness.'* Forensic awareness refers to **an offender's knowledge or understanding of the importance of forensic evidence (e.g., DNA, fingerprints, dental impressions) to police investigation.**[100]

Other examples are offenders wearing balaclavas and gloves. With the introduction of CCTV, offenders are known to wear a face covering. More recent considerations include offenders cleaning up a crime scene or 'staging' a crime scene. You will read more about that in the chapter *"Crime Scene Staging."*

Lochard's Exchange Principle has stood the test of scientific time for over one hundred years. Then the murder of Bruce Schuler came along,

---

[100] **Davies 1992**

where this scientific principle was thrown out with the baby's bath water.

In the case of Bruce Schuler, he left no forensic trace that he had ever been at Crime Scene One. As his body has never been found, it is not known if he took any forensic evidence away with him from either crime scene. Similarly, he left no forensic footprint on his journey from scene one to scene two. He did leave his forensic footprint at Crime Scene Two, including some curious trace evidence. I consider it to be suspicious trace evidence as you will read.

Stephen Struber and Dianne Wilson both left no forensic trace at scene one, and neither person took any forensic evidence away from there. Stephen Struber and Dianne Wilson left no forensic trace between that scene and scene two, and did not take any forensic evidence away with them from scene two.

There were two crime scenes and three individuals to leave evidence at and take evidence away from. Ten separate and distinct occasions where, if you accept Locard's Principle, trace evidence should have been found. Of those ten instances, trace evidence was found only once. Nine separate instances where a proven scientific principle failed spectacularly.

On the Crown case, Bruce Schuler ran from Crime Scene One to Crime Scene Two. It could be argued that area of approximately 140 metres was also a crime scene. Again, we do not know if Bruce Schuler took anything away from that crime scene, but he certainly did not leave anything behind. Neither did the Strubers, if they even had the time to go there, which seems unlikely. That would extrapolate the number of times the Principle failed to fifteen. What are the numerical chances of that happening in one investigation.

But it gets worse (for the Crown case). Palmerville Station was declared a Crime Scene. Scenes of Crime officers (SOCOS) were not only searching for evidence at, and in the gully, they searched both Struber vehicles, as well as the Homestead and all the outbuildings and outstations. That again extrapolates the number of opportunities to take and leave trace evidence. Consider the Struber 4x4 utilities for starters.

Regardless of whether one or both vehicles went to the burnt patches, no trace evidence was located in, or on either vehicle.

Because of the steep incline of the area where this supposedly occurred, the body would have needed to be strapped down to prevent it rolling off the vehicle. Another consideration.

The offenders allegedly moved a body using a vehicle. You would also expect to find trace evidence on the occupants, their clothes, their bodies, and their boots and so on. There was *no* blood, *no* DNA, *no* physical evidence, on or in the vehicles or on either of the offenders or their clothing.

And the same with the Homestead, the caravan Dianne was sleeping in, the outbuildings and other structures on the Station. No trace evidence was found. (Add countless instances to the calculations.)

I mention this elsewhere, but it is prudent to repeat it here. Apart from the claims of the prospectors, what evidence is there to link the Strubers to this crime?

Stephen Struber left school at fifteen. He was apparently very good with his hands at boiler making and mechanical work. Dianne Wilson had lived her entire life on Palmerville Station. She was home schooled to grade four level. Her favourite television program was 'Home and Away,' yet this couple was sufficiently skilled to defy a well-established scientific principle and destroy *all* forensic evidence.

What conclusions can be reached from this? Would it be statistically impossible for the principle to fail countless times, in such a short period of time and space, and in the one crime scene?

Was the police investigation so poor, significant forensic evidence was missed? The fact blood was found on leaves, ground cover and some rocks over that huge area would suggest otherwise[101].

Were the crime scenes swept by the offenders to remove all traces of evidence? There is a well document time constraint here, as given by the prospectors. It may have been possible for the Strubers to have removed all Schuler's personal belongings at the same time they

---

[101] Defence Admissions at trial

removed his body, but vital evidence was missed at Crime Scene Two. I do not believe the offenders had sufficient time to do all that and burn the ground cover as well. I doubted this couple were aware of the implications of forensic evidence and how to destroy it?

Was Crime Scene Two or both crime scenes staged? That is a possibility that appears was never considered. I discuss that in a later chapter appropriately called '*Crime Scene Staging.*'

What was the Strubers' motive for murdering Bruce Schuler? As you read, none was proffered. Revenge for the confrontation at the Croc Hole was a big call. As you read, Stephen Struber had a long history of evicting trespassers off the property. Judge Henry commented Schuler was killed because he was trespassing[102]. Zero to murder over a minor matter?

We will have to see what the evidence determines.

---

[102] J Henry Day 6

The only thing I regret Sarge

Who could forget Dan Bidner's remorseful comment to Detective O'Brien on Monday 9 July, when he was reporting the circumstances of the disappearance of their missing friend Bruce Schuler.

Bidner: '*And when it started up to move the second time, it turned around and drove back down the spur, along the river, back towards the homestead. The **only thing I regret, Sarge**, is I didn't lift my head up to, because I was scared, you know, worried.*'

'*But that's understandable.*'

Bidner: '*I didn't lift my head high to visually get a visual. I **lifted my head a little bit**, but I **didn't stand up**. And I just saw, like, the top bars of the car, you know, like the roof and the top bars.*'

Bidner was insinuating of course, had he stood up and had a proper look, he would have likely seen Bruce Schuler's lifeless body on the rear tray of the utility as it trundled past. But he was scared. This was a combat zone after all; shots were being fired, and the prospectors had brought metal detectors to a gun fight. Just as in the trenches of the Western Front of World War One and at Gallipoli, soldiers had to look over the parapet to fire, an invitation to cop a bullet to the head from an enemy sniper.

Twenty-four hours later, Dan Bidner repeated his version of events for his statement at Mareeba Police Complex. A written record of exactly what happened; something the investigators could rely on to determine exactly what happened and who was implicated. Something the prosecutor could rely on to prepare his prosecution. On this occasion he said:

'*Then from my position I saw the top of the ute. It was below me. I was looking down into the main Palmer River. I watched the vehicle* *disappear towards the homestead. I **did not stand up** and get a look at who was in it or who was on it…*

There it was again. Another positive claim that he did not stand up. A reliable witness. An honest witness. Another hint that had he stood up, he would have likely seen Bruce Schuler's lifeless body on the tray of the 4x4. If the vehicle was travelling away from him as he claimed, why didn't he stand up and see if anything was on the tray?

As you have read, that interview was also audio recorded. As well as the above which appeared in the statement, the below comments were recorded but were not added to the statement:

'Once that vehicle left, I rose from my, my position and I gingerly and carefully walked back, wondering whether they would, whether they would have left someone there, you know, like, he's gone back and left her, and then I thought to myself, I've never seen them separated, so I don't think they'd ever separate, you know, they always act as a pair, yep, to back each other up, um, which is their general, ah habit, from past experience'

How did he know so much about the Strubers? He had met them once. Were his comments true? There it was again. (He did not stand up). He rose from his position after the event. Three days later, Bidner was back at the crime scene doing a walk through. The re-enactment was videotaped. On that occasion he had this to say about looking over the parapet:

'As you can hear, it's getting louder and louder. I can hear it getting level with me.

*I rose to **my haunches.** I took my hat off and put it down there so as not to be seen. And as you can witness, you can just see the roof of that vehicle.'*

The witness version has changed from '*I lifted my head a little bit, but I didn't stand up,*' to '*I rose to my haunches*'. **In three days**. The witness has changed his version of events, significantly. But it gets worse. The problem with that dialogue, is that it was not what the video vision showed.

This witness is 193 centimetres tall (6'4"). The vision showed the witness rising to his haunches from his sitting position and then rise to his full height to enable him to see the roof of the vehicle. The video did not show his feet, but from his stance in the video, it was possible he was *even on his tiptoes.*

In the space of three days Bidner had moved from '*I did not stand up*' to '*I rose to my haunches*' whereas the witness could be clearly seen standing fully erect. Of course, he may not have been in exactly the same position as the day of the event, except he was emphatic he was in the same position. It appeared he changed his version to suit the circumstances. This significant evidence change was in the presence and hearing of the two detectives who had previously interviewed him only days before, but apparently, nothing was said.

This is a witness who was very specific and very precise with his language. On this occasion he had forgotten what he said two times previously, only shortly before. Two days later they returned and mapped the area with GPS mapping equipment and witness Bidner again confirmed his position on the ground.

The police and witness conducted a further re-enactment on 1 August 2012. On this occasion the video showed the witness standing his full height as the vehicle drove past.

'*I heard the vehicle start up. I got up off there, I was sitting there just below that peg and I* **walked up here** *as I could hear the vehicle coming along the river here; so, I got up here just to check the vehicle going past. And I just observed the top of the roof of the vehicle, and I observed it was the vehicle I observed at the first position I showed you.*'

Now Bidner has gone from '*I lifted my head a little bit, but I didn't stand up,*' to '*I rose to my haunches*' to '*I walked up here....*'

Was his complete change of evidence due to stress, trauma, memory fog, PTSD? I saw and heard none of that whilst reading the statement, listening to the audio and watching the videos. Many times. You may have heard of witnesses who lie in court to ensure a conviction. Was this witness lying even before he got to court? His evidence of what he saw did not alter, at all, and therefore there was no need to lie. Bidner's change of evidence did not further implicate the Strubers, so why change it?

But think about it. He had to see part of the vehicle but *not* see the whole utility. If he saw the utility tray, he would have had to say that he did or did not see Bruce Schuler's body, on the tray. Think about those implications. Up to that point and even beyond, the witnesses were not accusing the Strubers of murder, the police jumped to that conclusion. All the prospectors said was that they heard two shots, and their best mate was missing. But with police watching him during the re-enactment, it was obvious to all he *had* to stand up to see even a glimpse of the vehicle.

Forget the other 140 odd discrepancies for the moment and focus on this one discrepancy. Were the investigators and the prosecutor aware of it? It was as obvious as the nose on your face. Detectives O'Brien and Riles had surely told the other investigators of the changes in Bidner's testimony. The senior detective assigned the role of 'reader' would have read the statement and watched the re-enactment. If the investigators all said 'no, we didn't know about it', what does that tell you about the calibre of the investigation and prosecution. If all the investigators said 'yes, we knew about it', again what does that tell you about the calibre of the investigation and the prosecution.

Does a 'yes' mean they concluded Bidner was lying, or he was suffering PTSD? They must have concluded he was suffering PTSD because if they admitted he was lying, that would be a rabbit hole they would not have been keen to venture down. I wonder what blind Freddy would have made of Bidner's evidence? Detective Sergeant McLeish was already on the record to me disputing there were numerous inconsistencies with the prosecutors' evidence.

I am keen to hear his take on this inconsistency. Was this a minor discrepancy or a significant discrepancy in his view? I say it was a significant discrepancy. It went to Bidner's honesty, and his truthfulness, both of which he failed miserably.

A true believer might say' *that proves nothing. Maybe he was in the wrong position on the day the Struber vehicle drove past.*' And that was exactly what Bidner said three years later at trial. But it still didn't stop him changing his evidence. A true believer would have been disappointed by Bidner's evidence at trial.

Fast forward three years to July 2015, the murder trial. At examination-in-chief the following evidence was given:

Prosecutor:' *Did you see anything after the vehicle.*'

Bidner: '*After the vehicle - from where I was on that terrace, I had a slight view down into the river and I saw - witnessed the vehicle - I heard the vehicle drive off and I could hear it coming around my - from the gully's direction.*'

P:' *Yes.?*'

Bidner*:*' *And then go back down into the Palmer River and start driving along the riverbank, back along the way it came from.*'

P:' *And could you see the vehicle?*'

Bidner*:*' *And that's when I slightly lifted myself up from my position and I witnessed the top of that vehicle heading back to the homestead.*'

P: '*Did you see any other parts of the vehicle?*'

Bidner*:* '*No, just the cab. I didn't get high enough to witness the back tray or anything like that.*'

Prosecutor Rees had the police file including the re-enactment videos, the interview transcripts and the witness statements. Was there any alternate conclusion than the witness was lying.

Under cross examination, it could be considered Bidner's 'hour of shame':

Trevino:' *Going back to exhibit 2, do you see that position, N44?*

Bidner*:*' *Yes*'

T:' *Do you see the writing underneath? It says: Bidner hears second shot.*'

Bidner*:*' *Yep*'

T:' You dispute that's where you...?'

Bidner*:' yes. I dispute that.'*

T:' ...heard the second shot. You weren't at that location?

Bidner*: 'On the second shot, I was closer to my first position.'*

Despite three walk throughs, and confirmed by GPS mapping, by the time the matter reached court three years later, the witness decided he was not in that position when he heard the second shot. Was that because he realised he had changed his evidence? He would have been encouraged to read his statement before entering the witness box. *The 'I did not stand up*' comment was right there at point 83 of his statement.

T:' You say you saw or heard a car travelling down this road here, on this track near the river?'

Bidner*:' Yes.'*

T:' When you were at that location, N44, you were low to the ground?'

Bidner*:' Yes.'*

T:' You didn't stand up at any stage?'

Bidner*: 'Yes. I did.'*

T:' Until after the car had driven past?'

Bidner*:' No. I stood up to watch it drive past, to make sure that was the vehicle I heard, to make sure they were returning to the homestead or - to make sure that vehicle was leaving the area, so I felt safe to - '*

T:' You say that you..?'

Bidner*:' leave my position.'*

T:' You say that you stood up at that location?'

Bidner*:' Yes.'*

T:' And when you stood up, then you could see the cab?'

Bidner*: 'Yes.'*

T:' So do you mean the actual cab of the LandCruiser?'

Bidner*:' Yes.'*

T:' The whole of it?'

Bidner: 'Most of the cab. Yes.'

T:" Not just the top part?'

Bidner:' Just the - just the top part. Yes.'

T:' So your evidence today is that you stood up so you could get a look at it as it passed by?'

Bidner:' Yes.'

T:' Has that always been your evidence?'

Bidner:' Yes.'

T:' You gave your statement to police on the 10th of July 2012. I suggest that you said this:

I did not stand up and get a look at who was in it or who was on it.'

Bidner:" Yes.'

T:' Is that true?'

Bidner:' I didn't stand out of the gully, didn't - I don't mean - that's just a technical, like - "

T:' Well, we - just go back?

Bidner - Well. Let me put it to you. I was there; I stood up in the gully. The gully has a bench about two feet high on the edge of it. I didn't step onto that bench to get a better purchase for my look.'

T: 'I suggest to you —-'

Bidner: 'Had I gone up onto the edge of that gully and stood on there, that was what I meant by that statement. And I stick to that.'

T: 'I suggest what you said in your statement to police was:

I did not stand up.'

Bidner:' I just explained that to you.'

T: 'I did not stand up and get a look at who was in it or who was on it.'

Bidner: 'Yes'

T: 'Do you accept that you said that.'

Bidner: *'I - I may've. But meaning—.'*

T: *'Did you say it or not?'*

Bidner: *'Yes. I probably did say that, because it was always in my intention to say I didn't look higher to see the full view of the vehicle.'*

T: *'So, by stand up, you mean walk up to the top of the gully?'*

Bidner: *'Yes.'*

T: *'And do you accept that you go on to say in your statement, the 10th of July 2012:*

Once that vehicle left, I rose from my position.

Bidner: *'yes.'*

T: *'Well, aren't you meaning to imply that you were sitting down or low to the ground.'*

Bidner: *'How does that mean I'm sitting? I rose from my position; that doesn't mean I stood from my position. I rose from - whether I was on my haunches or whatever, I rose from my position, and I returned to where I was.'*

T: *'When you were—?'*

Bidner: *'To where Bruce was.'*

T: *'When you were asked by Detective Sergeant Nicholas O'Brien on the 9th of July —?'*

Bidner: *'Listen, that was not- that was not - that was a verbal conversation over the phone.'*

T: *'Yes?'*

Bidner: *'At about midnight.'*

T: *'It was at —?'*

Bidner: *'After talking to several policemen all night long.'*

T: *'It was after 9.10 at night?'*

Bidner: *'Yeah. I bet it was late, because I spoke to police from 6 o'clock till midnight that night.'*

T: 'You told Nicholas O'Brien that you regretted not getting - standing up- get a better look?'

Bidner: 'A better look, because then I might have seen Bruce on the back of that vehicle. That is correct.'

T: 'But what you told Nicholas O'Brien was you regretted not standing up to get a better look?'

Bidner: 'Yes. Not standing up to a better perch's position.'

T: 'In fact, you didn't stand up at that position. You were crouching low at it, weren't you.'

Bidner: 'That's your story mate. My story is I was standing there. I was squatting in that gully hiding.'

T: 'From your position it would have been impossible for you to see anything of the car driving…?'

Bidner: 'That's bullshit. when I showed the police my position on that day I said to them, as you can see - the police were standing beside me on the re-enactment and I said, As you can see from this position I can see that vehicle.'

T: 'Days later?'

Bidner: 'Days later.

T: 'After this car leaves you went back to the gully. Is that right?'

Bidner: 'Yeah, I've told you that several times.'

What did Mr Trevino have to say about witness Bidner and this portion of his evidence during summing up to the jury? He did not miss him: '*Bidner was prepared to argue, to dissemble, and to obfuscate on that issue. And you might think that that type of behaviour throws considerable doubt on the reliability of what he told you.*' It was disappointing the Defence barrister did not have the Court play the recording of the telephone call with O'Brien, and then play the video of the re-enactment, and then ask Bidner again to explain his movements.

None of the evidence Bidner gave regarding seeing the vehicle drive past his location proved the Strubers did or did not murder Bruce

Schuler, but it certainly cast strong doubt on his truthfulness and credibility as a witness. As well, Bidner was insinuating he spent all night up to midnight talking to police. He had two phone calls, a total of no more than thirty minutes, ending around 9.30 p.m.

If you accepted that Bidner was lying about that evidence, and that was likely the only conclusion that could be drawn, it begged the question if he lied about any of the other claims he made. Was there any reason why he needed to lie? If it was to ensure convictions were obtained, how would he explain the numerous discrepancies that occurred before the trial.

As you read just a few short chapters ago, the Crown made several admissions upon closing its case. Curiously, the Crown did not admit the evidence you just read; and I believe it was as strong or stronger than the denial Dan Bidner made about not returning to the point in the road where the alleged Struber vehicle did the u-turn. I note that neither Defence counsel objected to that Admission not being tendered.

Knocking on Heaven's Door

The discrepancies continued to mount, and this anomaly was of great concern to me.

The investigators were clearly aware of and ignored this clearly suspicious claim made by prospector Anderson. On the one hand the prospectors feared the Strubers, and worried they too may be stalked and shot, and in the same breath they were knocking on the door to the Strubers' *lair* at a time when they were claiming to be elsewhere. Illogical. Whilst it does not prove or disprove the Strubers were the offenders, the investigators must have realised the prospectors were being untruthful, repeatedly, and they seemingly ignored it.

Did Tremain Anderson walk to Palmerville homestead and knock on the door on Monday 9 July 2012 between 3.30 p.m. and 4.30 p.m. during his extensive searches for Bruce Schuler? If he made that claim up, what was his reasoning for so doing? I also wonder why police seemingly pretended it never happened. Bizarre.

This *is* the crux of the case. The witnesses' credibility, reliability and honesty. They had already been shown to be less than honest in relation to many aspects of the evidence.

The Palmerville Homestead is located on the southern side of the Palmer River, just as the prospectors' camp was. They were around two kilometres apart. The gully where Bruce Schuler was last seen was located 900 metres from the camp, on the northern side of the Palmer. You may recall the prospectors recounted how they had to remove their boots to wade across the river to go prospecting.

It is not necessary to detail every single time that Tremain Anderson claimed to have walked as far as opposite the homestead whilst looking for Bruce Schuler. There were a number. But here is just one.

In his Tuesday night statement at point 37 he said in part:

'Whilst Dan was gone, I had been back down the river and I was now looking for blood, scanning everywhere. I was freaking as it was 3.00 p.m. in the afternoon, and we had gun shots fired at around 10:00 a.m. and two men missing. I pretty much went to opposite Palmerville Station and yelled out, 'Bruce, Kevin. There were no replies, no nothing.'

And incidentally, that was the only time Tremain Anderson said he was also searching for Kevin. On all other occasions he only mentioned Bruce when he claimed he was searching.

To readers unaware of police procedures, in the Queensland Police Service at any rate, diaries were issued to detectives and notebooks to uniformed police and first responders. I expect other states had similar procedures. They were required to record their activities during their shift and to make, amongst other things, notes of events for later reference and court hearings. Perhaps notebooks and diaries have been phased out with the introduction of Ipads and BWC – body worn cameras.

During a significant investigation, such as Operation Kilo Principle, there would be regular briefings for all staff involved in the investigation. The briefings may be held morning and afternoon, daily, start and end of a shift or as required. It is usual for staff to make relevant notes in their diaries during those briefings. For instance, Detective Riles was not at Palmerville Station when he made the entry in his diary. He was at Mareeba conducting investigations from there. There would have also been regular briefings held at Mareeba for staff involved in Operation Kilo Principle. Briefings may also have been held at Cairns Police Station for police working from there.

Detective McLeish's entry on the second page of his diary after he started recording entries for Kilo Principle was as follows:

- *1000 - Briefing with 3 witnesses.*
- *Daniel BIDNER.*
- *Kevin 'Rusty' GROTH.*
- *Tremaine ANDERSON (sic).*

- 0930 - 1000 hrs - first shot fired.
- *Tremaine to homestead 1530 hrs.*
- Struber's ute not present.
- Yelled repeatedly - no one came out of house.
- NB Medical conditions for Schuler REDACTED.

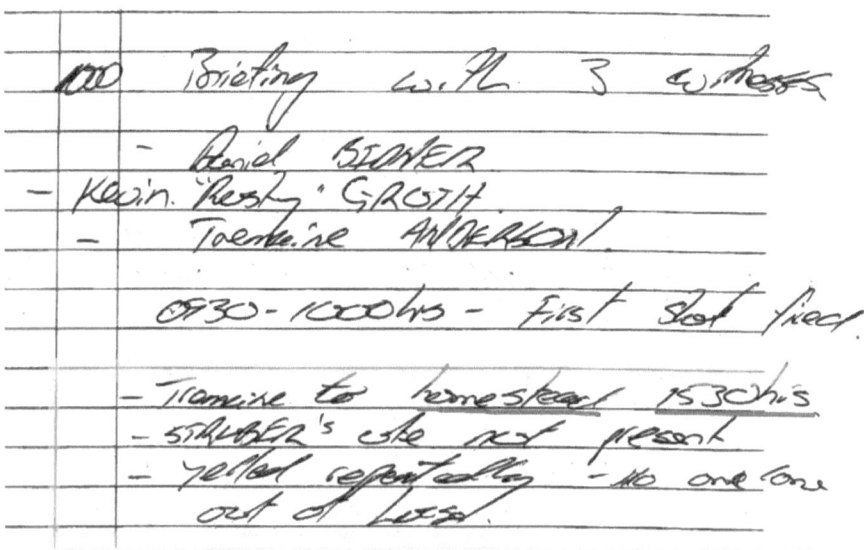

It would be difficult to arrive at any conclusion other than Tremain Anderson told Detective Sergeant McLeish personally of that visit to the homestead, and McLeish made contemporaneous notes of their names, the timing of the event and a significant occurrence such as going to the homestead. What, if anything, did Detective McLeish do with that information and why was it not in Anderson's statement. Was it considered irrelevant? Was it considered inappropriate or not in line with the Crown case?

Detective Sergeant Riles was called out on overtime to assist with the investigation on Tuesday 10 July 2012. He was working from Mareeba Police Station and was given a briefing on the disappearance of Bruce Schuler. The first page of his diary for that day recorded the briefing he attended. He noted relevant details of the disappearance. At the very bottom of that first page of his diary he wrote:

- *Anderson goes to homestead at **1630 hrs** (4.30pm) and can't find anyone.*

The other entries in the diary were factual. There would be no reason to believe that entry was also not factual. Riles then went on to obtain the lengthy statement from Dan Bidner on the Tuesday night, at Mareeba Station and diary entries for that event covered multiple pages. What did police investigators do with that information?

From what is known, nothing. It did not appear Tremain Anderson was ever challenged about that claim. It was apparently said Tuesday morning, but by Tuesday night the narrative had changed. That should have been a major red flag for investigators, but was seemingly ignored, along with many other red flags.

What are the implications if Anderson had in fact walked to Palmerville homestead? Firstly, the time factor. It would have taken at least two hours to walk there and back. I have viewed the re-enactment video of the drive from the homestead to Crime Scene One.

The ground is uneven, rough, the creek bed was very sandy. Anderson and Groth claimed they met up around 3.15 p.m. back at the riverbed camp when, on his claim to Detective McLeish, he would have been very close to, or at the Palmerville homestead.

And what of Officer Riles diary entry? He was told Anderson was at the homestead at 4.30 p.m. The prospectors claimed Dan Bidner returned from Maytown at 4.30 p.m. Anderson was one hour away at that point in time. Tremain Anderson was claiming two of their party were missing and feared captured or killed by Stephen Struber and Dianne Wilson. More significantly, Anderson claimed Struber to be armed and dangerous. He had shot at him before, twice. To suggest that he then walked to their 'lair' to confront them would be stretching the boundaries of credibility. He could have been knocking on Heaven's Door. Best to forget that scenario.

Were the Defence barristers aware of Anderson's claim? Apparently not. They should have had access to the police diaries, but the fact it was not raised in evidence would suggest they were not aware of this bizarre claim.

Once again, I do not consider that to be a minor discrepancy. I see it as a major red flag in a bunting of flags. It goes to the witnesses' credibility. Were they being truthful and honest?

Bruce Phone Home

And yet another discrepancy. Or was it? Everything is on the table for consideration. You have read about the note the prospectors placed under the driver's side wiper blade of Bruce Schuler's 4x4 telling him to call the prospectors at Maytown. By necessity, to validate the prospectors' claims, I needed to drill down into that claim, and verify it. Once again, it failed the sniff test.

The note was allegedly placed under the wiper blade on the Monday afternoon around 4.30 p.m. before the prospectors returned to Bidner's camp. It was written on A4 paper. Where did that size paper come from? Do prospectors usually carry A4 paper around with them? First problem. Was it perhaps written by Biden in Maytown whilst waiting for Anderson's 3 p.m. call? Problem solved. Except he told police they wrote the note in camp.

You may recall police recorded video and photographs of the note under the windscreen wiper. I placed that video along with photographs clipped from the video, on the Facebook group page and my YouTube channel. Once again, podcast listeners stepped up.

Listeners pointed out the inconsistency between the volume of debris that had accumulated on the passenger wiper blade, in comparison to the driver's wiper blade, and they were correct. The vehicle, based on the prospector's evidence, had sat parked and unmoved in that spot for around two days, by the time the police inspected it. The driver's wiper blade would have been disturbed when the note was placed under it, about twenty hours before. Or about halfway.

On that basis, the debris accumulated under the driver's wiper blade should have been approximately half the volume of debris under the passenger wiper blade. Upon inspection of the video and the photographs, it was evident the driver's side blade would be considered pristine, when compared to the debris on the left side blade. The only conclusion that could be reached, if the left side blade was considered the benchmark, was that the note had not sat there for almost one full day. Was the note placed there early Tuesday morning? If it was, why was there a need to lie about it?

And of concern, the same note said the prospectors had Bruce Schuler's dog with them, yet one officer's diary noted the dog was at the camp when police arrived on the Tuesday morning. Mistake? Or was the dog returned there Tuesday morning along with the note? Or never taken. To be accurate, the dog was never visible in the police video, nor was it mentioned in any other officer's notebook. Listeners questioned the wording in the note. *'We have the dog'*. Why wouldn't they write *'We have Red Dog?'* That I would consider a small discrepancy and hardly worth mentioning, but I do not see my role to pick and choose what is of no consequence. Was Dan Bidner aware at that time, Schuler did not have his satellite phone? If so, why write the note to call them? It tends to add weight to the suspicion the prospectors knew Bruce Schuler did not have his satellite phone with him, as they never tried to call him. Not once.

Kevin and Tremain meet up

It seemed innocuous enough. The two prospectors described how they met back at camp after an apparently traumatic event (although that too is a matter up for discussion in a later chapter). If all aspects of the prospector's testimony are under the microscope, then this event would also have to be closely examined. It too did not pass the sniff test. If you recall, Tremain and Kevin could also not agree on who was last in camp on the Sunday night, after prospecting in the afternoon.

The prospectors told police this story just one day after the event; it should have been still a vivid recollection. They then repeated it for the camera mere days later. Surely it was still a vivid memory. Of course, taken in isolation it is just one small anomaly; I nearly didn't add it. Remember what Prosecutor Rees told the jury, '*I concede there were inconsistencies.*'

Was he referring to this one? We will never know as that was the only mention he made of them. Maybe he knew there were a lot of inconsistencies? After all, his concession did not say, 'I concede there were a few minor inconsistencies.'

The time was apparently around 3.15 p.m. The location was the camp they had set up in the river, or perhaps 100 metres away from it toward the crossing, depending on whose version of events you accept. Groth had been missing for around six hours. Anderson had been heading out to do some more gold detecting to fill in time until Bidner returned from Maytown, or was he heading back to camp after changing his mind? Again, whichever version you accept.

On Tuesday night they gave their first account of the afternoon. At point 28 of his statement, Groth said this:

'I *left the trees around 3:00 p.m. because I* saw Tremain walk out in the open *near our camp. I then got up and grabbed my gear, detector and pick and proceeded to go to camp where Tremain was.* Tremain was a fair way in front of me sitting down having a drink. *Tremain said to me 'We been worried we've been looking for you.'*

There was certainly no confusion there. Kevin Groth was quite clear on where Anderson was when he first saw him. He even recalled what Tremain said to him and the fact he was having a beer.

The same night, Anderson said this at point 39 of his statement:' *I walked back across the river again towards the car about fifteen minutes later and next minute Kevin yells out, 'Oy.' I got a fright.* He was near the car. *I said, 'Bloody hell I have been searching for you all morning.'*

They could not both be correct. At least one of them was confused. Did the police investigators not challenge both and say, '*tell us again about meeting up?*'

Two days later Groth said this during the re-enactment:

'*then I'd seen about three o'clock I see somebody crossing the crossing there in the end of in the creek in the river and I watched that was Tremain* he's heading back to camp *walking straight out and open so once I seen him heading down through there yeah out and open he would never got challenged on even they'll be saying out to him anything like that I decided to get up and follow him in the camp yeah that was....* '

Groth followed him into camp he said. He didn't mention Tremain was sitting down having a beer by the time he arrived there.

Anderson said this the following day during his re-enactment,

'*I've come back across the main river crossing where we all proceeded from this morning. Back towards the car, sat down, had a beer. Anyway, and then Kevin's come out of the blue. Frightened the living day. Where did you come are from? I'm proceeding to give him a hard time. I've been looking for you all morning.*'

Anderson had now switched the narrative from Groth arriving first to him arriving back at camp first. Had they compared stories and aligned them? Did no police officer pick that up? Did they even read the Tuesday night statements and compare them to the re-enactments? Were they not concerned? Even their timing was out. Tremain said he phoned Dan Bidner around 3.15 p.m. and Dan said he was an hour away. Consistent with events so far. Kevin Groth even confirmed the telephone call between Anderson and Bidner. He then said, '*A short time later Danny arrived.*'[103]

Now, at the trial three years later, Anderson told the court at examination-in-chief that after bumping into Kevin, '*we went back to Bruce's car and just sat down and I think we had a beer each.*' He added that he then called Jo Bidner, and told her Rusty had turned up. Basically, word for word of what Kevin Groth had in his statement to police on 10 July 2012. For once, the prospectors were starting to align their evidence. Or read each other's statements.

Once again, those discrepancies go to their credibility. The suspicion of course is they just made up the versions on the fly.

---

[103] Statement by K Groth

Shots Fired

What did the jury hear or not hear, in respect of who fired the shots and what sort of weapons were used, that Monday Bruce Schuler went missing? Very little actually. In examination-in-chief, Dan Bidner told the jury he saw a .22 calibre lever action rifle, the same as was missing from the homestead. But that was nothing like what the prospectors told the police during their investigations.

And more importantly and relevant to the prosecution of Struber and Wilson, why were the jury not told details of the weapons fired?

If Struber and Wilson went to the area above Crime Scene One, which they strenuously denied, then it came down to the credibility of the witnesses. The witnesses said the Strubers were there. The Strubers said they were not. What did the witnesses see and hear? Let's explore it witness by witness. The main witness to the type of weapon used was Daniel Bidner.

None of the witnesses saw anyone fire a weapon, so it was purely speculation as to who fired the shots, and it was purely speculation that Bruce Schuler was even shot to death. Frankly, as you will read, you could not rely on Daniel Bidner to truthfully tell you who arrived in the gully, or if anyone apart from the prospectors was even there.

The very first interaction with the police on the Monday night, as you read, was with Officer Tome of Laura Police. He wrote this in his diary:

- *'BIDNER observed Stephen STRUBER and Dianne WILSON to exit the vehicle. Wilson was carrying a rifle. Struber & Wilson have walked over to the gully. BIDNER has squatted down & could not see.'*

The second interaction with the police was around two hours later with Acting Detective Sergeant O'Brien. Bidner said this:

Bidner: *'Long rifle, it was a rifle.'*

O'B: *'OK, yep, that's fine, yep.'*

Bidner: *'All I know, a long gun.'*

O'B: *'Yep.'*

Bidner: *'I thought it was a shottie (*shotgun*) myself, but the boys said, nah,'*

And by itself that would not be problematic. Traumatic event. Shot fired. Running and ducking for cover. So why was there a need to keep changing the narrative?

He told Officer Tome he squatted down and could not see. He told Officer O'Brien: *'then I saw her bring the gun out of the car and I went, oh, shit. So, I sort of, I got up and I thought I'll take the risk here of moving, you know what I mean?'*

To be fair, O'Brien's conversation was recorded, Tome was taking notes. We should give the witness the benefit of the doubt. Tome's notes were so comprehensive perhaps we shouldn't.

When Bidner was interviewed the following night, just twenty-four hours later, the audio captured the following:

'At that stage, the car stops quickly. Comes to a stop. Both doors bail. Before he even comes around the front of the car, I see her pull the gun from behind the seat.'

This was written between points 72 to 74:'

'Her door opened and she got out. Then she flicked the seat forward and then I saw her pull a gun from behind the seat. ...The gun had a black stick shape. I didn't know if it was a rifle or a shotgun but with that I turned while I was crouching and walked about 50 metres. ...It sounded like a shotgun going off.'

But later in the same audio recorded interview, the following conversation which again never made it to statement form, occurred:

Riles: *'She got out?*

Bidner: *'Yeah, she got out. I can see he's getting out too. Still turning the car off. She's a bit quicker than him. Her door first, his second. Then she's flicked the seat forward. And that's the last thing I saw.'*

R:' *Describe the gun for me.'*

Bidner:' *Oh mate. Black stick, that long. That's all I saw. Wouldn't know it was a rifle, a shotgun, what.'*

R: '*But how did you know that it was a rifle or a firearm?*'

Bidner: *'Because that's what she does. She keeps it there all the time bro.'*

Just to refresh your memory, Bidner met Dianne Wilson for the first time less than two weeks prior. How would he know that?

And as you will read later, Bidner apparently did see the sort of weapon Dianne was carrying, because he watched her load the weapon in an up and down motion, just as a Winchester lever action rifle is loaded.

It seemed to me on both Monday night phone calls, Bidner was quite explicit. He saw Dianne exit the vehicle with the gun, but as you read, that morphed.

Obviously, defence counsel had read the statements but had not listened to the audio nor read the police notebooks, or they would have been alerted to the changes in versions of events. Significantly, Bidner described the weapon as a black stick and was not sure what sort of rifle despite previously he was sure it was a shotgun.

He then said:' *It sounded like a shotgun going off,*' a̲nd as what was to become significant, he moved away 50 metres.

At the re-enactment conducted just three days later, on 13 July Bidner said this:

Bidner: *'I saw her, what looked to be her flipping the seat forward, like making the seat bow forward, and then reaching behind the seat for what to me, at this distance, was definitely a rifle.'*

R: *'Describe it further for me, if you can.'*

Bidner: *'I remember seeing a blackish coloured stock, a barrel, and a lighted coloured, a brownie lighted coloured stock.'*

The witness had graduated from a black stick, not sure whether it was a rifle or a shotgun to describing a rifle down to the colour of the stock.

Later in the same re-enactment:

Bidner: *'Well, I'd say it would have been close to something like my .357, because my .357 and my .22 are the only ones that have a lever action. Okay. And it looked a lot like my .357.*

R: *'Okay, and that's dimensions you're talking there? Dimensions, not colour. What's your experience with firearms?*

Bidner: *'I own three firearms, or four firearms. I own a pellet gun, I own a .357 Magnum rifle, I also own a .243 rifle, and a .22 Winchester Magnum.'*

At this point, Bidner is back to it being a rifle, not a shotgun. Now he is suggesting it was a lever action rifle. To explain, a lever action rifle is loaded in a downward and upward motion with the lever enclosed around the trigger. He was using his experience with firearms (which he denied as you will read) to suggest the weapon he saw was the size of his own .357 Magnum rifle. In comparison to a .22 lever action rifle, the .357 would be larger, sturdier, louder.

On 15 July 2012, when the crime scene was forensically mapped, the GPS calculated distance that Bidner first moved after seeing Dianne exit the vehicle was seventy-six metres. A long way from fifteen to twenty metres. A very long way. At trial, and under cross-examination, he disputed he was that far away and was much closer to his original position.

Later in the audio interview Bidner said this:

'And Tremain has seen them pull the gun many times. He has had it pointed at him on a couple of occasions and he reckons it is a lever action 30/30. But I wouldn't know that bro, I've never seen it.'

Bidner telling the police he had seen 'them' pull the gun many times would help reinforce a claim the Strubers were dangerous. To reinforce that threat with police, in his Tuesday night statement at point 72, Bidner said:' *As soon as I saw it come out of the car I thought "shit, she's got it. She's got the gun.'*

To my mind when he said, *'she's got the gun'* as opposed to *'she's got a gun'*, he was suggesting this was not the first time it had happened.

Tremain Anderson told police Dianne pointed a 30/30 rifle on him once, and on the second occasion he was behind a rock when Stephen Struber was firing a shotgun in his direction.

Which again raised the question as to why they would go on to Palmerville Station, and camp so close to the homestead if they were dangerous and known to pull rifles and point them at them. Or as Anderson would say,' *they would fire it over your head. That's what they do.'*

Bidner also had this to say:

'I find it ironic that you bastards turn up at my place with a bloody SWAT team for a bloody bit of personal cultivation you know and here's a bloody attempted murder and they turn up with six coppers in two cars for a bloody suspected murder. I find it ironic mate.'

One hundred kilograms of marihuana for personal use. Was Dan Bidner so drug-addled, so stoned on the day Schuler went missing, he had no idea what happened and consequently there were so many inconsistencies in his evidence? That may have been the case but listening to the audio and watching the video, I would strongly argue against that. He had total recall. His drug addled brain would also have had no impact on the disturbing lack of forensic evidence and other problems with the Crown case.

At the committal hearing in 2014 Bidner's evidence changed once again:'

'I cant be sure it was a gun but it sure as hell looked like a gun to me. I'm 100% sure it was a rifle yes'.

But then changed that to he was 100% sure it was a gun.

He made no mention of the firearm being a lever action rifle. He then told the court he moved about fifteen metres away. In his first statement he told police he moved fifty metres, and before that, he was 150 metres away from the Strubers, before amending that to fifty metres.

At trial in 2015, Bidner said:'

'I've seen her turn, flipped the seat as she got out. She's flipped the seat forward and got a gun out from behind the seat. What I presumed to be a gun…It was a black stick as far - you know, I couldn't tell what make, model or what, but it looked like a gun to me. …and to me it looked like she - she looked down at it like she was loading it or something. I'm not sure.'

P: *'So let me stop you there. You say she looked down at it, and then you're gesturing with your right hand?'*

Bidner*:' Yep'*

P:*' So you're indicating a downward and upward movement?'*

Bidner*:' Yes'*

Your Honour:*' Sort of with hand - almost like a handshake going down and back?'*

Bidner*: 'Yes'*

And with that, witness Bidner is back to the weapon being a lever action rifle, the same as the missing rifle and crucial to the Crown case. Yet in cross examination, the following exchange occurred when asked if he ever thought it was a shotgun he heard:'

'I did say that at one stage because I thought that boom sounded like a shotgun. I only said that out of the – what the sound of the gun was. But I'm no expert on guns. I'm just - it was a very loud boom.'

In response to a question where he described the weapon as a shotgun, to Detective O'Brien on the night of the 9th he replied:

'Maybe I did. Only through the sound.'

The prosecutor was obviously aware of witness Bidner's evidence. He knew Bidner told police he heard a shotgun, he believed it to be a shotgun, when he wasn't believing it to be a rifle, like his own .357 magnum rifle. But he would have been delighted the witness was now describing the missing rifle.

And then in response to a further question, Bidner stated he moved up to fifty metres away as per his original claim. Not fifteen to twenty metres as he stated just six months before at the committal proceedings.

And not surprisingly, Bidner was not asked by the prosecution the type of weapon he heard discharge. Was it a shotgun? A high calibre long rifle? A .22 lever action rifle? The jury never heard what type of firearm he heard discharged, except in cross-examination when he was denying it was a shotgun.

During cross-examination by Barrister Trevino, witness Bidner obfuscated, evaded and challenged his previous evidence.

When queried as to whether he had previously mentioned the up and down movement he replied: '*I may not have.*'

And when queried why he didn't mention it at the committal proceedings he said: '*Well, as I am now, I'm only answering the questions I am asked. And when I was asked, I wasn't asked to elaborate. I was strictly asked to answer the question.*'

T: '*The question was to describe all that you could remember about that incident, wasn't it?*'

Bidner: '*That's a technicality.*'

In a conversation in 2019 with former Laura policeman Bob Haydon, Bidner told him he now believed the rifle he saw Dianne with to be a high powered 30/30 rifle, Winchester lever action rifle, *the one she always carried.* By then of course, he was aware Anderson and Groth had described the weapon as a 30/30 or high calibre rifle.

George Wilson claimed they always carried a rifle in the utilities but next to the passenger, pointing down between the seats. Within easy reach. The seats and seat backs were too hard to move back and forward. There is no record the police ever tested whether it was possible to move the seat back forward on the unregistered LandCruiser.

Catherine Cummins lived and worked on Palmerville Station for lengthy periods between 2002 and 2006. She told police whenever anyone went out in a vehicle, there was always a weapon in the car for putting down injured stock and so on. It was not a big deal.

The witnesses who told police they had had confrontations with Stephen Struber and had seen a gun, it was usually in the cabin against the seat or him or Dianne holding the barrel. Obviously, the firearm would not have been seen if it was behind the seat.

Kevin Groth was the most credible of the three prospectors. Was that simply because he saw little, heard little, knew little and therefore could not be tripped up with discrepancies because he gave such minimal evidence? As you have read, Kevin Groth saw a Toyota with a different coloured headboard and heard a weapon discharge that Monday morning, before running off into the bush for six hours.

He never saw anyone, so he was unable to give any identification evidence. In fact, he was able to provide little evidence to support the Crown case. But the weapon he heard fired was very significant for the defence case. Except the jury never heard it.

When interviewed on 10 July 2012, he said this:'

'It sounded like a large calibre rifle to me and it sounded like it was fired in the air and not into the ground. The noise it made was not muffled it was clear and very loud. There is no way I could have been confused, it was definitely a high powered rifle.'

Three months later, when again interviewed, he said at point 13:

'In paragraph 22 of my statement dated 10 July 2012 I said that the gun shot noise I heard was in the air and not in the ground. I said this because just being around rifles a little bit, just the sound, it sounded clear, the shot. It didn't sound like it had hit anything, like into the ground I suppose you would hear a thud.'

The jury never heard any of that evidence. Why was that? From his statements to police, Kevin would be considered an experienced weapon owner and user. He would be giving qualified evidence. He was very specific in his wording to police including '*definitely*'.

He was that confident of what he heard, he reiterated it three months later. I wonder what would the jury have made of that evidence? If you accepted Groth's evidence, and why wouldn't you, all Dianne Wilson was guilty of was firing a high-powered weapon into the air. I would doubt a conviction would have even been recorded, if she was charged for that offence. A far cry from dying in prison for murder.

Detective Sergeant McLeish described Stephen Struber as a bully. On that claim, if Struber and Wilson were there, was Dianne Wilson a DV victim, being forced by Stephen Struber to shoot at Bruce Schuler or go along with whatever Stephen Struber demanded, potentially in fear of her own life and so instead, she fired into the air? Speculation I know, but the Crown started it.

Barrister Trevino commented on this aspect whilst summing up to the jury:' *Even if you accept the eyewitness evidence at face value – and I don't suggest that you would, but even if you could do that, the problem that remains for the Crown is that the evidence is incomplete. It cannot assist you at all as to what unlawful acts, if any, could possibly be attributed to Dianne after the point in time that Daniel Bidner claims to have walked away from the site of that gully.'*

You may recall after the second shot Kevin Groth told police he smelt gun smoke, the smell of burnt powder when he was about 300 metres away. Many podcast listeners were very sceptical of that claim. The jury did not hear the type of weapon fired but they were told did that Kevin Groth smelt gun powder.

Tremain Anderson's evidence in relation to the type of weapon used and seen on the Monday was also limited.

When he was interviewed by police on 10 July he said:

'*I then heard a loud gun shot. It sounded like a high-powered rifle. It was probably a 30/30 which is what I have seen Dianne with in the past.* '

Once again, reinforcing with the police that the Strubers always carried weapons, and used them. During his re-enactment, Anderson stated the gun shots were definitely a high-powered rifle, not a shotgun. You would have to ask yourself whether Bidner, Groth and Anderson were witnesses to the same shooting. Bidner initially claimed it was a shotgun. The other witnesses described it as a high-powered rifle.

Anderson told police he had grown up around weapons; he knew what they sounded like. He too would be considered a qualified witness. Why wasn't his evidence heard by the jury?

All the prospectors had years of experience with firearms. They would be qualified to tell the court what sort of weapon they heard fired. It would then be up to the jury to decide what happened at the crime scenes and what sort of weapons were used.

For the podcast, I had a lengthy conversation with Alex Krystic, a former Victorian Homicide Squad and Major Crime Squad detective, a former trainer at the Victorian Detective Training School and now the owner of a ballistics testing laboratory and a leading ballistics expert in Australia.

He confirmed there is a significant sound difference between a shotgun, a 30/30 rifle and a .357 handgun due to the speed at which the round travels. He also said the efficient range of a shot gun is fifteen metres. It is not known what distance Schuler was away from Dianne Wilson, but at the very least it would be fifteen metres, and of course, that would be assuming Schuler stayed still. It was up to four minutes between the utility stopping, and the first round being fired. Were Schuler and Wilson having a Mexican stand-off, or was Schuler running up the gully. I asked Alex Krystic of the claim that someone could smell gun powder (burnt gases) at 300 metres. He believed it was not likely, but possible.

The result was the jury were blissfully ignorant of all the firearm evidence.

What was the consequence of the shots fired evidence? The defence position was very simple. They were not there that day, as you read. What would the jury have made of that evidence? Would the jury have still considered the witnesses credible and truthful? Would they have considered it likely that it supported the claims of Stephen Struber and Dianne Wilson that they were not there.

If you are wondering why the jury never heard what sort of weapons were fired, consider the Crown Prosecutor's position. There were two weapons missing from the Palmerville homestead. A .22 Remington lever action rifle, and a .357 Magnum handgun. He needed the jury to accept they were the weapons used to murder Bruce Schuler.

But what had the witnesses told police? At the first crime scene, they heard the weapon fired as either a shotgun or a high-powered rifle, whilst the second shot was a high-powered rifle. As weapons owners and users, they were qualified to give that evidence. It should have been left to the jury to decide if they knew what sort of weapon they heard. How do you sell your case to the jury when the witnesses are describing weapons that do not fit the weapons that are missing? Easy. You do not ask them if they knew what sort of weapon they heard fired. But what about the two defence counsels? Why didn't they raise it with the jury. Barrister Trevino did raise the issue of a shotgun, but did not make a big issue of it.

And anyway, the claim of the two missing weapons being the murder weapons was nonsensical. What was the Crown alleging? They were saying there was a man missing, there were two shots fired, there were two weapons missing. Ipso facto, those weapons were used to murder Bruce.

Never mind the shots fired did not align with the missing weapons. Never mind that if Bruce Schuler had been murdered with a firearm, there would likely have been brain matter, blood and intestines everywhere. Far more than could be cleaned up, especially in the restricted time frame. The Strubers were clever enough to dispose of Schuler's remains never to be seen again. They believed he was alone, and therefore they were unseen. So why dispose of the weapons at all? As the body had been disposed of, they knew none of their weapons could be connected to the crime.

And how do you correlate all this unheard evidence with the journalist's quote of Detective Sergeant McLeish:' *'And of course that revolver is missing, and the Winchester .22 she used is missing, and they've gone missing because those bullets will be in Bruce's body.'*

Was Dan Bidner even there?

In the last chapter, you read about the weapon or weapons the Strubers were allegedly carrying when they allegedly stumbled across the prospectors. But that was only half the story. This chapter addresses the other half of the same story. Did Stephen Struber get out of the vehicle, or didn't he, when the vehicle first stopped? Dan Bidner changed his evidence on this matter so much I began to wonder if he was even there. Or scarier, was Stephen Struber even there? There were questions about whether Dan Bidner identified Stephen Struber or not as well when the vehicle stopped after supposedly hearing a dog bark, but they are addressed in the next chapter.

What do we know?

In the telephone call with Laura Police, Officer Tome recorded the following notes in his diary:

- *'BIDNER observed Stephen STRUBER and Dianne WILSON to exit the vehicle. Wilson was carrying a rifle. STRUBER & WILSON have **walked over to the gully**. BIDNER has squatted down & could not see.'*

And that wasn't a short step from the car to the edge of the gully. Closer to fifty metres. To put that in context, they both got out of the utility and walked about the same length as an Olympic-size swimming pool. Bidner then squatted down and didn't see anything further. He would have had a very good view of both offenders as they walked the length of a swimming pool.

That claim started to change within two hours and by the trial three years later, he agreed he did not even see Struber get out of the car. In the second interaction two hours later with Acting Detective Sergeant O'Brien, Bidner said this:

'But at one point my last vision was him and her getting out of the car, her with the gun. So I thought, nah, I seen that gun, I went, I know I'm going to make a move here. So I walked probably 50 metres away.'

Within two hours, Bidner has gone from watching Struber and Wilson walk fifty metres to the top of the gully and then squatting down, to not seeing him even get out of the car and moving fifty metres away.

When Bidner was interviewed the following night, just twenty-four hours later, the audio captured the following:

Bidner: *'At that stage, the car stops quickly. Comes to a stop. Both doors bail. Before he even comes around the front of the car, I see her pull the gun from behind the seat.'*

Bidner's statement was taken from the audio recording of his interview and somehow that evidence morphed into there being no mention of Stephen Struber exiting the vehicle. Not that you could blame Bidner for that, as the detective prepared the statement from the audio.

Later in the same audio recorded interview, the following conversation which again never made it to his statement was heard:

Bidner: *'Yeah, she got out. I can see he's getting out too. Still turning the car off. She's a bit quicker than him. Her door first, his second. Then she's flicked the seat forward. And that's the last thing I saw.'*

In a space of twenty-four hours, this witness has changed his version of events three times. This was not a minor inconsistency, not by any chance. At the re-enactment three days later, Bidner said both doors opened but never mentioned Struber's movements. Bidner turned and walked away before he saw anything further.

In the first week after the crime, witness Bidner had Stephen Struber exiting the vehicle at Crime Scene One. He even had Struber walking over to the edge of the gully.

Two weeks later, at his second re-enactment, Bidner told police his view of Stephen Struber was obscured, but he presumed it was him in the car, because they always travel together. How did he know that? He told police he did not witness Struber come around the front of the car because he was still getting out, as she was pulling the gun out.

At the committal hearing in 2014, Bidner's evidence changed once again, and he told the court he did not see the driver.

At trial in 2015, in response to a question by the Crown Prosecutor, Bidner said in part, '..*I mean, it looked like they were both getting out of the car but from my view I could only see Dianne.*' Mr Trevino for Dianne Wilson did ask him and he stated, '*I could see the driver exiting the vehicle, but that was – that was all.*' That was a huge change from watching him walk the length of an Olympic sized swimming pool.

Under cross examination by Mr Feeney there was considerable discussion about whether Bidner did or did not recognise Stephen Struber but no questions about whether Struber did or did not get out of the vehicle. Regrettably, it would seem Mr Feeney was not aware of the evidence as outlined above. Though this question and answer summarised the matter:

F:' *The fact is, Mr Bidner, you just didn't see Stephen Struber there on the 9th of July 2012, did you?*'

Bidner:' *not - not out of the vehicle. No.*'

Not out of the vehicle.

Just consider for a moment how many times Bidner had changed his evidence about whether Stephen Struber got out of the car or not.

On the Monday night he told Officer Tome that Struber got out and walked to the gully.

On the same night he told Detective O'Brien that Struber did get out of the car. He lost sight and did not see him any further than that.

The next night he said that Struber did get out of the vehicle and came around the front of the vehicle.

But in the audio of that same interview, he lost vision just after Struber got out.

At the first re-enactment he told police both doors opened but he did not mention Struber getting out of the vehicle, just Dianne. At the second re-enactment he said Struber got out of the car, but he did not witness him walk around the front of the vehicle.

At the committal hearing Bidner did not see Stephen Struber.

As you have just read, he told the court he did not see Stephen Struber out of the vehicle. I will ask the question again. Was Stephen Struber even at the One Mile on Monday 9 July 2012? Based on Dan Bidner's ever changing story, it was unlikely Struber and Bidner were present at the same gully, at the same time.

Stephen and Dianne were there!

Identification of the offenders at the crime scene is a pivotal part of any Crown case. The prospectors nailed it in this instance, despite what you just read in the preceding two chapters.

What did Dan Bidner see and not see?

In the Monday night phone call with officer Tome, Bidner stated he recognised Struber and Wilson pull up in the car. In the phone call the same night with Officer O'Brien, he said he could only see Dianne, not Stephen, but then went on to say he saw them in visual. Whatever that meant.

In his Tuesday night interview, he said he couldn't see who was driving. He identified the Struber vehicle as he had seen it many times. He described it including it had a flat tray and no sides. On the re-enactment on 13 July, he said he could not see the face of the driver. He was specifically questioned about that, and he confirmed he could not get a visual on the driver. Yet he had said on three occasions the driver had gotten out of the cab; on one occasion the driver walked around the front of the vehicle.

At trial in 2015, he said *'it looked like they were both getting out of the car'* but he could only see Dianne. Under cross examination from Mr Feeney on behalf of Stephen Struber, Bidner said he did see the driver of the car. He was able to identify him as Stephen Struber.

The Defence barrister then requested the court play the video re-enactment from 13 July 2012 in which Dan Bidner participated. After viewing that video in court, witness Bidner conceded he did not see Stephen Struber get out of the vehicle, but he 'thought' he was driving. After further extensive questioning regarding his comments and clarification from the video of 13 July, witness Bidner reluctantly retracted his claims, and he told the court he could not see who was driving the car.

Kevin Groth did not see anyone.

What did Tremain Anderson have to say about identification of the offenders? As you have read, Dan Bidner was able to identify Dianne Wilson and the Struber vehicle. His efforts at claiming Stephen Struber was at the crime scene failed.

Fortunately for the Crown, Tremain was able to identify the Struber vehicle and Stephen Struber at the crime scene. As you have read, he had two previous armed encounters with Struber and Wilson and as such was able to identify them, he said. Also, he had seen them driving around the property on numerous occasions over many years. Dianne with the 30/30 *'she always carried.'* Which was interesting because he apparently did have a prospector's license but had never sought permission from the owners of Palmerville Station to prospect on the property. On his first interaction with police on Monday night in a conversation with officer Tome, Anderson described a Toyota utility arrive that had no side boards. He knew this vehicle belonged to Stephen Struber.

When interviewed on the Tuesday night, he said when he heard the vehicle approaching, he *'knew'* it would be the Strubers. He recognised the car as it was *'the same one he always had.'* He saw a glimpse of Struber as he drove past and recognised him. Identification confirmed! He said Dianne Wilson was in the passenger seat, but the statement did not report that he identified her.

At his video re-enactment, when the vehicle drove up the track driven by a police officer and the video camera rolling, he was unable to see the face of the driver or the interior of the vehicle, but that didn't matter as he had identified Stephen Struber when he did drive up on the Monday! He also told police Dianne was always with him.

At the trial he identified the Struber vehicle, and both Stephen and Dianne. He was 100 per cent certain it was Stephen and Dianne. *'As plain as day.'*

Thus, the prospectors had proven Struber and Wilson to be present on the day. The prospectors heard two shots and from the evidence, it could be inferred they were fired by the Strubers, but the Strubers denied being there. Obviously, they were lying. Add to that the tyre tracks, the damage to the trees and anthill, the phone call Dianne Wilson made to homestead, and you have a compelling circumstantial case.

Until it was not.

A Hat for every occasion

What hat was Bruce Schuler wearing when he went missing? If you are wondering what difference it made, I can say the hat Bruce was wearing when he went missing is a giant piece of the puzzle. Along with the pick, the headphones, the backpack and the satellite phone. If you do stage a crime scene, you must be sure to 'disappear' all the accoutrements.

Bruce owned two hats for prospecting. Maybe more. A wide brimmed leather hat, and a dark blue cap emblazoned Minelab. Anyone who has used headphones, not just for gold detecting, would be aware it is uncomfortable, impracticable and almost impossible to wear headphones with a wide brimmed hat. If you wish to wear headphones, you wear a cap or nothing at all.

There are several photographs and videos of Bruce Schuler wearing Koss brand headphones along with the Minelab cap[104]. There are none of him wearing headphones with a wide brimmed hat. Billboards have been placed around Palmerville Station with Bruce Schuler's photograph on them, depicting him gold detecting. In that photograph, he was wearing a wide brimmed hat with a speaker attached to a shoulder harness.

All three witnesses said Bruce Schuler was wearing headphones the day he went missing. Bidner confirmed at trial Schuler was wearing the wide brimmed hat. He went further and claimed Bruce did not hear the Struber 4x4 approaching because of the headphones. A claim many gold prospectors challenged. Correctly, I believe.

Kevin Groth said during his re-enactment Bruce was wearing his wide brimmed hat the day he went missing. When police arrived on the

---

[104] Videos from Fiona Splitt and police photographs

scene on the Tuesday, they found Bruce Schuler's car locked. They took photographs through the windows. Lying on the seat was a pair of Koss brand headphones and Bruce's Minelab cap.

Whilst the police videographer was taking vision of the interior of the car, Tremain Anderson and Kevin Groth walked up and look in the window. Anderson can be heard to say,' *I told you he was wearing the other hat.*' That meant all three witnesses were claiming Bruce was wearing the wide brimmed hat whilst wearing headphones. Most unlikely.

What about the Koss brand headphones left behind on the car seat of the locked car? It is not uncommon for prospectors to have two sets of headphones. It would mean though that Bruce had two sets of Koss brand headphones. Having the headphones on the car seat whilst driving around would be inconvenient, especially with three big men on the front seat. On the prospectors' evidence, when they left camp that morning, Bruce had ignored the Koss headphones on the front seat and instead, retrieved another pair of Koss headphones likely from the rear section of his vehicle along with the wide brimmed hat.

If Bruce Schuler never went prospecting that morning and was murdered elsewhere, that would explain the headphones and cap being found in his locked vehicle. But what about his pick and satellite phone?

The two most damning accoutrements not accounted for were Bruce's prospecting pick and his satellite phone. A prospecting pick is an essential piece of a gold prospector's kit. When the metal detector sets off a signal, the pick is used to dig, scrape, and otherwise remove the surface dirt and vegetation to identify the source of the signal, and hopefully, a big piece of gold.

Prospectors usually own several picks. The picks generally have a steel head and a timber or steel shaft but there are many varieties on the market. To my knowledge, Bruce Schuler owned three picks. Perhaps he owned more. It would be pointless to leave camp without your pick; much like leaving camp without your water bottle, metal detector, handheld GPS device, satellite phone or backpack.

The prospectors told police, Bruce Schuler had a pick with him when he disappeared. Kevin Groth went further. During the walk through conducted on Thursday 12 July 2012, he was asked what equipment Schuler had with him when he went missing. Groth provided a detailed account of what Schuler was carrying, down to an apple and packets of chips. Very observant. Too bad he was not more observant of the vehicle and the occupants as they drove past him:

'he was carrying like a, like he had a metal detector, it was a GSX 5000, I think it's called, one of the latest mine lab detectors, with a coil, round coil, about so round, he had a pick, which was pretty distinctive, he broke it, broke the pick off, <u>he had to re-weld it</u>, so it's been welded, and he had a GPS on his belt, and his backpack, he had a backpack, because he'd rather use a backpack, because he could at least put a few bottles of water in the back, frozen bottles, and he had his battery for his his metal detector in that, and he had a couple of apples, an orange or something, a couple of packets of chips in there, because I had the same thing in mine.'

Plenty of kit right there to drop, lose or abandon in a frantic escape from deranged, armed lease holders hunting unarmed prospectors. It was noted Groth did not mention Bruce was carrying his satellite phone. Did he know by then that Bidner had Schuler's phone?

Tremain Anderson told police Schuler tied his GPS to his belt with a piece of twine and he described the whole set up as 'flimsy.' Yet, in his haste to escape a deranged killer, the twine did not break until halfway up the ravine at the Second Crime Scene. His DNA was found on that twine. Unless he had more than one piece of twine. But I digress. Kevin Groth was very specific. He told police Bruce was carrying a distinctive pick. It had been broken, which necessitated Bruce repairing it with a weld. The option would have been to replace it.

When Detective Sergeant McLeish photographed Bruce Schuler's 4x4 in the Palmer River camp, he took two photographs of the contents of the covered rear tray of the vehicle. Apart from the previously mentioned black carry bag, and other camp equipment including a swag, table and Esky there were two prospector's picks in the photo.

One of them had a bent pick head consistent with it having been welded.

In the video Dan Bidner took of the camp, the same pick could be seen standing on its pick head near the camp table. Confirmation right there that Bruce Schuler was using that pick on that trip. Photographs clipped from that video also showed the bent pick head. Without the luxury of examining the actual pick, it would be difficult to be absolute, but on the photographic evidence viewed, the pick head viewed in those photographs appeared to have been welded.

I sent photographs of the pick with the bent head to George Wilson. He is a long-time prospector. I did not provide him with any information but merely asked him his opinion of the pick in the photographs. This was his comment: *'Well, I'd say it's had some damage, because you can see there it looks a bit bent and looks like somebody's put it back and welded it.'* What are the chances of Bruce Schuler owning two picks that he repaired by welding? Kevin Groth said Bruce had that pick with him when he went missing; there is photographic evidence Bruce was using that pick on that trip; and that pick was still in the rear of his vehicle.

I wondered why a quantity of the belongings and items seen in the tray area of Schuler's vehicle were then photographed in the rear of Bidner's 4x4. I read in an officer's statement that the prospectors requested, and were given, permission to remove items from Schuler's vehicle.

The prospectors noted the same detail in their statements. Obviously, no examination, testing for blood or DNA was then possible, on the same day police were treating the case as a murder. Big opportunity lost right there.

Did Bruce Schuler own two backpacks? Possibly. Did he feel the need to carry two backpacks with him when he went prospecting? On the prospectors' evidence he did have that need. They said he was last seen wearing a backpack, yet a backpack was found behind the driver's seat of Schuler's car.

If it is accepted the detecting pick seen in the police photographs and Bidner video did belong to Bruce Schuler, he did not take it prospecting on the Monday yet used it on the Sunday. Add that to the hat, headphones, satellite phone and backpack he also did not take with him on the day he disappeared. Bruce Schuler had been prospecting for fifteen years. It is inconceivable he would go prospecting without his essential accoutrements. What really happened on Palmerville Station?

At what point do you decide there are so many discrepancies they are of concern?

Struck by a Bull

This is a significant story. If there was any suggestion Tremain Anderson was lying when relating these claims, then it would reflect poorly on his credibility as a witness.

As you read there were any number of prospectors, tourists and campers who responded to a call by police call for people who had interacted with Stephen Struber. They lined up to complain they were threatened, abused and intimidated by him (how dare he evict them for trespassing!).

What I did not find was a conga line of people wanting to complain Stephen Struber had assault them, pointed a weapon at them or fired a weapon at them. Except for Tremain Anderson. Which would not be unusual, except as you know he was also one of the three witnesses to the disappearance of Bruce Schuler.

After Bruce Schuler went missing, Anderson told police he had a '*few close calls with Struber over the years and once with Dianne*[105].' The first occasion would have been around the year 2000. He said he was wearing headphones and because of not hearing Struber approach, he never wore headphones from that day on. He claimed he was in a tourist area detecting but Struber claimed he was on his property. He initially thought he had been struck in the back by a charging bull that knocked him flat on the ground and broke his detector, but it turned out to be Stephen Struber. (Any number of listeners commented he would not be standing up if he was charged and struck by a bull), which seemed a reasonably accurate response.

Anderson was going to defend himself and fight Struber, but Dianne was pointing a 30/30 lever action rifle at his belly area. They then went

---

[105] Statement by T Anderson

their separate ways, but he did not make a complaint to police. Anderson claimed his second encounter was 2011, just a year before Schuler's disappearance.

He was fishing at the Croc Hole with his mate Dave Wright. As he cast his line, a shot hit the water just in front of where his fishing line hit the water. A second shot caused leaves above his head to start falling[106]. Then there was a third shot which sounded as if it hit the bank or the ground of the rock behind which he was fishing. He stated the shooter would not have seen him but would have seen his fishing line hit the water. He looked through the trees and saw three men.

He identified Stephen Struber and George Wilson. The third male could have been a female. Anderson did not make a complaint to police at the time. Tremain rode to his mate and told him about the shooting.

Dave Wright was far more descriptive of the incident. He confirmed he did not see anything but heard three shots. Tremain told him Stephen Struber was the shooter. After the Strubers left, they were concerned as to what to do.

They thought if they tried to leave the area, the Strubers may ambush and shoot them, because they would know where they were camped. (It was never explained how the Strubers would know where they were camped). From what I have read about Stephen Struber, if he knew where they were camped, he would have gone there. The pair rode back to their camp and decided to wait until morning. Tremain told him they were in a bit of trouble and that he (Struber) was a dangerous man. '*He also told me what he would do to our property if we weren't there. He told me he is capable of anything including smashing our equipment or burning our vehicles.*[107]'

The same conga line of people who complained to police about being evicted from Palmerville Station also neglected to complain about their vehicle being set on fire. Tremain Anderson was most unfortunate. He was the only prospector to be ever assaulted by Stephen Struber and

---

[106] Statement by T Anderson
[107] Statement by D Wright

now we find he was the only prospector aware that Stephen Struber would destroy property or set fire to motor vehicles.

Which of course begged the question:

Why would you continue to go on to Palmerville Station when the owners were that violent and that dangerous? Why would you camp within two kilometres of their homestead? Why would you knock on their door after your mate goes missing after shots fired? You would recall the claims by Coca Cola John. After his alleged beating at the hands of George Wilson, Coca Cola John never ventured again onto Palmerville Station. Not Tremain Anderson!

After allegedly being beaten and shot at by Stephen Struber, Tremain Anderson simply couldn't stay away from Palmerville Station. I was unable to put Tremain Anderson's allegations to Stephen Struber or Dianne Wilson due to Corrective Services regulations. I did put the allegations to George Wilson who categorically denied them. '*Never happened*' he said. He had never come across Tremain Anderson at the Croc Hole. He had evicted him from camps when he had been found trespassing on Palmerville Station land, but denied firearms were ever involved.

Not exactly 'a *few close calls with Struber over the years*' but concerning claims all the same. Clearly, either Tremain Anderson was lying, or George Wilson was lying about that incident at the Croc Hole. They could not both be correct. I hope Tremain was not lying, as his evidence was crucial to the convictions of Struber and Wilson, and if he lied about being shot at by Struber, he would be a totally unreliable witness. It came down to his word against George Wilson's word; just as it did twelve months later.

Why would Tremain Anderson lie? What possible motive could Tremain Anderson have for lying about Stephen Struber and Dianne Wilson being violent people willing to use a firearm to get their way. '*Brutish enforcer*' as the Cairns Post described him.

Was Tremain Anderson lying about the Strubers murdering Bruce Schuler? Was the Croc Hole incident made up to show Struber and

Wilson were dangerous individuals and likely capable of murder. There was no evidence to support that suggestion.

Dead or Alive?

If there was any doubt in those few short days after his disappearance whether Bruce was dead or alive, Tremain Anderson seemingly clarified that in his first re-enactment video. He was answering questions put to him by Detective Alina Bell. It was noted he started talking in the present tense, as Bruce still being alive, and then switched to the past tense as if Bruce was deceased. It appeared Tremain did not expect Bruce to return any time soon, and become one of his prospecting buddies.

Bell:' *How long have you known Bruce for?"*

Anderson:' *I have only met him once before I came out on this trip. And that was only briefly, one night at Dan's place. He had a truck and he was bringing a load of something into his camp. We do have mutual friends and that and I know people who know him and all the rest of it. Yeah, no, and then just this trip. Just the other week before we had gone up to Cradle myself, Bruce and Dan for a ride and a bit of detecting and yeah I just thought he was going to be one of the team you know cause we got on well he seemed...gold hadn't screwed with his brain he seemed like a nice guy, you know.'*

Author note – Anderson said he only met him once and yet in the same paragraph related how they went prospecting just the other week at Cradle Creek which was on Palmerville property. Trespassing again.

B:' *Had there been any disagreements or arguments between the four of you at all?'*

Anderson:' *Not a chance, no, not a chance he was a bloody he was a nice guy mate.'*

A good Barrister may argue switching tense was not evidence, and it may well not be. Body language experts may disagree with that

Barrister's assessment. This is an examination of all the prospectors claims and there are just these continuing questions about their evidence. A listener did make comment of the nervous laugh Anderson made when replying to the question regarding any disagreements.

Video does not lie

The power of social media!

The video evidence, had it been known at trial may have been a game changer. I will go further and suggest if the jury had heard and seen that evidence, there would have been a different trial outcome.

A quick refresher. Dan Bidner took two videos on the trip when Bruce Schuler went missing. Their existence did not become known for months. They were exhibits at trial and were played to the jury. One was two minutes forty seconds in length, filmed at 9.53 a.m. and the second thirty seconds in length, filmed at 5.13 p.m. Both were filmed on Sunday 8 July 2012. The time and date were not visible on the videos, and it is not clear (to me), how those times were determined. The police evidence matrix merely noted the videos were filmed Sunday 8 July 2012.

When I first read of the existence of those videos, my interest was immediately aroused. For several reasons. All three witnesses did not mention the videos existed, and they should have. After all, they would want police to know Bruce had been alive, and it was a legitimate trip. More importantly, the place where the first video was taken, on Fairlight Station was also not mentioned as a prospecting destination. How did all three prospectors forget to tell investigators they went there as part of their outing? Kevin Groth may have had an excuse, being a newbie on the location. But Dan Bidner and Tremain Anderson would have known where they were. Five kilometres past the Palmer River, they had to assemble their machines. How could they forget that?

Dan Bidner told police they arrived at the Palmer River to set up camp at lunchtime. That would prompt recall, right? He should have remembered what time he arrived, as he was asked only thirty hours later. By trial he had amended their arrival time to mid-afternoon.

How could he get it so wrong, when he related the story just one day later. It should be noted as well, arriving mid-afternoon and setting up camp would have severely limited the amount of detecting time available on the Palmer. '*Two went upstream, two went downstream. I knocked off about 4.30 p.m.,*' he told police.

If camp was set up around 3 p.m., the prospectors had a maximum of three hours detecting before dark. Anderson found gold forty-five minutes away from camp. He obviously did not walk to that exact spot, he detected to it, and then he had at least forty-five minutes' walk back to camp. How lucky was Tremain to find gold that day, when he spent at least ninety minutes walking to and from the location he found the gold.

The contents of the videos were typical home movie style. Innocent. In the first video, the camera pans over three prospectors setting up their detecting equipment, behind Bruce Schuler's Patrol, with Mount Emma in the background. In the area generally known as the '*Two-Mile gravel pit.*' Red Dog is visible.

Tremain Anderson was munching on a bag of possibly cocoa leaves. Was that the reason they did not want police to know about the existence of the video? To avoid a potential drug charge. As Dan Bidner can be heard say in the video, '*here we are hiding out in a little gully on Struberville.*' I have never been gold prospecting, but from comments from listeners it is possible to spend an entire day in one area. They seemed to spend about one hour there.

That little side excursion flew in the face of the reason why they went on to Palmerville Station in the first place? Because their neighbour had found ten ounces of gold. But the neighbour had not found ten ounces of gold at the Two-Mile gravel pit. He had found gold at the One Mile. So why go four kilometres away from the prize location? Absurd. Was that the reason the prospectors didn't want the videos found. Questions would be asked about why they went to the Two-Mile and not the One Mile?

The second video was of the prospectors' camp in the bed of the Palmer River. The video pans over the camp site, with a fire burning, a table, chairs and other camping equipment. The camera pans quickly over some men behind the trees, and you can hear talking. Fiona Splitt told me she could briefly hear Bruce's voice in that video. I posted both videos on the Facebook page I had created for my podcasting - *Graeme Crowley Podcast Investigations*. I also posted the videos on my YouTube channel, at the same time I released an episode on the '*Where is Bruce Schuler*' podcast.

I suspect the existence of the videos would never have become known except Kevin Groth commented on them in a further interview he gave police in September 2012, three months after his initial statement. He told police that Dan Bidner had a video recorder and had taken some video. Would the videos have ever seen the light of day except for the admission by Groth?

Bidner was duly questioned and yes, he had taken a video he said, he did not mention taking two videos. Small point and easily overlooked, or was there something in the video he did not want police to see? (Police were reading some statements at least, supporting claims they should have spotted discrepancies in the witnesses' claims).

Even at trial, Bidner was reluctant to admit he had taken a second video. He continued to deny knowledge of it. The prosecutor just gave up asking him questions about it, showed the court the video, and asked the witness if he had taken it, to which he obviously had to agree.

When I went looking for the details of the videos in the police file, all I could find was they were tendered in evidence as having been taken on Sunday 8 July 2012. I could not find a time. A person who attended court told me the times mentioned in court were 9.53 a.m. for the first video and 5.13 p.m. for the video in the riverbed camp. I could find no metadata on either video. I have little experience in that area and asked an expert in the field. He confirmed there was no metadata and stated there should have been. For those not familiar with the term, metadata just means information about the author, date created, file size and so on. It was later explained to me, it was likely the original videos were securely stored and copies, without metadata, were produced for court purposes.

I will deal with the first video. The two minute forty second video where the prospectors could be seen assembling their machines. Supposedly taken at 9.53 a.m. It was around a three-hour drive from Bidner's camp at Maytown. That would make their departure time 6.53 a.m. but Kevin Groth said they left at 9 a.m. Jo Bidner said they left around 7.45 a.m.

The witnesses said it took two-and one-half hours to reach the Palmer. The Two-Mile gravel pit was another twenty minutes past that. A prospector who had listened to the podcast and watched the videos, travelled to the exact same location and sent me his own video. He was of the opinion the Bidner video was taken in the morning. He took a video of that location at 8.30 a.m. The shadow lengths in his video did look similar to the shadow lengths in the Bidner video. That of course raises a very inconvenient question. If that was accurate, when was that first video taken? Sunday morning or Monday morning? If it was taken on the Sunday morning, when did the prospectors arrive on the Palmer? It couldn't have been taken Monday morning, could it? By 8.30 a.m. the Strubers were warming up the engine of their LandCruiser to go hunting prospectors.

Did all the prospectors go on to Palmerville Station on the Sunday morning or were some of them already there? Buried deep in Kevin Groth's statement of 10 July 2012, at point 13 was a single sentence: *'Bruce wanted to go out to where Danny was the next morning to do a bit of fossicking on the Palmer River.'*

Was that just a poor choice of words on Kevin Groth's part or was Bidner already on the Palmer. It was never clarified nor questioned. It would certainly explain why there were so many versions of what they all did on that Sunday. The day I described their evidence as a train wreck.

Just before publication of this book, Daniel Wood, a cyber security expert analysed the video and stated he believed the video was taken between 7 a.m. and 9 a.m. but closer to 7 a.m. That would be consistent with Schuler and Groth leaving Rosie's Gully early Sunday morning, driving to the Two-Mile and meeting Bidner and Anderson.

The visible contents of the rear of Schuler's 4x4 were compared with other known evidence. There appeared to be questions with many aspects of the contents, including what gear the prospectors took on the trip and so, on but nothing specific. The major question was whether there were four swags in Bruce Schuler's vehicle. There were enough inconsistencies in video one to arouse suspicion of the time of day it was taken, as well as the day it was taken.

In video two, the Palmer River prospectors camp, is where things become messy. Again, the video was said to be taken on the Sunday. Apparently at 5.13 p.m. according to evidence at trial I was told. Once again there was no metadata available.

The video was only thirty seconds in length. It panned across the riverbed, past a camping table, two chairs, a fire with a lot of ash around it, a prospector's pick, two gold detectors and other camping equipment. There were shadows visible, consistent with maybe one hour before sunset. Three prospectors can be briefly seen or heard in the brief video, and of course the videographer. I could never interpret what the prospectors were saying to each other, it was too quick. There were so many inconsistencies in that thirty second video, it was easy to conclude there was a problem with the time it was claimed taken. On the evidence given at trial, not all prospectors were back in camp at 5.13 p.m. In fact, Bidner should have been there by himself waiting for the others to return. They set up camp mid-afternoon and there was already a fire with a significant amount of ash around it. The whole video did not look right.

After posting the videos on social media, I would not describe the reaction by viewers as 'going viral' as the saying goes. But I would say the comments and messages from listeners erupted. The consensus was the video was taken in the morning, somewhere between 7.30 a.m. and 9.30 a.m. Birds could be heard singing in the background; they normally stop around 9 a.m. listeners told me.

The amount of visible ash around the fire was consistent with an overnight fire, others said, not a fire that had been burning for less than one hour. Viewers identified dew on the tyres on the roof rack of Schuler's Patrol. A listener was able to say the prospectors were talking about overnight condensation, dew, in the video audio. Upon relistening to the audio, I realised that was what they were talking about. Several prospectors, including one who camped in the bed of the Palmer River for six weeks, claimed the shadows were consistent with morning, not afternoon. Was that the reason Dan Bidner did not want the second video to see the light of day?

Ultimately, I spoke with four listeners who were also prospectors who knew the Palmer River area intimately. They were all confident video two was taken in the morning.

It was very hard to pin the prospectors down as to the time they went prospecting Monday morning, but likely 6.50 a.m. Notwithstanding, by the time that video was filmed, the prospectors should have been detecting for gold 900 metres away and bracing for the arrival of the Struber 4x4.

And why lie about it? Why claim the video was taken Sunday if it was taken Monday morning? *So what, yes, I took video Monday morning and then we headed off prospecting*. Was that because of the time factor? They said they liked to get out prospecting early to beat the heat. Dawdling around camp between 7.30 a.m. and 9.30 a.m. and then prospecting in the heat of the day was never going to float.

On the evidence of the four people I spoke with who know the location, it was possible the prospectors were still in camp at the time the Strubers were murdering Bruce Schuler. How does that work? Were those the actions of honest, credible witnesses just telling the story of how their best mate went missing? If accurate, this is disturbing evidence. That evidence also needs to be considered in the context of the Sunday night satellite telephone ping.

Was the video taken Sunday morning? If so, why not say so? But of course, they would then have had to amend the time (and day) they left

Maytown. I can see arguments why it would have been better to leave the videos buried.

What does that one single piece of the puzzle do for the credibility of the Crown's three main witnesses? The videos are important for the investigation, but for the Crown they are problematic. Catastrophic may be a better description. Another minor discrepancy not worth bothering about?

What would the jury have made of that evidence, had they seen and heard it? We shall never know of course, but I suspect it would not have ended well for the Crown.

I have often wondered what would be the Crown case if Bruce Schuler's body was found and he had been strangled, or stabbed to death? Would it be the case Prosecutor Rees would say,' *Forget I said the second shot was the killing shot. You can infer that after the Strubers shot at Schuler and missed, they stabbed him to death, and you can infer it was with a boning knife, the same knife Dianne always carried and used to slaughter cattle.*'

Daniel Wood, the cyber security expert, also analysed the second video and applied noise suppression software to it. He concluded the video was taken between 7.30 a.m. and 7.45 a.m. Daniel Bidner told police they left camp to go prospecting around 6.50 a.m.

Regardless of whether the video was filmed at 7.30 a.m. or 9 a.m., it is totally inconsistent with the claims and sworn testimony of the Crown witnesses.

The conversation in the video can now be heard as:

Voice 1*: 'What's the fucking go with no dew, normally this time of year you get some dew eh?' (*Believed to be Tremain Anderson*).*

Voice 2: *'Little bit of dew.' (*Believed to be Keving Groth).

You can view both videos taken by Dan Bidner, if you wish, on my YouTube channel @graemecrowley448

The Reader

A regular question I asked myself during my research into this case, and a regular question to me from listeners was along the lines of:

'What were the police doing? Were the police oblivious to the ever-changing story lines of the prospectors? Were they not concerned?'

As you read, Detective Sergeant McLeish disputed there were inconsistencies, and if there were, they were minor and to be expected. The prosecutor conceded there were inconsistencies.

I decided I would list the discrepancies with the prospectors' evidence I identified from my research, starting from the earliest date and progressing through in a chronological order. I identified 142 discrepancies in total. I listed them all, some minor or inconsequential, some significant or concerning. I sent copies to the families of Stephen Struber and Dianne Wilson, with a request for any information on any of the points, particularly inaccuracies. I decided I would send the list to recently retired, long serving police officers with investigative experience, and seek their thoughts.

Phil Notaro, a retired Queensland police officer was a regular listener to my podcasts. I emailed him the list of 142 concerns I had with the evidence, and asked him for his thoughts on the inconsistencies. This was his response, unedited:

I retired from the Qld Police Service in 2020. I served as a Qld Police Officer for 35 years and attained the rank of Senior Sgt. I served 15 years as a plain clothes investigator, including over 2 years as a Det Sgt at the Homicide Squad.

I have investigated over 28 murders. I have given evidence at the Magistrates, District and Supreme Courts, as well as Coroners Court.

I have prepared an extensive coronial brief in relation to a death in police custody and presented evidence for 5 straight days.

I have been asked to comment on the Bruce Schuler Case, in particular the discrepancies that have been identified by Graeme Crowley.

Firstly, I want it to make clear I have not conducted a full review of the evidence. Whilst I have read some material, I have not read every statement. I am merely commenting on the information that has been presented by Graeme in his Podcast. I have listened to every episode of the podcast (some episodes several times).

I will add I have never met Graeme Crowley in person. I have exchanged some emails over a period of several years and had one telephone conversation with him.

In relation to the discrepancies highlighted by Graeme.

While there are a few that could be better described as anomalies in the evidence, and some that are only minor in nature, in my experience there appears to be an abnormally high number of discrepancies in the evidence presented to the Supreme Court. I admit, it can be argued that the number of discrepancies is subjective and would vary from case to case (there is no magical number), but the higher the number of discrepancies then one must consider that a witness or witnesses are being untruthful. I would suggest that discrepancies carry more weight in a murder brief when

There is no body and

The case is purely 100% circumstantial without any physical evidence.

As an experienced investigator, in a murder investigation where there is no body located, and there is no physical evidence tying the suspect/offender to the scene, then the bar needs to be set pretty high to not only charge an offender with murder, but to secure a conviction.

I'm not seeing either in the Bruce Schuler case. One would expect, in any investigation, that there will be discrepancies in statements of witnesses. It is not uncommon. The last thing you want as an investigator is that witnesses recount the same incident exactly the same. This is very rare and will give rise to the suggestion of collusion.

Witnesses will present different "versions" of the same incident. This is expected as an investigator. Witnesses will have different perceptions. They will see the same incident differently. Many things can affect this, including stress. People's minds simply can "record" the same incident differently. That's human nature. This could relate to what they observed, what they did, what they saw or heard, it can affect times as well.

Again, I will say, there is no magical number of discrepancies that is acceptable. However, the greater the number of discrepancies between witnesses, then this gives rise to the suggestion that the witnesses are being dishonest.

One would expect that with a circumstantial brief, where there is no body and no physical evidence, then the direct evidence from eyewitnesses would be strong, cohesive and corroborative. After all, that's the entire crown case. Your eyewitnesses.

In circumstances such as the Schuler matter, where witnesses not only give varying versions of events but also alter their evidence time and time again, I'm not sure how they can be relied on to support a circumstantial brief. On face value, it appears there was some extremely sloppy police work. I am not aware of the identity of any of the police involved, but it does appear they lack the very basic investigative skills.

On a homicide investigation, a senior detective is assigned as "the reader". Their job is to read every statement in detail. Part of this process is to identify anomalies, discrepancies and highlight further lines of inquiries. This clearly has not been done in this case. Otherwise, many of the identified discrepancies would have been addressed or witness versions discounted. The three prospectors can only be described as extremely unreliable witnesses. I cannot fathom that in a circumstantial case there is no physical evidence that connects the Strubers with the alleged crime scene. These are just a few things that jump out at me.

That gave me solace. I was beginning to wonder if I was exaggerating, if I was focusing on the wrong issues. I did not know anyone who had an in-depth knowledge of the evidence whom I could bounce ideas off.

Scott Furlong was another recently retired Queensland police officer with significant detective experience. I had also never met Scott but had spoken with him on the telephone and we had exchanged emails. I had first heard of him when he was interviewed on another podcast which had been reviewing a murder investigation.

I was aware that as a then member of the Homicide Squad, he had been personally involved in the Schuler murder investigation and had spent time on the ground at Palmerville Station. He had told me in an earlier conversation he believed the Strubers were guilty. I was particularly interested in hearing his views, having been personally involved in investigating the case and familiar with the evidence. I wondered whether he was aware of the buried evidence. I wondered whether he would be defensive, or looking to deflect any personal blame or embarrassment, as my investigation results were very different to those of Operation Kilo Principle. He had separated from the Police Service, so I assumed not, but I really had no idea. I sent him the list of discrepancies and asked for his thoughts on the discrepancies.

Whereas Phil Notaro sent me a response of around 750 words as you have read, Scott replied with a nineteen-page document containing 5900 words. To say I was overwhelmed would be an understatement. Scott is currently studying for a law degree which may have helped explain it.

And whereas Phil had addressed my question, Scott had not. He titled his document *'Legal Argument: Guilt of Stephen Struber and Dianne Struber-Wilson in the Murder of Bruce Schuler.'* I wondered whether he misunderstood my question. I did note that in his reply he mentioned it was a stressful situation four times, and a traumatic event three times, which intrigued me. I recalled Detective McLeish made similar claims.

Scott quoted seven different legal cases a total of thirty-seven times, where circumstantial evidence was used to obtain a conviction. The crown had three witnesses who were able to give firsthand evidence.

The circumstantial evidence was secondary. It merely supported the claims made by the prospectors. Scott was satisfied the convictions were sound, and were well supported by circumstantial evidence, and despite '*the minor discrepancies in witness accounts.*'

I am well aware of how circumstantial evidence can be used to secure a conviction. I am also very aware of the potential problems with circumstantial evidence, if abused. I disagreed with Scott that the discrepancies in the prospectors' evidence were '*minor.*' On the contrary, I considered many of the discrepancies significant, disturbing and concerning.

What was I missing? In follow-up emails, Scott did agree with my assertion regarding witnesses. He stated in a lot of instances, it came down to interpretation of witnesses, by the investigators. For that reason, he preferred recorded interviews. Thankfully, many of the interviews in the Schuler murder were recorded, in the form of audio and video re-enactments.

I was not interested in whether the court had accepted the witnesses' testimony. Foremost in my mind was whether the prospectors were lying, and whether they had fabricated this entire story. I was interested in whether the Strubers were being honest when they said they were never at the One Mile location, not in the gully, and had nothing to do with the disappearance and murder of Bruce Schuler. Two ex-detectives, both former members of the Homicide Squad with two responses at the opposite end of the spectrum.

Scott Furlong's report is too long to place here; you will find it as Appendix E. I refer to Scott's report in the chapter '*A Very Stressful Situation, or was it?*'

Ghost Evidence

Perhaps no other incident had more impact on the outcome of this case, than the innocuous u-turn the alleged Struber vehicle performed that Monday. The evidence heard by the jury ended up being confusing and misleading, with this significant event being barely mentioned. I wondered whether that was on purpose. That evidence needs to be considered in the context of the Strubers claim that they were not even at the One Mile the day Bruce Schuler disappeared. Whilst reviewing the evidence, I had to bear in the mind the suspicion '*Was there a vehicle even there that Monday*,' and if there was, did it belong to the Strubers or a third party?

The Struber vehicle being there, on that ridge above where Schuler was last seen, and travelling to the Second Crime Scene was central to the Crown case. Apart from the three prospectors, that was the Crown case. Those aspects of the evidence were interwoven. Without one, the other didn't happen. The issues were also central to the Defence case. However, apart from '*we were not there, and we did not do it*', the Defence did not have any other strategy. Admittedly, with a defence such as that, there is little room to move. The defence counsel were aware of those issues, but I am not clear as to the depth of their understanding. I did request interviews with both defence counsel, but did not receive a reply to my emails. Accordingly, I must base my conclusions on the questions they asked, and did not ask during the trial.

Any evidence located by police and relevant to the charges before the court should be presented to the court. The prosecutor has a well-known obligation to present all evidence to the court[108].

---

[108] Qld Law Society. Rule 29 of Australian Solicitors' Conduct Rules

I have been involved in many cases during my career, both for the prosecution and defence. There had been instances in cases in which I was involved, where it was suspected that evidence had been buried, and had not seen the light of day. Never in my career, have I seen evidence that had seen the light of day and then be buried. Until now. The prospectors' statements contained evidence of the u-turn, in multiple instances, as I have shared with you. It was exculpatory evidence. The prosecutor had an obligation to present it to the court. He did not. It became ghost evidence. Why and how that happened are questions that have intrigued me.

It was not the case I went hunting for it and found it. I stumbled upon it. More accurately, I stumbled upon the fact it had vanished. I knew it existed. I had read it in statements. I had listened to, and read witness Bidner, asking Detective Riles if he should mark on the map where the vehicle turned around. I had watched the re-enactments with Detective Alina Bell pressing witness Anderson on the position the vehicle turned around, and why Anderson believed it had turned around. Then whilst reading the trial transcripts, it wasn't there. Where was it? The u-turn was not discussed. Where did it go? Part of the reason it successfully hid in plain sight I suspected, was because of the location of the crime.

If the u-turn had occurred at the intersection of Queen and Edward Streets, that was something everyone could grasp and comprehend. They would be able to orient themselves with the crime scene. They could picture it in their mind. But when the witnesses said '*it went up the road a bit, not far, and turned around*' it was open to interpretation, misuse and confusion. Your interpretation of the vehicle travelling a short distance up the road, may be different to my interpretation. But that was definitely not the only reason.

The waters were very muddied when it came to this part of the evidence. I am still not sure whether that was on purpose or accidental. I identified three separate and distinct issues with this aspect of the evidence:

a) Where did the Struber vehicle do a u-turn? (assuming the Struber vehicle was even there).

b) Did the Struber vehicle travel to crime scene two, the burnt vegetation area?
c) Did the Struber vehicle hit trees, a termite mound and leave tyre tracks travelling down and up the ravine?

For the Crown case to succeed, it had to have the Struber vehicle on the ridge above Crime Scene One, and it had to have the Struber vehicle going to the burnt vegetation or what I called Crime Scene Two. If both those aspects were not proven, their prosecution failed. The Crown proved its case by two witnesses telling the court they saw the vehicle on the track, identified it as the Struber vehicle, and identified the occupants as Stephen Struber and Dianne Wilson. The Crown further proved its case, by telling the jury the vehicle was *seen heading in the direction of the gully*. How quaint!

And along the way, it damaged trees, anthills and left tyre tracks all the way down the ravine. Of course, the Ezard evidence confused that evidence. The Crown never told the court when the tyre impressions were made, only when they were first observed, and the defence never asked. How did the Crown prove the Struber vehicle went to Crime Scene Two? The Crown prosecutor told the jury, they could infer the Struber vehicle went to Crime Scene Two, and an unscripted and unauthorised episode of *Star Trek* was born!

The Oxford Dictionary has this definition of infer:' *deduce or conclude (something) from evidence and reasoning rather than from explicit statements.*' The prosecutor was careful to never say the Struber went to Crime Scene Two. He inferred it, but he never said it. More dancing.

As an aside, during my research of the Singh family murders for that podcast, I noted the prosecutor's favourite word was '*distraction.*' Any shred of evidence that did not suit the Crown narrative, was a distraction. I don't recall reading the word '*infer*' at all in that trial. Maybe it was there. In the Schuler case, I have not come across '*distraction,*' but I sure have come across '*infer.*'

During my interview with Detective Sergeant McLeish, I told him I was struggling with the concept the vehicle went to Crime Scene Two because of the evidence of Bidner and Anderson. He said this: 'I *think you're sort of summarizing evidence to your advantage and I don't have the advantage of seeing the transcript now. But again, it's entirely reasonable to infer that. Entirely reasonable.*[109]' Well, Detective McLeish it may have been entirely reasonable to you to infer that, for me - not so much.

What did the jury hear? I suggest the jury heard all three of the above boxes were ticked, but in this order:

b) The unregistered Struber vehicle went to crime scene two by inference.

c) The vehicle struck trees and anthill, leaving tyre tracks along the way there.

a) The Struber vehicle turned around and went back toward the homestead.

Do you see the subtle difference?

What did counsel understand? The prosecutor was aware of the u-turn on the ridge line. That was obvious by the questions he asked witnesses, and more pointedly, the questions he did not ask witnesses. Hence, infer. The subject was on the radar of both defence counsel, but I am not satisfied they understood where exactly the alleged Struber vehicle performed the u-turn. My interpretation only, based on the questions not asked.

At one point, in the absence of the jury, Defence Barrister Feeney said in part,' *Then after some period of time the vehicle is heard to move and, it seems, stop again – a shot then sounds. It's not clear as to the path of the vehicle at that point – whether there's evidence of tracks showing a turn – and the vehicle leaves. It's seen to leave heading back in the general direction of where the homestead is although, of course, it's open country.*[110]'

That suggests that Barrister Feeney was aware the vehicle did turn around, but it also suggests he was unclear as to the location of the turnaround. The entire court staff had travelled to Palmerville Station.

---

[109] Interview with Det Sgt McLeish
[110] Day 6 -6 trial

It raises questions as to what was shown to them by police, and what was on display by police.

My investigations have revealed significant new evidence, and the following are the areas to focus on. When I say new, I should probably add that evidence was also hiding in plain sight, waiting to be discovered.

The u-turn was a separate and distinct event and was said to have occurred on the Monday.

Did the Struber vehicle drive to crime scene two, the burnt patches?

The tyre tracks across the ridge line and down the ravine, with the vehicle hitting the trees, anthill and leaving the tyre tracks, occurred at a separate time, likely the Tuesday or perhaps as late as Wednesday.

Placing the evidence at Crime Scene Two occurred at an undetermined time and date.

If there was a vehicle there that day, it completed a u-turn on the ridge line above the gully, and returned in the direction of the homestead. At least a day later, possibly longer, a vehicle left tyre tracks in the grass above crime scene two, collided with the trees and anthill whilst travelling to and from the bottom of the ravine. At some other time, evidence was left at crime scene two. As far as I am aware, the jury and the Defence counsels were blissfully unaware of those juicy little bits of information. More about that in the chapter, '*Trees, Pats and Tracks.*'

Due to the nature of what was and wasn't heard at trial, I will deal with the issues separately.

When the Struber vehicle performed a u-turn (a) will be the subject of this chapter.

Did the Struber vehicle (or the vehicle that was present) go to crime scene two (b) will be dealt with in the next chapter '*Teleporting.*'

Did a Struber vehicle leave the tracks down the ravine and hit the trees and termite mound (c) will be deconstructed in the chapter following, '*Trees, Pats and Tracks.*'

Placing of evidence (d) at Crime Scene Two will be covered in the chapter, '*Crime Scene Staging.*'

For once, witnesses Bidner and Anderson were quite aligned with their recall of what happened. But it would appear their versions did not align with the Crown narrative. What did Bidner and Anderson say? In overly simplistic terms, the Struber vehicle drove up, fired two shots and returned in the direction of the homestead.

Yes, there was a delay when the vehicle did nothing. Yes, the vehicle moved a short distance further up the track, and yes, witnesses heard a 'clang', but essentially that was the storyline. The problem with that storyline was that Bruce Schuler's blood and DNA were found a long way away, down a steep incline from where the u-turn occurred. The witnesses neither heard nor saw the vehicle go there and back again, and in the available time frame of less than thirty minutes.

The problem the Crown had was that they accepted the prospectors as honest witnesses. They had to accept all their evidence; they could not cherry pick which parts of their evidence suited their case. Therefore, they had to accept their claims the vehicle performed a u-turn and left the scene. How to deal with that inconvenient truth? Ignoring it was an option that worked well.

That left the jury having to infer the Struber vehicle went to Crime Scene Two. (There is that word again). The problem with that inference? The evidence clearly did not support it, but more about that in the next chapter, '*Teleporting.*'

More importantly, if it was shown the u-turn did occur, then it raised the obvious questions of how and when the Struber vehicle travelled to the second crime scene, how and when the vegetation was damaged, how and when the tyre tracks were made, how and when Bruce Schuler was murdered, how and when his body was removed, along with all his possessions, and how and when the crime scene was cleaned up. A lot of 'how and when' riding on one questionable u-turn. Better for the Crown case if the u-turn wasn't mentioned.

On all the evidence now available, there can be simply no suggestion the Struber vehicle (if it was even there), did not do a u-turn somewhere between twenty metres and eighty metres after leaving where the first shot was fired[111]. It would be ridiculous to suggest otherwise. (If only Queen and Edward streets were available).

If the reader accepts the vehicle did turn around and travel back in the direction of the homestead, never to be seen again that day as claimed by the witnesses, how did it then go to crime scene two? As time passed, witnesses Bidner and Anderson tried to distance themselves from the comments the vehicle did a u-turn, and that they went to where the vehicle performed the u-turn.

Groth was out of the picture by this time. Deep in the bush, not to return for almost six hours. However, when he did eventually surface, he corroborated Bidner and Anderson's claim the vehicle turned around and left the area. When he met up with Tremain Anderson somewhere around 3.15 p.m., they naturally discussed the day's events[112]. Groth told Anderson of running away after the first shot, or before, depending again on which version he gave that you accepted, and hiding out in the bush.

He then provided a garbled almost incoherent account to investigators, about the actions of the Strubers after the first shot. I do not suggest for a moment that was because of stress or trauma, that was the way he always spoke. I had watched and listened to his re-enactments videos countless times:

'I explained what I did and I said to Tremain what happened and he said 'the people went past where we first met after we departed from each other and went up there and done a u-turn and never came back.'
Not that the jury heard that. That was the sort of corroborating evidence the Crown did not need the jury to hear.

It must be remembered that Crime Scene Two was not discovered until late Wednesday afternoon[113]. Searches were conducted by Anderson on Monday, and police on Tuesday and Wednesday morning. *'Nothing of interest was found'* was the go-to comment in police notebooks and

---

[111] Based on evidence of witnesses Bidner & Anderson
[112] Statements by both T Anderson & K Groth
[113] Statement by police officer Vincent

statements. Crime Scene Two is covered in the chapter *'Crime Scene Staging.'* Police on the ground on Palmerville Station, had no idea of the direction that the Struber vehicle travelled that Monday. They were relying on the prospectors to tell them the movements of the Struber vehicle before, during and after the bushwhacking of Bruce Schuler. The prospectors dutifully recorded verbally, and in writing what they saw and heard. Repeatedly.

The issue was first canvassed in the Monday night phone call between Detective O'Brien and Daniel Bidner:

Bidner: *'And then they moved off. And then I heard the car, would have been like 20 minutes, again, half hour before that car moved the second time.'*

O'Brien *'OK.'*

Bidner: *'And when it started up to move the second time, it turned around and drove back down the spur, along the river, back towards the homestead.'*

And later in the same phone call:

Bidner:' *And then off it went back towards Palmerville Station.'*

O'B: *'Did it do a u-turn or just go straight ahead?'*

Bidner: *'A full u-turn.'*

O'B: *'Yep, OK, righto then.'*

Bidner:' *'And I even went and tracked that u-turn. Like, after they left, I went right. I'll go and see what they said to Bruce, you know what I mean?'*

And later in the same phone call Bidner said this:'

'We couldn't find any sign of blood or anything. But that's what I said to you. We did track where the car turned around. We went, yeah. I said, yeah, that's right, bro. I saw it.'

That conversation occurred twelve hours after the event, and as you will read shortly, witness Bidner strenuously denied he ever went to where the vehicle turned around. Not a case of memory fog or *'I'm sorry, I can't recall'*, he simply and repeatedly denied it had happened.

In his police interview the following night (Tuesday) Bidner said this:

79. *I then heard a vehicle start up and drive off. It didn't go far and stopped. It sounded like it only drove twenty yards and then maybe ten to fifteen minutes later there was a second gun shot.*

80. *For about twenty minutes to half an later I sat there thinking to myself:' What's going on?'*

81. *I couldn't hear anymore voices.*

82. *Then I thought I heard the clang again but the noise was further away from me then.*

83. *Then I hear the car start up again. From my position I heard the car start up and drive back the way it came from towards the homestead, heading in a westerly direction down the river.*

Once again, no doubt, no hesitation. Very specific, and as you have read, I had the opportunity to listen to the audio tapes. Many times.

Dan Bidner's interview with Detective Riles on the Tuesday night was audio recorded, and from that audio his statement was prepared. In the chapter '*Shots Fired*' you read some conversation that was captured on audio that did not find its way into his statement. The same happened with this part of his evidence. The audio captured the following which did not find its way into his statement, and by default, never heard by the jury:

Bidner: '*Do you think I should put where the car turned around?*'

Riles: '*You saw him turn around did you?*'

Bidner: '*No I didn't see him turn around.*'

R: '*So what did you..*'

Bidner: '*Well, we tracked it today with the other boys.*'

R: '*Oh did you. Did you see the track marks where he…*'

Bidner: '*Yeah one of the officers pointed it out.*'

R: '*Ah right, OK nah mate, we'll leave that off because that's your, this is your sighting of the day.*'

And that was a curious comment to make: '*Yeah one of the officers pointed it out.*' He repeatedly said he and Tremain went back on the Monday and saw where the alleged vehicle performed a u-turn. But then he had to have a police officer point out where the u-turn occurred. That didn't make sense. But it may be explained by a comment Bidner made to a journalist years later. He claimed a search helicopter flew low along the road and swept away the tracks.[114] And if that was the case, how did the police officer point them out?

I would argue with Detectives Riles' decision to leave out that significant evidence by that witness. That evidence was never mentioned again, anywhere. Ghost evidence. Of course, perhaps the police never went to the u-turn location at all as claimed by Bidner. Bidner did have a history of changing the facts to suit the circumstances. But what if the police did go to the spot where it was claimed the Struber vehicle did a u-turn?

As part of the investigation, that position would have been marked. It would have been forensically mapped. It would have been recorded in their statements. It would have been pointed out to the jury.

I cannot find where that happened.

Let us deconstruct that issue. Bidner initially said he and Tremain Anderson went to where the u-turn occurred, but they later denied that. The Crown admitted that conversation between Bidner and O'Brien had occurred[115].

Bidner told Detective Sergeant Riles and the court, that he went to the u-turn location the next day with police. Which may or may not have happened. I cannot find any records anywhere that Bidner did in fact go with police on the Tuesday, to the u-turn location. No entries in notebooks or diaries, no entries in police statements. There would appear to be three outcomes – none of which reflect well on the Crown case:

---

[114] Interview with Robert Reid
[115] Crown admission at closing of Crown case.

1. Bidner did not go with police on the Tuesday to the location of the u-turn. That would mean he lied under oath. That would explain why there were no police notes.
2. Bidner did go with police on the Tuesday to the location of the u-turn. Police noted the location, saw the tracks, took photographs, mapped the GPS point, and then buried that evidence and the jury never heard it.
3. Bidner did go with police on the Tuesday to the location of the u-turn. Police found no tyre tracks or other evidence to confirm a u-turn occurred. That would explain why there were no entries in police notebooks or diaries. Despite the rough terrain, that should have raised concerns, red flags. Where was the supporting evidence of the witnesses' claims that a vehicle had been on that track?

In his re-enactment three days later, he said this in relation to the vehicle's movements around the time of the second shot:

Bidner: *'I heard a vehicle start. I heard the vehicle come around to my right-hand side.'*

Riles: *'Yeah.'*

Bidner: *'And I heard the vehicle come along here.'*

By come along here, he meant travel back toward the river in the direction of the homestead. On this occasion he made no mention of it even travelling a short distance, before it turned around and headed back to the homestead. That fiasco, that lie, was covered in the chapter '*The only thing I regret Sarge.*'

At the committal hearing in 2014, Bidner again repeated the same story. He heard the first shot, the vehicle started up and travelled a short distance and stopped. He heard the second shot. Then nothing was heard for twenty to thirty minutes, and then the vehicle started up and returned in the direction of the homestead.

At the 2015 murder trial, how did Prosecutor Rees deal with Bidner's evidence at trial?

Prosecutor:' *Okay, and what did you hear after that?'*

Bidner:' *The vehicle start up and leave. And it went....'*

P:' *And from what direction-sorry, from what direction did you hear the vehicle?*

Bidner: 'From *the direction of Bruce.*'

Did the prosecutor just interrupt Bidner as he was about to tell the court the vehicle returned to the homestead? All his previous statements to police were at that very point, the vehicle turned around. How very fortunate for the Crown case. The questioning continued.

P:' *So the gully?'*

Bidner:' *The gully, yes.'*

P:' *Okay, Well, when you say the direction of Bruce, is that where you last saw Bruce?'*

Bidner:' *Yes. Yes.'*

P:' *Did you see anything after the vehicle ..?*

Bidner: *'After the vehicle – from where I was on that terrace I had a slight view down into the river and I saw – witnessed the vehicle – I heard the vehicle drive off and I could hear it coming around my – from the gully's direction.'*

And no questions about the vehicle turning around. It was an interesting selection of words by the prosecutor. '*So the gully?*' Was he suggesting the vehicle had been in the gully? Even though the jury had been there and saw the steep side of the gully rising fifteen to metres above where Schuler was allegedly prospecting? Or was he merely suggesting the vehicle had stopped near the gully?

And it was an interesting answer also from witness Bidner. '*From the direction of Bruce.*' Which was innocent enough, but he then added '*the gully, yes*'. Was Bidner changing his evidence to support the Crown case? That was it. No questions about the direction the vehicle took after the second shot, including the earlobe and whether the vehicle travelled up and down the ravine.

Was that the reason the prosecutor suggested to the jury Bruce may have been murdered where he was last seen? You know, where there was no evidence to place either Schuler, Struber or Wilson there. No blood, no DNA, no abandoned possessions, no disturbed earth and walls of the gully a steep ten metres or more high up which they would have had to drag a ninety-kilo dead weight.

How else do you explain the killer doing a u-turn in their vehicle? But he didn't explain the u-turn. He didn't mention it as you have read.

From this next question, perhaps even Prosecutor Rees was confused.

P:' *And the gully, where did that gully lead you? The gully you were in, you carried on detecting back to the camp. Is that correct.?*

Bidner: *'Yeah, but I wasn't in a gully then. I was running the high terraces.'*

Under cross examination at the 2015 trial, Daniel Peter Bidner was argumentative, obfuscating, evasive and deceitful. It was his second *'hour of shame'*:

Trevino:' *..that you went back to the gully to search?*

Bidner:*' No. Tremain did.'*

T: *'And you didn't follow Tremain?'*

Bidner:*' No.'*

T:*' You didn't do your own search?'*

Bidner:*' No.'*

T:*' You didn't go to that area and track where you say the vehicle did a u-turn?*

Bidner:*' I did that as I left. I did that the next day with the police.'*

T:*' You told the police about that, did you?*

Bidner:*' yes.'*

T:' *You didn't do it on the 9th of July in the afternoon?'*

Bidner:*' No.'*

T:*' Have you told anybody that you have?'*

Bidner:*' Not that I am aware of, no. I - I - I wouldn't have because I didn't do it.'*

T:*' Yeah. So you told Detective Sergeant O'Brien that you and Tremain went back?'*

Bidner:*' I said we - we went and had a look back meaning one of us went and looked back.'*

T:*' well, you said, he went back first, then you went back?'*

Bidner:*' Yeah. I went back to the car.'*

T:*' You told Nicholas O'Brien, in respect of the gully that when you were at the campsite in the crossing…?'*

Bidner:*' Yep.'*

T:*' you said about the gully: Me and Tremain went back.'*

Bidner:*' Yep?'*

T:*' Do you accept that you said that?'*

Bidner:*' Yeah, but I didn't mean as in me.'*

T:*' Then you said: I went back. I went back separately.'*

Bidner:*' I wouldn't have said that.'*

T:*' You didn't say that?'*

Bidner:*' Nuh. I might have said, we went back, meaning we had a look there.'*

T:*' Well, you told Nicholas O'Brien about a search Tremain did and a search that you did, I suggest to you, at the gully, on the afternoon of 9 July..?'*

Bidner:*' Not aware of that.'*

T:*' You told Nicholas O'Brien in your conversation with him: We…meaning you and Tremain. Did track where the car turned around?'*

Bidner:*' Not that day, we didn't.'*

T:*' Well, this is a conversation you had with Nicholas O'Brien on the 9th of July.'*

Bidner:*' yep.*

T:*' Do you accept that…?'*

Bidner: ' *Well, Tremain has returned to me and when we're sitting on that riverbank, he's told me that he's been back there, he's looked. I seen where the car turned around and all that. Doesn't mean I did it.* '

T: ' *You told...* '

Bidner: ' *I stayed - with the camp. I'm hoping on a return from one of the - Rusty or Bruce.*

T: ' *You told Detective Sergeant O'Brien that you went back to the gull on the afternoon on the 9th of July to search..* '

Bidner: ' *I've already told you, I've - if I've said that, I've meant Tremain's gone back and had a look.* '

That was another example of where witness Bidner had contrived his answers to suit the situation. He would appear to have no credibility at all as an honest witness. More importantly for this chapter, there were no questions about WHERE the vehicle turned around.

What was Tremain Anderson's recollection?

In providing his statement on the Tuesday night Tremain Anderson had this to say at point 31:

'*I heard the car stop and it would have been about two minutes since I saw it. I then heard a loud gun shot. It sounded like a high-powered rifle. It was probably a 30/30 which is what I have seen Dianne with, in the past. There was then probably a delay of say fifteen minutes in which time I kept walking through the scrub back towards the car. I then sat down again beside a tree and rolled a smoke and listened. The car then started up again and I heard it drive a little bit further up the road. From what I heard I assumed that it drove a little bit further up the gully where I had seen Bruce. I then heard another shot fire off. Then it was all quiet for about half an hour. I then heard the car start up again and I heard it travelling along the road. I could not see it from where I was, but from the noise it was travelling back down the river from the way it had originally come back towards the homestead, Palmerville Station.* '

On Friday 13 July, three days later Anderson participated in a walk through. Once again, the re-enactment was videotaped. This was part of that recording:

Anderson: *'And so I had the wind against me. So I had the wind coming this way. I couldn't hear. Bugger all, really. I heard the car pull up. I heard the shot. And then it was a half an hour of silence just with the wind. Then I heard the car start up again, turn around and proceed to head back the way it had come.'*

At that point in time, Detective Bell seemed determined to clarify whether the vehicle did turn around. Did she already understand the implications of that evidence for the Crown case?

Bell: *'Okay. Did you actually see it turn around and proceed back?'*

Anderson: *'No. But I heard it, plain as day, yeah.'*

B: *'Okay.'*

Anderson: *'Loud and plain as day.'*

B: *'So how come you believe it proceeded back the way it came?'*

Anderson: *'Well, it definitely come back down this track. Most definitely. And then later on in the day, like I explained in my statement, I run all the gullies and that right through to Palmerville Homestead and I seen it actually up on the road here where it had turned around.'*

That conversation was videotaped. They were on the spur line, a long way away from crime scene two, and Anderson was telling Detective Alina Bell the vehicle turned around *'just up there.'* He told her he went and observed the turn around location.

B: *'What did you see?'*

Anderson: *'I just seen where the tracks had turned around.'*

There was no video of the police and the witness then going to that location.

At the 2015 murder trial the prosecutor asked Anderson to recount everything he did after he met up with Bidner back at camp. Anderson provided a detailed account of going back to the gully where Bruce was last seen; running all the gullies he said. He even went down as far

323

as the homestead, on the opposite side of the river. He made no mention of going to the tracks where the vehicle made the u-turn.

Just as Bidner had his hour of shame (or two), Tremain Colin Anderson also had his 'hour of dishonest evidence' shame. This exchange occurred:

Feeney: '*Daniel Bidner did his own search?*'

Anderson: *'Not to my knowledge.'*

F: '*Did he come back with you to the gully?*'

Anderson: *'No. I went back on my own.'*

F: '*Did you go and go back to the gully and track a u-turn- or where you thought the vehicle had done a u-turn in that gully, with Daniel Bidner?*'

Anderson: *'No, I - because that was further up. I actually raced back to where Bruce was and ran up and down the gully looking for blood, or anything.'*

F: '*So you didn't even go to- further up the gully, where you heard the vehicle drive?*'

Anderson: *'Yeah, I didn't go up via the road, but I ran via the gully.'*

F: '*So you certainly didn't track any U-tun?*'

Anderson: *'No I didn't.'*

F: *'that the vehicle had done?'*

Anderson: *'I - I - I didn't follow it up the road to physically see a u-turn.'*

F: '*And it follows that you wouldn't have told Dan Bidner anything about attempting to track a u-turn of the vehicle when you came back to the camp at the crossing?*'

Anderson: *'No. I - I - I obviously looked for tracks on the road, but my attention was more focused in the gully.'*

F: *'You didn't tell him about tracking a u-turn that this vehicle had done?'*

Anderson: *'I don't recall, mate.'*

That exchange made a mockery of an answer he gave when questioned about Dianne, earlier in the trial.

Anderson: *'Sir, I am under oath, and I will endeavour to tell the truth to the best of my ability, and I'm telling you now both those people were there.'*

(Author note - to clarify potential confusion. The gully Bruce Schuler allegedly ran up was narrow with steep V sides. No vehicle could access it or drive up it. The vehicle had to drive along the spur on the ridge above the gully. When you read a witness or barrister talking about the gully, they were talking about the vehicle driving along the ridge line. It is only when you drive along the Ear Lobe and then descend the steep ravine do you get close to the gully. The jury had been to Palmerville Station so hopefully they understood the questions and their relativity to the scene. As Anderson said in response to a question - *I obviously looked for tracks on the road, but my attention was more focused in the gully.'*)

By that time, both Bidner and Anderson should have lost any credibility they had as honest and truthful witnesses. It also raises a significant and disturbing question. If you have one witness lying at a murder trial you have concerns, and of course you wonder about the motives of the witness for lying. But what do you have if you have two witnesses lying in the same murder trial. Witnesses who are 'almost family.' A conspiracy comes to mind. If they were both lying, the only commonality, it seemed was to ensure Struber and Wilson were convicted of the murder of Bruce Schuler. What could their motive be for that?

It is important to note what happened when the prosecutor closed the Crown case on day six of the trial. A procedural matter, but very significant. The Crown '*accepted*' some facts were not in dispute, just as you may recall the Defence had done at the start of the Crown case.

This was one of them, a conversation between Dan Bidner and Nick O'Brien:

(b) *the u-turn, like, after they left. I went, Right, I will go and see what they said to Bruce";*

(c) But after I went back to the car and waiting a while, me and Tremain - oh, Tremain went back first. I also went back. So we both - we went back to see the site separately. We did track where the car turned around. We went - yeah'.

The Crown was accepting that conversation had occurred despite Bidner strenuously denying it had. There can be only two conclusions – Bidner was lying or Bidner was mistaken. Did the jury even understand that? As I wrote earlier, the Crown did not admit '*The only thing I regret Sarge*" lie which was as strong as, or stronger than the u-turn evidence. Why didn't the Defence counsel jump up and down? By accepting the evidence, there was no necessity to call witnesses to prove the conversation had occurred, and therefore no need to discuss that pesky, inconvenient u-turn business. How good for the Crown!

The entire crime scene area was forensically mapped on Sunday 15 July 2012, just two days after the first re-enactment by Bidner and Anderson. Just two days after Bidner and Anderson repeatedly told investigators the Struber utility did a u-turn on the track, and returned to the homestead.

Obviously, the map produced by the Queensland Police Service should have showed exactly where the utility did that u-turn. But did it? The nodal points consisted of numbers N1 to N57. I have not been provided with, nor can I find a document which described each N point. I suggest the nodal point that appeared to be numbered N1, is where the u-turn occurred, based on the evidence provided by Anderson and Bidner. The N1 nodal point is very close to the X point, marked in the photograph in the chapter '*Crime Scene Location*.'

If there was no N point depicting the u-turn, why would that be? The jury attendance at the crime scene was not videotaped nor recorded in any manner, to my understanding. Was the jury shown where the vehicle did the u-turn? And if not, why not? It certainly wasn't mentioned in summing up. You know, along the lines of '*you will recall when we walked the crime scene at Palmerville Station, you were shown where it was claimed the Struber vehicle turned around and returned in the direction of the homestead.*'

How did Crown Prosecutor Rees deal with the u-turn evidence in summing up to the jury? Easily. He did not refer to it. But he did have the Struber vehicle heading in the direction of the gully I refer to as Crime Scene Two. These are some of his comments in summing up to the jury:

'This is an inferential case- sorry, circumstantial case full of inferences, and here, the crown cannot say who did what. The inference is that both accused arrived at the gully.'

Shortly afterward he added, *' There are multiple inferences.'*

You will note he did not say the accused drove to the gully. More dancing. How very convenient for the Crown case to say they *arrived* at the gully. It reminds me of that quote by Mark Twain, *'Never let the truth get in the way of a good story.'*

'Anderson tells you he heard the vehicle go off in a northerly direction.'

That was correct, Mr Prosecutor. But to be accurate, your next comment should have been, *'the witnesses then said the vehicle performed a u-turn and returned in the direction of the homestead.'*

But you didn't do that. As you never presented that evidence to the jury, there was no obligation for you to say that, was there? Instead, you danced around the subject and asked the jury to infer the Strubers arrived at the burnt patches.

'The second shot - which direction did they say it came from? Well, Daniel Bidner says it come from the direction of Bruce. The last place he saw Bruce was in the gully. Anderson says it came from the direction where the vehicle was further up the road. Again, remember, he said the vehicle moved north.'

Correct, Mr Prosecutor, until the u-turn.

'Tremain hears the vehicle start up again and heads in the direction of the gully.'

Same here Mr Prosecutor. More dancing.

Dan Bidner says he heard the vehicle start up and leave from that position he was in, he could see the cab. It was heading back to the homestead.'

That was correct, but if you '*inferred*' the vehicle had driven to the burnt patches then naturally, it would be heading back to the homestead, at some point.

'*The vehicle is heard driving in the direction of the burnt patches.*'

Again, correct Mr Prosecutor, but only part of the story. More dancing.

At page 16 he said this:'

The witnesses put Struber and Wilson at the gully. Dianne is seen with a firearm. A shot is heard after she is seen. All three of them hear that shot. Stephen is seen driving that vehicle. The vehicle is heard driving to the direction of the burnt patches[116].

That is all correct as you have read, but it was incomplete. Once again, I point out the prosecutor was very selective with his words. At no stage did he say the vehicle drove TO the burnt patches. The prosecutor was careful not to ask either of the prospector's questions about the Struber vehicle going to the burnt patches. The jury had to infer that. Because there was no evidence the vehicle did that.

These comments by Judge Henry, were said in the absence of the jury,' *The evidence was, as I recollect it, consistent with the sound of the vehicle moving in, very generally, that direction, not specifically so, though. That's probably about as high as you could put it.*[117]'

How did the Defence barristers deal with the u-turn? Mr Feeney, Barrister for Stephen Struber did not mention it. Mr Trevino for Dianne Wilson said this in summing up:

'The *third matter is the search (indistinct) u-turn. You might think that this inconsistency in Mr Bidner's account is denial in respect of his earlier statement and the inconsistency all of that evidence has with Mr Anderson's account is quite concerning and troubling. It certainly doesn't fit with the Crown theory about the significance of those tracks*

---

[116] Prosecutor summing up at Trial
[117] J. Henry day 6-8

that you can see in exhibit 2. Mr Bidner spoke about a u-turn and tracking a u-turn. I asked Mr Anderson about whether he imparted this information to Mr Bidner about tracking the u-turn on his own separately from Mr Bidner and you will remember that he knew nothing about it. Why was Mr Bidner so concerned to deny that - to deny that he had been back to the gully and that he'd seen those tracks and in fact there were u-turn tracks. The other most unusual, incongruous or mysterious feature in their evidence is this: the fact that neither hears any shouting yelling or screaming.'

Regrettably, I do not think Mr Trevino understood the importance of the location of the u-turn evidence. He seemed more focused on proving Bidner denied going to the site of the u-turn. By referencing the tracks, it suggested he was talking about the tracks to the burnt vegetation. It appears at no point did anyone on the defence team say words to the effect:' *If the vehicle did a u-turn along the track as the witnesses said, how did it then go to crime scene two*."

Teleporting

Teleporting - (especially in science fiction) transport or be transported across space and distance instantly. Did Stephen Struber and Dianne Wilson somehow end up in a live episode of Star Trek? Is there any logical explanation for what came next?

You have just read there was significant evidence that the Struber vehicle, or whoever's vehicle it was, or if there was even a vehicle there, did a u-turn after the two shots were fired. If you accept that evidence, then the next obvious question is: *'How then did the Strubers travel to crime scene two, murder Bruce and remove his body, along with all his possessions?* It did not appear to have been considered relevant for the Crown case, but it was obviously critical to the investigation.

As an investigator, you need to understand every single aspect of how the murder occurred. If you do not, amongst other things, you run the risk of being tripped up by witnesses who are lying. Teleporting was one option for the Strubers to go to and from the burnt patches, but unlikely. The obvious explanation of course, was the Strubers drove their utility from scene one to scene two, murdered Bruce, loaded his body and possessions on the tray of their utility (the clang), and returned to the homestead. The only problem with that scenario was the evidence given by the witnesses to police, and the evidence given at trial, did not support that option, and an inference was born. One of many.

The unnamed track from the Palmer River past the gully where Bruce Schuler was last seen went for about four kilometres before it joined up with a road. After leaving the riverbed, the track went up a steep incline, and then along the spur below which to the left was the gully where Bruce Schuler was last seen. As mentioned, the distance from

Crime Scene One to Crime Scene Two, by road, was approximately 200 metres made up of travelling in three separate and distinct directions.

Leaving the area above the first scene, the Strubers needed to drive approximately eighty metres along the spur line, following the track and mainly in a northerly direction. As Prosecutor Rees was prone to say, '*The vehicle is heard driving to the direction of the burnt patches.*' As I have commented before, but I will remind you, whilst travelling along the spur the vision down into the gully was very limited.

I have often wondered how the Strubers even knew where Bruce Schuler ran to. What was Bruce Schuler doing in that time? If you accept the police scenario, he was wounded but not bleeding. What a bizarre murder indeed. Yet, Schuler had only managed to run 140 metres in around fifteen minutes. It should have taken him less than five minutes. Even with all the baggage he had. What was he doing? He apparently didn't dump any of his belongings to lighten his load. After travelling north for eighty metres along the spur, there was a track off to the left known as the '*Ear Lobe*', called that for obvious reason. On the evidence of the prospectors, the Struber vehicle did not even make it as far as the turn off to the Ear Lobe. (Author note- it may help to revisit the photograph in the chapter *Crime Scene Location* to orientate yourself).

The jury heard about some clangs, but not that clanger. Once the Strubers turned left onto the Ear Lobe, they would have needed to have driven a further eighty metres, before heading down a steep incline for about forty metres, to arrive at the burnt areas of vegetation (Crime Scene Two).

And of course, to return to where they started from required driving in the reverse direction. Driving down and up the steep ravine would have required the LandCruiser to be in four-wheel drive, low range first gear with the engine revving loudly and the vehicle straining under the difficulty of negotiating the steep incline. With the brakes in poor condition and no hand brake. Due to the incline of the hill, it would have been necessary to strap Bruce Schuler's body down, to prevent it from falling off. More time required, and more opportunity to transfer trace evidence such as DNA.

And the vehicle unable to be put into reverse gear or it would be locked in reverse. As Detective Camp said, he was travelling at about five kph when traversing the ravine. So, in total, the Struber vehicle, after the second shot, would have driven roughly 300 metres, up and down a steep ravine, the Strubers had to load Schuler's body onto the tray of the utility and strap it down, collect his detector and anything else laying around, burnt the vegetation to destroy evidence, and then returned back past the prospectors on the ridgeline. In the process, they did not leave any footprints, boot prints, drag marks, scuff marks (Bruce did weight ninety kilograms after all) or evidence of their even being there.

At trial, Bidner was asked if the first shot was fired from the middle of the gully, and he replied he did not know. As you have read, there was no evidence Schuler, Struber or Wilson were ever in the gully known as the first crime scene.

However, the prosecutor seemed intent on placing Struber and/or Wilson in the gully. He knew the logistics of that. He had been there. Climbing down and up the steep sides of the gully. Did Bruce Schuler just stand there and watch her climbing down with a weapon but saying nothing? Yet that is exactly what he must have done. On the Crown case, Dianne then fired the shot at Schuler and injured him, some four minutes later. That defies comprehension. Yet Anderson said the first shot was as if it went down the gully. Groth said it was in the air, and as you read, was it a shotgun or high powered rifle they all heard.

In the last chapter you read the witnesses consistently said the vehicle performed a u-turn, after travelling a maximum of about twenty to eighty metres, after leaving the ridge above Crime Scene One.

Bidner was clear and precise throughout all interview and re-enactments on his evidence. As I have said, Bidner presented as a credible, confident witness. He never stumbled over his words or recollections. However, he was never challenged about the discrepancies either, and that was how he gave his evidence on the direction the vehicle travelled. Even the court bailiff commented Bidner and Anderson were good witnesses.

Bidner was asked whether he thought the vehicle had travelled 300 metres, and he replied he believed it travelled no more than 100 metres. Did that not raise red flags for the defence counsel and what about the prosecution? They had walked that ground. They could see it was more than 100 metres to the ridge line and the ravine. What were they doing?

He did not tell the police he heard the engine revving loudly, and roaring as it drove down and then back up a steep incline, in 4x4 low range first gear at five kph. The vehicle was stationery for twenty to thirty minutes on their claims; could they have done everything alleged in that time frame?

I address this comment in the next chapter, but he also never commented that he saw or smelt smoke coming from the ravine. How much time would it have taken to murder Bruce, carry (I won't say drag because that would have disturbed the earth) his body, and place on the tray of the 4x4, collect all his possessions, and burning various areas.

How did Bidner's evidence compare with the evidence provided by Tremain Anderson?' How did Prosecutor Rees address Anderson's evidence at the murder trial?

Prosecutor:' *Did you hear anything whilst you were in this little gully?'*

Anderson:' *I heard the vehicle stop. So pretty much when the vehicle pulled up, I pulled up.'*

P:' *Then what happened?''*

Anderson:' *There was just a little bit of a delay, then I heard another loud gunshot.'*

P: '*I should ask this. The first shot you heard, from what direction did you hear that shot.?*

Anderson: *'The first one?'*

P: '*Yes.'*

Anderson: *'meaning - well it presumed to that it - it was downstream - it was shooting downstream or down into the gully.'*

P: *'So it was coming from the direction of the gully?'*

Witness Anderson told the court the shot was fired into the gully. That couldn't be clearer. The prosecutor wanted Anderson telling the court the first shot had come from the direction of the gully, just as Bidner had said. You can read Anderson's reply.

Anderson: *'No. No. It was coming from the - it was coming from where the vehicle was for sure.'*

That was inconvenient for the prosecutor.

P: *'Now, the second shot, in which direction did you hear that come from?'*

Anderson: *'It was definitely coming from where the vehicle was. There was - the second shot was where the vehicle was, further up the road.'*

Another inconvenient answer for the prosecutor.

P: 'You didn't see the vehicle, though did you?'

Anderson: 'At the - no.'

Was the prosecutor challenging his own witness as to the direction the shot came from? But Anderson couldn't be any clearer. The shot came from where the vehicle was on the road. Further up the road.

P: *'What did you do after you heard the second shot?'*

Anderson: *'I just sat there for a little bit longer, and I think I actually moved a little bit just into the thicker shrubbery very near to where I first was sat.'*

P: *'And how long were you sat there?'*

Anderson: *'Probably about 15 minutes, half an hour. Coming onto half an hour.'*

P: *'Did you hear anything else after the second shot?'*

Anderson: *'No. I didn't.'*

No clang heard, yet Bidner was a lot further away than Anderson was.

P: *'What's the next thing that happened?'*

Anderson: *'Well, after about half an hour, the vehicle started up again and seemed to - seems to be heading back towards the river.'*

P: *' And you say that because of the noise, is that correct?'*

Anderson: *'That's correct?'*

Witness Anderson said he saw the vehicle tracks where the Struber utility turned around. He later retracted that claim as you have read. He did not tell police, the video camera or the jury he heard the vehicle travel any great distance. The vehicle would have had to travel 300 metres or more to reach crime Scene Two and return. He did not say he heard the engine revving loudly and roaring as it drove down and then back up a steep incline in 4x4 low range first gear at five kph.

And as with Bidner, he did not see or smell smoke. If Anderson had been asked how far or where he walked to reach the place the vehicle turned around, I believe he would have said he walked a short distance up the track to where the u-turn was. If you can believe Bidner, that is exactly where he went the next day with police officers

Police found no evidence of a vehicle doing a three-point-turn at the bottom of the ravine, below the burnt patches. Did the vehicle simply drive in and reverse out? The re-enactment video was shown to the jury, and the three-point turn was clearly visible in that video. Had Anderson said he had gone to that location, he would have had to walk around two hundred and fifty metres up and down a steep incline. He would have seen burnt patches. I am sure he would have mentioned that. Remember, on Tuesday the tracks down the ravine and the burnt patches had been neither seen nor found. More about that in the next chapter.

The fact neither Bidner nor Anderson told police they heard the Struber vehicle's engine roaring loudly for an extended time is significant evidence the Struber vehicle did not drive down or up the ravine.

At the JCU presentation in 2018, the videotape of the vehicle driving up and down the ravine was played to the audience. An audience member told me she could hear the engine revving loudly to make it up the ravine. She said stones and gravel were being thrown up by the spinning wheels and the grass was being flattened and burnt in the process.

Detective Sergeant Camp told the murder trial he had to drive up the slope in four-wheel drive, low range, first gear. He told the court he had to *'give it a little bit'* of accelerator to make it up the slope. For those readers not familiar with four-wheel driving, he was in the lowest gear possible.

How was the matter addressed in cross-examination? Barely at all as you heard in the last chapter.

When Tremain Anderson gave evidence-in-chief he tried to walk back his claims he repeatedly told police, about the vehicle turning around and heading back in the direction of the homestead. When asked what the next thing was to happen, he replied: *'The vehicle started up again and seemed to – seemed to be heading back towards the river.'* Yet he told Detective Bell it was *'plain as day'* that the vehicle turned around and travelled back toward the river.

As well as what was said in the last chapter, the prosecutor added this in summing up. For continuity I will include what was said in the last chapter:

'The witnesses put Struber and Wilson at the gully. Dianne is seen with a firearm. A shot is heard after she is seen. All three of them hear that shot. Stephen is seen driving that vehicle. The vehicle is heard driving to the direction of the burnt patches. (That inaccuracy has been addressed). *There was a second shot. There are tyre marks in the grass. Bruce Schuler's DNA is found in the burnt patches. Bruce was six foot and 87 kilos.*

*Inferentially (*there is that word again*), you may think Dianne is not going to be able to handle that body on her own. Inferentially, you may also think that after the first shot, if you conclude Dianne has taken that shot, Stephen Struber knew her intentions, and then they go off and do the second shot, or there is a second shot. (*and no mention of how they carried the body to the vehicle without leaving drag marks or disturbing the vegetation.) *There are scrape marks matching the accused's vehicle in the termite mound. (*Sorry Mr Prosecutor, the scrape marks did not match the accused's vehicle). *There is Bruce's DNA* on *the bailing twine. You heard he used it to secure his pickaxe.'* (Correct, evidence he was there, but not the Strubers).

I will deal with the prosecutor's jumbling up of the words '*consistent*', '*correspond*' and '*matching*' when it comes to the tyre tracks and anthill marks in the next chapter. Once again, the prosecutor carefully danced around the Struber vehicle going to the burnt patches. '*The vehicle is seen driving to the direction of the burnt patches.*'

In further summing up, the prosecutor had this to say:

'*Mr Schuler was shot in the region wherever he was last seen,* (and in case you have forgotten I will remind you), you know the First Crime Scene, where there was no blood or other forensic or physical evidence that Schuler was ever there, *made his way to where the burnt patches are, then there was a second shot, and as I say, ladies and gentlemen, the kill shot, you may infer.*'

In the absence of the jury, there was legal argument about whether the Struber unregistered 4x4 could even drive up and down the steep ravine. You may recall the police mechanic said he could not get the unregistered 4x4 into first or second gear in two-wheel drive, four-wheel high range, or four-wheel low range gear. The vehicle also had poor brakes and no handbrake. It is generally known you can not traverse steep, rough country in third gear.

Detective Camp said he was in first gear four-wheel drive extreme low range travelling at five kph. George Wilson and Stephen Struber both told the court it was difficult to engage first or second gear but it could be done, if you were careful. If you remember, I spoke with George Wilson who said it could not be put into reverse as it would then require removal of the top of the gearbox to disengage it. Detective Camp told the court he could not recall if he had any trouble putting it into first or second gear.

When Stephen Struber gave evidence, he told the court he was awaiting gearbox parts to repair the vehicle which arrived between the disappearance of Bruce Schuler and his second arrest on 31 October 2012.

The argument about whether the 4x4 could go up and down the ravine, covered twenty-three pages of court transcript, and a lot of court time, with the barristers concluding the vehicle could traverse the ravine, provided it was in low range first gear crawling along with the engine revving loudly. The argument about whether the 4x4 did go up and down the ravine covered zero pages of transcript. Not one barrister asked any witness whether they saw or heard the 4x4 driving up or down the ravine!

Not one.

Judge Henry understood the issue. At one point, in the absence of the jury he said this:

'See there's two issues, I think, here. One is whether or not a vehicle of the kind with which we're dealing here could actually be driven up and down the slope at all....But another issue is whether, in fact, the vehicle that we're concerned with here went up and down that slope on the day in question.[118]*'*

It was a bizarre situation where the evidence clearly showed the vehicle had not driven up or down the slope, but no witnesses were asked about that.

The jury were asked to infer it had. If the jury had heard the u-turn evidence, would they have concluded teleporting may have been the only option for the Strubers to go to and from the burnt patches? From researching this case and evidence that wasn't heard by the jury, there was no other option available to the Strubers.

---

[118] J Hendry day 5-64

Trees, Pats and Tracks

If the reader accepts the premise that the vehicle, owned by Struber, or if there was a vehicle even there, did make a u-turn and ipso facto, did not go to the Second Crime Scene, it raises more questions than answers. Add to that Senior Constable Ezard's fresh tyre evidence, and the findings of the Court of Appeal that the unregistered Struber ute could not have left the tyre tracks down the ravine, why would we even discuss the trees, cow pats and tyre tracks? Nevertheless, here we are.

What evidence did the police find on the ridge above the gully, down the ravine and at the area I have designated Crime Scene Two? It also raises the questions of when did this occur and how much of that evidence was linked to this crime?

As you read, there was an ear lobe track running off to the left of the main track. Think of it as two tracks in a semi-circular shape meeting at the middle. Thus, the Ear Lobe. There was evidence gathered from both tracks. On that evidence the Struber vehicle travelled on both sides of the Ear Lobe in an anticlockwise direction. So potentially it travelled an estimated 300 metres or more, that no witnesses heard or saw. On the same evidence, it was the registered Struber vehicle not the unregistered ute that left the tracks in the grass. The registered ute was the one with the tub on the back. The one the prospectors never said they saw at all.

On the right-hand track was a broken tree, scratches on a tree, gouges on two trees, gouges on a termite mound, and a struck tree. On the left-hand track were two fallen trees, a struck termite mound, two cowpats with tyre tracks in them, and two struck trees.

Once the two roads rejoined, the flat country disappeared down the ravine. When Police and SES searched this area, once they were alerted to the tyre tracks on the Wednesday afternoon, blood and a piece of twine were found nearby on a leaf, and further down the ravine burnt patches, the film canister and green fibre were found.

In total there were five burnt patches about twenty centimetres in size - burnt patches not much bigger than a dinner plate. The two 'main' burn patches could be covered by a blanket.

Four partially burnt matches were found in one of the charred patches, of which one of those matches had Bruce Schuler's DNA on it. A partially burnt match was also later recovered from the cabin of Bruce Schuler's locked 4x4.

What evidence was found in this entire area to connect Stephen or Dianne Struber to it? Nothing. No physical evidence; no forensic evidence. No personal belongings. The jury was required to infer that the Struber vehicle went down the ravine. There was then circumstantial evidence (since discredited) that may or may not have connected both of their vehicles to the area. To refresh the reader's memory, the police evidence suggested the damage to the saplings and the anthill may have been caused by the unregistered Struber ute.

The tracks down the ravine were consistent with having been caused by the registered Struber ute. Or the marks and tracks may have been caused by another 4x4 vehicle with a similar chassis altogether. If you accept the Crown case, the Strubers were so careful, so particular, to erase all evidence at scene one and the gully leading to scene two, as well as leaving no evidence on the ridge line implicating them or their vehicle. (Forensic awareness).

The Strubers then left a trail of breadcrumbs across the Ear Lobe and down the ravine that Hansel and Gretel would have been proud of. As well, apparently taking the film canister and twine from Bruce Schuler's body, and then dumping or carelessly dropping them on the ground[119].

The Crown claimed the killers burnt those patches of vegetation to destroy evidence of blood. They had gone to the trouble of burning five different patches, but there was no evidence about when they did that

---

[119] Interview with Det Sgt McLeish

or had the time to do that. There is also the question why they did not just burn the entire area, to ensure they destroyed all blood and other evidence. It is notable that none of the prospectors said they saw or smelt smoke. Add to that, there were no footprints, boot prints, drag marks or other evidence of how they managed to lift Bruce Schuler's body onto the tray of their vehicle. How many separate trips would it take to carry the body, collect the detector and all accessories. Maybe teleporting was an option?

Bruce Schuler's Nissan Patrol was examined for damage to the bulbar. The vehicle could not be eliminated as the vehicle that caused the damage to the trees on the Ear Lobe. The undercarriage was not examined to see if there was damage consistent with striking a termite mound.

The two Struber vehicles were examined at the homestead. But not for potential damage to the bulbar. They were examined for tyre comparisons with the cow pats and chassis damage consistent with striking a termite mound.

At this point it is relevant to refer you back to the admissions at trial by the defence, and I repeat, would Stephen Struber and Dianne Wilson have even understood what they were admitting to? The defendants would be taking advice from their barristers in those matters.

The significant areas of those admissions relating to the trees and tyres are repeated here for reference. **Bold** has been used for emphasis.

The points have been numbered for ease of reference.

1.) 'The gouge marks are **consistent with being made** by a metal component on the undercarriage of the unregistered Toyota Land Cruiser owned by the accused.'
2.) 'An examination of the gouge marks established a **positive comparison** between test marks, the cast taken from the vehicle, and test marks, cast taken from termite mounds.'
3.) 'The marks present within the termite mound **was consistent with having been caused by an object such as the underneath of a vehicle** or a similar type of tool capable of leaving such a mark.'

4.) 'These **impressions correspond in class characteristics, tread design and wear** to the tyres on the unregistered Toyota.'

5.) 'LandCruiser owned by the accused and **could have been made by the tyres on that vehicle or any other tyre** with similar tread characteristics.'

Because they were admissions, no witnesses were called to give evidence regarding them. As a result, there was no opportunity for Defence barristers to examine those witnesses on the validity and accuracy of that evidence.

The first obvious comment regarding those admissions was that nowhere was it said the marks or impressions were identical to the vehicles or tyres. That is very important and relevant. If the wording was that the marks were **identical**, that put it beyond doubt that it was a Struber vehicle that made them. The words used were '**consistent**', '**correspond**' and '**could have.**' A Struber vehicle may have made the marks or impressions or as was written '**any other tyre with similar tread characteristics**.' The underneath of Strubers 4x4 may have made the gouge or impressions or likely, **any other LandCruiser** utility the same as the Strubers. It was a circumstantial case after all.

Taken literally, that meant the Struber unregistered utility may or may not have caused the gauge marks as claimed in point one; that the vehicle may or may not have caused the marks on the termite mounts as claimed in point three; that the impressions referred to in points four and five may or may not have been made by the Struber vehicle.

As you read, Prosecutor Rees decided the tyre treads **matched** the impressions in the pats, and the gouge in the anthill **matched** the mark in the chassis of the Struber unregistered vehicle[120]. A synonym for **matching** is **identical.** What were the defence counsel doing? Why were they not jumping to their feet to pull the prosecutor into line? Was the jury confused? Or did they just conclude it **was** the Struber vehicle

---

[120] Crown summing up at trial

that was on the ridgeline, because the prosecutor said it was. (Graham Stafford will have someone to compare notes with).[121]

To have a successful circumstantial case, the Crown must link the various circumstantial points of evidence together, to form an unbreakable connection, like the individual links that comprise a steel chain. Therein lies the problem for the Crown with the Struber and Wilson case. What other circumstantial evidence?

What exactly did the jury hear at trial about the trees, pats and tracks?

The admissions the defence accepted as outlined above covered the trees, pats and tracks. The jury could conclude the Struber vehicle may have caused that evidence. Or did cause the evidence, if they accepted the words of prosecutor Rees. To that time in the trial, all the jury knew about the gearbox in the unregistered Struber LandCruiser was that a police mechanic could not engage first or second gear in any range and then they heard and saw Detective Sergeant Camp drive the same unregistered Struber utility down and up the ravine with no difficulty. He had to be in four-wheel drive, low range first gear travelling at about 5 kph but he had no problem traversing the slope.

The jury also heard George Wilson say you could get the ute into first gear, but it was difficult. Officer Camp gave evidence that tracks were observed across the flat country above the ravine and down the slope at about 1.40 p.m. on Wednesday 11 July 2012 by SES volunteers. Following that, the damage to the saplings and anthill were observed on the flat ground above the ravine. Two cow pats were seen to be flattened with tyre impressions in them. Burnt patches of grass were found on the side of the slope and at the base of the ravine, near the gully Bruce Schuler was last seen in.

A clear plastic film canister was located about ten metres from one of the burnt patches. Burnt matchsticks were visible in another burnt patch, and a piece of black bailing twine was located. On the 14th of July after further searches, another drop of blood was found[122].

---

[121] Murder of Leanne Holland 1991
[122] Statement by Det Sgt Camp

In summing up, Defence Barrister Mr Feeney for Stephen Struber had very little to say about that evidence. He did urge the jury to take a close look at the evidence. He did comment it would not be surprising if Bruce Schuler lit a fire whilst prospecting, and perhaps a minor mishap resulted in his blood and DNA being found.

Which of course could be entirely possible, and entirely impossible on the evidence of the prospectors. He also pointed out the age of the tracks was not known. It was just inferred they were made by the Strubers.

Defence Barrister Mr Trevino for Dianne Wilson spent some time addressing the jury on this aspect of the evidence. He pointed out to the jury there was no evidence given as to when the tracks were made, and they could have been there for days; and there was no evidence of a connection between the tyre tracks and the burnt patches.

As to the burnt patch, well, it was not located until the 11th of July and that was after the defendants had been taken from the property. We simply don't know if the tracks came before the burnt patch or the other way around.'

That was a very valid point. He pointed out Bruce Schuler could be connected to those patches and other located evidence in that area. He reminded the jury of the comment by barrister Feeney of a possible mishap by Schuler in that location.

He finished by pointing out the damage to the anthill or the impressions in the cow pats could have been made by any similar vehicle.

Mr Trevino had this very telling comment to make:

'The crown rely on 2 items to suggest that they were made by the unregistered LandCruiser. The mould of the termite mound and the cowpat bushes. But neither of those matters take the Crown very far in analysis. In respect of the termite mound, read the whole of that paragraph, because it finishes with essentially any tool for the underneath of any vehicle could have caused that scraping. In respect of the mould in the cowpat, that could have been made by any vehicle with a tyre with similar tread characteristics. So ultimately, I suggest

to you that the forensic evidence proves very little apart from, perhaps, Mr Schuler's presence in that gully.'

What did prosecutor Rees have to say to the jury in summing up?

On page ten of his summing up, Prosecutor Rees told the jury the gouge marks in the termite mound were consistent with being made by the unregistered LandCruiser. By page sixteen of the same summing up, he had the gouge marks **matching** the Struber vehicle. He then went onto say that the tyre impressions were **identical** to the impressions in the cowpats (shades of the Holland case all over again).

What did he say exactly? *'Cowpats with tyre impressions that match unregistered LandCruiser.'* He added *'The inference is that there can be no doubt that this vehicle was driven in that area.'* An error he repeated at the Court of Appeal hearing in 2016 when he submitted:

'Tyre marks matching the accused's vehicle were located coming from the direction of the top of the slope/steep embankment.'

It was a bizarre situation where the forensic evidence found the unregistered LandCruiser did not leave the tyre impressions in the cow pats, but the jury was asked to infer that it had. You must ask yourself this question. If the Struber vehicle did not leave the tyre tracks in the bush, did not knock over the saplings and did not damage the anthill, who did, and when?

And of course, as retired police officer Bob Haydon commented, but no one pointed out to the jury, Bruce Schuler had perfect cover in the gully. He could have hidden there all day from the Strubers. Instead, he chose to run towards the shooters, up a steep forty-five-degree incline, carrying many loosely held items.

There are so many holes in the evidence I do not believe any conclusion can be reached other than it likely did not occur in the way the police claimed.

Perhaps the answer lies in the next chapter *'Crime Scene Staging.'*

Crime Scene Staging

Criminologists do study Crime Scene Staging (CSS). They have concluded it does occur, in one form or another. In a recent article by Dr Claire Ferguson of New England University and Dr Wayne Petherick of Bond University they wrote this:

'Staging is a specific form of precautionary act, and one of many that offenders may carry out in order to distance themselves from the crime. According to the literature, this type of precautionary act is not uncommon in criminal investigations (Geberth, 2006; Hazelwood & Napier, 2004).'

Crime scene staging is not a recent invention. It has likely been around, in one form or another since time immemorial. It is probable, that with advanced investigator training, the introduction of photography and videography, and investigators being trained to be conscious of it, crime scene staging is more likely to be noted, observed or suspected now than in previous decades and centuries.

Did crime scene staging occur in the murder of Bruce Schuler? That is a question that has long troubled me. Is there evidence of crime scene staging? Yes, I believe there is strong evidence it did occur.

You will recall there was NO evidence of either Bruce Schuler, Dianne Wilson or Stephen Struber ever being at the location I designated as Crime Scene One. No evidence at all. No abandoned physical possessions. No blood, no DNA, no sign of a struggle or drag marks, no tyre impressions, no footprints, no ammunition or shell casings. Nothing. What are the chances of three persons not leaving something at the scene, and at least two of them not taking something away from the scene?

What are the chances of Bruce Schuler running away in fear, carrying a significant number of bulky, loosely held possessions, and not dropping a single item? That just defies comprehension. Add to that, no forensic or physical evidence was located between Scene One and Scene Two. I suggest criminologists would describe it as a 'classic' example of a staged crime scene. Except there was nothing to stage. What evidence, apart from the word of the three prospectors whose credibility is in tatters, existed to prove Schuler had ever been at the bottom of the gully and the Strubers' had been on the ridge line above?

Allow me to put it this way. How hard would it be to stage the first scene? It would be this simple, this easy. Dig a hole in the ground at the bottom of the gully and then tell police *'That is where we last saw Bruce Schuler.'*

In my discussion with Detective Sergeant McLeish, he told me their investigations suggested Bruce Schuler was wounded at the first crime scene and then made his way to the burnt patches. Sorry Sergeant, I find that claim nonsense. Where is the evidence, apart from the word of your two less than credible witnesses?

What about the second scene? Was there evidence of it also being staged? I believe the evidence showing scene two was staged to be more compelling than scene one.

Small blood stains on leaves and rocks identified as coming from Bruce Schuler were found. What about brain fragments, pieces of bone or body organs, or large pools of blood? Especially if Bruce Schuler had been shot at close range by a .357 magnum handgun as alleged by police. The .357 magnum was designed in the USA in the 1930's to combat gangsters who were using submachine guns, particularly the Thompson SMG. A .357 round was designed to go through an engine block.

If such a bullet struck Bruce Schuler it would have left a very large exit wound and taken with it a large amount of blood and bodily organs or brain matter. The shock from a high velocity bullet such as the .357 round, even a flesh wound, can be enough to kill. Depending on the angle of fire obviously, there would be a strong chance of finding that spent shell in the dirt. A metal detector was used to cover the area and only an old bullet round was found.

Police claimed the burnt patches destroyed the forensic evidence. That may be the case but the location of those burnt patches was not consistent with Bruce Schuler being murdered in that location. They were spread over a considerable area and halfway up the steep incline. *'Was that because he was staggering around after being shot'*? Except there were no footprints, drag marks or trampled grass consistent with that claim.

Tremain Anderson described the twine Bruce Schuler used to secure his GPS to his belt as *'flimsy'*.[123] Of all the possessions he carried, he dropped a small film canister, some twine and an old slug. Detective McLeish informed me that Bruce Schuler did not drop anything. The possessions had been taken from his body by the offenders. That claim is nonsensical. Again, no blood, no disturbance of the vegetation.

The offenders took items from his body and then left them behind to be found, and in the process not leaving their DNA but they transferred the victims DNA. When I queried Detective McLeish about the lack of drag marks, he explained the area had been burnt by the offenders. When I queried the suggestion that a fire would have destroyed drag marks, he commented that he didn't know if there were drag or scuff marks[124]. I have repeatedly asked 'How do you carry or drag a ninety-kilogram dead weight without leaving any evidence at all? Particularly where one of the lifters is a small-framed woman.

How hard would it be to stage the second crime scene? Let's explore that. First, there were tyre tracks down to the crime scene but no footprints, boot marks, scuff prints etc. I do not claim to have all the answers, but this scenario seemed possible - the offenders drive down there, throw out the items of Schulers, pour out some of Schuler's blood from a container, pour accelerant out of the car windows and throw matches to light it. The matches came from Schuler's car so one

---

[123] Interview with DSC Bell
[124] Interview with det Sgt B McLeish

match had his DNA on it as you will read shortly, and then they drive out.

Schuler's DNA was identified on one of four partially burnt matches. How did that get there? According to Fiona Splitt, he hated prospectors lighting fires. So was he there detecting and he lit fires. That would go against Fiona's claims. It also made no sense. When was he there? Did he run up there after he was shot at (and wounded) and then light fires to go prospecting? Ridiculous.

There were similarly burnt matches found in his locked vehicle. Forensic awareness? Had he been prospecting in that location prior to him going missing? According to the other prospectors none of them had been in that location. So how did it get there? Perhaps the murder did occur there, but not at the time or in the circumstances we have heard described.

Did the investigators ask themselves how Bruce Schuler's DNA found its way onto a burnt match at that crime scene? According to Detective Sergeant McLeish, Schuler's DNA found its way on to the matches because the offenders had been carrying Schuler's body and had transferred his DNA to the burnt match, but not their own DNA? Struber and Wilson had expertly managed to ensure Bruce Schuler's DNA did not get on their bodies, their clothes, their vehicles and their house but they managed to transfer HIS DNA onto a match. What are the mathematical chances of that happening?

There was no doubt a vehicle drove across the Ear Lobe and down the slope. The unanswered, ignored or brushed aside question was, when? Was that another matter best left alone? (Ghost evidence?). There is also the question of what the jury was told or not told?

You will recall prosecutor Rees said the tyre tracks *matched* the Struber vehicle and the gouge mark on the chassis *matched* the gouge in the termite mound. You read where Senior Constable Ezard concluded the tyre tracks were *similar* to the registered Struber 4x4, not the unregistered vehicle and a forensic scientist said the gouge marks were consistent with having been caused by an object such as the underneath of a vehicle. How do those conclusions morph into *matched*?

I spoke with George Wilson. You will recall George. It was claimed he was heading to a meeting with police with a dead body under a tarpaulin on the back of his ute. He had lived almost his entire life on Palmerville Station. He was hoping to buy Palmerville Station. He may not be a trained investigator, but he is a very experienced stockman and bushman.

He saw those burnt patches. He examined the entire area. In fact, after the arrest of Struber and Wilson, solicitor Ann English asked him to go there and look for potential evidence. He found more burnt matches which were passed to police. He told me that from his view of what he saw, he believed the burnt areas were designed to attract attention, not destroy evidence.

And as you read in the chapter 'Teleporting', there was no evidence the Struber LandCruiser even went to the second scene. You had to infer it. There was no evidence of drag marks, footprints, disturbed earth or anything else you would expect to see when a man and a very small woman drag or otherwise get a ninety-kilogram dead weight onto the tray of a vehicle.

And then make several back-and-forth trips picking up the metal detector, pick, GPS, backpack and any other accessories. Except the film cannister. Which they took from the victim, according to Detective Sergeant McLeish but then abandoned, to be found as evidence.

I have no doubt the Crown could mount a persuasive argument that the crime scenes were not staged. If that was the only discrepancy in this case, I may be persuaded to accept their argument.

How and when did those burnt patches get there on the side and bottom of that steep ravine? Police conducted several foot searches of the area on the Tuesday and Wednesday morning and countless helicopter searches. The police first found the burnt patches late Wednesday afternoon. If the Strubers were responsible, the only time available to them would have been on the Monday night.

Does that mean they left Bruce Schuler's body there and collected it later; or went back to clean up the crime scene, yet Anderson saw nothing and found nothing at the first scene, or along the way to what would become the second crime scene. That may be an option. Before or after Stephen Struber was calling his brother of course. The Strubers were arrested and taken from the property Tuesday night and did not return for around one week.

Were the jury and probably the defence counsel aware of when the burnt patches first appeared? There is no evidence to suggest they were. You read where Defence Barrister Travino told the jury there was no evidence of the age of the tracks. After all, it was the Crown case the Strubers left those tracks, knocked over the sapling and collided with the anthill on the way to and from Crime Scene Two.

Whilst researching the evidence, it was difficult to pin down when the tracks, pats and trees were first noticed. Until now. It was a case of trawling through all police and witness statements, and all police diaries and notebooks, and collating and cross checking the evidence.

What do we know about the burnt patches and the tyre tracks? We know the entire area was flooded with police on the Tuesday and Wednesday searching for Bruce Schuler, and evidence of what happened to him. We know the first time the tracks were mentioned by police was on Wednesday 11 July 2012. Two full days after Schuler went missing.

We know the prospectors never claimed to have seen them. We know initial searches by police never noticed them. We know helicopters were flying in that very location, at tree top level, scanning the ground for signs of Bruce Schuler. They were not seen from the air. Senior Constable Vincent wrote that at about 1.40 p.m. on that Wenesday, he observed what appeared to be recent vehicle tracks in the grass about 100 metres past the mining equipment, on the left-hand side of the track. He followed the tracks for about 100 metres, and they disappeared over a ridge, down a steep embankment, toward the dry gully. He saw the tracks went down and back up the embankment.

But he was not the only officer to search that area. Senior Constable Soles searched that same area the day before, Tuesday. This is what he put in his statement:

'10. Shortly after 12 midday we walked upon an old mining plant on a ridge, leading to and from this ridge was a vehicle track. Adjacent to this ridge was a gully, this gully was then described by BIDNER as being the last place he saw SCHULER. A foot search of this location was then conducted. I was then informed that location was identified as a crime scene.

11. I personally conducted a search adjacent to the vehicle tracks, I did not find anything related to the investigation.'

A search adjacent to the vehicle tracks found nothing. To clarify, he was searching adjacent to the vehicle track that ran alongside the gully all the way to the main road. So, a day before Vincent found the tracks in the exact same location, they were not there. They both mentioned the old mining plant. Officer Lauder was more specific.

Senior Constable Lauder covered the same ground on Tuesday 10 July 2012, but he was clearer as to what he wrote in his statement: *'9. That location was down in a dry gully or creek bed with steep walls on either side. I walked from that location up the dry creek bed with steep walls on either side. I walked from that location up the dry creek bed for about 500 metres before turning back and returning to the same point. I then climbed back up out of the gully and <u>walked up the roadway that runs beside the gully for about the same distance.</u> I then returned and took up with the others.'* From the wording of his statement, he walked along the exact same route officer Vincent walked (although he did not mention the mining equipment).

Officer O'Brien wrote in his diary that on that Tuesday he went with Bidner and other police to where Schuler was last seen:

- *'Conduct search of area used by Struber. Nil evidence found.'*

Quite an unusual comment – *area used by Struber*. Did he mean the road? Detective Sergeant McLeish wrote in his statement that at about 9.10 a.m. that Wednesday morning he and other police returned to the 'primary crime scene' and conducted a further foot search but nothing of interest was located. If they were searching *the area used by Struber* they would have been on top of the tracks. In his notebook he wrote that after that search, they:

- '*drove track out to main road.*'

That track went along the ridge above the gully, past the old mining equipment, past the track to the left known as the earlobe, to the main road. Straight past where the tracks were eventually seen. Once he reached the main road he would have turned right and crossed the Palmer River, the same crossing used by the prospectors.

Officer Messer, who was in charge of Search and Rescue, recorded in his diary that at 3.50 p.m. he was informed the following had been found:

- '*clothing, film canister, matches burnt fire, blood on leaves.*'

That was the first and only ever mention of clothing being found at Crime Scene Two or in the vicinity. What was the clothing found, where di it come from and was it connected with this investigation?

Officer Nick O'Brien recorded many notes in his diary. He wrote that, with others, they went to the last know place where Schuler was seen and searched the gully left and right. He also wrote this:

- '*O'BRIEN/BIDNER/TOME walked right to end, back along roadway to original place where STRUBER vehicle first observed.*'

Of course, he could have meant they walked the gully back down to the river and walked up the road where Struber allegedly drove. If he was referring to walking in the other direction, once again they would have walked on top of the tracks found on the Wednesday.

Officer Pettman noted that after the C.I.B returned from the initial walk to the scene with witness Bidner, the CI.B then drove to the crime scene. That would be the reverse direction to that mentioned by McLeish above, except this also occurred on the Tuesday. Once again, no mention of seeing tracks.

Do not forget, Dan Bidner told Officer Riles on the Tuesday night, and repeated it in evidence, that he and police officers went to the place the vehicle did the u-turn on the Tuesday, well before 2 p.m. That is in the exact same area where the tracks were found Wednesday. Yet those police did not notice them. The obvious conclusion was there were no tracks there on Tuesday afternoon.

I also read the SERT officers were taken to the gully where Schuler was last seen on the morning of Wednesday 11 July. There is no record of where they searched or didn't search, but they were driven there by road. It is likely some of them searched the spur line, some the gully.

What conclusions can we reach from that? I suggest we cannot conclude the burnt patches, and the tyre tracks occurred at the same time. We CAN conclude, based on the evidence of all the above officers, particularly Lauder and Vincent, that the tyre tracks in the grass, 100 metres past the old mining equipment were NOT visible at about 1 p.m. on Tuesday 10 July 2012, but they WERE visible on Wednesday at 1.40 p.m.

Therefore, they were not there when the Strubers supposedly drove to Crime Scene Two. I believe we can conclude the burnt patches, the blood, matches and film canister were consistent with some staging or 'forensic awareness' happening in that part of the crime scene.

Who could have made them between 1 p.m. Tuesday and 1.40 p.m. Wednesday? As I wrote previously, if the Strubers were up there Tuesday afternoon, they would have been seen and heard by police and prospectors alike. By 6 p.m. Tuesday, they would have been more focused on the armed police outside their home. From that point on, they were in custody and removed from the property.

The prospectors were on their way to Mareeba from around 2 p.m. that Tuesday. Were the tyre tracks even associated with this murder? You would have to conclude they were. They went to the burnt patches where Schuler's blood was found. So, who made them?

Was that area guarded by police overnight?

The obvious question is *'why was the jury not told that?'*

The evidence regarding the tyre tracks and the burnt patches was so disconnected, so disjointed, was it possible a police vehicle or SES vehicle made those tracks across the flat terrain and down the ravine, whilst transporting searchers to or from the area?

Perhaps the driver was not aware of it or did not want to own the mistake. To further confuse the entire scene, were the tracks in the grass separate to the tracks in the area where the saplings were knocked over and the anthill damaged? There was a lot of traffic in the area, transporting searchers around.

I am aware of at least one police vehicle driving along the tracks on Thursday 12 July 2012 until they were radioed and advised to stop and reverse out. Who is to say another police or SES vehicle was not spotted, and drove down the ravine?[125]

And then there was this significant evidence that again, the jury never heard. As you read, there were burnt patches found on the side of the ravine. No one knew when the grass was burnt, but one officer described them as freshly burnt areas. The prospectors did not give evidence they saw or smelt smoke on the Monday, or the Tuesday. Neither did police on the Tuesday.

A member of a road repair gang had a very specific recollection of the smoke and gave police a very detailed statement nine days later. He recalled Tuesday 10 July 2012. He saw several police vehicles go through the road works before lunch. He then had lunch and went back to work.

He heard from a co-worker on the two-way radio of smoke to the northwest. He went to a high ridge and saw what he described as a chimney of white smoke. He described that as strange as nothing burns white in the bush. He said the smoke was only visible for about ten minutes[126].

He believed it was likely an accelerant was used as that causes the smoke to be usually quite white. This smoke was apparently coming from the direction where Bruce Schuler was last seen. The road worker told his supervisor, and another worker as noted in his statement, but no statements were obtained from either of them.

---

[125] Notebook of Officer Lauder 24/7/12
[126] Statement D Ryan

Whilst no time was mentioned apart from having lunch it would appear the time was between perhaps 12 p.m. and 1 p.m. that he sighted the smoke on the Tuesday. The only people in the area at that time were the police and the prospectors.

Had the Strubers driven up to the Ear Lobe and down the ravine on that day, at that time, they would have almost run over the police at the scene. At the very least, their presence would have been heard by all, and everyone would have seen or smelt the smoke.

Could the witness have been out by a day? His statement was nine days later. He associated the fire with the police presence. Could he have been referring to the Monday around 1 p.m.? The Strubers were long gone by then. The only ones around the crime scene were the prospectors. There was another witness who saw the smoke and contacted police. He gave a statement also. He thought he saw the smoke on the Monday.

Investigators engaged the services of an arborist. He viewed the police photographs of the saplings knocked over by a vehicle. From those photographs, he estimated they were damaged on the Sunday night or Monday[127].

We know the Struber vehicle did not go down the ravine. That estimation by the arborist may be consistent with the trees being damaged on the Monday, at the same time the white smoke was observed.

What have we learnt from all of this? It was a very confusing crime scene in which nothing made sense. I am of the belief all three events occurred at separate times. That is, the u-turn was one specific event. At some other point in time, the tyre tracks across the ridge and down the ravine, including the damaged trees and cow pads were made. At some other random time, someone set fire to some vegetation and dropped a film canister and blood.

---

[127] Statement by W Taylor.

Window Dressing

Whatever your thoughts on Kevin 'Rusty' Groth, he was central to this story. As I have said, without him, his companions may have been considered snake oil salesmen. Whatever his involvement, his evidence does deserve consideration.

I have only had one conversation with Kevin Groth. A twenty-five-minute telephone call in December 2023. He told me he had told the police and the court everything he knew. He knew nothing else. He denied being involved in the murder of Bruce Schuler. He has not spoken to Dan Bidner or Tremain Anderson for over nine years, not long after the court case, and then only Dan, not Tremain.

When I asked him if they knew where he lived, he told me that at the time of the trial, there were cars moving around out on the farm where he was living, so he moved into town. He told me they do not know where he now lives. Kevin did not understand the meaning of an Indemnity against Prosecution. I explained it to him, and I told him I had a criminal solicitor on standby who would act on his behalf and approach the prosecution for an Indemnity against Prosecution in exchange for telling them what happened on Palmerville Station. He declined and said he had told the police everything he knew. At the end of the call, we agreed to stay in touch.

He has not responded to further calls or messages. After the information about the Sunday night satellite phone call became known, I begged him to contact me and tell me what he knew. I have not heard from him.

Dan Bidner and Tremain Anderson have ignored messages to call me.

A Very Stressful Situation, or was it?

Was the murder of Bruce Schuler a stressful and traumatic event for the prospectors? A reasonable question. A reasonable answer could be that witnessing a murder or shooting would be a very traumatic event for everyone involved. Ordinarily, reviewing whether a violent criminal event was stressful or traumatic would not even be considered. Why this time?

With so many questionable claims by the witnesses, the never-ending discrepancies, the ever-changing story line, I considered exploring whether it was traumatic for the prospectors a valid question. I wanted to test whether the prospectors' actions after the event were consistent with it being a stressful event.

Without doubt, people will react differently to a stressful or traumatic event. There are a myriad of studies and examples of how people can and do respond to trauma and stress. There were three witnesses. It may be possible we could see three different responses to the unfolding calamity around them. I have spoken personally to two of the police investigators involved in the Bruce Schuler murder, Detective Sergeant Brad McLeish and former Detective Sergeant Scott Furlong.

In an interview with Detective Sergeant Brad McLeish, he said: '*it is entirely plausible that three witnesses under a high-stress situation are going to have inconsistencies in their statements and their versions and their evidence.*' In the same interview:' *Again, witnesses have just heard gunshots in a high-stress situation who have seen two people they know to be violent and have used weapons before running for their lives.*'

I asked former Detective Sergeant Furlong for his opinion on the discrepancies. He wrote a nineteen-page report which was more advising that the convictions were sound, and the evidence was solid.

He provided case law where various courts, including the High Court found that discrepancies in witness testimony should not automatically discredit the reliability of the evidence, especially in cases involving traumatic events.

He wrote: '*Minor variations in recollection are natural and do not undermine the core facts if the essential narrative remains consistent and is corroborated by other evidence. In this case, the discrepancies highlighted by the defence involve minor details, such as the precise timeline of events or specific actions of individuals.*'

He concluded it was a stressful and traumatic event and mentioned that four times and three times respectively in his report. You can find Scott's report: '*Legal Argument: Guilt of Stephen Struber and Diane (sic) Struber-Wilson in the Murder of Bruce Schuler*' as Appendix E.

Both police were satisfied that the event was traumatic and stressful and the actions by the prospectors was normal, to be expected and consistent with having experienced a traumatic event. With no disrespect to Brad or Scott, I considered that their claims it was a stressful and traumatic event needed fact checking.

Firstly, I do not agree with Scott Furlong's conclusions regarding the discrepancies being minor. I believe the discrepancies I have identified and outlined were central to the events of that day, as well as days before and after. Stressful or traumatic event aside, I believe there are too many discrepancies, and they are far from minor. To my mind, they challenge the credibility of the prospectors, and I am suspicious of their motives. As such, I need to explore them and satisfy myself they were of no consequence to the events of those days.

What would be reasonable conduct after hearing two shots in the bush, and your friend goes missing, would obviously be open for discussion. I believe the companions would likely regroup at the riverbed camp and wait and see who does or doesn't arrive back. I would expect immediate calls to Bruce Schuler's satellite phone. I would expect immediate calls to friends for advice. Should we call police? What should we do? Did those things happen?

Anderson and Bidner gold detected their way back to camp. Even though Kevin Groth did not immediately reappear, there was never any apparent concern for his welfare. The prospectors focused on Bruce Schuler. They went looking for Bruce Schuler, and calling out for Bruce Schuler.

If the prospectors did not regroup or return to the riverbed camp, I would have expected the prospectors to return to the last known point where they were all together. The gully where the gold had been found. The Struber ute by that time had disappeared and apparently no longer a threat. Would it be obvious to regroup there? In any event, the prospectors did neither of those things.

McLeish said the witnesses were *running for their lives*. Were they? Tremain Anderson rolled a smoke whilst the violent offenders were less than 100 metres away. Dan Bidner was dreaming of going fishing. They both detected for gold immediately after the event, even though Tremain Anderson was concerned Struber may be on foot, and stalking them[128].

McLeish also said as you read, '*.... have seen two people they know to be violent and have used weapons before running for their lives.*' The prospectors knew them to be violent, but that did not stop them trespassing on Palmerville Station and setting up camp literally under the nose of the people they knew to be violent. There is that '*running for their lives*' again. I did not read, see or hear a similar comment anywhere, particularly from the prospectors.

Scott Furlong's dissertation on the quality of the convictions is a matter for the lawyers. I am exploring the conduct of the witnesses. As I mentioned, he considered the discrepancies minor.

Was Kevin Groth traumatised or stressed by the event? He had started leaving the area before the first shot. He said he had been warned to hide if he saw anyone coming, because the Strubers had previously fired over the head of Tremain Anderson. '*That is what they do. They scare you.*' And then he forgot the reason he was told to hide, and

---

[128] Re-enactment by T Tremain

rambled on about not wanting to give away his prospecting position, because others will want to search there also.

By the second shot, he was 300 metres away. At trial, he was asked how he was feeling at that time. He replied:' *It's a bit – yeah - nerve-wracking.*' Really? Later, when asked again, he said,' *Oh, a bit worried and that.*' Not '*I was scared for my life! I was out of my mind! I was thinking we were all going to die.*' It was just nerve wracking.

He then wandered around the bush for six hours. He even had a sleep. What traumatic event did he witness or was he a victim of? Did he ever receive counselling? Kevin Groth had been told they were not welcome on the property, and he had been warned Struber fired over your head to scare you. He was aware the landowners wanted them gone, yet it took him six hours to get back to camp; after hearing no further shots; and being around only two kilometres from the camp.

What about Dan Bidner and Tremain Anderson? Anderson had recent experience of the Strubers allegedly firing over his head. He knew he was not welcome on their property. On his own words, Struber fired over their head to scare them. As he told the camera in his first re-enactment, Tremain said:' *And the reality is, you're not going to sit there. Even if the guy is only scaring me, he's still got a gun and he's a nasty person. Yep.*' What was his traumatic moment?

And Dan Bidner similarly. He knew of the threats. Stephen Struber firing over their heads should have come as no great surprise to them. They were obviously not worried about camping in the river, not far from the homestead. Would they have wanted police protection as soon as possible, to extract themselves and head home? He was wishing he had a fishing line.

But the police investigators had decided, for whatever reason, it was a stressful and traumatic event. That needed assessment. I asked Artificial Intelligence this question: '*How do witnesses react in high stress situations?*'

This was the reply:

Eyewitnesses in high-stress situations often exhibit a range of reactions due to the intense pressure they experience. Stress can significantly affect their perception, memory, and behaviour.

Some common reactions include

Narrowed focus (tunnel vision): *Witnesses may focus on a particular detail (like a weapon) while missing other important information.*

Memory distortion: *High stress can impair the accuracy of their recollection, causing them to confuse details or misidentify people. Stress may also cause memory gaps.*

Fight, flight, or freeze responses: *Some witnesses may attempt to act or escape the situation, while others may freeze in place, unable to react.*

Increased emotional responses: *Witnesses may become overwhelmed with emotions like fear, anxiety, or confusion, which can cloud their judgment and recall.*

Physiological responses: *Stress can lead to increased heart rate, rapid breathing, and adrenaline surges, which may affect their ability to process events clearly.*

Despite these challenges, some witnesses may demonstrate remarkable recall in certain situations, though overall, high stress tends to reduce the reliability of their testimony.

Warnings signs of stress in adults may include:

Crying spells or bursts of anger.

Difficulty eating.

Losing interest in daily activities.

Increasing physical distress symptoms such as headaches or stomach pains.

Fatigue.

Feeling guilty, helpless, or hopeless.

Avoiding family and friends.

How can you identify a person who is experiencing stress?

Physical signs of stress

Difficulty breathing.

Panic attacks.

Blurred eyesight or sore eyes.

Sleep problems.

Fatigue.

Muscle aches and headaches.

Chest pains and high blood pressure.

Indigestion or heartburn.

Plenty to work with there. I considered the evidence. What traumatic event did the prospectors participate in? They heard two gunshots some distance away from them, in the bush. They saw nothing. No violence, no blood. They did not hear screams, shouts, cries for help. On the distances recorded in the forensic map, Tremain Anderson was eighty metres away from the weapon when it discharged. I have queried elsewhere his claims his ears were ringing from the shot, and I wondered about the honesty of that claim. Dan Bidner was 200 metres away and Kevin Groth was a whopping 300 metres away, in the bush.

I then considered the points made by Artificial Intelligence against the conduct and statements made by the three prospectors. I was fortunate that I was able to listen to lengthy audio files and watch all video interviews with the prospectors. I did not see any of the symptoms or signs suggested by Artificial Intelligence in the statements, in the audio files or in the video files. Quite the opposite.

Bidner or Anderson liked to video record their own prospecting trips. Hence the two videos taken that trip. I was also able to access five other videos where Bidner and/or Anderson were filmed prospecting on other occasions; Bruce Schuler appeared in one video wearing his blue cap and Koss headphones. Bidner and/or Anderson was present when a fire was lit to enable the gold detectors to get closer to the earth, on Palmerville property. That fire got away from them and raced up the spur.

One video was of a fishing trip where a good catch of Barramundi resulted, but I cannot confirm that was at the Croc Hole. I would go so far as to say their conduct, their speech, their actions were no different to their conduct, speech and actions whilst being recorded by police.

As you read, prospectors Bidner and Anderson went gold detecting immediately after the shooting. Or perhaps not, depending on which of their versions you accept as the truth, after expressing concern that Stephen Struber may have been dropped off by Dianne Wilson, and he could have been on foot, armed and hunting them, *Deliverance* Style[129]. In that situation, gold detecting, with the machine squealing loudly as neither wore headphones, standing up in the open, would be considered entirely inappropriate and entirely inconsistent with being in a stressful or traumatic situation. Was there any suggestion of memory distortion in those original comments? Quite the opposite.

Watching and listening to the audio and video files, both Dan Bidner and Tremain Anderson present as credible witnesses. The interviews were strong, forthright, direct, no hesitation or confusion apparent. If you wondered whether Dan Bidner suffered any memory fog from the stress and trauma, look no further than his statement taken the next night, Tuesday. Point 70 read,'….I ~~think~~ Bruce's dog barked.' The word 'heard' had been handwritten above 'think'. There were three other handwritten amendments in the same statement. Another example is the Monday night phone conversation between Dan Bidner and Nick O'Brien, particularly the second half, where Dan Bidner corrected him in comments.

I did not detect any sense of urgency. Bidner had to tell the whole story, 'setting the scene'. It was not until around the ten-minute mark of that conversation he mentioned he was scared, and finally, at the eleven minute twenty-nine second mark he told the police officer his friend was missing. *'All I can hear is my heart beating*.' And straight back to setting the scene. At the nineteen-minute mark he said:' *We're worried hey.*' And once again, straight back to the scene.

---

[129] Re-enactment by T Anderson

And when officer O'Brien commented that he understood Bidner would be stressed and upset did Bidner add to it? Embellish it? No, he just agreed. Contrary to Bidner's evidence at trial that he was talking to police from 6 p.m. to midnight, he had two phone calls. One with officer Tome at 7 p.m. that lasted around ten minutes and the call with officer O'Brien at 9 p.m. that lasted twenty-five minutes.

When listening to the phone call Dan Bidner had on the Monday night phone call with Detective O'Brien, he did not sound traumatised, worried, concerned, or fearful. There was no suggestion of memory fog, confusion, uncertainty, trauma, stress. Quite the opposite. That call after all, was the equivalent of a 000 call. A very calm 000 call.

Whilst waiting for the 'frantic' searches by Tremain Anderson to find Bruce Schuler, Dan Bidner was wishing he had a fishing line as *'the fish were jumping'* in the Palmer River. Was that evidence of being stressed or traumatised? The prospectors had a satellite phone. They did not attempt to phone Bruce, Police or family to alert them to what had just happened, for around ten hours. If you accept that Tremain Anderson physically went to the homestead, was that the actions of someone in fear of their lives from two people he knew to be violent, and he had just heard them fire two rounds from a high-powered weapon?

A lot of comments come to mind when I think of Bidner and Anderson; having a poor memory or memory recall problems are not included. We are fortunate that early interviews with the witnesses were recorded by audio and video interviews. Their response to questions was very matter of fact.

I was able to listen to the interview on the Tuesday night with Detective Riles that lasted two hours and forty minutes. Riles asked Dan Bidner to relate the events from the previous morning. Instead Bidner started from twelve months before when Bruce Schuler bought a lease up the road.

He was there to tell the officer of a potential murder, but he wanted to set the narrative. He went through the whole story of Kevin Groth never having found a piece of gold, and he was given the prime prospecting area. There was even light-hearted banter during the audio interview with officer Riles.

I was able to watch and listen to the video recorded re-enactments. None of the witnesses exhibited any of the above signs as suggested by Artificial Intelligence. On the balance of probability, at least one of the witnesses should have been exhibiting some signs of trauma or stress. Anderson laughed in the video re-enactment when commenting that his ears were still ringing from the gun shot.

The prospectors' post event reactions were totally inconsistent with a traumatic or stressful event. Police did not make any comment, verbal or written in their notebooks or statements, that the witnesses were shocked, traumatised or apparently stressed. They were not crying, hugging each other, seeking solace.

As you may be aware, survivors of a traumatic event are known to shun others and seek out the company of the persons who went through the traumatic event with them. *Brothers-in-arms* is a phrase that comes to mind. That did not happen in this instance. Whilst Bidner and Anderson have remained in contact, Kevin Groth has no contact with either of them.

As of 2023 the last time he had spoken to them both was at the 2015 trial. He recalled speaking with Dan Bidner again, about twelve months after that[130]. I would take a guess that there was no contact between 2012 and 2015 either, except where there had to be.

I received numerous comments from listeners during and after the podcast. I felt this one was particularly relevant:

- Telling a story in chronological order can be a sign of deception or a rehearsed story, as most people start with the most important part of the story and add other detail afterwards.
- Dan started the day before, in the second interview even when he was directed to start the day of by the interviewer.

---

[130] Interview 2023 with K Groth

- Dan mentioned "we argued about whether it was 9:30 or 10" which is confirmation that they discussed each other's versions of events before speaking to police.
- Switching tense could be a sign of deception or a rehearsed story, as the person may be focusing on the narrative and not genuinely recalling something.
- Both Dan and Tremain switched to present tense a few times during their stories.
- Neither Dan nor Tremain provided an actual description of Steve and Dianne.
- They both explained why they believed they knew it was them, but did not actually describe their height, clothing, hair colour etc.
- The police did not seem to press them on this.
- They both used distancing and vague language regarding "the incident", despite being very specific about other details. This can be another sign of deception.
- Tremain was very descriptive when he was able to drive the narrative, but became vague in response to specific questions.
- Each time the interviewer asked something, he seemed to be thrown off guard or become nervous.
- Tremain said he couldn't hear much because he didn't turn his detector off, but his ears were "ringing" from the gun shot.
- Tremain laughed (nervously?) when the interviewer asked if there were any arguments.
- They all seemed to include some similar detail that didn't seem particularly relevant, such as the story of finding the gold or explaining they couldn't be close to each other because the detectors interfere with each other.
- By itself, the trauma or otherwise of the prospectors may be of no consequence. I found an ever increasing and concerning list of discrepancies. Again, by themselves they may be nothing. Combined, to my view, they paint a very disturbing picture of deceit and dishonesty by the prospectors.

RoboCop

In 2024 I was released a podcast called "Who Killed Sarah Brown.' That podcast covered the death of Sarah Brown in Gympie, Queensland in 2021. The police investigation quickly concluded Sarah Brown took her own life by hanging. The coroner agreed and the file was closed. There were a lot of unanswered questions swirling around that outcome, and I mean a lot. I researched and released ten episodes on the case.

During that podcast, I was contacted by an Australian couple living in Bulgaria. They consulted to European based businesses on IT matters and the benefits of using Artificial Intelligence to improve their business. The couple were following the Sarah Brown case via the podcast and were keen to help. They offered to have Artificial Intelligence analyse the evidence in the case. Sarah's mother and I were both enthusiastic about the offer, and jumped at the opportunity. We nicknamed the computer program RoboCop after a 1987 hit movie about a part human, part robot policeman.

Witness statements, audio interviews, photographs, videos and all necessary material gathered from the investigation was emailed to them. The process took around two months, and eventually a report comprising 135 pages was received on the results of the Artificial Intelligence analysis. For the podcast I focused on the Final Summary which comprised seven pages.

RoboCop considered five scenarios that may have explained Sarah's death. After analysing the evidence, RoboCop suggested the most likely scenario was Scenario 2: *Foul play by Someone in Sarah's Circle, with a Staged Suicide.*

RoboCop concluded the likelihood of Sarah Brown taking her own life was a less than one percent chance (0.00001875%). It also believed there was more than an eighty percent chance someone in Sarah's circle was involved in her death. RoboCop went on to name those it believed involved or complicit in Sarah's death. In 2025, the Queensland Coroner announced they were reopening the case into Sarah Brown's death.

Fast forward to the podcast "Where is Bruce Schuler.' The significance of the discrepancies in the prospectors' evidence had not escaped me. I pondered what RoboCop would make of the prospectors ever changing story lines. The Bulgarian Australians were willing to undertake the research. This was a much bigger undertaking than Sarah Brown with many more statements, audio interviews, and re-enactments. The whole exercise was made more complicated by the bush setting and the lack of landmarks to reference witness claims to. Ultimately, the RoboCop consultants were commissioned to analyse five separate facets of the case:

The prospectors witness statements.

Specific events that occurred after Bruce Schuler's disappearance.

The prospector's behaviour and language.

Discrepancies between the prospectors' statements and re-enactments.

The prospectors trial testimony.

As there were three prospectors, this required the evidence of each prospector to be analysed individually and together. It was a huge undertaking and took weeks. Robocop ultimately generated a 193-page report of its findings. The report did come with a qualifier. The podcast episode was also again titled RoboCop. The episode focused on a five-page summary of the report which I have included here:

Analysis of witness statements:

Potential signs of deception identified include excessive detail in irrelevant areas, conflicting behavioural details, lack of personal involvement, inconsistent dates, over-explanation of behaviour, redundant or contradictory information, appeals to authority. The report concludes that there are numerous indicators of potential deception by all three witnesses, but no clear proof of lying. Possible motives for lying or withholding information are explored: fear of legal consequences, protection of others, self-interest, personal insecurity, and unwillingness to cooperate.

Tremain Anderson:

Seeking retribution, fear of legal consequences and avoiding conflict are the most likely motivations, based on his excessive detail and attempts to appear cooperative.

Dan Bidner

Seeking retribution is the most likely motivation, given his vague statements and past conflicts with key figures.

Kevin Groth

Embarrassment and self-preservation are the most likely motivations, given his over-explanation of behaviour after hearing gunshots.

Analysis of Specific Events

The report examines the prospectors' actions after hearing gunshots and their failure to immediately search for Bruce. Their continued prospecting could be a way to downplay their responsibility, conceal fear, or create a narrative of normalcy. If the prospectors were involved in Bruce's disappearance, their behaviour, including lack of concern and attempts to blame Stephen Struber, could indicate a coordinated effort to cover their tracks. Discrepancies in the prospectors' descriptions of the weapon used (high-powered rifle vs. shotgun) are noted.

Analysis of the prospectors' activities upon arrival on Palmerville Station on 8th July 2012 reveals inconsistencies in their accounts of their arrival time, and who went in what direction, and the times they returned from prospecting. Examination of the information about Bruce's satellite phone shows that the prospectors believed he had it in his car but did not mention finding or using it. The report highlights the prospectors' lack of explanation for their delayed search for Bruce.

Dan Bidner's initial vague description of the weapon Dianne Struber was holding ("black stick shape") is contrasted with later, more definitive statements. Dan Bidner's behaviour, including checking Bruce's location then continuing prospecting, is particularly suspicious. Dan Bidner's downplaying of gold and money as potential factors is noted as unusual.

Analysis of the instructions given to Kevin Groth to hide if he encountered anyone highlights the prospectors' prior encounters with Stephen Struber and their fear of him. Kevin Groth's strong and repeated declarations of innocence are highlighted as potentially defensive.

Discrepancies and Suspicions

Key inconsistencies in the witness statements include the timing of gunshots, the number of shots heard, and the weapon used. The prospectors' narrative about being absorbed in prospecting and losing track of time is highlighted as a convenient way to explain their delayed response and minimise suspicion. Further discrepancies include inconsistent timelines, lack of immediate concern, and potential financial motives. The report concludes that while there is no direct evidence implicating the prospectors, their inconsistencies, delayed responses, pre-emptive defensiveness, and potential motives suggest a possibility of involvement. The prospectors' actions could be interpreted as attempts to create an alibi, control the narrative, and shift blame onto Stephen Struber and Dianne Wilson

Deeper Analysis of Witness Behaviour and Language

The report analyses the prospectors' statements for signs of evasiveness, including distancing language, shifting responsibility, lack of ownership, overuse of generalisations, inconsistencies, excessive detail, omissions, overemphasis on routine, and emotional inconsistency.

The report concludes that each prospector's statement contains multiple signs of potential evasiveness, suggesting they may be withholding information or actions related to Bruce's disappearance. The prospectors' statements are further analysed for signs of obfuscation, including feigning forgetfulness, presenting conflicting versions, overly agreeable demeanour, deflecting attention, pleading ignorance, exaggerating confusion, emotional detachment, repetitive responses, and attempts to control the narrative. The report highlights the prospectors' use of specific language and behavioural cues that suggest potential deception or attempts to obscure their involvement.

Examples include:

Tremain Anderson:

detached language, focus on prospecting as avoidance,

and inconsistent emotional responses.

Dan Bidner:

detachment and focus on logistics, emotional repression,

and lack of emotional engagement in language.

Kevin Groth:

over-emphasis on self-preservation, calmness despite claiming fear, and language focused on self-oriented actions.

The report notes the prospectors' inconsistent emotional responses, suggesting they may be suppressing true feelings or obscuring involvement. Their over reliance on irrelevant factual details and the minimisation of Bruce's role is also highlighted as potential indicators of deception.

Further analysis identifies patterns of behaviour suggesting coordination among the prospectors, including:

Consistent fear-based behaviour:

All three men claiming fear to justify inaction suggests possible premeditation.

Over justification of inaction:

Excessive explanations for their behaviour after hearing gunshots could indicate attempts to cover up suspicious actions.

Echoing of key details:

Similar descriptions of the vehicle, gunshots, and Bruce's dog suggest they may have rehearsed their stories.

Linguistic hedging and vagueness:

Use of uncertain language suggests a lack of confidence in their accounts or attempts to avoid being pinned down.

Disjointed emotions:

Inconsistent emotional responses, ranging from casual to fearful, suggest their emotions may be fabricated.

The report concludes that the prospectors' coordinated behaviour, linguistic cues, and inconsistent emotions suggest a possible attempt to create a plausible but fabricated narrative to avoid suspicion.

Analysis of Discrepancies Between Witness Statements and Re-enactments

The report compares **Daniel Bidner's** witness statement with his re-enactments, identifying inconsistencies in timeline, event descriptions, and tone. Key discrepancies include differences in the reported time of Bruce's disappearance, details about Dianne Struber's actions, visibility of Stephen Struber, and emotional tone.

Similar inconsistencies are found between **Kevin Groth's** witness statement and his re-enactments. Key discrepancies include differences in the description of the vehicle, reasons for hiding, movements after hearing gunshots, and level of detail about equipment.

The report highlights specific examples of repeated language, unusual phrasing, and formal terms used by the prospectors, suggesting possible rehearsal or external influence. These include the use of words like "gesture," "fawn-coloured," "vehicle of interest," and "last visual position." Other inconsistencies in language and behaviour include dramatic descriptions, overly precise phrasing, and repetition of similar phrases.

The report concludes that the prospectors' language patterns suggest possible coordination or rehearsal to align their stories.

Analysis of Trial Testimony

The report analyses the trial testimonies of Tremain Anderson, Dan Bidner, and Kevin Groth, identifying signs of potential deception or withholding information.

These include inconsistent responses, over-explaining details, hedging language, lack of sensory detail, combative behaviour, evasive answers, memory gaps, and attempts to shift blame or responsibility.

The report acknowledges the complexity of interpreting human behaviour but notes that the witnesses' strange actions and shifting testimonies suggest they may be hiding information.

Conclusion

The report concludes that Bruce Schuler's disappearance remains uncertain but highlights several elements suggesting foul play. The inconsistent testimonies and suspicious behaviour point to the possibility that the witnesses are not being truthful, and that Stephen Struber and Dianne Wilson could have been framed as scapegoats and are innocent of the murder of Bruce Schuler.

While there is no definitive proof, the inconsistencies and suspicious actions suggest deeper involvement by the witnesses. The report then included 20 points that could suggest the Strubers may be innocent of the disappearance of Bruce Schuler.

Lack of Direct Evidence Linking the Strubers to the Disappearance:

The sources do not present any concrete evidence directly linking the Strubers to Bruce Schuler's disappearance. No physical evidence, such as DNA, fingerprints, or weapons, ties them to the scene or any harm that may have befallen Bruce.

Prospectors' Inconsistent and Suspicious Behaviour:

The inconsistencies in the statements and actions of the three prospectors—Tremain Anderson, Kevin Groth, and Dan Bidner—raise significant doubts about their credibility and suggest they might be concealing information or involved in Bruce's disappearance. Their strange behaviour, particularly continuing to prospect after hearing gunshots, casts suspicion on their potential role in the events.

Potentially Fabricated or Exaggerated Gunshot Story:

While the prospectors claim to have heard gunshots, their accounts are inconsistent regarding the number of shots, the type of weapon used, and their reactions. This lack of consistency, combined with their other suspicious behaviours, raises the possibility that the gunshot story was fabricated or exaggerated to mislead investigators or create a false narrative.

Shifting Blame and Creating a Scapegoat:

The prospectors consistently point to Stephen Struber as a potential threat, highlighting his past confrontations and aggressive reputation. This focus on Struber as the likely culprit could be a deliberate attempt to deflect suspicion from themselves. By creating a scapegoat, they could divert attention away from their own potential involvement in Bruce's disappearance.

Motive for the Prospectors:

The sources explore potential motives for the prospectors' involvement in Bruce's disappearance, including disputes over gold or claims, personal conflicts, fear of legal consequences related to illegal activities, or an accidental death and subsequent cover-up. These motives suggest that the prospectors had reasons to harm Bruce or conceal his disappearance.

Dan Bidner's Unusual Comment About Robbery:

Dan Bidner's statement downplaying the possibility of robbery, seems unusual and could be interpreted as an attempt to pre-emptively dismiss a potential motive for him and the other two prospectors. By suggesting robbery is unlikely, Bidner may be trying to divert attention away from a financial motive.

Kevin Groth's Overly Defensive Statements:

Kevin Groth's repeated and emphatic assertions of innocence, even when not directly accused, appear defensive and raise suspicions. This behaviour could suggest an attempt to overcompensate for guilt or a fear of being implicated in Bruce's disappearance.

Discrepancies in Describing the Vehicle:

While all the prospectors describe Struber's vehicle, their accounts contain inconsistencies. For example, they use the unusual term "fawn-coloured" and the phrase "vehicle of interest," which sounds like legal jargon, suggesting possible rehearsal or external influence. These inconsistencies raise questions about the accuracy and spontaneity of their observations.

Lack of Clarity Regarding Bruce's Last Known Location:

The prospectors provide conflicting information about Bruce's last known location and their own movements, making it difficult to establish a clear timeline of events. These inconsistencies could be intentional attempts to obscure their involvement or knowledge of what happened to Bruce.

Tremain Anderson's Lack of Urgency:

Despite hearing gunshots and knowing Bruce was missing, Tremain Anderson continued prospecting for an extended period. This lack of urgency in searching for Bruce seems out of character and could suggest that he wasn't genuinely concerned about Bruce's safety, possibly because he already knew what happened.

Dan Bidner's Passive Role in the Search:

Dan Bidner's relatively passive role in searching for Bruce, despite being aware of potential danger and having past confrontations with Struber, raises questions about his true concern. His lack of initiative in trying to locate Bruce could indicate that he knew Bruce wouldn't be found.

Dan Bidner's Conflicting Accounts of Dianne Struber's Actions:

Dan Bidner provides varying descriptions of Dianne Struber's actions when the vehicle stopped. Initially, he claims she retrieved a stick-like object, then a gun and later she looked down at the gun and made a loading action with her hands. These discrepancies raise doubts about the accuracy of their observations and suggest possible exaggeration or fabrication.

Dan Bidner's Changing Statements About Seeing Stephen Struber:

Dan Bidner's statements about seeing Stephen Struber in the vehicle change over time. He initially claims to have only seen Dianne and just assumed the other person was Stephen but later expresses more certainty. These inconsistencies suggest that he might be altering his story or making assumptions to fit a specific narrative.

Focus on Fear and Self-Preservation:

All three prospectors emphasise their fear of Stephen Struber as a justification for their actions, such as hiding or avoiding confrontation. This consistent focus on fear could be a coordinated effort to downplay their own responsibility and create a narrative that deflects suspicion away from them.

Lack of Detailed Emotional Responses:

Despite the gravity of the situation, the prospectors often lack detailed emotional responses in their accounts. Their language and behaviour suggest emotional detachment or suppression, which could be a sign of guilt or an attempt to conceal true feelings.

Overuse of Factual Details and Minimisation of Bruce's Role:

The prospectors often provide excessive factual details about irrelevant matters such as borrowing a cable from Bruce for a detector. They also minimise Bruce's role in their narratives. This could be a subconscious attempt to distance themselves from Bruce and his disappearance, potentially indicating guilt or knowledge of what happened.

Tremain Anderson's Memory Gaps During Trial:

During his trial testimony, Tremain Anderson displays significant memory gaps, particularly regarding the names of key people and the vehicle's registration number. He often replied, "I can't really recall", "I don't remember" in the trial. These lapses in memory could be intentional attempts to avoid providing potentially incriminating information or to create distance between himself and other involved individuals.

Kevin Groth's Inconsistent Timeline and Over-Explaining:

Kevin Groth's testimony is marked by an inconsistent timeline and a tendency to over-explain irrelevant details. He corrects himself on dates, provides unnecessary information about his clothing, and hedges his language when discussing critical moments, all of which suggest uncertainty or potential fabrication.

Kevin Groth's Exaggerated Self-Preservation:

Kevin Groth's actions after hearing the gunshots, particularly his extended hiding and lack of immediate concern for Bruce's safety, suggest an exaggerated focus on self-preservation. This behaviour could indicate that he knew more than he was revealing and was prioritising his own safety over finding Bruce.

Lack of Physical Evidence to Support Any Theory:

The absence of physical evidence, such as a body, personal belongings, or forensic material, makes it difficult to confirm or deny any of the accounts provided. This lack of tangible proof creates ambiguity and allows for multiple interpretations, including the possibility that the prospectors' involvement is more significant than they admit.

It's important to note that these points highlight the possibility of the Strubers' innocence based on the inconsistencies and suspicious behaviours of the prospectors. However, the absence of concrete evidence against the Strubers does not automatically equate to their innocence. The case remains complex, and further investigation is necessary to determine the truth behind Bruce Schuler's disappearance.

Back to Court 2025

As this book goes to print, an Appeal is being prepared to have the convictions of Dianne Wilson and Stephen Struber return to the Queensland Court of Appeal. After the Court of Appeal hearing in 2016, followed by the Application for Leave to Appeal in the High Court, that was the end of the legal road for Dianne Wilson and Stephen Struber. The only way to appeal their convictions after that is by a Petition for Pardon to the Queensland Attorney General, and many convicted persons do just that, seek a pardon from the Governor of Queensland.

Practically, any Petition the Queensland Governor receives is forwarded to the Queensland Government and lands on the desk of the Attorney General. I have been a critic of that process for many years. The Attorney General may be our first law maker, but they are also a politician. I need go no further than raise the issue of Law and Order.

If the Queensland Government of the day takes the moral high ground on Law and Order, as they are prone to do, what position does the Attorney General adopt? Do they follow the Party lines to retain their seat, or do they refer an application by a 'dangerous convicted murderer' to the Court of Appeal? You will read shortly a classic example regarding the Leanne Holland case. I can only suggest the Attorney General does not want to make a decision that would be unpalatable to the Government. When I last wrote to the Attorney General and pointed out she was breaking her own laws by refusing to hold an Inquest into the murder of Leanne Holland, she replied to my correspondence but ignored that claim.

In 2024, legislation was passed in the Queensland Government to permit Petitioners to by-pass the Attorney General and go directly to the Court of Appeal. It is not as simple as that, but I am sure you get the gist. I am not suggesting for a moment the Queensland Government took any notice of my constant whingeing about having the Attorney General in the loop, but I am certainly glad they listened to someone.

Another case I am involved in is that of Massimo Sica. I recorded a thirty-three-episode podcast on the brutal Singh triple murders for which Max Sica is serving a life sentence. His appeal is the first case to go to the Court of Appeal having by-passed the Attorney General. Massimo Sica, convicted of those murders will have his day in court.

As I have seen the explosive new evidence uncovered in that case by retired solicitor Jeff Johnson, who has been working pro bono on the case for six years, and which has been included in my podcast, I will be watching that Appeal with interest.

And I believe the Struber and Wilson Appeal will be the second case to reach the Court of Appeal under the new legislation.

What options does the Court of Appeal have?

They would ordinarily have three options open to them in an Appeal application but in this instance, they would have six options, as there are two Petitioners. I will discuss it as if it is one, for simplicity.

The Court can dismiss the Application and the conviction stands.

They can accept the Application, quash the conviction and order a new trial.

They can accept the Application, quash the conviction and enter a verdict of Not Guilty.

Of course, as there are two Applicants they could give the same result for both, or they could refuse one and grant the other and so on. What does that mean? If the Application is refused, the applicants would be returned to prison to serve out their sentence, which is to die in custody or give up the body of Bruce Schuler.

If the convictions were quashed and a new trail ordered, it would then be up to the DPP to decide whether they would prosecute the defendants again. If the convictions were quashed and verdicts of Not

Guilty entered, the defendants would be released from prison, and they could get on with their lives.

You have read the evidence as it now stands. What do you believe the outcome of the Appeal to the Court of Appeal should be, and do you believe that outcome, whatever it maybe, should apply to one or both defendants?

I have been down this rocky road before, and it is a rough ride.

Graham Stuart Stafford had his conviction for the murder of Leanne Holland quashed in 2009. The Court of Appeal ruled on a two to one majority that the conviction be quashed, and a retrial ordered. The dissenting Justice recommended a finding of Not Guilty be entered. The DPP then publicly stated they would not be retrying Mr Stafford. A finding which was expected, because the circumstantial evidence that convicted Graham Stafford was in tatters after the evidence was properly examined for the first time, after his conviction in 1992. Because of the ruling, Graham Stafford was not entitled to apply for compensation for the fifteen years imprisonment he had served. He was technically in legal limbo; not Innocent, not Guilty. The DPP could prosecute him again if they so chose.

The Queensland Police Service took the moral high ground. The QPS declared they would not be reopening the investigation as they 'knew' who murdered Leanne Holland. After a groundswell of public opinion, the QPS very reluctantly agreed to review the case. Not reinvestigate, review. As the well-known quip goes, 'Police marking their own scorecard, what could possibly go wrong.'

The QPS reviewed their own original investigation. After the two years it took to undertake the review, the QPS gave themselves the equivalent of a Google five-star review. They had gotten it right the first time they found; Graham Stafford had murdered Leanne Holland, and he acted alone, despite the findings of the Court of Appeal and despite the contents of their own Review Report. Yes, the finding was at odds with the contents of the report.

The QPS then refused to release the Review Report to Graham Stafford, his solicitors or anyone else under Right to Information legislation. When the groundswell of adverse public opinion continued, a high-ranking member of the QPS leaked the five hundred + page report to a commercial television station which broadcast a pro-police story based on the untested police findings.

A brilliant move by the QPS! All public interest waned. No more pesky journalists calling on police to release their findings. No investigation was ever commenced or actioned by the QPS to identify the leaker, despite the QPS having a notorious reputation for doing just that. Several years later, the QPS ultimately released a redacted copy of the report to Graham Stafford. Around 370 pages out of some 530 pages. I cover the 370 pages in an episode of the podcast "*Who Killed Leanne Holland'* and concluded the report was very self-serving and at odds with the Report finding. The QPS continue to refuse to release the balance of the report to this day.

Graham Stafford has been requesting an Inquest be held into the death of Leanne Holland to identify the killer since 2010 (our original investigations identified three persons of interest in the murder who were more likely to have murdered Leanne Holland than Graham Stafford).

To add insult to injury, the Queensland Police Service has consistently recommended to the coroner no inquest be held – *Not in the public interest*, they said. That position changed in 2023 at which time they declared they would support an Inquest.

There have been several requests for an inquest dating back to 2010, which is obligatory in Queensland where a violent death has occurred. Just recently (2025), a listener to the podcast '*Who Killed Leanne Holland*' wrote to me, and advised they had written to the Attorney General requesting an Inquest be held into the death of Leanne Holland.

The listener has now forwarded me the reply they received. The matter '*is still under consideration by the State Coroner.*' An Inquest has been under consideration from 2010 to 2025. How much time does the Coroner need to decide a matter? Do they not have KPI's? Do they answer to no one?

I can say my patience with the Queensland Government, the Queensland Police Service and the Judiciary in general has been sorely tested over the years. I will be watching with interest the Court of Appeal hearing into all cases when they occur.

MOJ

Were the convictions of Dianne Wilson and Stephen Struber a malicious prosecution and Miscarriage of Justice? I am sufficiently disturbed by so many aspects of this case including but not limited to the hasty and inadequate police investigation, the amount of evidence the jury did not hear, the ever-changing story line of the three main witnesses I believe this case should return to the Court of Appeal urgently to address those very questions.

This case is very important for the Queensland Judicial system. If the jury reached the correct verdict, perhaps the Queensland Police Service and the Office of Director of Public Prosecutions need to address how to deal with ever-changing evidence as occurred in this case. When such evidence is not presented to the jury, it leads to questions and concerns within the community about due process.

If Dianne Wilson and Stephen Struber were wrongfully convicted, it is probably the biggest MOJ this country has ever seen. Two innocent people convicted of murder and sentenced to die in prison, courtesy of legislation enacted specifically because of their convictions. As of 2025, the Strubers' have been incarcerated for ten years. They continue to proclaim their innocence. They have lost their home, their business and their income and have been vilified by the police and the media. *'Bonney and Clyde', 'Wolf Creek Killer', 'Brutish Enforcer.'*

The most common question I am asked is:' What do you think happened to Bruce Schuler.'

After almost two years of research into the case my standard answer is along these lines,' I do not know what happened on Palmerville

Station. What I can say is that whatever happened to Bruce Schuler, that was not the story that played out in the Cairns Supreme Court in 2015. (I never comment the murder occurred on the Monday because it is possible it occurred before that day).

Whatever your own thoughts on this case, Kevin Groth is at the centre of it.

Was he merely in the wrong place at the wrong time and witnessed the Strubers murder Bruce Schuler? The evidence does not support that version of events. Although to be fair to Kevin Groth, he never said the Strubers murdered Bruce Schuler. He never said anyone murdered Bruce Schuler. Neither did the other prospectors.

Was Kevin Groth in the wrong place at the wrong time and witnessed someone else murder Bruce Schuler? He did describe the headboard of the Toyota vehicle as an orangey rusty colour to police. At trial he went back to it being beige, in line with the description given by his co-prospectors, and then in cross-examination he agreed with the suggestion it could have been an orangey rusty colour. If there was another vehicle and another killer present that day, and if it did not belong to the Strubers, then who was it? The only ones who could answer that question would be Dan Bidner and Tremain Anderson.

Was Kevin Groth in a conspiracy with Dan Bidner and Tremain Anderson to murder Bruce Schuler? He had only met them the day before. No connection or common thread between all three witnesses was ever identified. Without that link, it would be very unlikely Groth would agree on the spot to murder his friend of twenty years.

Was Kevin Groth threatened to remain silent, or he would suffer the same fate as Bruce Schuler? There is some suspicion that may have occurred. Suspicion only, not evidence. His disappearance for six hours after hearing the gun shots was bordering on the absurd. If he was told to '*head bush and you will see nothing and hear nothing other than two gun shots,*' he played that to perfection.

As you may recall, I referred to Groth as Sgt Schultz in the podcast. Kevin Groth mentioned to me he was concerned by the number of vehicles moving around his place before the 2015 trial. If that was what happened, he has kept that secret for thirteen years.

I do not believe we know what happened on Palmerville Station at the time Bruce Schuler disappeared. To borrow the line by Prosecutor Nigel Rees, blind Freddy can see there are serious problems with the evidence in this case.

Answers may come if and when Crime Scene Three is discovered or identified. I have no idea where crime scene three is but the first place I would be searching would be in the vicinity of where Bruce Schuler's satellite phone pinged at 7.33 p.m. on Sunday 8 July 2025.

Are there any **STAND OUT** issues in this case for me? Probably too many to list. But here are a few obvious ones:

- The reason they went prospecting was based on a lie. I can only conclude Bruce Schuler was lured there.
- The two videos taken by Dan Bidner are a game changer.
- The left-behind accoutrements, especially the detecting pick, are very telling.
- The Ghost Evidence is irrefutable.
- The lies, the discrepancies, the obfuscation of the witnesses is compelling.
- The complete lack of evidence to implicate Stephen Struber and Dianne Wilson leaves me shaking my head as to why they were even charged, let alone convicted.

You may recall in the chapter styled '*Where is Bruce Schuler Podcast*', I wrote about the factors that can cause a Miscarriages of Justice. It is appropriate to explore those factors, now that the evidence in this case has been laid out:

Tunnel Vision by Investigators:

There were three instances where yes, I believe there was tunnel vision by investigators. Acting Detective Sergeant Nick O'Brien wrote this comment in his diary: '*Name (redacted) stated he believed nominated witnesses' story*'. That was on the very first night of the investigation.

Even before he had spoken to the first witness. That suggested to me, he went into this investigation believing the Strubers were guilty. The next night, despite there being no body, no conclusive proof Schuler was even dead, no admissions and no real evidence, he arrested Dianne Wilson and Stephen Struber for murder.

Detective O'Brien had the phone call with witness Daniel Bidner on Monday 9 July 2012, fortunately recorded. Four days later he was present when Bidner performed a re-enactment of his movements on the Monday. It must have been obvious to O'Brien and by default, the rest of the investigation team, that Bidner had changed his evidence in several key areas. I can only conclude the investigators chose to ignore the altered evidence.

Detective Sergeant McLeish was quoted by a journalist in 2015 after the convictions as saying: '*I was sure from day one that they were responsible for Bruce Schuler's disappearance.*' Unless the journalist misquoted him, I believe that comment would be accurate.

I am comfortable in concluding there was likely some tunnel vision happening in this investigation.

Witness Misidentification:

The only witnesses who placed Struber and Wilson at the crime scene were Bidner and Anderson. They each identified one offender and they both identified the Struber vehicle at the scene. Both witnesses were pressed hard by defence counsel on the identification of the offenders, but they remained firm.

There was of course the issue where Bidner had to retract his claim that he identified Stephen Struber at the scene, but apart from that, there was probably no doubt in the mind of the jurors the prospectors had identified the Strubers as the offenders.

Was that misidentification? No, it wasn't, but this aspect must be considered in the context of the next factor.

Witnesses lying under Oath:

Did Kevin Groth lie under oath? I do not believe there is evidence to support that suggestion. Did he tell everything the court everything he knew about the events? For example, the satellite phone ping. That is open for consideration. However, he was not there to simply tell the court anything. He was there to answer specific questions. Had he been asked further questions, who knows what would have come out.

Did witnesses Bidner and Anderson lie under oath? I think a more accurate question would be *'How much lying did Bidner and Anderson do under Oath?'* You have read multiple examples of where the only reasonable conclusion you could reach was that they were lying under Oath. So, I ask this question - were those witnesses lying when they identified both Strubers at the crime scene? Or to put it another way, were Dianne Wilson and Stephen Struber even at the One Mile on Monday 9 July 2012 killing Bruce Schuler, or were they at the big dam about eight kilometres to the south as they insisted?

Poor Police Procedures or Investigation:

I suggest unhesitatingly there was poor police procedures and poor investigation techniques in this investigation. I could go into multiple examples, but I will simply refer you to three chapters I wrote: *'The Reader,' 'The Weapons,'* and *'Ezard's concerns.'* Enough said.

Misconduct by police and/or prosecutors:

I refer you to the chapters *'Ghost Evidence,' 'Teleporting'* and *'Trees, Pats and Tracks.'* I suggest the trial would have had a different outcome if the jury had heard all the evidence. Was that misconduct, or more accurately, misconduct by whom?

Poor legal representation of the defendants.

I believe there was evidence the defence counsel were not completely across the evidence. I have been told the Defence teams were not provided with the entire brief of evidence. If they had been across the evidence, the jury would have been told about the exact location the alleged Struber utility performed a u-turn.

And when you have multiple factors aligning like the planets, you have a breeding ground for an MOJ. I suggest in this case, the planets were well and truly aligned.

What is the position now? Apart from a potential Miscarriage of Justice it begs the question '*What evidence is there now to prove Dianne Wilson and Stephen Struber murdered Bruce Schuler?*'

As you know, the Crown case relied on the evidence of the prospectors and the forensic evidence at the burnt patches or Crime Scene Two.

If you remove the prospectors from the equation, and I believe there is every reason to not accept any of their evidence, as they simply have no credibility, you are left with the sketchy forensic evidence at the burnt patches. If you accept the matters raised in '*Crime Scene Staging*', the burnt patches was *not* a crime scene. None of which proved the Strubers were even there. What is left?

Nothing.

Very similar to the Leanne Holland murder. Once you removed the perjured evidence and the fabricated evidence from that case, the rest of the circumstantial evidence collapsed like a house of cards.

In this instance, there was never a house of cards to start with; more like a gunyah. What happened on Palmerville Station? Why and how did the wheels fall off the police bus?

I believe the evidence showed two snake oil salesmen were peddling their wares. They never said Stephen Struber and Dianne Wilson murdered Bruce Schuler. Others jumped to that conclusion. The salesmen were dangling a big lump of iron pyrite - fool's gold, and some fools fell for it.

And no one lived happily ever after.

I believe Stephen Struber and Dianne Wilson will never give up the location of Bruce Schuler's remains, because they do not know. We will never know where those remains lay until we determine what happened to Bruce Schuler on Palmerville Station, on or about Monday 9 July 2012.

These muddled, disorganised, doubtful convictions desperately need to return to the Queensland Court of Appeal. The murder of Bruce

Schuler needs to be reinvestigated, by properly supervised police not tainted by this mess.

We have not heard the last of the murder of Bruce Schuler. It will play out in the courts, in the media and in discussions in communities, particularly in FNQ.

Thank you for reading.

Graeme Crowley

You can contact me at the following:

www.graemecrowleyinvestigates.com.au

graeme5353@live.com

Facebook: GraemeCrowleyPodcastInvestigations

Appendix A

DISCREPANCIES IN EVIDENCE

Name References

DB = Dan Bidner
TA = Tremain Anderson
KG = Kevin Groth
BS = Bruce Schuler
SS = Stephen Struber
DW = Dianne Wilson
CS1 = Crime Scene One
CS2 = Crime Scene Two
PVStn = Palmerville Station

- The reason for going on the detecting trip was a ruse. There was never 10oz of gold found at the One Mile.
- The prospectors only planned 1 night trip. (a long way to go for 1 day prospecting)
- DB told police he had never been on PVStn. This was a lie. He had been going there for years. He lived nearby!
- Two prospectors were previously randomly approached by BS to go prospecting on PVStn but were 'nervous' and declined.
- The prospectors could not align their stories of events on the Sunday, leading to suspicion it was dramatically different to what was claimed.
- BS black bag had 3 pairs jocks & socks. 2 shorts & shirts. 1 long sleep shirt and trousers. A lot of clothing for 1 night trip.

- According to Jo Bidner, the prospectors left after a 'quick cuppa' of KG and BS arriving at Maytown at 7.30 a.m., whereas according to KG, they left at 9 a.m. after others had breakfast.
- According to DB, the prospectors went straight to PVStn river bed and set up camp, arriving at lunchtime.
- By trial, this changed to mid-afternoon.
- According to KG, they stopped along the way, with TA pointing out points of interest, and it took 2.5 hours to get there.
- TA said they went straight to Palmer River after leaving Maytown.
- None of the prospectors told police they went onto Fairlight Station, 4 klms past river crossing & prospecting there from 1-3 hrs.
- Going to that location was inconsistent with the reason for going to PVStn – because 10 oz of gold was found.
- This only came to light from DB video 1; (court told video timed 9.53 a.m. No meta data recovered).
- It is 3 hours drive from Maytown to Fairlight,
- yet video timed 9.53a.m.?
- After arriving in river to set up camp, all 3 prospectors could not agree on who went in which direction prospecting.
- TA said he was last back in camp that afternoon.
- KG said he was last back in camp.
- DB took video of camp – video 2 (court told video timed 5.15 p.m. but no meta data recovered).
- Bidner denied knowledge of this video until forced to agree.
- Riverbed video 2 was definitely filmed between approx. 7.30 a.m. and 9.30 a.m. The day it was filmed is not known.
- According to prospectors, they were allegedly prospecting and hiding from the Strubers.
- If video 2 was taken Sunday morning, all prospectors claimed they were at Maytown, over 1 ½ hrs away.
- Bidner & Anderson recounted numerous stories of how dangerous S & W were. Why then camp less than 2 klms from their homestead 'under their nose?'

- Police noted GPS ping was 12 klms to the east and consistent with the MP camp, which was correct if using the main road. The ping was 4 klms away from river camp, in a straight line.
- That information only became known on Saturday 14 July 2012. The same day the search for Bruce Schuler was abandoned.
- The same day BS satellite phone 'found.'
- That area where the phone pinged was never searched.
- Evidence showed prospectors left camp before 7 a.m. yet times given by prospectors varied erratically.
- Whilst prospecting for gold, DB said he was absent for 2 hours before returning to meet up point.
- TA said he was gone 20 minutes before returning to meet up point.
- KG said he was gone 40 minutes before returning to meet up point.
- Yet they all arrived there at same time and denied seeing each other.
- Despite many variations, Struber vehicle allegedly came along at 9.30 a.m., they claimed.
- Strubers utility would have left wheel marks in the sandy river showing travelling in both directions. Police investigations silent on whether tracks found or not.
- When S & W arrived, DB said he didn't have time to warn BS but clearly he had at least 2 minutes notice of utility arriving.
- On their evidence, DB & TA should have seen each other at that time, but denied doing so?
- When shot fired, DB heard a shotgun; KG heard a large calibre rifle fired into the air; TA heard a 30/30 rifle.
- The jury was not told this.
- KG forgot the reason why he hid from vehicle.
- Some heard a clang after first shot, some heard the clang after second shot, DB heard clang after both shots.
- The number of times SS did or did not get out of the vehicle earned a full chapter.
- The type of weapon DB saw occupied a full chapter.
- No evidence to connect BS, SS or DW to CS1. No physical evidence, no forensic evidence, apart from witnesses.

- No yelling, swearing, calling out, cries of pain, arguing heard during this time.
- There is a strong argument, therefore, that CS1 was staged. There was nothing to see apart from 2 prospectors claiming they were there.
- Distance by road from where utility stopped at CS1 to CS2 was 200 metres
- After shot and waiting period, ute drives off and goes about 20 metres and stopped.
- TA & DB repeatedly said ute then did a u-turn and headed back in direction of the homestead. This occupied a full chapter in book.
- Groth headed bush before 1st shot. He did not return to camp until 3 p.m. He was probably never more than 2 klms from camp during that 5.5 hour time.
- All prospectors remained in the area the rest of the day and did not hear or see the utility again.
- Groth was a VERY reluctant witness.
- His only evidence was to the colour of the roof of the ute which changed.
- He heard 2 gun shots. He had NO other evidence to give, apart from smelling gunpowder at 300 metres which was considered to be absurd.
- In a later interview he repeated his belief the high calibre rifle was fired into the air, not the ground.
- On his evidence, DW did not shoot BS or shoot at BS instead over his head.
- None of this evidence, including type of weapon etc heard by jury.
- DB said in 1 version he went directly back to riverbed camp after shots fired. He 'considered' detecting but 'no, he wanted to make sure BS was OK.'
- On his next version, DB met up with TA and they spent **2 -3 minutes** discussing shooting & then both detected their way back to camp.
- At trial, DB said they spent **15 minutes** discussing shooting before parting company.

- At re-enactment TA said he and DB spoke for **30 minutes** when meeting up after the shooting.
- Red dog had 'apparently' swum the river and was, on one version, beside BS ute and on another, cowering under BS ute (which DB claimed he could see from across the river). Many, many people challenged this claim and said dog would have followed the body.
- Police notebook records BS walked back to camp and found dog there.
- TA went to the spot where the ute did a u-turn and saw tracks in the dirt. He denied this at trial.
- Db told police in recorded interview he went back to where vehicle did u-turn. He strenuously denied this at trial.
- There were so many changes by prospectors it was impossible to prepare a timeline of events.
- TA said went as far as opposite PVStn homestead looking for BS. He denied actually going to PVStn homestead.
- A police diary recorded TA went to homestead at 3.30 p.m. TA told them no car present and after persistent yelling, no one came out of the homestead. This was covered in a full chapter.
- 2nd police diary recorded time attendance at homestead as 4.30 p.m. At least 1hr walk back to camp, yet they left area at 4.30 p.m.
- A witness gave statement TA told him he went to homestead.
- A further person was apparently told TA went to homestead; no statement was taken from him.
- TA & KG met up around 3 p.m. at camp. Their versions of where they met, how they met differ significantly. Confirmed by both. Yet he was at homestead at either 3.30 p.m. or 4.30 p.m.
- Why would TA go to homestead when he consistently claimed they were dangerous.
- DB told investigators the Monday night he left for Maytown between 12 p.m. and 12.30 p.m.
- DB later told detective he didn't leave for Maytown (at least 1 hr trip) until 1.30 p.m.
- Elsewhere DB stated he arrived at Maytown at 1.30 p.m.
- Elsewhere DB stated he arrived at Maytown at 2.30 p.m.

- DB said he arrived back at scene between 4.30 p.m.
- At 4.30 p.m. prospectors left a note on BS windscreen and returned to Maytown. In note, said they took BS dog.
- In his notebook, Det McLeish recorded when he arrived at camp on the Tuesday, the dog and BS ute were both there.
- Comparison of police photographs of windscreen wiper blades on BS vehicle shows passenger side blade covered in debris (vehicle apparently unmoved 40 hrs). Driver side blade with note to BS under it was 'pristine', yet note apparently there for 20 hrs.
- TA called a friend and told him they heard 3 gun shots. A claim he disputed at trial, but crown accepted he had said that.
- Prospectors did not attempt to call BS on his satellite phone at any time that day even though they were aware he had a satellite phone.
- Prospectors waited 9 hrs to call homestead.
- In phone message to Homestead, TA makes no allegations, does not mention any names, does not claim BS missing. He does not mention seeing Stephen & Dianne at gully shooting at them.
- In 2nd phone message he does not even mention rifle shots.
- Prospectors waited 10 hours to call Police.
- On Monday night, in recorded telephone call with detective, DB stated only regret he did not stand up to see if BS was on rear tray of ute. This was covered in a full chapter.
- DB initially said in his statement (taken the next day) they called the homestead before leaving the riverbed. This later changed to they called the homestead from DB property at Maytown.
- Very obscured view of gully from ridge where vehicle was. S & W would have literally 'no idea' which direction BS would have/could have gone.
- No evidence was found between CS1 and CS2 to connect anyone to there, including prospectors, Schuler or Strubers.
- Small drops of BS blood found at CS2 - on grass & leaves, a film canister, 2 rocks and old slug. A burnt match with BS DNA found in on eburnt patches of grass.
- On minimal evidence at CS2, was it also staged?

- This CS was up out of gully'- BS literally ran toward the shooter by heading up out of the gully, rather than away from shooter. Other prospectors ran away from shooter.
- Given the steep incline, the 4x4 had to travel at 5 kph. BS would have seen and heard it. DB & TA would have heard it. KG may also have heard it. NO one told police they heard vehicle go to CS2.
- This entire area was searched the following day Tuesday 10 July, nothing was found.
- The area was searched again the next day, Wednesday morning and nothing was found. Burnt grass, burnt matches etc found Wednesday afternoon.
- At least 1 burnt match found in BS ute.
- Damaged trees found, which police claimed were consistent with having being caused by S & W vehicle. Admissions were made by defence regarding this evidence.
- The evidence of the arborist placed the tree damage as Sunday 8th night or Monday morning 9th. That was not consistent with the evidence the S & W vehicle did not go to CS2, during Monday daytime. As it must have gone there Monday night.
- Tyre patterns in cow pats police claimed were consistent with S & W unregistered vehicle. No evidence when this occurred. This changed in evidence and at appeal. Admissions were made by defence regarding this evidence.
- Damage to anthill consistent with Strubers vehicle claimed by police. Admissions were made by defence regarding this evidence.
- Prosecutor told jury they could infer S & W went to CS 2.
- No drag marks, no blood trail, no disturbed earth, nothing to suggest S & W carried/dragged body (90kg) to tray (clang evidence).
- No DNA, blood, physical evidence connected S & W to either CS1 or between CS2. No evidence found on persons, personal clothing, either vehicle, boots, houses, firearms, etc.
- Distance from where vehicle turned around to CS2 was close to 100M. How did S & W get there then? How did they get BS away? When did they go to CS2?
- Prosecutor was careful not to mention ute turned around.

- In GPS mapping of evidence points shown to jury, there was no GPS point where ute did a u-turn. Were jury told vehicle did a u-turn?
- ute only had 3rd and 4th gear. 1st and 2nd gear inoperable. The descent to and from CS2 is very steep. Too steep for 3rd only. Police mechanic unable to select 1st and 2nd in any range.
- S & W were awaiting gearbox parts for ute. When parts arrived (after murder) the gearbox was repaired and by Oct 2012 when reenactment done, ute could easily drive up and down steep incline.
- That evidence not heard by jury until SS gave evidence.
- Prospectors gave evidence BS was wearing headphones at time of disappearance. KOSS brand headphones found in his locked vehicle.
- 5 days before disappearance, BS was videoed prospecting with KOSS brand headphones. He may have had backup pair of headphones, maybe not.
- Witnesses said BS had his GPS with him when he went missing but not his sat phone.
- On the evidence, BS left one of his most valuable possessions (satphone) in the unlocked back tray of his ute in a black bag with his clothes, not locked in the cabin whilst away prospecting.
- BS had a detecting pick that had been welded. KG said he had it with him when he went missing.
- In police photographs, 2 of BS picks visible in rear of ute, including welded pick.
- Prospectors claimed he was wearing wide brimmed hat when he went missing. He usually only wore cap when he used headphones. Cap found in locked vehicle. Wide brimmed hat impractical for wearing headphones.
- On Wednesday DB changed all 4 tyres on his 4x4 in Mareeba. He told police on 1 October he had a puncture and mixed tread so needed to replace tyres.
- He later told journalist Robert Reid he was pinged by police for defective vehicle.

- On Saturday, 14 July 2012, QPS attended DB property on prearranged search. The black bag was not found, nor handed over to police.
- From there, police went to BS camp. Whilst on the way, they met BS neighbour (Silver) on the track who had just left BS hut. He handed over BS rifle he had taken for safe keeping. (this weapon apparently always left behind driver's seat in his 4x4. Was rifle left in camp on this occasion?
- 2 hrs later, Silver arrived back at BS camp and handed over black bag he informed he had just picked up from DB. In it, was BS satellite phone.
- That was documented in diaries but no statements taken, and for all intents, the satellite phone was found at BS camp.
- S & W continue to deny involvement in the murder and 'refuse' to state where BS body can be located. They are aware of the nobody, no parole legislation and understand the consequences.
- Audio recorders and tracking devices placed in S & W house and vehicles, but no evidence ever recovered.
- Aboriginal tracker brought in concluded events must have occurred elsewhere as no evidence found to support claims.
- After police called for witnesses of confrontations with S & W, apparently 200 people came forward. Around 30 statements taken. Of those, 17 complained of intimidation when found trespassing. Some saw firearms and were afraid. Only people who ever claimed they were physically assaulted by S & W were DB & TA.
- DB clearly obfuscating and evasive in trial evidence.
- Lack of concern by the prospectors and delay in calling police.
- Police claim discrepancies in witness evidence due to highly stressed situation.
- Watching and listening to prospectors in recorded video and audio interviews suggested exactly opposite- witnesses not stressed at all.
- Their conduct in those videos was the same as shown in videos filmed by them before BS disappearance.
- Neighbour Bert Callaghan – told police he did not see Strubers on the Monday; he told 4 people he did see Strubers on the Monday.

One witness he told the same day he allegedly told police he didn't see anything. Bert now deceased.
- TA claiming his ears were ringing from gunshot and laughed about it. A person must be very close to a firearm to have ears ringing, TA was at least 100 metres was from the Strubers at the time of the alleged discharge.
- TA had a sat phone with him that day, yet he never tried calling BS, nor did they call police for 9+ hrs.
- Artificial Intelligence analysed statements and evidence. A 192-page report expressed concern regarding the 3 prospectors and their evidence.

Appendix B

Full List of Admissions by Defence at Trial:

Vehicles

Toyota LandCruiser, unregistered. The internal and external areas of the vehicle were examined for the presence of blood. No apparent bloodstains were observed, and no presumptive results for blood were obtained. Located in the cabin was a .22 bolt action Norinco rifle, a Harrington & Richardson firearm in a leather case and spent cartridge cases. Toyota LandCruiser, registration 730HRO. The internal and external areas of the vehicle were examined for the presence of blood. No apparent bloodstains were observed, and no presumptive results for blood were obtained. Located in the cabin was a bolt action firearm with scopes and unspent cartridge cases and a firearm magazine.

Clothes

A blue long sleeve shirt and dark denim jeans were seized from Wilson and Struber and tested for traces of human blood. Both items tested negative. A blue Bisley work shirt and blue torn off shirts were seized from Struber and tested for traces of human blood. Both items tested negative.

DNA testing

DNA STR profiling. STR - short tandem repeat - profiling is the standard technique currently in use for forensic DNA analysis. Deoxyribonucleic DNA is a complex chemical found in almost all cells of the body. It carries genetic information which governs a person's physical and biochemical characteristics. Half of a person's DNA is inherited from their mother and half from their father. A person's DNA is the same in almost all cell types in their body so that DNA recovered from someone's blood will normally be the same as DNA from their hair roots, saliva or skin cells.

Except for identical twins, each person's total DNA is unique to themselves, although current DNA STR profiling techniques do not allow the analysis of the whole of someone's DNA. Instead, specific regions - loci - of the DNA are tested which contain short sequences of DNA STRs repeated a number of times end to end. The number of times a particular STR is repeated at each locus region of DNA will tend to vary between people, and it is these differences which allow DNA from different people to be compared. A method known as the Polymerase Chain Reaction - PCR - is used to amplify specific STR regions of the DNA to produce many copies of the original DNA template. In this way minute amounts of DNA isolated from small or degraded samples can be greatly increased to potentially yield a sufficient quantity of DNA to obtain a DNA profile. Swabs from an empty film canister, G20, botanical matter, G18, black twine, G15, leaf, G21, Rock 1 and Rock 3 match, G19, the DNA profile of Bruce Schuler.

Photographs

On the 11h of July 2012 photographs were taken by a Scenes of Crime officer of the following. Unregistered beige coloured Toyota Land Cruiser parked in front of the homestead. Beige Toyota Land Cruiser, registration 730-HRU parked approximately one kilometre from the homestead. Tyre tracks in bushland, Palmerville Station homestead. On the 13th of July 2012 photographs, location of leaf, map reference G21, general views of the burnt patches. Firearm projector, map reference G18. Anthill and scrap marks. 14th of July 2012, photographs were taken of the damaged trees, anthill and tyre tracks in grass bushland. Markers one to 12 indicate tyre tracks in the grass leading from the bushland down the ravine to the levelled-out ground. Marker 13 denotes the location of the green fibre and bloodstained leaf. Markers 14 and 15 denote the location of the larger burnt grass area where the partially burnt matchsticks were located. Marker 6 denotes the knocked over termite mound.

Map titled Palmerville River Station

The map produced has been marked with the last known position of Bruce Schuler according to Daniel Bidner. The positions marked on the map of Kevin Groth, Daniel Bidner and Tremain Anderson are positions described by themselves. Map references N18, last known location of Bruce Schuler. The area between N18 and N13 was searched. No human blood was detected. No projectiles were detected. Tyre tracks from N10 to N13 to N15. G11, broken saplings. G16, termite mounds that had been knocked over and had gouge marks. The gouge marks are consistent with being made by a metal component on the undercarriage of the unregistered Toyota Land Cruiser owned by the accused.

An examination of the gouge marks established a positive comparison between test marks, the cast taken from the vehicle, and test marks, cast taken from termite mounds. This established that the metal surface of the underneath of the Land Cruiser responsible for these test marks are capable of leaving reproducible marks. The marks present within the termite mound was consistent with having been caused by an object such as the underneath of a vehicle or a similar type of tool capable of leaving such a mark.

G21, leaves with blood matching the DNA of Bruce Schuler. G19, area of burnt grass and vegetation. Located in this area were four partially burnt matchsticks. One of these matches the DNA profile match of Bruce Schuler.

Bloodstains were observed on several rocks. The bloodstains matched the DNA profile of Bruce Schuler. G18, bloodstaining was observed in the ground cover. The ground cover in that area consisted of grass, leaves and other botanical material. The blood matched the DNA profile of Bruce Schuler. A damaged projectile was found. The projectile slug was old and had not been recently fired.

G17, smaller area of burnt grass. G1, knocked down tree with gouges in the bark and grease marks on the exposed wood. G2, knocked down tree with gouges in the bark. G3, scratches in termite mound. G4 and G5, gouges in the bark of two trees that were parallel to one another on either side of the tyre tracks. G6, scratches on the top of the surface of a termite mound. G7, cow pat and tyre impressions. These impressions correspond in class characteristics, tread design and wear to the tyres on the unregistered Toyota

Land Cruiser owned by the accused and could have been made by the tyres on that vehicle or any other tyre with similar treat characteristics. G8, gouges in the bark of a tree. G9, gouges in the bark of a tree. G10, gouges in the bark of a tree. G11, two knocked down trees. G12, damage to tree and termite mound. G15, piece of black twine. The DNA profile matches that of Bruce Schuler. G20, empty white film canister. The DNA profile matches that of Bruce Schuler.

Telephone Call:

On the 12th of July 2012 at approximately 9.27 am Dianne Wilson-Struber telephoned Palmerville Station homestead from a pay phone at Lawson Street, Mareeba and had the following conversation with Detective Sergeant Goen.

Goen:	Hello.
Wilson-Struber:	Hello.
Goen:	Hello.
Wilson-Struber:	Is this Palmerville Station?
Goen:	Yes, it is.
Wilson-Struber:	Is this the police?
Goen:	Yes.
Wilson-Struber:	You're doing a search for a person?
Goen:	Yes.
Wilson-Struber:	I have some information.
Goen:	Okay.

Wilson-Struber:	You're looking in the wrong spot.
Goen:	Okay, where do you think we should be searching?
Wilson-Struber:	12 to 15Ks to the east of there.
Goen: Okay.	Who am I speaking with?
Wilson-Struber:	I don't want to give my name.
Goen:	Okay then. Why do you say we are looking in the wrong spot?
Wilson-Struber:	I have someone that was involved.
Goen:	Okay. If that's the case we would like to speak to your friend to help them. We might be able to sort this out.
Goen:	Are you there?

The call was then terminated. The call lasted 86 seconds.

Weapons

The schedule titled Seize and Missing Firearms is a list of firearms that were seized and/or are missing from Palmerville Station. Pages 2 to 6 are photographs of the seized weapons listed in the Seize and Missing Firearms Schedule.

Witness

It is formally admitted that Berty Lyndon Callaghan is the neighbour of Dianne Struber - Wilson and Stephen Struber. He is profoundly deaf and did not see or hear anything on the 9th and 19th of July 2012 from his neighbour's property.

Full List of Admissions

by Crown at Trial:

1) Daniel Bidner was interviewed by Detective Sergeant Nicholas O'Brien on the 9th of July 2012,

2) the interview was conducted by telephone and commenced at 9.10 p.m.,

3) Daniel Bidner has said the following:

(a) "At the very same moment, I heard Bruce's dog bark, and at the same time, Bruce said, 'Quiet."

(b) "I even went to track the u-turn, like, after they left. I went, 'Right, I will go and see what they said to Bruce.'

(c) "But after I went back to the car and waiting a while, me and Tremain - oh, Tremain went back first. I also went back. So we both - we went back to see the site separately. We did track where the car turned around. We went - yeah."

4) Walter Randall receives a telephone call from Tremain Anderson on the afternoon of the 9th of July 2012. Tremain Anderson said to Walter Randall that he had heard two gunshots being fired and then another shot a bit later.'

Appendix C

PALMERVILLE

Behind The Crime 2018 Presents

The Gold Prospector Who Vanished

Good evening, I am Detective Sergeant Alina BELL and tonight we will be discussing the investigation that took place, into the death of Bruce SCHULER. I was the arresting officer, along with Detective Sergeant Brad McLEISH.

Sergeant Lesley WALKER the Scientific Officer and Principal Crown Prosecutor Nigel REES will also be speaking tonight. I will cover the investigation; Sergeant WALKER will discuss the forensic side of the investigation and Crown Prosecutor REES will go through the court proceedings.

Then we will hear from Fiona SCHULER, the wife of Bruce SCHULER. She will be discussing how she got the 'No body no parole' legislation passed in parliament.

Before we proceed, I would like to mention in advance that the presentation focuses on the investigation and the subject matter will be presented in a very factual manner, on that note I would also like to acknowledge the family and friends of Bruce who have attended and realise that this presentation could be confronting. Also, if you have any questions during the presentation feel free to ask as we proceed.

Homicides	2012	2013	2014	2015	2016	2017
Queensland	55	40	52	56	41	41
Brisbane Region	12	6	11	12	7	12
Northern Region	11	4	17	11	12	11
Far North District	7	2	16	4	5	10
Cairns Division	2	0	9	4	1	2

Before we begin, I thought I would enlighten you on the statistics of homicides that occur in Queensland yearly. As you can see the table represents homicides in Queensland, the Brisbane region, Northern region, Far North district and the Cairns Division. You will note that in 2014 the numbers for homicides in Cairns was high, however this was due to the tragic death of 8 children.

The murder of Bruce SCHULER was code named Operation Kilo Principle. The two accused and convicted were Stephen STRUBER and Dianne WILSON.

STRUBER and WILSON owned and ran, Palmerville Station. The property previously belonged to Dianne's parents.

Bruce SCHULER was 48years of age. He was the husband of Fiona SCHULER and the father to Lisa and Bruce Jnr.

Daniel BIDNER, Tremaine ANDERSON and Kevin GROTH were the key witnesses in this matter. Witness BIDNER and ANDERSON had previously had altercations with STRUBER and WILSON whilst allegedly being on their land.

Witness GROTH and SCHULER did not know STRUBER and WILSON.

Bruce SCHULER, the gold prospector who vanished. Many may ask how one can just disappear.

Well firstly you must understand the environment in which this occurred. Palmerville Station, the cattle property is 1360 square kilometres. Cooktown is the closest midsize township, 139kilometres to the North.

Due to its heritage and location gold mining is still a frequent past time for many in the area. There were several mining permits issued for people to prospect specific areas of Palmerville Station when the murder of Bruce SCHULER occurred.

STRUBER and WILSON had a well-documented history of opposing such leases and having confrontations with trespassers upon the property. There had been rumours of them shooting at Trespasses over the years, however no formal complaints were made to Police.

STRUBER also had a long history of disputes with the Cook Shire Council after a portion of his land was resumed by the State Government for the purpose of building gazetted roads that ran through Palmerville.

On the morning of the 8th day of July 2012 Bruce SCHULER, Daniel BIDNER, Tremaine ANDERSON and Kevin GROTH travelled from Daniel BIDNERS residence to the Laura / Maytown Road, Palmer River Crossing situated within the confines of Palmerville Station.

This location is about one kilometre East of Palmerville Station Homestead.

ANDERSON travelled to this location on his trail bike and SCHULER, BIDNER and GROTH travelled in SCHULER'S 2004 Nissan Patrol Utility.

A camp site was established on the banks of the Palmer River so that neither the camp nor SCHULER's vehicle could be seen from the Palmer River Crossing Road.

That afternoon BIDNER, ANDERSON, GROTH and SCHULER commenced prospecting for gold and later returned to the camp.

At approximately 7:30am the following morning, Monday 9th July 2012, BIDNER, ANDERSON, GROTH and SCHULER walked in a westerly direction along the Palmer River. They walked to a gully and from this position they all then moved off in different directions to commence prospecting.

At about 10:30am witness Daniel BIDNER returned to a ridge line above the same gully that SCHULER was prospecting in. BIDNER observed that SCHULER's dog was next to him. BIDNER then observed one of the owners of Palmerville Station, Dianne WILSON in the passenger seat of a Toyota single cab ute. BIDNER had a clear view of WILSON, but he was unable to observe the driver of the vehicle.

WILSON gestured with her hand indicating that there was something down in the gully, this was where SCHULER was prospecting for gold. The vehicle stopped suddenly above where SCHULER was prospecting.

Witness Tremaine ANDERSON was prospecting on the ridge above SCHULER and opposite to where BIDNER was positioned.

Witness ANDERSON observed SCHULER prospecting in the gully below the ridge line where he was prospecting two minutes before, he heard a vehicle. Witness ANDERSON observed the vehicle drive up the bank of the river, following the road that ran from the Palmerville Homestead along the Palmer River towards where he and SCHULER were prospecting. Witness ANDERSON stated that he identified STRUBER as the drive of the vehicle as he drove past, however he did not see the passenger. ANDERSON decamped and stopped and crouched in a gully. Witness ANDERSON heard the car stop and approximately two minutes later he heard a loud gunshot which sounded like a high-powered rifle. Approximately fifteen minutes later ANDERSON heard the car start up again and heard it drive a little bit further up the road before he heard another gun shot. Witness ANDERSON stated that it was then quite for about half an hour. He then heard the car start up again and heard it travelling back along the same road.

Witness GROTH had left the gully area where SCHULER was prospecting, he headed along the ridge line where he heard a vehicle that sounded like a Toyota Diesel motor. GROTH stated that he could see the top of the vehicle and that it looked like a Ute, beige in colour. GROTH observed the vehicle travelling along the Palmer River towards the gully area where SCHULER was last sighted. GROTH stated that a minute or two later he heard a rifle shot. GROTH stated that it sounded like a large calibre rifle. GROTH stated that five to ten minutes later he heard a second gun shot.

After the vehicle was heard to leave the area, witnesses BIDNER, ANDERSON and GROTH made their separate ways back to the location where they had camped the night before and where SCHULER's vehicle was parked. At this time, they realised that SCHULER was missing. SCHULER had the keys to the vehicle and as such witness BIDNER had to return to his residence on ANDERSON's motor bike to retrieve another vehicle. During this time witness ANDERSON re-attended the area where SCHULER was last seen and did not locate any trace of him. ANDERSON also walked towards the Palmerville Station homestead however did not locate any sign of SCHULER. Witness ANDERSON also did not sight STRUBER or WILSON.

This aerial map depicts where the three witnesses were positioned, where Bruce SCHULER was last seen and where his DNA was later located.

This area was treated as our primary crime scene.

The photographs and aerial view do not adequately display the steep ridge lines and nature of the terrain.

The distance from SCHULER to where his blood was later located was 150metres.

The distances, line of sight from BIDNER to WILSON was a 100meters.

ANDERSON was 30 meters away from where STRUBER and WILSONS vehicle was parked.

At approximately 4:30pm, 6hours after the gun shots, SCHULER still had not returned to his vehicle. Witness BIDNER, ANDERSON and GROTH then decided to head back to the main camp and left a note for SCHULER on his vehicle advising him that they had his dog and to contact them ASAP upon his return.

After returning to BIDNERS, at approximately 6.16pm ANDERSON rang STRUBER's home number. No person answered and ANDERSON left a message.

I am camped in the river; I haven't seen my mate since this morning. I heard a couple of rifle shots. If I don't hear from him in the next half an hour, I am calling the police".

ANDERSON left a second message at 6.19pm.

"I am camped in the river, haven't seen my mate since this morning. If I don't hear from him in half an hour, I am calling the police".

Police listened to the Telstra home phone 101 messages during the execution of the crime scene warrant. This was the first time that police had accessed the message bank for the homestead landline since executing the search warrant. Police believe that as the messages were in the "saved messages", it suggests that they had been previously listened to by Struber and/or Wilson.

At this time the three witnesses were of the belief that SCHULER had just been taken by STRUBER and WILSON and that perhaps they were holding him for trespassing and that they had contacted the Police. They thought the gun shots were just warnings and were unaware of the sinister reality of what really had occurred.

On the 10th of July 2012, the investigation into the disappearance of at this time missing person SCHULER commenced. Police travelled to Maytown and spoke at length to the three witnesses to ascertain fully their movements and recollections of Monday 9th July 2012.

Police then travelled to Palmerville Station, and a preliminary search was conducted in the area in which SCHULER was last seen. SCHULER, or any indication of his presence, was not located.

At approximately 6:45pm that evening Police executed a search warrant at Palmerville Station. STRUBER and WILSON were arrested for murder and placed in custody. The only comment made was to say that they had not discharged any firearms in recent days and that they had not seen any persons in recent days. There was no re-action observed by either party. No statements or pleas of innocence.

When arrested both appeared to have blood droplets on their clothing. They were transported from Palmerville Station to the Mareeba Police Station for questioning. After seeking legal advice STRUBER and WILSON refused to participate in an electronic record of interview.

Non-intimate Forensic Procedure Orders were conducted on both STRUBER and WILSON.

During the FPO STRUBER made reference to the waterways being damaged and his cattle business being detrimentally affected by the prospectors.

WILSON stated during the examination that they had been castrating cattle that day. The Stock Squad located evidence at the property to indicate that cattle had been recently castrated. Presumptive tests confirmed that the blood located on STRUBER and WILSON and their clothing was from a bovine source.

STRUBER and WILSON were released from Police custody on the $11^{th\ of}$ July 2012 without charge. They were both refusing to provide versions and at that time Police had not located any further evidence linking them to this crime.

Police obtained typed statements and conducted video recorded re-enactments with the three witnesses at Palmerville Station. There versions remained consistent.

Witness BIDNER and ANDERSON also viewed Police photo boards. BIDNER identified WILSON as being the passenger of the vehicle and ANDERSON identified STRUBER as being the driver of the vehicle.

Police also conducted non-intimate forensic procedures on the three witnesses. Their hands were swabbed for gun residue testing, all of which was negative.

Police made application to a Magistrate for a crime scene warrant on the $10^{th \, of}$ July 2012.

The crime scene was declared to be fifty kilometres around the home stead and was due to expire 7days later.

Whilst the crime scene warrant was in effect, Police conducted forensic examinations and investigative searches of the homestead, sheds and vehicles.

An extensive aerial search utilising two helicopters and an extensive land search of the property for missing person SCHULER was also conducted over the following days. Specialist trained search and rescue Police attended the scene and with the assistance of SES, foot, horse, vehicle and helicopter searches were commenced.

A statistical search area of 19km radius from the last known position of SCHULER was established based on lost person behaviour statistics showing that 97% of deceased persons moved from a murder scene were located within 19km of this scene and 100% of these deceased persons were located within 136m from a road or end of a track, generally found in debris piles, dead ends, overgrown gullies, canyons or waterways.

Waterways and mine shafts in the area were also extensively searched.

Neither SCHULER nor any of his property (GPS, metal detector, watch, necklace etc.) was located.

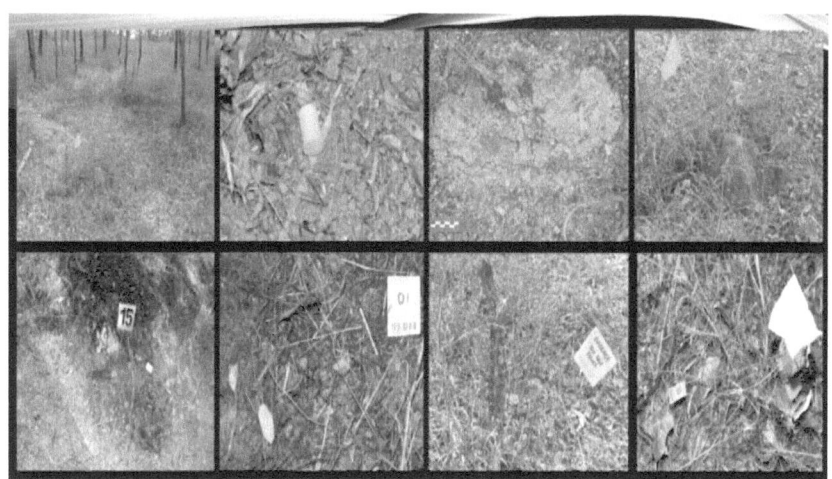

On the 13th day of July, whilst searching in the vicinity of the gully area where SCHULER was last sighted, Police did locate evidence to indicate that SCHULER had met with foul play. Within 140m of where SCHULER was last seen, Police located a set of tyre tracks that led off the (main) roadway and down a steep embankment into the same gully where SCHULER was last sighted. Examinations were conducted of the tyre tracks. Tyre tracks at the scene were consistent with that of the vehicle of STRUBER and WILSON.

Near the bottom of the gully where SCHULER was last seen and where the vehicle tracks end, Police located two small sections of grass that had been recently burnt. Nearby to these burnt sections Police located a small film canister that is commonly used by prospectors to store metals (gold) they locate. It was known that SCHULER kept one of these canisters on his person, SCHULER'S DNA was located on this canister. In the burnt areas of grass Police located what presumptive tests by Scientific Officers at the scene indicated was human blood. DNA tests later confirmed that the blood belonged to SCHULER.

Bailing twine, tyre impressions in cow pats, a gauge out of a termite mound and knocked over damaged trees were also identified. The Bailing Twine had SCHULER'S DNA on it, the tyre impressions in the cow pat corresponded in class characterises (thread design and wear) to STRUBER and WILSONS vehicle. The damaged trees were identified by an arborist as being knocked over between the evening of the 8/7 and the morning of the 9/7. A Scientific officer gave an opinion that the marks in the termite mound were consistent with STRUBER and WILSONS vehicle or a similar type of tool capable of leaving such a mark".

On the 12th day of July 2012 Schuler's vehicle was seized as an exhibit and conveyed back to Cairns Police Station for forensic analysis. No evidence was located.

Schuler's camp was also searched by investigators with DNA comparison exhibits seized namely razors, toothbrushes for analysis.

On the 12th of July a female called Palmerville Station. She stated, "Is this the Palmerville Station? Is this the Police? You're doing a search for a person. I have some information and you're looking in the wrong spot, 12 to 15 km's east of there. I don't want to give my name. I know someone that was involved".

Police conducted a reverse charge call records and identified that the call came from a phone box at Mareeba. Police arranged for the phone box to be forensically examined, and a door knock of nearby houses was conducted. Police identified that a nearby address was that of WILSONS stepsister and that WILSON had been staying at this address since her release from Police custody.

Whilst obtaining investigative statements from witnesses, Police also identified that WILSON had been dropped off at this phone box on the date in question. Police confirmed the timings with a download of the witnesses' mobile phone as they made a corresponding call at the same time.

Police then tuw WILSON who admitted to using the phone box however denied calling Palmerville Homestead. WILSONS solicitor attended and indicated that WILSON would not answer further questions, however the solicitor confirmed that it was WILSON who called Palmerville Station. ENGLISH indicated that WILSON had done this out of frustration, that the Police were looking at the wrong people responsible and that the Police should be looking at drug users who were mining in the area.

Police thoroughly searched this area, that was identified as 'Cradle Creek'. This area was situated fifteen kilometres to the east of Palmerville Station. Maps for the area in the vicinity of Palmerville homestead, indicated that the location as described by Wilson was Cradle Creek. Nothing of interest was located.

Police concluded that WILSON had made this phone call to direct Police away from the property, perhaps to the next-door neighbours so that she could return as whilst the crime scene warrant was in effect, STRUBER and WILSON were not allowed to return to the property. Cradle Creek was also an area that was known to be utilised by BIDNER.

During the investigation STRUBER and WILSON regularly alluded to the fact that our key witnesses were behind this crime. This avenue of investigation was explored and found improbable.

During the investigation it was also identified that WILSON had grown up on the property and had only left the property a handful of times to travel to Mareeba for supplies. Therefore, she was quite out of her comfort zone, being removed from the property.

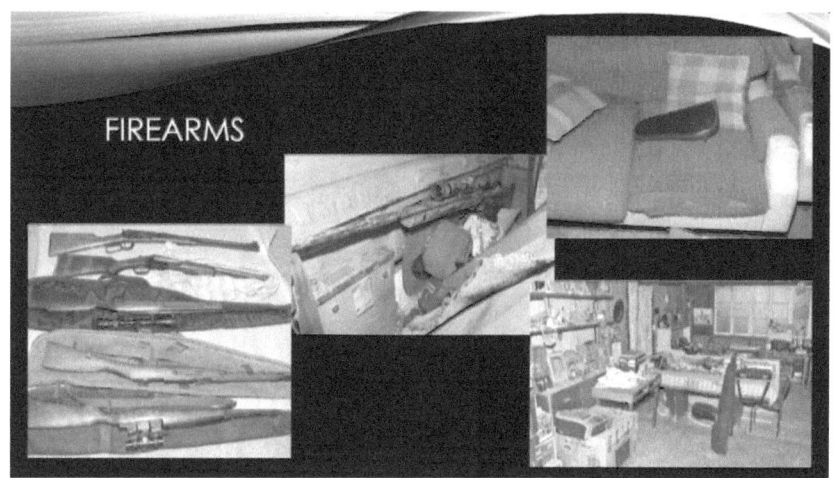

Police inquiries established that STRUBER had a Queensland weapons licence, he was licenced to possess a handgun, however his licence for rifles had expired. WILSON was not a weapon licence holder. The brother of WILSON, George also had a weapons licence and had a number of firearms registered to him that were kept at Palmerville Station.

On the 10th July when STRUBER and WILSON were initially arrested STRUBER stated that there were two firearms in the broken down Toyota Land cruiser on a track near the airstrip. He stated there was a 308 rifle and pistol in the vehicle. When Police located the vehicle, it was locked, in working order. A 308 rifle was located; however, the pistol was not.

Police located the .357 revolver empty leather case on a couch in the homestead.

There were numerous other firearms seized, some registered and other not.

During the investigation it was also identified that a .22 rifle registered to the brother of WILSON was missing from the homestead.

STRUBER was questioned about the missing .357 handgun however he refused to supply a response as to where it was located. He was later formally directed to produce it and when he failed to comply, he was charged with 'Contravene direction or requirement of Police' PPRA.

Police never located the handgun that STRUBER claimed was in the broken down vehicle, two rifles registered to STRUBER and WILSON or the rifle registered to WILSONS brother, George.

Witnesses had provided statements to Police indicating that STRUBER carried the handgun on his person whilst patrolling the property. Police also were aware that WILSON was known to use George's rifle. George stated that he stored the firearm at the homestead and that if WILSON needed a gun to shoot, she would loan his because she had not learnt to use a bigger gun. George stated that only he and Wilson had access to the safe where the firearm was stored.

The investigation indicated that firearms were used in the course of the suspected killing of Schuler, therefore the fact that the .357 handgun and rifles were outstanding allowed the inference to be drawn that they were associated with the killing for which STRUBER and WILSON were suspects. Police were of the belief that STRUBER and WILSON had disposed of them after the incident.

STRUBER and WILSON later claimed that Police stole the handgun, and the rifle registered to WILSONS brother. This allegation was investigated and found to be unsubstantiated.

On the afternoon of the 15th July 2012 SES personnel departed and the search for Schuler moved from a search and rescue operation to a search operation. It had been determined that the survivability of Schuler was no longer possible.

For the next two days Police continued their investigations and searches for Schuler, however nothing of interest was located. On the 17th day of July, the Crime Scene at Palmerville Station was discontinued and all Police departed.

Operation Kilo Principle continued, and further investigative avenues were pursued. A number of entities were identified that had been involved in interactions with Struber and Wilson.

These witnesses reported confrontations between themselves and STRUBER and WILSON. These persons also stated that some of these confrontations included STRUBER and WILSON presenting firearms.

Witness ANDERSON stated that he was detecting on Palmerville approximately 20years prior when WILSON confronted him with a rifle, aiming it at his stomach, demanding he got off the property.

VIDEO RECORDED CONVERSATION

- Wilson: Will I get it?
- Struber: Hey?
- Wilson: Will I get it?
- Struber: Please yourself. He's an ignorant arsehole.
- Bidner (distant): What, are you getting the gun out are ya?
- Struber: He's got plenty of witnesses.
- Wilson: "If those other c---- weren't there I'd stop and get the gun out and I'd .....ui... between the eyes".

Witness BIDNER had an altercation with STRUBER and WILSON a few weeks prior to SCHULER disappearing. BIDNER stated that WILSON was recording this on a video camera and when Police executed a search warrant, they located the recording of this incident.

On the recording BIDNER indicated to WILSON that he would be on Palmerville Station next week, which was around the offence date.

Some of the conversation captured on the video camera when STRUBER and WILSON were back at their vehicle:

Wilson: Will I get it?

Struber: Hey?

Wilson: Will I get it?

Struber: Please yourself. He's an ignorant arsehole.

Bidner (distant): What, are you getting the gun out are ya?

Struber: He's got plenty of witnesses.

WILSON is then heard to say,

"If those other C's weren't there I'd stop and get the gun out and I'd .....ui... between the eyes".

432

CRIME SCENE WARRANT TWO (2), THREE (3) & FOUR (4)

Upon departing Palmerville Station on 17 July 2012 Police completed a comprehensive review of the initial forensic examinations and investigation. It was determined further crime scene examinations and searches were required necessitating the utilisation of specialist staff from the Australian Federal Police and Queensland Police Service officers based in Brisbane.

Police obtained a second crime scene warrant for Palmerville Station and on the 31st July 2012 it was executed upon STRUBER and WILSON, along with George WILSON. They were all removed from the property. Further re-enactments with the three witnesses, utilising STRUBER and WILSONS motor vehicle was conducted. Video recording of the incident location utilising 'Spheron' (3d video recording device) was also obtained. Acoustic examinations and further mapping of the offence location, incorporating terrain was conducted. Mechanical examinations of STRUBER and WILSONS alleged broken down vehicle and the utilisation of an Australian Federal Police firearms detection dog to search for the missing .357 firearm and Schuler's outstanding G.P.S, backpack, pick, metal detector, watch and neck chain. The forensic examinations and searches were completed on 2 August 2012 and nothing of interest was located.

A third crime scene warrant was executed on the 15th August 2012. The determination to obtain a further crime scene warrant was based upon the fact that .357 hand gun registered to Struber had not been located and the Winchester lever action rifle registered to George Wilson was un-accounted for. Items of clothing being worn by Struber and Wilson as described by the witnesses had also not been located. A land search of the area referred to as cradle creek was also required. This was in response to the phone call by Wilson to the homestead upon their initial arrest.

The forensic examinations and searches were completed on 18 August 2012 and nothing of interest was located.

The fourth crime scene warrant was executed on the 6th October 2012. Further searches and forensic examinations were conducted. The forensic examinations and searches were completed on 12 October 2012 and nothing of interest was located.

During the execution of the crime scene warrants, STRUBER and WILSON were always removed from the property. On theses occasions they were transported back to their requested area in separate vehicles where Police attempted to build some rapport with them. STRUBER refused to speak with Police at all and WILSON had very little to say.

As well as conducting further crime scene warrants police also used a number of other investigation techniques including listening and tracking devices as well as having the behavioural specialist unit review recordings of interactions that Police had with STRUBER and WILSON.

Other methods were also utilised however will not be discussed due to revealing Police methodologies.

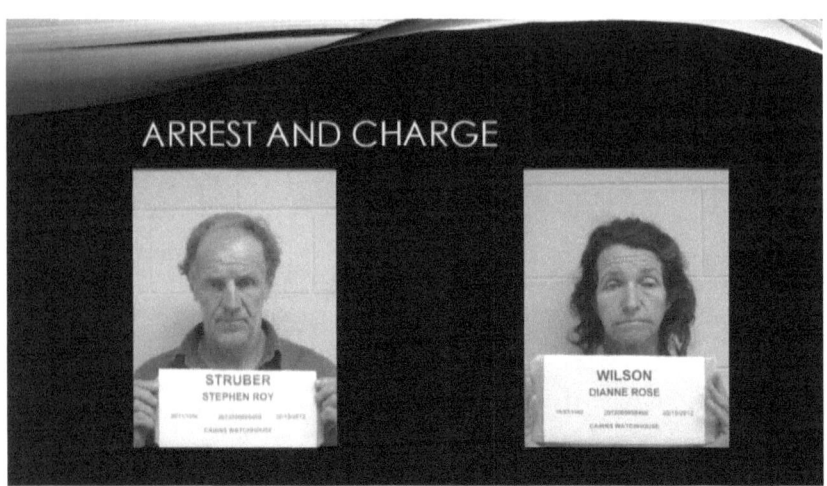

On Tuesday the 30th of October 2012 Detectives McLEISH and I, along with other Police returned to Palmerville Station and located and arrested STRUBER and WILSON. They were returned to the Cairns WH where they were charged with Murder and Misconduct with a Corpse.

They both refused to participate in EROI's. Bail was objected to however they were later released on bail after a supreme court application.

Crown Prosecutor Nigel REES will discuss the trial, and appeal in further detail. He had the difficult job of convincing a jury of STRUBER and WILSONS guilt in a murder case without a body or any direct forensic evidence linking the couple to it.

The two-week trail took place in the Supreme Court in Cairns in July 2015. Struber and Wilson were found guilty of murder and were sentenced to life imprisonment.

Fiona, SCHULER'S wife read a victim impact statement to the court asking how someone could have so little regard for human life and made reference to STRUBER and WILSON discarding Bruce like a piece of rubbish. During this STRUBER and WILSON'S facial expressions remained lifeless and neither displayed a hint of remorse.

After the guilty verdict Detective Sergeant McLEISH and I attended the Cairns Watch house to ask STRUBER and WILSON one last time where SCHULER was located. Neither made a sound and both stared stonily ahead through the bars as though we were not there.

On this day Fiona also declared that it was not the end, that they needed to bring Bruce home and they needed to make it happen. Which is when she commenced pushing for the no body, no parole legislation to be passed in parliament.

Fiona successfully had the legislation passed, however to no avail to bringing Bruce home.

Detective Sergeant McLEISH and I once again approached STRUBER and WILSON at their respective prisons, only once again to be confronted by their cold, un-responsive demeanour.

Bruce Schuler

29.12.1963 – 9.7.2012

Appendix D

Correspondence to QPS, ODPP, and both Defence Counsel via Legal Aid Queensland.

Hello Brad

I hope this finds you well.

I am extending an invitation to you and to prosecutor Nigel Rees to participate in a recorded audio interview for a forthcoming episode of my podcast "Where is Bruce Schuler".

I would appreciate if **you could forward my email** to prosecutor Rees to enable him to reply to me directly.

I would like to discuss the following matters:

In the diaries of 2 police officers, it was noted crown witness Tremain Anderson claimed he went to the Palmerville homestead on the afternoon of Monday 9 July 2012 whilst looking for Bruce Schuler. That was never recorded in any statement and was not mentioned at trial. Did he walk there? Did he drive there? What time did he go there? What time did he arrive back at the camp site? The prospectors were supposedly in fear of Stephen Struber. Why was that information not made known to the jury? Were there any concern as to the reliability, credibility and truthfulness of the witness after this change of version of events?

Crown witness Dan Bidner gave 3 VERY different versions of the one incident to police over 3 consecutive days when referring to his actions when the Struber ute drove past him returning to the homestead. His audio is in episode 8 of my podcast "Where is Bruce Schuler", recorded by QPS and therefore known to both QPS and DPP.

How did investigators conclude the witness was reliable, truthful and credible after hearing those differing versions?

At trial, under cross-examination, when being questioned regarding that very matter, the only conclusion that could be reached was the witness was obfuscating when answering the questions. Were you as investigators and prosecutor concerned at the way he answered questions regarding that matter? Did you consider at that time whether he was a reliable, credible and truthful witness?

Who made the decision not to inform the jury of his 3 significantly different versions of that event?

Who made the decision not to inform the jury of his 3 significantly different versions of that event?

Crown witnesses Bidner and Anderson repeatedly told police the Struber ute did a u-turn after the second gun shot and travelled in the direction of the homestead. Witness Groth corroborated those claims. Those claims were never raised at trial. Who made the decision not to inform the jury of that significant information?

At no time were the versions of the crown witnesses ever disputed. Therefore, on what basis could it be 'reasonably inferred' the Struber ute drove down the ravine to the second crime when the crown witnesses specifically and clearly stated the ute turned around and travelled in the direction of the homestead and never went down the ravine. The witnesses remained in the area for the remainder of the day and the ute was NOT heard to return to the crime scenes.

Who made the decision NOT to mark the spot on diagrams and maps produced by police of the spot where the Struber ute performed a U turn and returned in the direction of the homestead. Apart from being seen by the crown witnesses, it was noted in audio recordings that several police pointed out the U turn location also.

Crown witness Dan Bidner gave 2 VERY different versions of the one incident to police over 3 consecutive days when referring to returning to the camp after the second gun shot. Who decided to accept the "he prospected his way back to the camp site" as opposed to "he didn't prospect his way back to the camp site". Who made the decision not to inform the jury of these conflicting versions of his movements on the day.

When he gave that evidence, were you concerned that he had also given a contradictory statement as to what he did on the way back to camp.

I take it the QPS and DPP were not concerned with the credibility and truthfulness of the witness after those conflicting versions became known. On what basis did the QPS and DPP decide the witnesses were credible, honest and truthful.

There were significant discrepancies given by crown witnesses Anderson and Groth of their meeting around 3pm on Monday 9 July 2012 near the camp site. Whose version was ultimately accepted as accurate? Were the QPS and DPP concerned with the reliability, credibility and truthfulness of the witness after hearing of their different versions of that meeting?

Bruce Schuler had a satellite phone in his possession. In your police brief the following was written for an entry on Saturday 14 July 2012: " At approximately 11am I forwarded a request to obtain satellite telephone information belonging to the missing person for phone ending in digits 58681, including last known location and usage. I subsequently received a latitude and longitude of -16.0051S and 144.1279E as the last point on 8 July 2012 at 9.33 GMT. Reverse call data was not available. This location is consistent with the missing person's camp located near Palmerville Station, approximately 120miles NNW of Cairns. When plotted, I determined this to be approximately 12 klms to the east of the missing persons LKP. Who made the decision not to disclose this information to the jury?

09.33GMT on 8 July 2012 was 7.30pm eastern Australian time 8 July 2012. I do not agree with the above calculation. I say it is around 3.5 klms to the east of Bruce's LNP in a straight line, or around 5 klms by road not 12 klms. It may be possible the officer calculated the distance from the homestead. Either way, the 3 prospectors claimed they remained around the riverbed all night, near where Bruce Schuler's vehicle was found. There was NO mention of Bruce leaving the group that night and making a satellite call some 5 klms away, and why would he? I am told the GPS coordinates is very rugged country. What was Bruce doing 5 klms to the east in very rugged country? Do you care to comment? Was a foot search of those GPS coordinates conducted after they became known. Were the prosecutors questioned as to why Bruce Schuler would be there at 7.33pm on the Sunday night when they claimed they were in camp on the riverbed?

It was accepted witness Anderson told Walter Randall he heard 3 shots that day. Were you concerned Anderson was an honest, reliable and credible witness?

The crown witnesses repeatedly told QPS they were waiting for a phone call from Bruce Schuler on his satellite phone. Yet, this phone was in possession of witness Daniel Bidner from 9 July 2012 - 14 July 2012. This phone was apparently handed to Det Sgt McLeish by third party named CS. Yet Det Sgt McLeish did not take a statement from CS. He also recorded in his statement that he seized the satellite phone from the camp of Bruce Schuler. Which version was the truth?

The above matters are not the only matters of concern as to the truthfulness, credibility and honesty of the crown witnesses. I am not inclined to provide other examples of discrepancies in their evidence, although many exist. If the above matters are not enough to cause sufficient concern, it would be unlikely to sway you with any further amount of discrepancies. I consider the above shows a disturbing course of conduct by the crown witnesses. In view of the conflicting accounts of the crown witnesses, do you still maintain they were credible, reliable and truthful witnesses?

In light of all the evidence now being aired, can you now advise what evidence exactly points to Stephen Struber and Dianne Wilson being the killers of Bruce Schuler?

Would you support this case being referred to the Court of Appeal for consideration as a miscarriage of justice?

If no, how do you explain the concerning and disturbing variations in the evidence of the crown witnesses.

I look forward to hearing from you and prosecutor Rees.

Graeme Crowley

Correspondence to Both Defence Counsel via Legal Aid Queensland

Greetings

You acted for **Dianne Wilson Struber (Legal Aid Qld)** and **Stephen Struber (Richardson & Assoc)** at their Cairns Supreme Court trial on a charge of murder commencing on 13 July 2015.

I would kindly ask you forward this email to J Trevino, barrister who acted for Wilson-Struber and to P J Feeney, barrister who acted for Stephen Struber for the purposes of requesting an interview.

I am broadcasting a podcast on the murder of Bruce Schuler at Palmerville Station Qld in 2012 and the conviction of the above 2 defendants at Cairns in 2015.

I would like to extend an invitation to both parties to participate in an recorded audio interview for a forthcoming episode of my podcast "Where is Bruce Schuler".

I would like to discuss the following matters:

In the diaries of 2 police officers, it was noted crown witness Tremain Anderson claimed he went to the Palmerville homestead on the afternoon of Monday 9 July 2012 whilst looking for Bruce Schuler. That was never recorded in any statement and was not mentioned at trial. The prospectors were supposedly in fear of Stephen Struber. That information was available in disclosure. Why was the witness not cross examined on that claim.

Crown witness Dan Bidner gave 3 VERY different versions of the one incident to police over 3 consecutive days when referring to his actions when the Struber ute drove past him returning to the homestead. His audio is contained in episode 8 of my podcast "Where is Bruce Schuler", recorded by QPS and therefore was available in disclosure. Why was the witness not cross examined on those ever changing versions of events?

There were significant discrepancies given by crown witnesses Anderson and Groth of their meeting around 3pm on Monday 9 July 2012 near the camp site. That information was available in disclosure. Why were the witnesses not cross examined on those ever changing versions of events?

A call was made on Bruce Schuler's satellite phone at 7.33pm on Sunday 8 July 2012 in a location 5 klms from the camp the prospectors claimed to be in at the time. That information was available in disclosure. Why were the witnesses not cross examined on that satellite call. What was Bruce Schuler doing 5 klms away from the camp when the prospectors made no mention of it.

If, after considering the information that is now available, would you support this case being referred to the Court of Appeal for consideration as a miscarriage of justice?

I look forward to hearing from you.

Graeme Crowley

Appendix E

Legal Argument: Guilt of Stephen Struber and Diane (sic) Struber-Wilson in the Murder of Bruce Schuler

The conviction of Stephen Struber and Diane Struber-Wilson for the murder of Bruce Schuler hinges on strong circumstantial evidence. The defence has attempted to challenge this by highlighting discrepancies in the timeline, witness testimonies, and the absence of direct physical evidence, such as the victim's body. However, Queensland law allows for conviction based on circumstantial evidence, provided that the evidence, taken as a whole, excludes any reasonable hypothesis consistent with innocence. This legal principle, affirmed in *Shepherd v The Queen* (1990) 170 CLR 573, forms the foundation of the prosecution's case.

The Role of Circumstantial Evidence in Criminal Convictions

Circumstantial evidence is indirect evidence that implies a fact through inference, and under Queensland law, it can be used to secure a conviction if it meets the legal threshold of proof beyond reasonable doubt. As the High Court established in *Shepherd v The Queen* (1990) 170 CLR 573, the prosecution need not exclude every conceivable hypothesis of innocence, but it must exclude those that are reasonably consistent with the evidence. This doctrine emphasises that the evidence must be viewed collectively, not in isolation, and the jury must be satisfied that guilt is the only rational conclusion that can be drawn from the circumstances.

In this case, the key circumstantial evidence includes:

Tyre tracks at the crime scene that match the Strubers' vehicle, placing them in the vicinity where Bruce Schuler disappeared.

Witness testimony, which consistently places Struber and Wilson at the scene around the time of Schuler's disappearance. These witnesses observed suspicious behaviour by Struber and Wilson, such as driving erratically and leaving the area shortly after the prospectors heard gunshots.

Burnt matches found at the crime scene with traces of Schuler's DNA, which suggests an attempt by the accused to destroy evidence after the crime.

Geographic damage to the landscape, including damaged trees and anthills, which aligns with the movement of Struber's vehicle in the area, further corroborating their presence near the scene of the murder.

While the defence argued that circumstantial evidence lacks the certainty of direct evidence, courts have long recognised its probative value when properly contextualised. The Queensland Court of Appeal in *R v Hytch* [2005] QCA 216 held that circumstantial evidence can sustain a conviction even when the victim's body is missing, provided that the totality of the evidence clearly indicates that the victim is dead and that the accused is responsible. In this case, despite the absence of Schuler's body, the circumstantial evidence leads to a strong inference that he was killed by Struber and Wilson, and no reasonable alternative explanation exists for his disappearance.

Addressing Discrepancies in Witness Testimony

The defence has raised concerns about inconsistencies in witness testimony, particularly regarding the timeline of events and the actions of Struber and Wilson on the day of Schuler's disappearance. It is important to address the legal significance of such discrepancies.

In *Domican v The Queen* (1992) 173 CLR 555, the High Court emphasised that discrepancies in witness testimony should not automatically discredit the reliability of the evidence, especially in cases involving traumatic events. Minor variations in recollection are natural and do not undermine the core facts if the essential narrative remains consistent and is corroborated by other evidence. The Court held that the jury must evaluate whether the discrepancies are material to the case and whether they affect the overall reliability of the witness's testimony.

In this case, the discrepancies highlighted by the defence involve minor details, such as the precise timeline of events or specific actions of individuals. These variations are to be expected in cases where witnesses are recounting events that occurred under stressful circumstances. What remains consistent, however, are the key elements of the testimony:

Witnesses consistently placed Struber and Wilson at the scene near the time of the murder.

Witnesses observed Struber and Wilson engaging in suspicious behavior, such as hastily leaving the area after gunshots were heard.

The circumstantial evidence, such as the tyre tracks, burnt matches with Schuler's DNA, and damage to the landscape, corroborates the witness accounts.

Thus, while the defence may attempt to cast doubt on the reliability of the witness testimony by pointing to minor discrepancies, these inconsistencies do not materially affect the prosecution's case. The jury was entitled to conclude that the core facts, supported by corroborating evidence, were reliable.

Post-Offence Conduct as Evidence of Guilt

Post-offence conduct, including attempts to mislead authorities or destroy evidence, can be admitted as evidence of consciousness of guilt. In *Edwards v The Queen* (1993) 178 CLR 193, the High Court held that actions taken by the accused after the commission of a crime—such as fleeing the scene, lying to police, or attempting to conceal evidence—can be indicative of guilt if properly explained to the jury. The Court emphasised that post-offence conduct must be evaluated in light of the totality of the evidence and must be carefully explained to the jury to avoid undue prejudice.

In this case, Struber and Wilson engaged in several actions after the murder that point to a consciousness of guilt:

Burning evidence: The burnt matches found at the scene with traces of Schuler's DNA suggest that the Strubers attempted to destroy evidence linking them to the crime.

Evasive behavior: Despite being placed at the scene by multiple witnesses, Struber and Wilson denied any involvement in Schuler's disappearance. Their refusal to cooperate with investigators and their attempts to shift attention away from themselves further suggest that they were aware of their guilt.

These actions align with the principles established in *Edwards* and should be viewed as further evidence supporting the inference of guilt. The jury was entitled to consider Struber and Wilson's post-offence conduct in evaluating their culpability.

The Significance of Ms. Wilson-Struber's Phone Call

On 12 July 2012, Ms. Diane Wilson-Struber made a phone call to the police, advising them to search "12 to 15 kilometres east" of where they were currently searching and hinting that she had information about the crime. She refused to provide her name, and the call was terminated after just 86 seconds. This phone call is highly indicative of consciousness of guilt and aligns with the legal principles outlined in *Edwards v The Queen* (1993) 178 CLR 193, which established that misleading or evasive behavior can be admissible as evidence of guilt.

Ms. Wilson-Struber's cryptic statements and refusal to cooperate with police suggest that she was attempting to divert the investigation away from the actual location of Schuler's body, while maintaining some degree of control over the situation. This behavior is consistent with someone who knows they are guilty and is attempting to avoid detection. The fact that she hinted at having information but refused to disclose her identity further supports the inference that she was trying to protect herself and Struber from being implicated in the crime.

The Impact of No Body, No Parole Legislation

The defence may argue that the absence of Bruce Schuler's body weakens the Crown's case. However, Queensland's "no body, no parole" legislation, introduced after this case, underscores the principle that a conviction can still be secured without a body if the circumstantial evidence is strong enough to exclude any reasonable hypothesis of innocence. The High Court in *R v Baden-Clay* [2016] HCA 35 affirmed that in cases relying on circumstantial evidence, the jury must be satisfied that guilt is the only rational conclusion that can be drawn from the facts.

In this case, the jury carefully considered the circumstantial evidence—including the tyre tracks, the burnt matches containing Schuler's DNA, and the consistent witness testimony placing Struber and Wilson at the scene—and concluded that Struber and Wilson were responsible for Schuler's death. The absence of a body, while significant, does not preclude a conviction where the circumstantial evidence strongly points to the accused's involvement, as it does in this case.

Corroboration of Key Evidence and the Testimony of Stephen May

The defence raised the issue of corroboration, but Queensland law under s 632 *Criminal Code Act* 1899 (Qld) does not require corroboration for a conviction, provided the jury is satisfied beyond a reasonable doubt of the accused's guilt. However, in this case, there was corroborative evidence, particularly from forensic findings and witness testimony.

The testimony of Stephen May, who came forward after the convictions and stated that he saw a body in a vehicle near the Palmer River around the time of Schuler's disappearance, provides further corroboration of the circumstantial evidence. As the High Court explained in *R v Baskerville* [1916] 2 KB 658, corroboration strengthens or supports other evidence. May's statement aligns with the witness accounts and forensic evidence, adding weight to the prosecution's case.

May's testimony, although provided after the trial, reinforces the overall narrative and supports the conclusion that Struber and Wilson were involved in Schuler's murder. Moreover, the corroborative evidence, including the physical evidence of tyre tracks, damage to the landscape, and Schuler's DNA on the burnt matches, strengthens the prosecution's case and makes the jury's conclusion more probable.

Missing Firearms and Incriminating Implications

The schedule of seized and missing firearms from Palmerville Station is another crucial piece of circumstantial evidence. The murder of Bruce Schuler involved the use of a firearm, and the fact that several firearms were unaccounted for raises suspicion that Struber and Wilson may have disposed of the weapon used in the murder. In *R v Baden-Clay* [2016] HCA 35, the High Court held that attempts to dispose of or conceal evidence, such as firearms, can be indicative of guilt if viewed in the broader context of the case.

The missing firearms from Palmerville Station provide further support for the inference that Struber and Wilson were attempting to cover up their involvement in the murder. The concealment or loss of firearms fits within a broader pattern of post-offence conduct aimed at hiding their culpability.

Lack of Motive or Evidence for Daniel Bidner, Tremain Anderson, and Kevin (Rusty) Groth

There is no credible evidence or identified motive suggesting that Daniel Bidner, Tremain Anderson, or Kevin (Rusty) Groth had any involvement in the murder of Bruce Schuler. Motive is a crucial element in establishing a link between suspects and a crime. In this case, there is no history of animosity, disputes, or personal conflicts between these individuals and Schuler that would have led them to commit such a violent act. Additionally, none of the forensic evidence, such as tyre tracks, DNA, or witness testimony, links Bidner, Anderson, or Groth to the scene of the crime. The lack of incriminating evidence against these individuals further weakens any suggestion that they could be involved in the murder. Instead, the circumstantial evidence consistently points towards Struber and Wilson, both of whom had clear territorial motivations and were present at the scene.

Mode of Homicide

The mode of homicide in Bruce Schuler's case is suggested to be shooting, based on the fact that multiple witnesses heard gunshots around the time of Schuler's disappearance and the proximity of Struber and Wilson, known to have access to firearms. The absence of a body complicates the determination of the exact mechanism of death, but circumstantial evidence strongly suggests that Schuler was shot, and attempts were made to destroy evidence, as indicated by the burnt matches with traces of his DNA. The presence of firearms at Palmerville Station and the discovery of missing firearms further supports the theory that the murder weapon was a firearm, and the mode of homicide likely involved shooting. Given the forensic evidence and post-offence conduct, the inference is that Struber and Wilson used a firearm to kill Schuler and then disposed of the body to cover up their crime.

The conviction of Stephen Struber and Diane Struber-Wilson for the murder of Bruce Schuler is well-supported by substantial circumstantial evidence. The tyre tracks, witness testimony, burnt matches with Schuler's DNA, geographic damage, post-offence conduct, and corroborative testimony from Stephen May all point to their involvement in Schuler's death. Despite the absence of a body and minor discrepancies in witness accounts, the overwhelming weight of the evidence justifies their conviction.

The jury was properly directed to consider whether the evidence excluded all reasonable explanations consistent with innocence, and they reasonably concluded that guilt was the only rational conclusion. Ultimately, the Qld Court of Appeals also accepted the Crown case.

Discrepancies	Response with Legal Analysis
1. DB never been there before, but stated he had been going for 10 years	The inconsistency in DB's statements about his prior visits to Palmerville—first claiming never to have been there and later stating he had been going for ten years—raises concerns about credibility. However, this discrepancy must be assessed in terms of materiality to the case. According to *Domican v The Queen* (1992) 173 CLR 555, discrepancies only undermine a case if they are material to the facts in issue. In this context, the core issue is

Discrepancies	Response with Legal Analysis
	whether Struber and Wilson are responsible for Bruce Schuler's murder, not DB's history at Palmerville. While notable, this inconsistency does not affect the core forensic evidence implicating Struber and Wilson, such as tyre tracks, DNA on burnt matches, and witness testimony.
	The distinction between a witness's credibility and the reliability of their evidence is key. In *R v Perera* [1986] 1 Qd R 211, the court emphasised that juries must determine whether discrepancies affect the reliability of the evidence. DB's inconsistent statements may raise questions about his credibility, but they do not undermine the corroborative forensic evidence that connects Struber and Wilson to the crime. As held in *Shepherd v The Queen* (1990) 170 CLR 573, circumstantial evidence can be sufficient to secure a conviction if it excludes any reasonable hypothesis consistent with innocence, regardless of minor inconsistencies in witness testimony.
	It is also plausible that DB's inconsistent account was motivated by reasons unrelated to the crime, such as a desire to avoid admitting to prior trespassing or other illegal activities. The High Court in *Edwards v The Queen* (1993) 178 CLR 193 recognised that motives for dishonesty not directly connected to the crime itself do not necessarily undermine a witness's testimony regarding key facts. Therefore, DB's inconsistency

Discrepancies	Response with Legal Analysis
	could be explained by a desire to avoid incriminating himself in other activities, which does not diminish the validity of the core forensic evidence implicating Struber and Wilson.
	While the ten-year discrepancy in DB's statements is significant, it does not bear directly on the facts of the case and does not affect the forensic evidence that supports the prosecution's case against Struber and Wilson. Courts have consistently held that discrepancies affecting a witness's credibility, particularly when unrelated to the crime, do not necessarily undermine the overall case. As such, this inconsistency can be acknowledged without weakening the circumstantial and forensic evidence that supports the conviction of Struber and Wilson for Bruce Schuler's murder.
2. One-night trip seems unusual for the distance travelled	While traveling a significant distance for a one-night trip may appear unusual, this fact does not affect the substantive issues in the case. Whether or not the trip was unusual does not negate the forensic evidence placing Struber and Wilson at the scene of the murder. The court's focus remains on the sufficiency of the evidence connecting the accused to the crime. As emphasised in *Shepherd v The Queen* (1990) 170 CLR 573, circumstantial evidence must exclude any reasonable hypothesis consistent with innocence. The duration of the trip is

Discrepancies	Response with Legal Analysis
	irrelevant to the question of whether Struber and Wilson are guilty of the murder.
3. DB's neighbour's 10oz gold find not confirmed	The issue of whether DB's neighbour found 10oz of gold is peripheral to the central facts of the case. Even if this gold find were never confirmed, it does not bear on the forensic evidence directly implicating Struber and Wilson in BS's disappearance. The court, in *R v Baden-Clay* [2016] HCA 35, emphasised that for circumstantial evidence to support a conviction, the jury must be satisfied that the accused's guilt is the only rational conclusion that can be drawn. The alleged gold find does not present an alternative explanation for the events that transpired and therefore has no bearing on the case's key issues.
4. Other prospectors declined DB's invitation due to nervousness	The refusal of other prospectors to join DB due to nervousness does not support or refute the central question of Struber and Wilson's involvement in the murder. Nervousness about trespassing on private property is a plausible reason for declining such an invitation, but it has no direct connection to the forensic and circumstantial evidence implicating Struber and Wilson. The law recognises that unrelated behaviour, such as DB inviting others, does not detract from the specific evidence of the crime. *R v Hytch* [2005] QCA 216 reinforces that circumstantial evidence can sustain a conviction when no direct evidence exists, provided that the totality of evidence points

454

Discrepancies	Response with Legal Analysis
	to the accused's guilt beyond a reasonable doubt.
5. BS's bag contained multiple sets of clothes for one night	Overpacking multiple sets of clothes for a one-night trip, while unusual, is not evidence that impacts the case against Struber and Wilson. Individuals often pack extra clothing for various reasons, and this fact does not bear on the forensic evidence or the timeline of events. The Queensland Court of Appeal in *R v Hytch* made it clear that circumstantial evidence can support a conviction if it is consistent with the overall narrative of the crime and excludes any hypothesis consistent with innocence. Here, the key facts—Struber and Wilson being present at the scene and the forensic evidence linking them to Schuler's death—are far more relevant than the contents of BS's bag.
6-9. Discrepancies in timing of arrival at DB camp and departure	Timing discrepancies, such as whether the group left camp at 7:30 am or 9:00 am, are typical in witness testimony, especially when witnesses are recalling events under stress. As in *Domican v The Queen*, courts acknowledge that minor differences in testimony about specific timings do not necessarily undermine the overall reliability of the witnesses. The key issue here is the prospectors' presence at the scene and the subsequent events leading to BS's disappearance, which are supported by forensic evidence. *Shepherd v The Queen* establishes that circumstantial evidence can

Discrepancies	Response with Legal Analysis
	be sufficient if it collectively points to guilt, regardless of small timing discrepancies.
10-11. Travel time discrepancies (2.5 hrs vs direct)	Variations in travel time (e.g., whether the trip took 2.5 hours or if they went directly to Palmerville) reflect normal differences in memory and perception. These discrepancies are not material to the core facts. The circumstantial evidence, such as the tyre tracks, DNA on the burnt matches, and damage to the landscape caused by Struber and Wilson's vehicle, remains intact. The legal principle from *Domican v The Queen* applies: minor inconsistencies in witness testimony do not detract from the broader, consistent narrative that supports the prosecution's case.
12-17. Inconsistent times of video recordings	The timing of the video recordings, whether they were taken in the morning or afternoon, is a secondary issue. The focus of the case rests on the circumstantial evidence linking Struber and Wilson to BS's murder. Even if the videos were taken earlier than stated, they do not contradict the key evidence—tyre tracks, DNA evidence, and witness testimony—that placed Struber and Wilson at the scene. The Queensland Court of Appeal in *R v Hytch* [2005] clarified that circumstantial evidence can support a conviction, even when there are discrepancies in ancillary details, such as video timing, provided the totality of the evidence is consistent with the prosecution's narrative.

Discrepancies	Response with Legal Analysis
18-24. Disagreement over who went prospecting in which direction	The inability of the prospectors to agree on who went in which direction during prospecting is not unusual and does not diminish the case against Struber and Wilson. As outlined in *Domican v The Queen*, discrepancies in witness accounts, especially over minor details like direction or prospecting location, are expected. What is important is that the core facts—the presence of Struber and Wilson at the scene and the subsequent disappearance of BS—are corroborated by physical and forensic evidence. This evidence includes the tyre tracks, the damaged trees, and the burnt matches with BS's DNA, which together form a strong circumstantial case for Struber and Wilson's guilt.
25-30. DB deflecting video 2; other prospectors questioning video times	DB's reluctance to admit taking Video 2 may indicate concerns about being locked into a specific timeline. However, this deflection does not undermine the circumstantial and forensic evidence implicating Struber and Wilson. Even if discrepancies exist about the exact timing of the video, this does not change the fact that the evidence—such as tyre tracks and DNA—points strongly to Struber and Wilson's involvement in the crime. The court in *Shepherd v The Queen* affirmed that circumstantial evidence must be considered as a whole, and inconsistencies in peripheral details, like the timing of a video, do not invalidate the overall strength of the prosecution's case.

Discrepancies	Response with Legal Analysis
31-34. Misreporting of satellite phone GPS ping location	The discrepancy regarding the satellite phone GPS ping's location (whether it was near the prospectors' camp or 5 km away) is a minor error that does not affect the outcome of the case. The primary issue is the forensic evidence linking Struber and Wilson to the crime scene, which remains strong. As outlined in *R v Baden-Clay* [2016], the jury must consider the entirety of the evidence to determine whether guilt is the only rational conclusion. In this case, the forensic findings, such as the DNA on burnt matches and the physical evidence at the scene, provide compelling proof of Struber and Wilson's guilt, despite the misreported GPS data.
35-44. Inconsistent accounts of waking and departure times	Witnesses provided inconsistent accounts of when they woke up and left camp, but these discrepancies are common in cases where traumatic events are being recalled. As held in *Domican v The Queen*, minor inconsistencies regarding timing are not sufficient to discredit witness testimony. What remains crucial is that the prospectors were present in the area at the relevant time and that forensic evidence, including tyre tracks and DNA, corroborates the timeline of events leading to BS's disappearance. The law does not require witnesses to perfectly recall every detail; rather, the court must assess whether the core facts are reliable and supported by the evidence.

Discrepancies	Response with Legal Analysis
45-54. Not seeing/hearing each other in the gully	DB, TA, and BS not seeing or hearing each other in the gully could be due to environmental factors such as terrain, wind, or distractions. While these discrepancies might raise questions, they do not undermine the core evidence implicating Struber and Wilson. The forensic evidence, such as the physical damage to the landscape, tyre tracks, and DNA on the burnt matches, provides a consistent narrative of the crime. In cases relying on circumstantial evidence, the High Court in *Shepherd v The Queen* emphasized that the jury must be satisfied that the circumstantial evidence, when viewed as a whole, excludes any reasonable hypothesis of innocence. Here, the forensic evidence outweighs minor inconsistencies in witness testimony.
55-58. Reasons for scattering when S & W arrived	The differing reasons given by the prospectors for hiding (fear of Struber and Wilson or a desire to protect their prospecting spots) are not material to the main issue of Struber and Wilson's involvement in BS's disappearance. The High Court's ruling in *Edwards v The Queen* (1993) 178 CLR 193 established that post-offence conduct, such as evasive actions or inconsistent explanations, could be indicative of guilt. However, the reasons for the prospectors' actions are secondary to the forensic evidence, which provides the clearest link to Struber and Wilson's guilt. The tyre tracks, tree damage,

Discrepancies	Response with Legal Analysis
	and DNA evidence remain crucial in establishing their involvement in the crime.
59-63. Different accounts of hearing gunshots	The variations in witness descriptions of the type of gunshots heard (e.g., shotgun vs. rifle) are to be expected in high-stress situations. Witnesses often perceive such events differently, especially when startled. As noted in *Domican v The Queen*, discrepancies in witness descriptions of peripheral details do not undermine the credibility of the core facts, which in this case are supported by forensic evidence. The important fact remains that gunshots were heard, placing Struber and Wilson at the scene. The physical evidence, such as the tyre tracks and damage to the landscape, corroborates the witnesses' testimony, making the type of gun used less significant.
64-69. Inconsistencies in weapon type and W's actions	DB's changing description of the weapon carried by W (from a long arm to a shotgun to a black stick) reflects typical memory issues in high-stress situations. As seen in *Domican v The Queen*, memory inconsistencies regarding peripheral details like the type of weapon do not discredit the core facts, especially when corroborated by physical evidence. The key facts remain that witnesses observed Struber and Wilson behaving suspiciously, and forensic evidence, such as tyre tracks and DNA on burnt matches, links them to BS's disappearance. These facts are far more significant than the variation in descriptions of the weapon. Additionally, in *R*

Discrepancies	Response with Legal Analysis
	v Perera [1986] 1 Qd R 211, the court held that juries must assess whether the evidence allows for any reasonable inference other than guilt, which is not the case here.
70-72. Movement of the ute	Discrepancies in the witnesses' descriptions of the ute's movements (e.g., how far it travelled or where it stopped) are minor and do not undermine the case against Struber and Wilson. The physical evidence—tyre tracks matching Struber's vehicle, damage to the trees caused by the ute, and the location of the burnt matches—provides objective proof of the vehicle's presence and movements. In *R v Hytch* [2005] QCA 216, the court ruled that circumstantial evidence, such as tyre tracks and physical damage, can establish guilt when it aligns with the prosecution's narrative. Here, the evidence strongly supports the prosecution's version of events, making minor discrepancies in movement irrelevant to the outcome.
73-82. Ute driving and shots fired	Variations in witness accounts of how far the ute travelled and when the shots were fired are minor discrepancies that do not significantly affect the case. The critical issue is that witnesses heard gunshots and observed Struber and Wilson's suspicious behaviour. Forensic evidence, such as the damaged trees, burnt matches with BS's DNA, and tyre tracks consistent with Struber's vehicle, corroborates these observations. As outlined in *Shepherd v The Queen* (1990), circumstantial evidence must be viewed

Discrepancies	Response with Legal Analysis
	collectively, and minor discrepancies in witness testimony do not diminish the overall strength of the evidence. The physical evidence and consistent narrative remain compelling, despite the minor variations in testimony regarding the sequence of events.
83-110. Conflicting accounts of prospectors returning to camp	The prospectors' differing accounts of when they returned to camp and how they searched for BS reflect typical variations in memory. These discrepancies are not uncommon, particularly when recalling events after a traumatic incident. In *Domican v The Queen*, the court made it clear that minor inconsistencies in testimony are expected and do not undermine the core facts of the case. Here, the physical evidence—tyre tracks, damaged trees, and burnt matches with BS's DNA—provides objective support for the prosecution's case. The timeline discrepancies are peripheral and do not alter the fact that Struber and Wilson were implicated by the forensic evidence. Additionally, under *s 632 of the Criminal Code (Qld)*, the jury can convict based on uncorroborated testimony, provided they are convinced beyond a reasonable doubt. The forensic evidence, however, corroborates the key witness testimony, reinforcing the conviction.
122-126. Subsequent searches and	The searches conducted on July 10 and 11 uncovered critical evidence, including burnt grass, damaged trees, and tyre tracks, all of which linked Struber and Wilson's vehicle to

Discrepancies	Response with Legal Analysis
damaged trees found	the scene of the crime. These objective findings corroborate the witness testimony and provide physical evidence of Struber and Wilson's involvement. In *R v Hytch* [2005], the court held that circumstantial evidence, such as physical damage and forensic traces, could form a compelling case when viewed collectively. The damage to the trees and the matching tyre tracks are consistent with the prosecution's narrative that Struber and Wilson used their vehicle to move BS's body, providing further support for their conviction.
127-137. Absence of DNA or blood at CS1 and CS2	The absence of large amounts of DNA or blood at Crime Scenes 1 and 2 does not preclude a conviction. As the Queensland Court of Appeal emphasized in *R v Hytch*, circumstantial evidence can sustain a conviction, even when direct physical evidence is limited. The presence of small drops of BS's blood at Crime Scene 2, as well as the burnt matches containing BS's DNA, are critical pieces of forensic evidence that tie Struber and Wilson to the crime. Additionally, the physical evidence of tyre tracks, damage to the trees, and geographic features linked to Struber's vehicle further corroborate the prosecution's case. The High Court in *Shepherd v The Queen* affirmed that circumstantial evidence must be viewed in its entirety, and the forensic evidence here provides a strong foundation for the conviction, even without more substantial amounts of DNA or blood.

Discrepancies	Response with Legal Analysis
169-170. DB's possible motive to implicate Struber & Wilson	The suggestion that DB had a motive to implicate Struber and Wilson due to a previous drug raid or an earlier confrontation is speculative and unsupported by the evidence. While motive can play a role in criminal cases, it is not determinative. As the High Court noted in *Edwards v The Queen* (1993), post-offence conduct or alleged motives must be carefully weighed, but the presence of motive alone does not establish guilt or innocence. In this case, the circumstantial and forensic evidence—tyre tracks, DNA on burnt matches, and damaged trees—provides a far stronger basis for Struber and Wilson's conviction than any potential motive for DB to implicate them falsely. Additionally, under *s 632 Criminal Code (Qld)*, the jury is entitled to convict based on the weight of the evidence, and here, the overwhelming weight of the physical evidence points to Struber and Wilson's guilt.

Appendix F

16-08-2022

Dear Lisa Schuler,

Thank you for writing to me, my appologies for not answering sooner. I would like to say, I'm not the crazy person that people say I am. I appreciate how confronting it must be for you to write to me. I did not shoot your father and if I did I would have said so from the very start.

There are persons out there that know what happened and as far as I know some are still on the property. These people are not the poor prospectors/miners that they innocently claim to be.

These persons have been trafficking drugs internationally from around this area for over 35 years, they use mining & prospecting as a cover. We would always avoid them and where they were as much as possible because we feared for our own safety.

When someone reported them to the police they confronted and threatened us saying they were going to "sort us out" because they believed it was us. The question remains unanswered as to who actually reported them and enraged them.

These same individuals also began to chase tourists off our property claiming ownership and threatening them with firearms. As a result we, as the legit owners were accused of this conduct despite having no part in it.

These individuals would travel around the property in 4WD vehicles including one which closely resembled our own. Only days after the incident on the 4th of July their vehicle was parked up on the property with a water pump in the back, I noted the only difference from ours was that it had wider tires. Another vehicle had its tires changed right after the incident despite there being an active investigation.

Another point I have noted is that despite having a satelite phone with them, the individuals with your father waited 9 hours before reporting anything to police. I would think any normal person would have called the police immediatley.

Lisa, I sincerely regret that I am unable to help you find your father. You have my deepest sympathies for the loss and trauma you have experienced as a result of his disappearance. I believe we both need closure & if I ever find out anything that could provide the answers needed I will not hesitate to contact the police and yourself.

Sincerely,
Wilson,
Diane Struber